DYNAMIC PATTERNS IN COMMUNICATION PROCESSES

James H. Watt
C. Arthur VanLear

DYNAMIC PATTERNS IN COMMUNICATION PROCESSES

SAGE Publications
International Educational and Professional Publisher
Thousand Oaks   London   New Delhi

For information address:

SAGE Publications, Inc.
2455 Teller Road
Thousand Oaks, California 91320
E-mail: order@sagepub.com

SAGE Publications Ltd.
6 Bonhill Street
London EC2A 4PU
United Kingdom

SAGE Publications India Pvt. Ltd.
M-32 Market
Greater Kailash I
New Delhi 110 048 India

Printed in the United States of America

Library of Congress Cataloging-in-Publication Data

Main entry under title:

Dynamic patterns in communication processes / editors, James H. Watt and C. Arthur VanLear.
    p. cm.
    Includes bibliographical references and index.
    ISBN 0-8039-5619-3 (alk. paper). — ISBN 0-8039-5620-7 (pbk.: alk. paper)
    1. Interpersonal communication. 2. Communication—Psychological aspects. I. Watt, James H. II. VanLear, C. Arthur.
    BF637.C45D96   1996
    302.2—dc20   Po 00227   96-4448

This book is printed on acid-free paper.

96 97 98 99 10 9 8 7 6 5 4 3 2 1

Sage Production Editor: Astrid Virding
Sage Copy Editor: Joyce Kuhn
Sage Typesetter: Janelle LeMaster

Contents

PART

Some Ideas and Speculations

What, then, is time? If no one asks me, I know what it is. If I wish to explain it to him who asks me, I do not know.

—Saint Augustine, *Confessions, Book XI* (circa 400)

The how an actual entity becomes constitutes what that actual entity is. . . . Its "being" is constituted by its "becoming."

—Alfred North Whitehead, *Process and Reality* (1929)

For tribal man space was the uncontrollable mystery. For technological man it is time that occupies the same role.

—Marshall McLuhan, *The Mechanical Bride* (1951)

Time is the substance from which I am made. Time is a river which carries me along, but I am the river; it is a tiger that devours me, but I am the tiger; it is a fire that consumes me, but I am the fire.

—Jorge Luis Borges, "A New Refutation of Time" (1964)

The illimitable, silent, never-resting thing called Time, rolling, rushing on, swift, silent, like an all-embracing ocean-tide, on which we and all the universe swim like exhalations, like apparitions which are, and then are not: this is forever very literally a miracle; a thing to strike us dumb, for we have no word to speak about it.

—Thomas Carlyle, *On Heroes and Hero-Worship,*
Lecture 1, "The Hero as Divinity" (1841)

A Partial Map
to a Wide Territory

C. ARTHUR VaNLEAR
JAMES H. WATT

This book is centered around the theme of dynamic communication processes. Although there has been general agreement for at least 35 years that communication should be studied as a process not a condition, the implication that change over time must be included in our understanding of communication has only slowly become an important criterion in communication research. On a positive note, there lately has been some movement toward the development of dynamic theories of communication and some increase in the number of empirical studies that include over-time observations.

However, there has been very little general, systematic examination of dynamic processes in the specific context of communication. Paradigms and methodological procedures used by communication researchers have been borrowed from engineering, statistics, econometrics, and systems science and applied as intact solutions to the study of specific communication situations. There has been only modest generalization of approaches and methods to different subdisciplines within the broad area of human communication. Although it is evident that there are ideas about dynamic processes that cut across different subdisciplines, the approaches developed in one area have not generally migrated to other areas. Researchers are frequently unaware of the similarity of their work to that of others in different areas of communication. They are often unaware of dynamic system theories and methodologies that might provide significant benefit to their research programs. We believe that this situation has developed because attention to dynamic communication systems has been narrowly focused. Consideration of the over-time behavior of communication processes is normally done only in the context of a single theory or phenomenon. As a result, the exposure of communication researchers to the range of dynamic concepts and methodologies has been spotty. There has been little recognition of the basic similarities among the problems being studied in different areas of communication research.

This book is aimed at partially rectifying this situation by bringing together a series of contributions from the researchers doing the best work in a variety of subdisciplines of communication research. But casting a wide net has its penalty. When a very helpful anonymous reviewer first saw the description of the breadth of chapters in this volume, that person was understandably confused about the interconnections among the contributions and reported a "lost in space" feeling. Both of us are familiar with that sensation (too familiar, really), so in a rush of enthusiasm, we agreed to write a summary chapter that would make some of the linkages among the contributions clearer to the reader. This task turns out to be fairly easy to talk about but a lot harder to do. Nevertheless, that is the goal of the present chapter.

The difficulty in describing current ideas and work in dynamic communication processes does not stem from a lack of interconnections; rather, it is the opposite. There are many ways to approach the study of dynamic communication processes, and most approaches have some instructive merit. Still, a volume devoted to a topic area as broad as that addressed in this book is difficult to navigate without some road map that identifies major features and regularities on the conceptual landscape. The problem is deciding on the method of representing the intellectual latitude and longitude, so to speak, and of classifying the landmarks.

This chapter offers two basic ways of mapping ideas about dynamic communication processes. First, the works of researchers recognized as the pioneers in this field are examined to reveal the issues and approaches that characterize the current state of the art. The contributors to this volume are innovators and leaders in conceptualizing and researching dynamic communication processes. The chapters in this volume are described and contrasted on a number of dimensions, and with any luck, some useful generalizations will emerge.

The second method is to find the fundamental ideas and procedures that are used by these pioneers. These common grounds provide the orientation needed to contrast different approaches to the study of communication processes. We'll describe some basic ways that time can be included in communication theories and empirical research.

Classifying and Contrasting Contributions

One classification of similarities and differences appears in the structure of this volume. However, there are many ways other than the one we have chosen in which we could have organized the chapters of this book. After considering several different lineups, we finally decided to divide the volume into three main units that roughly correspond to the categories of concepts, tools, and applications.

In the first section, some general conceptual and metatheoretical issues related to communication processes are addressed. Since you are reading it, you have probably figured out that this chapter is attempting to provide a conceptual and methodological map for the rest of the book (and thus for the general area of dynamic communication theories). VanLear's chapter reviews the evolution of the concept of communication as process over the past 40 years and concludes with some very general and basic assumptions about viewing communication as a process. Monge and Kalman develop the metaphor of communication processes as windows and panes to explicate the concepts of sequentiality, simultaneity, and synchronicity in human communication. The concepts in the VanLear and the Monge and Kalman chapters are general and abstract enough to cut across the various domains (mass, organizational, persuasive, group, and interpersonal communication) and methods in the heterogeneous discipline of human communication.

Although most of the other chapters in this book present ideas and models that can apply to some extent across a variety of content areas, they tend to be more tied to a specific communication setting or problem than are the chapters in the first section. The purpose of this initial section is not to constrain scholars by presenting a single correct way of conceptualizing dynamic process but to learn from the intellectual history of this central concept and use that history as a heuristic springboard for useful ways of conceptualizing time and process in communication. The second section focuses on the tools and techniques used to model communication as process. Again, where most of the contributors discuss methodological issues associated with applying and testing their models, the chapters in this unit focus primarily on fundamental methodological issues (sampling, measurement, assessing residuals, and experimentation) as they relate to modeling communication as a dynamic process.

Arundale develops criteria that are necessary for indexing patterns over time in communication research. How do we measure time? How finely must we segment or punctuate the temporal stream? How long must the time series be to draw valid conclusions about dynamic patterns? Arundale provides precise guidelines for answering these questions.

If we conceptualize time as continuous, how can we derive communication measures that are isomorphic with that conceptualization? West and Biocca review some methods for measuring responses to communication stimuli as continuous and provide methods for analyzing such data. Although their methods usually have been applied to mass communication processes, they are really quite general and could easily be used to study dyadic nonverbal communication, for example.

Time series texts typically provide methods for assessing the pattern of autocorrelations in a whole data set (see the next section of this chapter). The chapter by Nass and Moon offers a "localized autocorrelation diagnostic statistic" (*LADS*) as one method for examining clusters of the most extreme residuals from a regression analysis of time series data. This interesting and very general tool provides a way of finding anomalous patterns within a smaller region of a time series that may indicate the presence of some new communication process. It is an exploratory procedure that can be used to spur theoretical thinking in any area of communication.

The analysis of data from an experimental (or quasi-experimental) design is usually straightforward if the dependent variable (effect) is represented by a single (or small number of) value(s). However, if the effect of a manipulation is expected to take the form of a change in dynamic process (*e.g.,* the frequency or amplitude of a cycle), then the use of traditional ANOVA techniques (even repeated measures ANOVA) is unlikely to be the most appropriate analytical tool. Watt demonstrates how to use Fourier transforms and harmonic analysis of time series in an experimental design to uncover the effects of experimental manipulations on cyclical processes. This procedure can be used to study any type of communication process that results in periodicities (and can be generalized to include any experimental effects that are functions of time).

Corman shows how cellular automata can model processes that produce unintended consequences in organizational communication. Cellular automata are a very powerful set of models that can be used to describe the complex consequences of relatively simple dynamic rules in a variety of communication contexts.

The final and largest section of this book consists of specific applications of general methods and models to the substantive subdisciplines of communication: organizational, mass, persuasive, and interpersonal communication. Although these methods and models are developed as specific applications to substantive issues within a given domain, in almost all cases they can easily be applied to other areas of communication.

Theories of self-organizing systems have a long and illustrious history in the field of communication. Contractor and Grant's application of these ideas to the emergence of shared interpretations in organizations indicates there is still great potential for this approach if we are willing to go beyond traditional linear methods of modeling. The potential for the application of similar methods in contexts other than organizations seems promising.

In their chapter, Barnett and Cho demonstrate that a cyclical model accounts for a substantial portion of the variance of television viewing. The notion of regular embedded cycles of behavior adjusted for social events as a model for communication has application beyond the context of television viewing. On a more microscopic level, Meadowcroft shows how attention to television viewing can also be represented by a model of harmonic cycles.

Cybernetics has a long history as a metaphor for communication systems. Kaplowitz and Fink use the spring as their model for cognitive oscillations in persuasion and attitude change. Because the mathematics of spring physics is well known, it provides a useful heuristic analog for modeling a damped oscillating communication process. Other concepts from physics may provide a useful starting point for theory in differing areas of communication. For example, the Meadowcroft chapter discusses the idea of "attention inertia."

Buder uses deterministic cycles of variables from speech science to demonstrate how dyadic coordination can be modeled as synchrony of deterministic physiological cycles. A clear example of cross-spectral comparison is given. A similar paradigm is described by Warner in her review of evidence for cycles of communication behavior, physiological cycles, their linkage to each other, and relational outcomes.

Finally, Cappella shows how to use time domain ARIMA techniques to model mutual adaptation (reciprocity and compensation) of vocal and kinesic behavior in dyadic interaction. The nature and extent of mutual adaptation are shown to have important relational consequences.

There are, of course, other ways of classifying and grouping these chapters than in the three areas just discussed. A major distinction can be made between the methods used to analyze the basic time series observations that these authors use as the basis of their discussions. Some conceptualize and analyze process primarily in the "time domain" (Cappella; Nass and Moon), where the state of a process at the current time point is used to predict its subsequent states. Others conceptualize process in the "frequency domain," where time series data are converted to a series of periodically cycling functions and then used to analyze the process (Buder; Meadowcroft; Warner; Watt). Still others discuss both.

Another distinction can be made between linear process models and nonlinear models. Most of the chapters treat process as nonlinear; that is, the variables in the process (including time) are linked with mathematical functions that are not simple proportions. However, they differ in the ways in which they deviate from linearity. Many of the chapters picture communication as a cyclical process and provide ways of assessing cycles (Barnett and Cho; Buder; Kaplowitz and Fink; Meadowcroft; Warner; Watt). Other chapters focus on circular causality and feedback loops (Cappella; Contractor and Grant). Still others extend the concept of nonlinear process to nonlinear dynamic systems capable of chaos (Kaplowitz and Fink; VanLear; West and Biocca).

This book can be used in different ways, according to the needs of the reader. If one is using it primarily for its theoretical/conceptual contributions, the first and third sections plus the West and Biocca chapter are the most relevant. If one is interested to learn more about the techniques of process modeling, this chapter plus the second and third sections are the most useful. We asked our contributors to be tutorial whenever possible, and they have provided clear descriptions of methods and procedures where space permitted. When authors in an edited volume are left relatively free to determine their own content and approach, a certain amount of discontinuity and redundancy is inevitable. We believe that this disadvantage is more than offset by the insights gained by having some of the best process theorists and researchers in our field set their own agendas.

Common Ideas and Methods

The preceding discussion has outlined some ways of differentiating and classifying the intellectual contributions of the authors in this volume. Underlying much of the discussion, however, are some common ideas, themes, and procedures. The remainder of this chapter focuses on some ideas common to many of the chapters in this book.

Level of Measurement and Unitizing Time

Variables, including time, can be measured at the nominal, ordinal, interval, or ratio level of measurement. Observations taken in nominal time are not very interesting, as all that can be said about them is that they are not simultaneous.

By common understanding, temporal measurement consists minimally of observations sequenced in time. This ordinal level of measurement introduces the idea of "before" and "after" to the observations. It is often called "event time."

There are valid reasons for choosing to analyze event time. First, and most obviously, events may be the object of interest. We may be more interested in how events are sequenced, patterned, or connected to each other than with their duration or latency of onset. For example, when assessing relational dimensions, we may be concerned with the pattern of interaction that occurs *between* participants but not with the duration or latency *within* each speaker's turn at talk. Second, we often perceive and think of time not as a continuous stream but as a series of events. Therefore, by unitizing time by a series of events rather than by ticks of the clock we may be treating it more like social actors sometimes do in their everyday lives. Events (and, therefore, event time) may be more phenomenally real to our subjects than precise units of time in some cases. If the basis of cycles and dynamic patterns is the way people act

TABLE 1.1   Times Series Analyses Available for Different Types of Data

	Event Time	*Clock Time*
Discrete-level measurement	Lag sequential analysis Markov chain analysis Information theory Log linear Cellular automata	Semi-Markov analysis Dummy-coded time series Event history analysis
Continuous-level measurement	Event history analysis Repeated measures ANOVA LISREL and structural equations Cross lag panel path analysis	Trend analysis Time series regression ARIMA Fourier analysis Cross-spectral analysis

toward or punctuate events, then we may actually be better able to uncover such patterns using event time than clock time.

When time is described with an interval metric such as seconds, minutes, or days, it is both an interval and ratio level measurement. Introducing the idea of quantity to time transforms it into "clock time." Obviously there are cases in which clock time is the most appropriate or even the necessary method of unitizing time. Sometimes, we are interested in the duration and/or latency of events as the primary indicators of some phenomenon. Further, the onset or continuation of events can be coded and graphed onto a continuous temporal metric, thus allowing us to observe patterns of events. Sometimes, the assumed basis of temporal patterns is a continuous temporal phenomenon like our "biological clock" or the earth's rotation on its axis or orbit about the sun. Treating time as continuous affords very precise measurement. Finally, certain analytical techniques assume that time is treated as continuous. The most appropriate method depends on the issues and variables under study, the nature of the data, practical constraints, and so forth.

One can always move from interval/ratio levels of measurement to ordinal but not vice-versa. That is, observations taken in event time can be analyzed only according to their temporal ordering alone. Most time series techniques make assumptions about how time is measured and the level of measurement of variables. Table 1.1 describes what techniques are generally appropriate with what type of data.

Arundale (this volume) provides a detailed discussion of these issues, using illustrations from other chapters in this volume to illustrate the different ways of treating time.

Stationarity and Change

One of the most basic issues in time series analysis is whether the data exhibit stability or change over time. Indeed, this is often the reason for conducting longitudinal research and time series analysis in the first place. However, this is not always a simple issue. What may appear to be change in the short term may be a stable cycle in the long term. Change may occur at one level of analysis or order of complexity, whereas processes assessed at other levels may be stationary (see VanLear, this volume).

Standard time series texts often make the distinction between stationarity of level, stationarity of variance, and stationarity of process (McCleary & Hay, 1980). System theorists make similar distinctions between first-order and second-order change (VanLear, this volume). Most standard time series analyses assume stationarity of process (second order) if not stationarity of level (although if one has a long enough time series process stationarity can be, and often is, tested empirically; see Watt, 1994). For example, the types of adaptation processes studied by Cappella (this volume) test and control for changes in level (trend or drift) but assume stationarity of process (reciprocity or compensation) over time.

Homogeneity of Processes

Power in time series analysis may come from having a lot of data over an extended period of time for each case, instead of a large number of separate cases. This permits researchers to have a great deal of confidence about the adequacy of their description or model of the process for each case. However, it is usually important to compare the model of processes across cases for homogeneity. Variations in process across cases may point out the need for a multiple-sequence model (VanLear, 1983, this volume) or could suggest the presence of exogenous causal variables (Watt, this volume).

When insufficient data per case are available, time series must be pooled to assess temporal processes (Sayrs, 1989), and homogeneity is assumed. When sufficient data are present, homogeneity of process should be tested. VanLear (1991) and Cappella (this volume) have used meta-analytic techniques to test for homogeneity of process.

Three Paradigms for Dynamic
Modeling of Communication Processes

In the discipline of communication, quantitative methods have been approached in two ways. The first, and most popular, is to view quantitative methods as a set of tools applied to answer substantive questions about communication. Whereas it is important that the assumptions of the statistical method used are consistent with the underlying theoretical and metatheoretical assumptions, there is no explicit contention that the nature of the statistical technique is analogous to characteristics of the communication process. For example, most researchers who use ANOVA do not argue that communication is like an ANOVA equation.

The other approach to quantitative research and the one adopted by many of the authors in the present volume is to treat the quantitative technique as a *model* of the communication process. The argument of this approach is that the mathematical equations of the technique are isomorphic representations or mathematical analogs of the very process under investigation. The quantitative technique is not simply a tool used to test substantive theory but is an integral part of the theory itself.

In this section, three different paradigms for dynamic modeling are discussed. These three do not come close to exhausting the possibilities, even those represented in this book, yet are representative of the kinds of dynamic models of communication available. Because the authors in this volume are often interested in breaking new ground, there are times when the basics or fundamentals are assumed or omitted. This chapter explicates some of the ideas and techniques not covered in other chapters.

The first paradigm is the sequential analysis of discrete data popularized in communication by people like Aubrey Fisher (1978a, 1978b) using information theory statistics, lag sequential, and Markov analyses. The second is the analysis of multiple continuous time series in continuous time in the "time domain" (see Cappella, this volume) using ARIMA techniques. The final paradigm is the analysis of continuous data in continuous time in the "frequency domain" using Fourier and cross-spectral analyses (Buder, this volume; Watt, this volume).

Sequential Analysis of Discrete Data

This approach is explicated here in detail because (a) it is a very popular and useful method for dealing with process (see VanLear, this volume, for the theoretical background) and (b) none of this book's authors address these methods in depth.

One way to think about a time series of sequentially ordered events is with information theory. To what extent can knowing the nature of an event at time $t + 0$ "reduce our uncertainty" regarding the nature of an event at time $t + 1$? Will knowing the nature of an event at $t + 0$ and $t + 1$ significantly reduce our uncertainty about the nature of an event at $t + 2$? The answers to these questions lie in the amount of redundancy or pattern in the sequence of events. Information theory statistics (Attneave, 1959; Krippendorff, 1986) include the H function (a measure of uncertainty based on binary "information bits") and stereotopy or S, a standardized index of the average amount of structure (redundancy) in a sequence at a given level of complexity ranging from 1.0 (absolute predictability) to 0.0 (total randomness). Uncertainty regarding an event in a sequence is reduced by knowledge of each prior event [$S_i < S_{i(j)} < S_{i, j(k)}$, etc.], but there will be a point at which the incremental increase will not be significant.

If the data consist of a series of events coded by a dichotomous category system, then one frequently used method of describing the series is through lag sequential analysis. The misapplications of lag sequential analysis are legend. Too often, the series from different subjects or cases (often of different lengths) are pooled together with no test for homogeneity or stationarity. Long higher-order lagged sequences are often tested as if each lag were statistically independent, with no controls for autocorrelation. Likewise, when between-subjects grouping variables or experimental conditions are used, differences between levels are often assessed by "eyeballing" the differences in the z scores rather than by a formal test of difference.

Current reviewers are unlikely to be very charitable with the continued misapplication of this technique. Allison and Liker (1982) critique the use of Sackett's (1979) z score and proposed an alternative z that has become the new standard. Morley (1986) offers several other solutions to the problems of lag sequential analysis. Using meta-analytic procedures, he shows how to convert Allison and Liker's zs to *phi* coefficients that can be used as indices of the sequential structure for each case unbiased by the number of time periods (z scores are, of course, sensitive to the number of observations in a sequence). Likewise, because these *phi* coefficients are product moment coefficients one can use simple partial correlations for controlling for the effect of $t + 1$ when assessing the effect of $t + 0$ on $t + 2$, and so forth. A Fisher's Z transformation of the *phi* coefficients makes them good measures of the amount of sequential dependency in the series of a given individual or relationship that can then be used both to aggregate the data from the series of many cases and to test hypotheses using more conventional statistical tests like ANOVA and regression (VanLear & Zietlow, 1990).

As indicated, lag sequential analyses often fail to test for the homogeneity or stationarity of sequential structure before pooling data across dyads or across time. Further, even when these assumptions are met, lag sequential analysis is best suited for dichotomous data, and often our categorization of events must be more complex than can be represented by a dichotomous category system. In such situations, the use of Markov analysis may be appropriate. A simple Markov model makes three testable assumptions. First, it assumes that the data exhibit first-order sequential structure—that is, that knowledge of the event at time $t + 0$ increases our ability to predict the nature of the event at $t + 1$, and knowing $t + 1$ increases our ability to predict the nature of $t + 2$, but knowing $t + 0$ does not improve our ability to predict $t + 2$ beyond the reduction of uncertainty from knowing $t + 1$ [$S_i < S_{i(j)}$, but $S_{i(j)} = S_{i, j(k)}$]. Of course, if the sequence exhibits structure at higher orders of Markovity, then more complex models can be constructed.

Construction of the simple Markov model requires two types of matrices. Let V stand for the "absolute state probability vector." The elements of V are the probabilities p of each type of event i occurring. Then, $\Sigma p_i = 1$.

The second matrix, the T or transition matrix, is composed of the "transition probabilities." Its elements (p_{ij}) indicate the probability of any particular event i at a particular time t being followed by a particular kind of event j out of a finite set of possible events at time $t + 1$. By convention, the rows of the T matrix are the antecedent events i and the columns are the possible subsequent events j so that p_{ij} is the probability of being in state j at time $t + 1$, if the event at time t was i. The elements of each row sum to 1.

The assumptions of stationarity and homogeneity basically require that the transition probabilities are constant across time and across different cases. For example, let us assume that we have time series for several media viewers watching TV each night for several months. For each program they watch (half-hour or hour), we code what network they are watching. The analysis of sequential structure shows that if they are watching network A at time t they are more likely to continue to watch A at $t + 1$ than if they were watching network N at time t, in which case they would be more likely to watch N at $t + 1$, and so on. Assume that the analysis shows that this sequential dependency is a first-order Markov chain. The assumption of stationarity is that the transition probabilities (p_{ij}) are the same when we start the study as later in the study and on different nights of the week. The assumption of homogeneity is that the transition probabilities are basically the same across different cases. Note that there is no assumption that the state probabilities remain constant over time. In fact, this is what we want to predict: the probability of being in a particular state at a particular point in time.

If we let ^{t+0}V stand for the initial distribution of the state probabilities at time t and ^{t+1}V stand for the state probabilities at $t + 1$. Assuming homogeneity and stationarity (T is constant), ^{t+1}V is a function of ^{t+0}V and T. If T is constant, a first-order Markov chain has the following properties (Hewes, 1975; VanLear, 1983):

$$^{t+1}V = ^{t+0}V(T)$$

[1-1]

$$^{t+2}V = ^{t+1}V(T),\ \text{and so on.}$$

This reduces to

$$^{t+n}V = ^{t+0}V(T^n)$$

[1-2]

Therefore, Equation 1-2 shows that one can predict the probability of being in any state in the finite set of states at any point in time if one knows the initial probabilities (^{t+0}V) and the transition probabilities (T), given the assumptions of first-order stationarity and homogeneity. For a finite realization of a nominal sequential time series, these assumptions can be tested given adequate data (Anderson & Goodman, 1957; Kullback, Kupperman, & Ku, 1962). The test for stationarity consists of testing the transition probabilities at different points in time against the composite T matrix representing the transition probabilities at all points in time pooled with a likelihood ratio chi square (Anderson & Goodman, 1957). The test for homogeneity is also a likelihood ratio chi square which tests for differences between the transition probabilities for each case against the composite T matrix for all cases pooled (Kullback et al., 1962). If each individual case or time does not have sufficient data for these tests, one can test successive powers or T for convergence. If the T matrix fails to converge, then at least one of the assumptions must be invalid (Hewes, 1985).

There are several types of Markov processes that conform to these three assumptions (Raush, 1972). Absorbing chains move inexorably toward a given state or set of states. A regular chain has transition probabilities such that it is possible to go from every state to every other state with sufficient time. In a cyclical chain there is a discernible pattern such that certain states tend to recur only at periodic intervals.

In practice, many (possibly most) data sets do not meet the assumptions of stationarity and/or homogeneity. When homogeneity is rejected, this may indicate that different cases operate according to different processes rather than simply being characterized by differences in the probabilities of being in different states (VanLear & Zietlow, 1990; Williamson & Fitzpatrick, 1985). If we can explain the variation in temporal processes across systems/cases, then we have a more interesting (albeit more complex) model of temporal processes. Likewise, variation in transition probabilities over time may be evidence of process change in development (Fisher & Drecksel, 1983; VanLear, 1987). Our models of communication development must incorporate process changes as well as simple changes in state probabilities.

One strategy that researchers often employ is to use Markov tests of order, stationarity, and homogeneity to determine what the general model will look like and then use the lag sequential z scores, *phi* and partial *phi* coefficients to describe specific patterns and sequences.

Of course, information theory, Markov chains, and lag sequential analysis are not the only methods of discrete sequential analysis of process. Log linear methods (Bishop, Fienberg, & Holland, 1975) and cellular automata (Corman, this volume) can be used to model discrete data in event time.

Analysis of Continuous Data
in the Time Domain: ARIMA

When modeling continuous data over time one must first choose whether to operate in the "time domain" or the "frequency domain." The time domain treats "data directly as a graph of measurement against time" (Gottman, 1981, p. 12), whereas the frequency domain treats the time series as a spectrum that can be decomposed into sinusoidal (sine and cosine) functions of various frequencies. Time domain analysis is more common in communication research, so we will deal with it first.

Research questions in the time domain are formulated directly in terms of time, as predictions of the present or future value of a single variable from the past values of the same variable (univariate models) or of a different time series variable (bivariate and multivariate models). Usually, one wishes to assess the effect of one time series on a contemporaneous time series. One would like to know if a measurement in one series at time t can predict the value of the other series at some future time, such as $t + 1$.

Although simple correlational techniques like autocorrelation (the correlation between a variable's current value and its value at time points in the past, called time lags), cross-lagged correlations (correlation of two variables with each other at differing time lags for each), and time-lagged regressions have been used in the past to model over-time processes, use of simple correlations is a questionable practice. Generally, one cannot simply correlate the measurements of one series on the simultaneous and lagged measures of the other series because a time series usually exhibits some form of serial dependency within itself over time. In a time series each observation is not independently selected, nor is each observation statistically independent of its neighboring observations. This produces "correlated error" (the same unmeasured factors producing errors of prediction in one observation produce similar errors in neighboring observations) that violates the assumptions of most standard statistical tests.

It also makes it difficult to determine the meaning of correlations between observations in two contemporaneous series. There are two ways in which this occurs. First, the scores of two time series may be spuriously correlated because they are both effected by a similar temporal process. For example, self-disclosures generally tend to become more intimate with time for successful relationships (Altman & Taylor, 1973), and this presumably is true for both partners to the relationship. If the time series of intimacy scores of person A is correlated with the time series of intimacy scores for person B, the correlation may make it appear that A's intimacy effected B's intimacy such that when A increased in intimacy so did B when in reality the relationship was due to the fact that both A's and B's intimacy was effected in the same way by time. Likewise, satisfaction and trust are likely to increase with time for successful relationships (VanLear & Trujillo, 1986), thereby producing an artificially high correlation between time series of these variables.

ARIMA is a time domain stochastic modeling technique that deals with these problems. ARIMA is an acronym for a group of models called AutoRegressive, Integrative, Moving Average processes. As a stochastic technique, one of the most important assumptions of ARIMA analysis is that the best predictor of the present is the immediate past, with the effects of the past diminishing as they become more remote in time.

Temporal processes that cumulate over time are called integrative processes. These include "deterministic" processes like trends and stochastic processes such as "drift." These produce nonstationary time series that are not permitted in most statistical modeling procedures (although modeling procedures for nonstationary series exist; cf. Phillips & Ouliaris, 1990). In ARIMA analyses, these integrative processes are usually extracted from the data by "differencing" the series, that is, by subtracting some prior value of the series from the current value. More complex integrative processes can be extracted from the series by differencing an already differenced series.

Differencing a series tends to increase its stationarity by removing the effects that accumulate over long time spans. If the cumulative processes being removed by differencing are theoretically important, some other procedure such as trend estimation or dynamic curve fitting might be more appropriate than differencing (see Watt, 1994), as differencing will control for the cumulative process but will not model it in an interpretable way. ARIMA assumes that a time series is stationary in level, variance, and process. Differencing can create a process that is stationary in level. If a series is nonstationary in variance because of ceiling or floor effect, it can often be corrected with a log transformation.

Aside from integrative processes, there is another reason why correlations between two contemporaneous time series can be misleading. For example, assume that series X affects series Y, but series Y does not affect series X. Changes in series X at time t produce synchronous changes in Y at t but at no other time lag. Further, assume that X_t predicts X_{t+1} and Y_t affects Y_{t+1} (there is autocorrelation in both series at time lag 1). Because X_t affects X_{t+1} and X_{t+1} affects Y_{t+1}, then Y_{t+1} is indirectly influenced by X_t and directly influenced by X_{t+1}. There will be an apparent (and spurious) correlation between X_t and Y_{t+1}, due to autocorrelation. If all serial dependency is removed from both series X and Y (that is, autocorrelation within each series is controlled, a process called "prewhitening"), the cross correlations will not display such spurious and misleading patterns. This is the basis for a procedure generally called Granger causal inference (cf. Granger, 1980).

Two types of serial dependency that can be represented by ARIMA models (and removed, if prewhitening is the goal) are autoregression (AR) and moving average (MA) processes.

An autoregressive process predicts current values of a time series by values of the same series at one or more previous time points. It can be symbolically described by the following equation:

$$\hat{X}_t = B_1 X_{t-p} + B_0 \qquad [1\text{-}3]$$

where $\hat{X}_t$ is the predicted value of X at time t; B_1 is a maximum likelihood regression coefficient; X_{t-p} is the value of X at time lag p; and B_0 is the value of X at the time of origin.

Autoregressive and moving average processes are identified by examining patterns of autocorrelation function (ACF), the correlation between X_t and X_{t+k}, where k is a time lag that ranges from 1 to a reasonably large number of lags that presumably span the period in which any effect might occur, and the partial autocorrelation function (PACF), the correlations between successive observations k units apart, controlling for the effects of intermediate lags (cf. McCleary & Hay, 1980; SPSS, Inc., 1993).

Autoregressive processes show an exponentially decreasing pattern of autocorrelations, as at each time lag, the effect is the product of previous effects times the autocorrelation. For example, see Figure 1.1a. In this process, the series has a simple lag-1 autocorrelation of .70. A change in X at time t of 1 standard unit will be seen at X_{t+1} as a change of .7 units, at X_{t+2} of $(.7)(.7) = .49$ units, at X_{t+3} of $(.49)(.7) = .336$, etc. However, the PACF will show only a single spike (Figure 1.1b) as controlling for the effect at X_{t+1} due to a change at X_t interrupts the chain autocorrelation effects by holding X_{t+1} constant for all subsequent lags, so the partial correlations of X_t with X_{t+2}, X_{t+3}, and so on are all zero. The lag of the PACF spike is the order (the time lag at which the effect occurs) of the autoregressive process.

Moving average processes, unlike autoregressive processes, are characterized by a persistence of the effects of any change at X_t. A moving average process predicts current values of X from a weighted average of past errors in prediction. Thus, any corrections made to the prediction

(text continues on page 24)

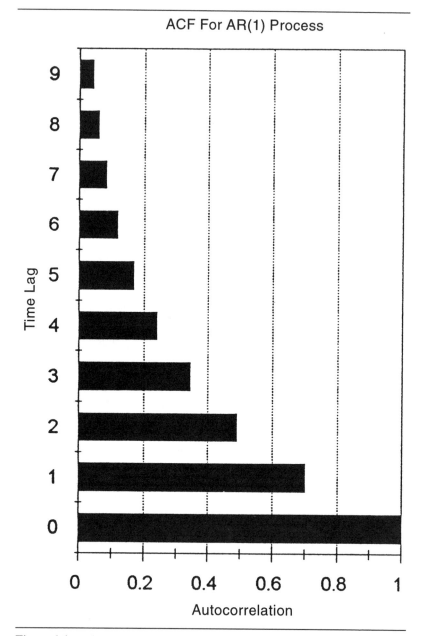

Figure 1.1a.   Autocorrelation function (ACF) for autoregressive process of
lag 1 [AR(1)].

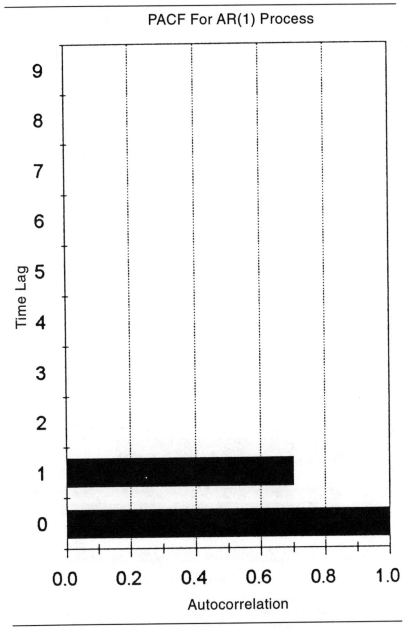

Figure 1.1b. Partial autocorrelation function (PACF) for autoregressive process of lag 1 [AR(1)].

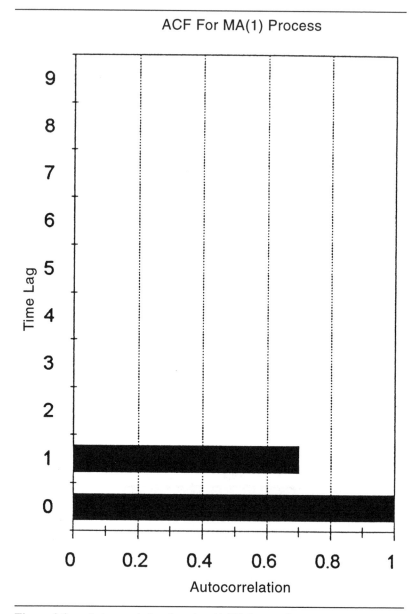

Figure 1.1c.   Autocorrelation function (ACF) for moving average process of lag 1 [MA(1)].

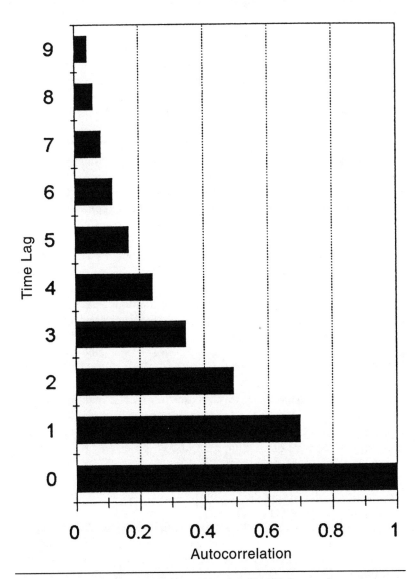

Figure 1.1d. Partial autocorrelation function (PACF) for moving average process of lag 1 [MA(1)].

of X_t will persist through future predicted values of X. A moving average process can be represented by the following equation:

$$\hat{X}_t = a_t - B_1 a_{t-p} \qquad [1\text{-}4]$$

where $\hat{X}_t$ is the predicted value of X at time t, a_t is the error residual between the predicted value of X without the moving average process and its actual value, a_{t-p} is the error of estimation at time lag p, and B_1 is a moving average coefficient estimated by a nonlinear likelihood procedure (Box & Jenkins, 1976).

A moving average process at time lag p has ACFs and PACFs that look like Figures 1.1c and 1.1d. Note that these are the opposite of the comparable plots for an autoregressive process. In a moving average process, the ACF is significant only at the time lag corresponding to the order of the process, whereas the PACF diminishes exponentially. This is due to the persistence of the moving average effects. Controlling for intermediate time lags does not remove the correlation of X in subsequent time points with the moving average adjustment made at time t.

Multiple orders of autoregression and moving average processes are possible in a single model, by extending the simple Equations 1-3 and 1-4 to multiple time lags, and combining them into a single predictive equation. Combination models are referred to in shorthand as ARIMA (a; i; m) models, where a is the order or orders of the autoregressive model, i is the order(s) of the integrative process (the number of differencing operations necessary), and m is the order(s) of the moving average process. Thus an ARIMA (2, 3; 1; 1, 3) model would contain autoregressive processes at time lags of 2 and 3; a single integrative process at time lag 1; and moving average processes at time lags of 1 and 3. Most communication processes are much simpler than this example and are often composed of first-order AR, MA, and/or I processes.

The basic idea behind an ARIMA analysis is to conduct an iterative process of (a) identifying the appropriate processes and their orders by plotting the raw time series, the ACFs, and the PACFs, (b) fitting what appears to be the best ARIMA model (estimation), and (c) testing the residual series for and remaining serial dependency (diagnosis) by recomputing the ACFs and PACFs on the residuals to the current ARIMA model. Once the residuals of all series are white noise processes (no significant ACF or PACF values), cross correlations (CCFs) between time series variables can be computed. Once serial dependency is removed the pattern of CCFs should show which series leads and which lags the other.

The reader should note the general similarity between the ACFs and PACFs and the *phi*s and partial *phi*s generated by Morley's (1986) revised lag sequential procedures. The same issues of order, stationarity and homogeneity from Markov analysis are also issues in ARIMA and other time series analyses. The chapters by Nass and Moon and by Cappella in this volume take a time domain approach to the analysis of time series data.

Analysis of Continuous Data in the Frequency Domain: Fourier and Cross-Spectral Analysis

Frequency domain analyses rely on a powerful mathematical fact: Any function, regardless of its complexity, can be represented by a weighted sum of simple sine and cosine (sinusoidal) periodic functions. A periodic function has several parameters. Amplitude R is the height of the cycle from zenith to baseline. The frequency ω (usually measured in radians per unit time) is the number of full repetitions the function makes in a single unit of time, and the *period* of the function is the time it takes to complete a single cycle. An example of such a cycle is shown in Figure 1.2. The algebraic representation of the function in the figure is

$$y = R \sin (\omega t + \phi), \qquad [1\text{-}5]$$

where R is the maximum amplitude, ω is the frequency in radians, and ϕ is the *phase angle* in radians with respect to the time origin.

Fourier Transforms and Periodograms

Since any series of observations taken over time can be considered a function of time (from a mathematical viewpoint, at least), any time series can be described by a set of weights representing the amplitudes and frequencies of a set of sinusoids. This set of weights is called a Fourier transform. Fourier transforms were developed by the French mathematician Joseph Fourier (1768-1830). If a set of frequencies is chosen for a discrete set of time-sequenced data of N points so that

$$\omega_j = \frac{2\pi j}{N}, \; 0 < j < \frac{N}{2}, \qquad [1\text{-}6]$$

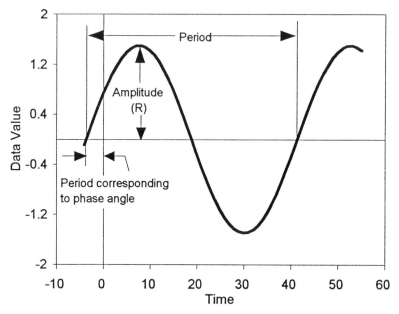

Figure 1.2. A periodic function.

it can be shown that the sinusoids at these frequencies are orthogonal and hence independent. These orthogonal frequencies are called the Fourier frequencies. Basic time series analysis references such as Brillinger (1975) and Bloomfield (1976) give detailed proofs of the derivation of their properties and of the following mathematical identities.

The amplitude and phase angle of a single sinusoid can be transformed into a function of two parameters. The cosine (A) and sine (B) coefficients corresponding to the Fourier frequencies in a time series can be defined as shown in Equation 1-7.

$$A_0 = \frac{1}{N} \sum_{t=0}^{N-1} X_t = \overline{X},$$

$$A_j = \frac{2}{N} \sum_{t=0}^{N-1} X_t \cos(\omega_j t), \qquad 0 < j < \frac{N}{2}, \qquad [1\text{-}7]$$

$$B_j = \frac{2}{N} \sum_{t=0}^{N-1} X_t \sin(\omega_j t), \qquad 0 < j < \frac{N}{2},$$

$$A_{\frac{N}{2}} = \frac{1}{N} \sum_{t=0}^{N-1} (-1)^t X_t, \text{ if } N \text{ is even} \qquad [1\text{-}7 \text{ cont'd}]$$

$$= 0 \text{ if } N \text{ is odd}.$$

The first cosine coefficient is simply the mean of the series. The last cosine coefficient (at $t = N/2$), if N is even, corresponds to a Fourier frequency of π radians, at which frequency the value of the cosine will be either positive or negative unity at each time point. If N is odd, the last data point does not correspond to a Fourier frequency, and thus there is no cosine coefficient.

The A and B coefficients are computed at each Fourier frequency j by evaluating the above sums. The resulting set of coefficients is called the discrete Fourier transform (DFT) of the time series. Conceptually, it describes a series of periodic components that, when added together, produce a continuous function that passes through each point in the discrete time series. Figure 1.3 shows how three sinusoids at Fourier frequencies, when added together, approximate a square periodic function.

In practice, the A and B coefficients are computed by more efficient methods than the evaluation of sums. The "Fast Fourier Transform" developed and refined by Tukey and others (Tukey, 1967) uses mathematical identities to simplify and speed up the computation process, while producing the same results.

Any time series can be represented by its DFT, with no loss of information from the original data. The original N data points have been transformed into $N - 1$ sine and cosine coefficients (since A and B are jointly defined by the amplitude and phase of the component, they represent only 1 degree of freedom) plus the zero frequency term (the mean of the series). N data points are thus represented by coefficients representing N degrees of freedom, resulting in no information loss. The original data points can be recovered by inverting the transform:

$$X_t = A_0 + \sum_{j=1}^{\frac{N}{2}-1} [A_j \cos(\omega_j t) + B_j \sin(\omega_j t)] - A_{\frac{N}{2}} \qquad [1\text{-}8]$$

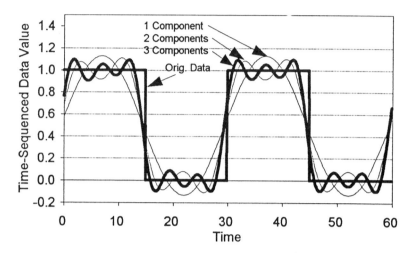

Figure 1.3.   Approximation of a nonsinusoidal function by a summation of Fourier components.

The amplitudes of the Fourier coefficients can be plotted against the Fourier frequencies to create a *periodogram* (see Figure 1.4). This plot is useful in finding strong periodicities in the data, which appear as peaks in the plot. Even if the periodicity does not fall on one of the orthogonal Fourier frequencies, nearby Fourier frequencies in the periodogram will have large amplitudes. Peaks in amplitude are often more visible when the periodogram is "smoothed" by some curve-fitting procedure. When a periodogram is presented in this fashion, it is called a *spectrum*, and the procedure of creating DFT's and examining their smoothed periodograms is called spectral analysis.

Periodograms can be used to study relationships between two time series variables. Multiplying the values of two periodograms gives a cross-periodogram (or when smoothed, a cross-spectrum). The values of a cross-periodogram will show a peak only when frequency elements in both original periodograms are high. Thus, a cross-periodogram or cross-spectrum plot will point out periodicities that are common to both time series values. This is the equivalent of establishing covariance between two static variables.

The values of two periodograms can also be subtracted from each other to create a *difference periodogram* (or, in a smoothed version, a differ-

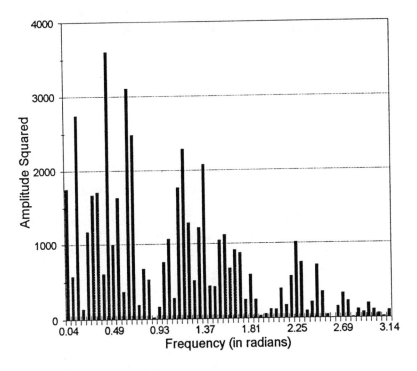

Figure 1.4. A typical periodogram.

ence spectrum). The values of this periodogram isolate periodic components that are present in one series but not in the other. Difference periodograms are valuable for hypothesis testing (see Watt, this volume).

Modeling Periodicities in Data

Any time series (even random white noise) can be decomposed into
a set of orthogonal Fourier frequencies, with an associated periodogram.
But usually the purpose of the time series analysis is to provide a
parsimonious description of a long time series, focusing on a small
number of periodic components, or to establish the cointegration (covariance) of two series in order to examine the relationship between two
time series variables. Examining the full spectrum, cross-spectrum, or
difference spectrum will give a full qualitative view of the situation but

is generally not sufficiently parsimonious for formal modeling. Methods for modeling periodicities must be introduced.

The strongest amplitude found in a discrete Fourier transform (at a Fourier frequency) may not represent the maximum amplitude of the strongest periodicity in the data, however. Fourier frequencies are defined for their property of orthogonality, with no regard for direct representation of any single periodicity within the data. Strong periodic components at non-Fourier frequencies will be seen as several moderately strong DFT coefficients at the Fourier frequencies that are near the frequency of the periodicities or are at integer multiples of the frequency (harmonics). For this reason, periodograms provide only a starting point for the estimation of strong periodic components in a model of the time series.

To find the optimum periodic model coefficients for a series of discrete data points, the sum of squares of the residual values about a series of periodic components must be minimized. The function to be minimized at any single frequency ω is

$$SS(X, A, B, \omega) = \sum_{t=1}^{N} [X_t - \overline{X} - A \cos(\omega t) - B \sin(\omega t)]^2 . \quad [1\text{-}9]$$

Bloomfield (1976) provides a very readable presentation of the solution to minimization. For any fixed ω, the least squared error estimates of the parameters are approximately given by

$$\overline{X} = \frac{1}{N} \sum_{t=1}^{N} X_t ,$$

$$\hat{A} = \frac{2}{N} \sum_{t=1}^{N} (X_t - \overline{X}) \cos(\omega t) , \quad [1\text{-}10]$$

$$\hat{B} = \frac{2}{N} \sum_{t=1}^{N} (X_t - \overline{X}) \sin(\omega t) .$$

The exact solutions for $\hat{A}$ and $\hat{B}$ are also given in Bloomfield and are computationally difficult. The above approximations are generally accurate to at least four significant digits. This is more than sufficient for most applications.

$\hat{A}$ and $\hat{B}$ have additional properties which make them useful in estimating the ω that will best fit the data. The amplitude R of the fitted periodic component is described by the following equation. This is the value usually used to create the periodogram.

$$R(\omega)^2 = A(\omega)^2 + B(\omega)^2 .$$ [1-11]

The amplitude of the periodogram at frequencies near the strongest periodic component in the data describes an inverted U. It is possible to find the value for ω that maximizes the amplitude R in the neighborhood of ω by numerical methods such as Newton's (cf. Conte, 1965). The frequency is adjusted computationally to produce the maximum value for $R(\omega)$ in the neighborhood of the starting value of ω (see Watt, this volume, for a more detailed description of this). As there are a number of local maxima in the periodogram, it is important to choose an initial value for ω that is close to the real maximum amplitude in the periodogram. This starting value of ω is obtained by choosing the strongest frequency in the DFT. After numerical adjustment, the final ω, with its associated A and B coefficients, represents the least squared error estimate of the best periodic model that contains only a single frequency.

Estimates of A, B, and ω can also be found for models made up of more than one periodic component. The sum of squares minimization is a simple extension of that outlined above.

A time series can, therefore, be decomposed into a parsimonious process model by an iterative stepwise process. This procedure is discussed in detail in Watt (1994). A summary of the process is given below.

1. Identify the fundamental frequency through analysis of a DFT periodogram.
2. Estimate the least squares values for A, B, and ω, as in Equations 1-9 and 1-10.
3. Compute the sums of squares for explained variance and for residual error, and determine if the model explains a significant amount of variance in the original series.
4. If the model explains significant and meaningful variance, extract the residuals around this periodic model.

5. Construct a DFT for this residual series, compute its DFT, and repeat Steps 2-5 until additional components add no significant or sizable explanation of variance in the series.

This procedure can be accomplished with standard statistical packages or with special purpose packages such as FATS (Watt, 1988). As with stepwise linear regression or factor analysis, each component added to the model increases the variance explained; therefore, if enough components are included in the model, the original series will be reproduced exactly. Of course, the goal is to adequately reconstruct the series with as few components as possible. The incremental increase due to each component can be determined and graphed much like a scree test.

Using Frequency Domain Techniques
to Represent Processes

It has been shown by the Wiener-Khintchine theorem that time domain and frequency domain analyses are mathematically equivalent. However, pragmatically speaking, the types of questions each addresses and the ways they view time series are different.

Both stochastic and deterministic processes can be reconstructed by Fourier analysis. A deterministic process will produce more regular cycles that can be reconstructed by fewer functions (Gottman, 1981; Buder, this volume). Further, a model built using data from the first half of a long series should adequately "forecast" the data for the second half of the series if the function is deterministic. This is analogous to the issue of stationarity in the other two paradigms.

As with the other two techniques, the appropriate model can be generated for the series representing each case if there are enough observations. The researcher must then test the homogeneity of the model so generated across cases.

In addition to the inductive descriptive approach outlined above, an a priori cyclical model (based on either theory or prior research) can be fit to a data set and tested for significance. If one has a model that predicts the appearance of cycles of a certain frequency, that model can be tested against an observed time series (see Barnett & Cho, this volume).

Two time series can also be correlated in the frequency domain. In the descriptive analysis (univariate), the time series are decomposed into a set of orthogonal components of varying frequencies. Each component, at a given frequency, will have a phase and amplitude (or cosine and sine coefficient) for each co-occurring series. The methods outlined by Watt (1994, this volume) can be used to identify common periodic components in both series (when the object is to find coordinated behavior between the two series) or to identify periodic components that appear strongly in one series but not in the other (when the object is to establish the effect of an independent variable that is present in one series and absent in the other).

Conclusion

One can choose to combine the approaches presented above. For example, one could use Fourier or spectral analysis to model the major deterministic patterns in the data. Cross-spectral analysis could be used to determine the extent to which the major patterns were coordinated across communicators or variables (Buder, this volume). Then, one could use stochastic techniques to model mutual adaptation as described in Cappella's chapter. The general strategy of first modeling cumulative processes that produce nonstationarity, followed by modeling periodicities in the frequency domain, followed finally by modeling stochastic processes in the time domain is suggested by Watt (1994).

Certainly, other "paradigms" might be added to the ones reviewed here. Most notably, nonlinear dynamic system that use "chaos" mathematics to model apparently random behavior as deterministic may have some real value (see VanLear, West & Biocca, Kaplowitz & Fink, all this volume).

Our intention in developing this book has been to produce a multipurpose volume. This book can be read by scholars and students interested in the conceptual and theoretical implications of viewing communication as a process. As such, it would make a useful addition to course readings in a graduate seminar in communication theory. Likewise, this volume could be used in a methods seminar to help students explore ways of modeling communication dynamics. It is our hope that the strong efforts of the contributors to this book will spur more use of dynamic analysis in investigating communication phenomena.

Communication Process
Approaches and Models

Patterns, Cycles, and Dynamic Coordination

C. ARTHUR VANLEAR

> If we accept the concept of process, we view the events and relationships
> as dynamic, on-going, ever-changing, continuous. . . . We mean that it
> does not have a beginning, an end, a fixed sequence of events. . . . The
> ingredients within a process interact; each affects all of the others.
>
> —Berlo (1960, p. 24)

Nearly every basic communication text for the past 35 years has
instructed students that "communication is a process." This is usually
accompanied by some prose inspired from Berlo's (1960) book describing it as dynamic, ever moving, in flux, and without end. Despite its
centrality as an assumption, there is little agreement about the implications of a process view of communication (Alexander, 1975; Berlo,
1977; Smith, 1972).

Johnson and Proctor (1992) recently called for us to abandon the
notion of communication as a process. Apparently they asked their

introductory students to define a "process" and provide an example after reading their book's definition. When most of the students provided definitions that were, in Johnson and Proctor's view, "mechanistic" and "linear" and only a few provided answers that the teachers deemed sufficiently "Berlo-esque," they concluded that it was time to abandon the assumption that communication is a process.

I do not believe that Johnson and Proctor's pedagogical failure is sufficient warrant for abandoning one of our most central assumptions. If anything it highlights the fact that most people tend to think in linear terms and tend to accommodate concepts to their way of thinking. If one tries to explain "relativity" to undergraduates, one encounters similar problems. However, no one has suggested that Einstein's ideas are not useful because they are hard for undergraduates to understand. What is necessary is to move from vague metaphorical references to "dynamic flux" to more precise principles and operationalizations. Berlo (1977) himself chided scholars for treating "process as mystery" and proposed some suggestions for empirical research on process. The research programs described in this book are good examples of dynamic models that move us well beyond "process as mystery."

This chapter provides a brief historical survey of process models of communication. I focus especially on decision emergence in small groups and relationship emergence because of my own research interests. This review is then used to focus attention on several issues and assumptions that I believe are important for constructing process models of communication.

Conceptualizing Dynamic Patterns

The search for pattern is a central goal of science. The identification of pattern is prerequisite to both prediction and explanation and is, therefore, the focus of most of our description. Pattern can be recognized as a redundancy across space and across time. If we recognize a pattern across a large enough number of cases, it permits us to "generalize" to other unobserved cases. If we recognize a pattern over a long enough period of time, it permits us to "predict" it will continue into the future. The science of communication requires the identification of patterns across cases (people, relationships, groups, organizations, societies, etc.) and across time. The central theme of this book is the identification and modeling of these dynamic patterns in space-time.

The identification and explication of communication as a *process* is most often credited to Schramm (1954) and Berlo (1960). Berlo's quote at the beginning of this chapter is often used as the quintessential definition of process. Berlo (1960, 1977) borrowed freely from the philosophy of Whitehead (1929) who contended that "how an actual entity becomes constitutes what that actual entity is. . . . Its 'being' is constituted by its 'becoming' " (pp. 34-35). Although the field has been almost unanimous in its acceptance that "communication is a process," there has been no such unanimity or agreement about what that means when faced with the pragmatics of doing communication research. If I were to review the arguments of every scholar who has lamented the lack of "true" process research I would have space for little else. Yet I am not so downcast as my colleagues. This assumption has been father, mother, and/or midwife to many of the most important models and theories of communication over the past 35 years and has spawned a number of methodological advances (many of which are reviewed in this volume). Research too is a process without a final ideal or ultimate end state.

The Linear Mechanistic Approach to Process

> Absolute, true, and mathematical time, of itself, and from its own nature, flows equably without relation to anything external, and by another name is called duration.
>
> —Isaac Newton, *Philosophiae Naturalis Principia Mathematica* (1687/1959)

Perhaps the most typical dynamic pattern observed in the social and behavioral sciences is covariation: If X, then Y. *One* of the requirements of causal explanation is that the covariation between cause and effect be temporally sequenced such that the cause precedes the effect. When covariation is temporally ordered and the history of the variables can be controlled, it can provide the basis of prediction—for example, Granger causality (Cappella, this volume; Monge & Kalman, this volume).

The linear mechanistic model claims to represent process by recognizing the *mutual causality* inherent in communication systems (Fisher,

1978b). The roles of senders and receivers are arbitrary designations because every sender is a receiver and every receiver a sender. Every cause is recognized as an effect of something and every effect is a cause. One could, theoretically, trace the chain of causes and effects back an infinite distance. Further, because so many variables work together to produce a given effect, perfect prediction is only an ideal. Therefore, errors in prediction result not only from measurement and sampling error but from unmeasured causal variables. Complex, multivariate, structural equation models are likely to be a preferred technique of this school of process researchers.

This way of conceptualizing process has often been presented as a rhetorical foil to show how *not* to do "true" process research. Smith (1972) is particularly contemptuous of the mechanistic model as linear, deterministic, archaic, and, worst of all, Newtonian. He argues that a mechanistic view of process is consistent with an archaic Newtonian view of the world that separates matter from energy and process, that clings to the ideal of objectivity in the face of Heisenberg's (1930) demonstration of its impossibility, and that embraces linear causal determinism instead of quantum relativism as a model for science.[1]

Smith suggests that process as Whitehead and Berlo conceive of it recognizes that the nature of a phenomenon is constituted by the processes that bring it into being rather than a materialistic structure and is, therefore, more consistent with 20th-century relativism. Smith contends that taking a Whiteheadian approach to process implies (a) recognizing an inherent limitation to the objectivity of knowledge, (b) that one can accept a number of differing explanations so long as they derive from differing perspectives (apparently the mechanistic view is not among the list of acceptable perspectives), and (c) that a holistic perspective offers a more complete view than the summative accumulation of knowledge offered by the traditional view of science.

Despite Smith's (1972) critique about 25 ago, most current approaches to process research would still probably be identified as relatively mechanistic. If Johnson and Proctor's (1992) experiment demonstrated anything, it was that most people tend to think of process in linear, mechanistic, Newtonian terms. If, as Smith claims, reality is constructed rather than objectively given, most people seem to construct a Newtonian view of process. Although many of us realize in the back of our minds that the apparently material objects we work with everyday owe their natures to the dynamic flux of quantum physics, it often pays us to pretend that matter and energy are separate and that the world is made up of at least semipermanent structures. Just as Newtonian physics usually works well enough for engineers, architects, carpenters, and the rest of us in our everyday life, so too a Newtonian view of communication processes may be quite capable of providing many useful, if limited, insights into the pragmatic functioning of communication in the everyday world.[2]

The Stochastic Open Systems
Perspective on Process

One of the most popular responses to critiques of the mechanistic approach like Smith's was a view of process that combined an open systems perspective (von Bertalanffy, 1968) with information theory and a stochastic view of process.[3] A system is defined as "a whole which functions as a whole by virtue of the interdependence of its parts" (Rapoport, 1968, p. xvii). This implies the key assumption of a systems perspective, "holism," which in turn implies the principles of "nonsummativity" ("the whole is different from the sum of its parts"). The characteristics of the system emerge from the processes and interrelationships of its elements (Fisher, 1978a, 1978b).

Systems are constituted by the dynamic interrelationships of smaller subsystems (which are composed of smaller interrelating systems, etc.) and are nested within larger suprasystems. Because each of these system levels is "open," it exchanges matter/energy/information across systems boundaries in highly complex ways.

Open systems are capable of both growth or change and stability. The key to a system's stability is its self-correcting negative feedback process. Negative feedback is a deviation counteraction process such that when system values are perturbed or exceed some critical level (e.g., they get too high) corrective action is initiated to bring the levels back within the functional parameters of the system; if the values deviate too far in the other direction (e.g., they get too low), the self-correcting process is again activated. In this way a dynamic equilibrium (homeostasis) is achieved. A thermostat is the classic mechanistic example of a negative feedback process.

Open systems are also capable of growth and change, and this may occur either as the result of recalibration of an existing steady state to a new level of homeostasis with different baseline parameters or through positive feedback (deviation amplifying) processes. In a positive feedback process, change in one part of the system leads to change in another part that leads to more change. Change feeds on itself to produce an exponential increase in the *rate* of change in the system. Some clearly mechanistic models are presented as systems models. The systems approach discussed here differs from a mechanistic systems model in several important ways. First, it is viewed as an open system. As such, it is capable of growth and change. Change could be either equifinal (different initial conditions can produce the same end state) or multifinal (the same initial conditions can produce different end states). The initial conditions of an open system (the initial characteristics and configurations of its parts) do not *determine* the end state of the system. The outcome of an open system is contingent upon the complex interaction of inputs and internal system processes that are themselves always evolving. Nonlinear relationships, complex interactions, and stochastic probability are viewed as more appropriate models than simple additive linear equations.

Information theory (Cherry, 1957; Shannon & Weaver, 1949) was wedded to systems theory ideas (Bateson, 1972) early on. Dynamic patterns are often defined in terms of information—"the reduction of uncertainty" (Cherry, 1957; Fisher, 1978a; Shannon & Weaver, 1949). If a temporal pattern is present, then knowledge of an event at time t can reduce one's uncertainty of an event at time $t + 1$ (see VanLear & Watt, this volume).

Smith (1972), Hawes (1973), Berlo (1977), and Fisher (1978b) have argued that modeling communication as a stochastic process avoids the problem of mechanistic causal determinism. Fisher (1978b) contends that people are capable of choices from a universe of alternatives. These choices may be *constrained* (not determined) by a combination of past choices, the choices of others, and rules (whether tacit or explicit). These constraints make certain choices more probable than others and therefore set up redundant sequences of behavior (a "pattern"). The more redundant the sequence (pattern), the less uncertainty. Rules, constraint, pattern, and information are all linked by the same mathematical definition. In this perspective, a stochastic model is required not just because there is always measurement and sampling error and not because there are too many unmeasured "causal" variables but because behavior is the result of constraints (rules) on *choices*, not necessary and sufficient causal forces (laws) (Fisher, 1978b). Therefore, patterns are inherently probabilistic.[4]

> Verbal and nonverbal behaviors are transformed into verbal and nonverbal symbols when the behaviors are ordered or patterned. It is their patterning that gives them "meaning." When others recognize the patterns, they can share in the use of those symbols making possible human communication. (Hawes, 1973, p. 15)

In this perspective, communication behaviors are considered in terms of their "pragmatic function" (Watzlawick, Beavin, & Jackson, 1967). The function of a behavior is what it accomplishes, and a communication function is always accomplished vis-à-vis another person. Therefore,

> if the function of a symbol is to be determined, the relationship binding the symbol users must be defined. . . . All communication interacts [pairs of concatenous behaviors by separate interactors] conceal, repeat or disclose information about the relationships among symbol users enacting the symbol systems. (Hawes, 1973, p. 17)

By identifying redundant patterns of functional behaviors (e.g., interacts and longer sequences), Hawes (1973) argued that one can uncover the "typified," "in order to," and "because motives" in human communication systems.

Hawes (1972a, 1972b) had participants in medical interviews help develop a category system for identifying the functions of their communicative behaviors. He then used "stimulated recall" to allow the participants to code their own behaviors into that system, preserving the temporal sequence of behaviors.[5] Likewise, Fisher (1977) used "transactional coding rules" which recognize that the function of an act can only be identified when placed in its interactional context (the ongoing stream of behavior). Using Markov chain statistics and information theory, these researchers were able to identify the redundant patterns of interaction.[6] Self-coding through stimulated recall and "transactional coding rules" were these researchers' approach to Whitehead's (1929) argument that an entity's being is constituted by its becoming: The meaning of behavior is constituted and revealed in its interactional history and context.

Patterns of Mutual Adaptation

Scholars operating from the systems perspective have often used Bateson's (1972) distinction between symmetrical and complementary interaction patterns. Bateson (1972) argued that the most basic elements of form and pattern (including dynamic patterns) can be characterized by their relative symmetry or complementarity depending on whether two parts or aspects of a system achieved functional integration in the system although maximizing similarity or difference. His applications of these patterns to social systems consisted of patterns of mutual adaptation between groups and between individuals. According to Bateson, interaction can be identified as symmetrical (the exchange of functionally similar behaviors) or complementary (the exchange of functionally dissimilar behaviors). Either of these patterns, if employed exclusively, can be progressive (i.e., deviation amplifying), or in Bateson's terms, "schismogenic," and can lead to the destruction of the system.

For example, if boasting by one party leads to boasting by the other, which in turn leads to more boasting by the first party, the "symmetrical schismogenesis" can cause the system to spiral out of control. If one party (A) blames the other (B) for a problem and party B blames A, the situation can escalate to violence or termination of the relationship. Such symmetrical progressions can be used to explain patterns from the arms race to marital conflict in which each partner to the relationship vies for the "one-up" position and refuses to defer to the other. However, complementary interaction can also be "schismogenic." For example, when one group or person (A) engages in exhibitionism and the other (B) in spectatorship, the more exhibitionist A becomes the more intense B's spectatorship, and the more intense B's spectatorship the more exhibitionist A becomes. Such complementary patterns could explain, say, violence in hockey or sex and violence on TV. Likewise, Edna Rogers describes a pattern of ridged complementarity of relational control that has been linked to relational problems (Rogers & Bagarozzi, 1983; VanLear & Zietlow, 1990; Watzlawick et al., 1967).

Schismogenesis results when the symmetrical or complementary pattern maintains itself and escalates in intensity or extremity. However, if escalating symmetry is restrained or punctuated by a period of complementarity and if complementary patterns are interspersed with periods of symmetry, then a larger metapattern called a "parallel" relationship emerges (Fisher & Drecksel, 1983; Lederer & Jackson, 1968). Research to date indicates that ridged or escalating patterns (symmetrical or complementary) tend to be dysfunctional for relational systems, whereas more flexible patterns like the parallel relationship are more satisfying (Gottman, 1979b; Rogers & Bagarozzi, 1983; Van-Lear & Zietlow, 1990). Schismogenic patterns are examples of Weick's (1979) contention that tightly coupled systems are not always desirable.

Other scholars have used the concepts of reciprocity and compensation (Burgoon, Dillman, & Stern, 1991, 1993; Cappella, this volume) to describe patterns of mutual adaptation similar to symmetry and complementarity. Burgoon et al. (1993) define reciprocity as "the process of behavioral adaptation in which one responds, in a similar direction, to a partner's behaviors with behaviors of comparable functional value" and interpersonal compensation as "the process of behavioral adaptation in which one responds with behaviors of comparable functional value but in the opposite direction" (p. 302). Comparable functional value means that the behaviors relate to the same functional dimension of communication.

Although there is an obvious similarity between the reciprocity/compensation distinction and the patterns of symmetry and complementarity, the terms reciprocity and compensation do *not* necessarily imply potentially schismogenic patterns. Likewise, scholars who use the reciprocity/compensation terminology are less likely to cast their explanations in open systems terms than scholars using Bateson's (1972) concepts. For example, reciprocity and compensation have been posited to be the result of "expectancy violations" (Burgoon, 1978, 1983) or a "discrepancy-arousal" relationship (Cappella & Greene, 1982, 1984).

Patterns such as symmetry and complementarity or reciprocity and compensation are usually referred to as patterns of *mutual* adaptation. However, the degree of influence can be either symmetrical (*mutually* adaptive) or asymmetrical (when one person's behavior dominates or entrains the other's). These patterns of mutual or asymmetric adaptation can be discriminated by time series analysis regardless of the functions of the behaviors being coded or measured and are of major theoretical importance (Cappella, this volume).

Uniphasic Versus Multiple Sequence Processes

Despite Berlo's (1960) claim that viewing communication as a process implies that it does not have "a fixed sequence of events" (p. 24), many process models, even those proposed from an open systems perspective, pictured communication as passing through a unitary phasic sequence. Much like Piaget's (Piaget & Inhelder, 1969) theory of child development, developmental stage or phase models have been forwarded for group decision making (Bales & Strodtbeck, 1951; Fisher, 1970; Mabry, 1975), conflict development (Ellis & Fisher, 1975), and relationship development (Altman & Taylor, 1973; Honeycutt, Cantrill, & Greene, 1989; Knapp, 1978; VanLear & Trujillo, 1986). The logic behind these "functional phasic models" goes something like this:

- Certain social phenomena (e.g., group decisions, relationships) do not spring spontaneously into being in their final form. They must be developed.
- Communication and its associated functions are necessary for a developed mature group decision, relationship, and so on.
- These phenomena tend to develop through a series of stages or phases because certain communication functions are prerequisite for efficient or effective movement from one stage to the next.
- Because progression through the phases is functionally efficacious, social norms tend to support the phasic structure and such phases are learned as social scripts or schemata.

For example, relationships are often pictured as emerging through a series of developmental stages (Altman & Taylor, 1973; Knapp, 1978; VanLear & Trujillo, 1986). Communicators first meet, present an opening line, and engage in stereotyped interaction (orientation). Next, they engage in searching for commonalities, small talk, and reduction of uncertainty (exploration). Then, they expand their breadth and depth of communication, make more mutual positive judgments about each other, and increase their involvement in each others' lives (interpersonal growth). Empirical research provided some support for this view of relationship development (Altman & Taylor, 1973; Knapp, Ellis, & Williams, 1980; VanLear & Trujillo, 1986).

Likewise, phases of group decision emergence were hypothesized because it is most efficacious if groups first define the problem and orient themselves to it (orientation), next, debate alternative ideas and possibilities (conflict), then develop the necessary consensus behind the preferred solution (emergence), and finally, secure commitment from members to that decision (reinforcement) (Fisher, 1970). Early studies looking at both the relative frequency of certain communication behaviors over time (Bales & Strodtbeck, 1951; Mabry, 1975) and systematic variations in interaction patterns (Fisher, 1970), generally tended to support such a phasic model of group decision emergence.

Poole (1981) argued that this model had not been adequately tested nor compared against an alternative multiple-sequence model. Poole (1981, 1983) presented evidence that although many groups do follow this phasic sequence other groups deviate from it in a variety of ways, suggesting that a multiple-sequence model is a more appropriate view of group decision emergence.

Likewise, the idea of a uniphasic model has been challenged in other contexts, including "social confrontation" (Newell & Stutman, 1988) and relationship emergence (Baxter & Wilmot, 1983; Delia, 1980; Huston, Surra, Fitzgerald, & Cate, 1981). The argument is that many different courses of action are available to people as they jointly enact social episodes and relationships. It is inevitable that some people will choose not to follow the normative sequence of events. Likewise, variations in goals and situational factors also lead to variations in trajectories or courses of development. If "end states" are multifinal, then multiple sequences are to be expected. In fact, from this perspective, if a state of being is always in the process of becoming, as Whitehead contends, then end states are merely the latest "snapshot" of a continually evolving process.

Structuration

Giddens (1984) argues that social structures are created by the very people who are subject to and constrained by them. Every time we pattern our behavior according to a rule we participate in recreating and strengthening the social order. If no one conforms to the rule (e.g., the former 55-mph speed limit), than it is no longer the rule de facto. Social structures are not, therefore, given a priori but are emergent and enacted. The nature of a social phenomenon is defined by the process that brings it into being. Structuration offers one view of Whitehead's (1929) contention that being is constituted by becoming and is often cited by proponents of a multiple-sequence model.

Linear Versus Cyclical Patterns

They are not changed from their first estate; But by their change their being doe dilate: And turning to themselves at length againe, Do work

their owne perfection so by fate; Then over them Change doth not rule
and raigne; But they raigne over change, and do their states maintaine.

—Edmund Spenser "Mutabilitie cantos,"
Faerie Queene (1552-1599)

One might expect that the definition of a "linear" process would be
rather *straightforward* (no pun intended). However, sometimes the term
linear process is used to refer to a precise mathematical function like a
linear regression trend or to additive equations (linear algebra). In other
cases, it is used to refer to any process that has a direction or end state
—phasic models are viewed as linear processes, although the variable
trends that comprise them are usually curvilinear. One discussion
(Werner & Baxter, 1994) even refers to any process characterized by
change as linear. Here, I generally use the term linear to refer to a
unidirectional process (see Figure 2.1a). Curvilinear refers to trends
that evidence a bend in the regression equation (exponential or logarith-
mic). Werner and Haggard (1985) define a cyclical pattern as "the
cessation and recurrence of similar activities and feelings, or, in other
cases, to a cycle in which behavior progresses repeatedly from a point
of origin, through a pattern, and back to the same or very similar point
of origin" (pp. 62-63). Although, strictly speaking, a quadratic trend
could be called a cycle because variable values return to previous levels, I generally reserve the term cycle for processes in which there are
at least two zeniths and two nadirs and can be expected to recur
periodically.

Traditional social and behavioral models have tended to focus on
linear directional models both for describing variable relationships and
for describing change over time. However, there are sound theoretical
reasons to model communication processes as cyclical.

The Epistemology of Cycles

Altman, Vinsel, and Brown (1981) argue for a "dialectic" model of
relationship development. A dialectic is a dynamic tension between
opposites. Dialectic scholars contend that people regularly experience
a dynamic tension between such polar opposite desires as "stability
versus change," "openness versus closedness" (Altman et al., 1981;
Baxter, 1988), autonomy versus dependence, dominance versus deference, and so forth. *One* way such competing tendencies can manifest
themselves is in cyclical alternation over time.

A systems perspective may also call for us to expect cyclical patterns over time (VanLear, 1991). Human social systems are capable of both stability and change. Stability of systems is often modeled as self-correcting negative feedback (deviation counteraction) or dynamic equilibrium (homeostasis), whereas change is conceived as positive feedback (morphogenesis), growth, or recalibration. Central to most systems approaches is the identification and explanation of the self-correcting properties of systems.

Unrestricted continual growth is usually untenable. There are probably upper and lower limits to most variables and system processes. Relationships may suffer from a lack of intimacy or from too much (VanLear, 1991). If groups avoid conflict, their decisions may suffer from "group think," but when conflict becomes excessive, this too can be detrimental (Fisher, 1980). One needs to be assertive and exercise leadership, but there are times when subordination and deference to others is called for. The media may become more and more sensational in response to their audience's demand; however, there may be certain boundaries of propriety and acceptability that, if exceeded, could create a backlash and lead to regulation and restrictions. When the upper threshold is reached, the system must reduce that variable value or risk destruction; however, when the lower level is reached, the system must increase the variable level or dissolve. By cyclical alternation, dynamic equilibrium is achieved (Fisher & Drecksel, 1983).

For example, reciprocal increases in the intimacy level of self-disclosure is usually thought to index growth in an interpersonal relationship. Person A's disclosures are responded to by disclosures by person B, which in turn elicits further disclosure from person A, such that each person increases the breadth (amount) and depth (intimacy) of their self-revelations. However, if this process were to continue unrestrained, both parties would soon reach a point where they would be revealing a large amount of highly sensitive information about themselves. There is a threshold of intimacy in most relationships beyond which it is uncomfortable, inappropriate, or even dangerous to exceed, and when that threshold is reached, self-disclosure may begin to mutually decline. However, excessive avoidance of disclosure and prolonged restraint for a long time could imply lack of trust, create uncertainty, and stifle further growth in the relationship. Just as a thermostat regulates the temperature in a room to keep it from getting too hot or too cold, interpersonal system processes regulate the intimacy level of the relationship not by a static lack of variance but through cyclical variation over time (VanLear, 1991). Systems may recalibrate so that the threshold is raised or lowered, but it is unlikely that linear progress is an adequate model of system change.

Regularity and Complexity of Cycles

Although there are bound to be some irregularities, VanLear (1991) provides several reasons to expect regularity in behavioral cycles:

> First, people like a degree of predictability and stability in their social lives and the pacing of communication cycles may provide them with that continuity. Second, people have natural physiological rhythms which may manifest in regular behavioral cycles (Chapple, 1970; Warner, 1991). Finally, our social lives are structured around regular periodic social activities. We often go to work, school, church, bowling, lunch, coffee, or meetings at regular times. In the course of these activities we often see the same people and engage in a regular sequence of interaction. These regularities may provide the contexts and constraints that entrain communication behaviors into predictable cycles. (p. 341)

The regularity of these cycles in turn permit us to coordinate our behavior with others by timing and matching (or compensating) our periodic behaviors to theirs (cf. Buder, Warner, this volume). People punctuate their lives into regular events and seasons on which they impose ritualistic beginnings and endings.

Obviously, these various sources of cyclical activity have different frequencies. At the level of historical processes for whole cultures or societies, one might expect cycles with frequencies spanning decades, centuries, or even millennia ("Those who do not know history are doomed to repeat it"). Other social institutions or organizations as well as individuals may have "life cycles" that span decades. The seasons of the year produce regular cyclical activity as does the 7-day week and the 24-hour day (Duck, Rutt, Hurst, & Strejc, 1991; see also Barnett & Cho, this volume). Conversations, meetings, and other regular events are structured into beginnings, middles, and endings that are repetitively enacted over time with regular encounters. And our physiological rhythms (Warner, this volume) and attention spans (see Meadowcroft, this volume) can create very short duration cycles spanning only minutes or seconds. One implication is that different variables and processes can produce cycles of different frequencies. Another possible implication is that communication processes can be thought of as a series of nested cycles of different frequencies embedded within each other.

Another variation is that the frequency (and therefore, the period) of a cyclical process can systematically change over time. A system can "recalibrate" by an increase or decrease in the "baseline" level of functioning. A system can change by a systematic increase or decrease (i.e., a dissipative or damped system) or periodic variation in the amplitude of cyclical behavior. Finally, a complex system can display variations of both frequency and amplitude over its life cycle. Some variations in developmental trajectories are illustrated in Figures 2.1a-2.1f.

For example, Altman et al. (1981) argue that during relationship development partners to a relationship experience a dialectic tension between "openness" and "closedness." This tension is hypothesized to produce cycles of openness and closedness that systematically varied in frequency and amplitude. Newly formed relationships undergo frequent (short) openness/closedness cycles of relatively small amplitude. As relationships progress, cycling is less frequent (Baxter & Wilmot, 1983) but of much greater amplitude (VanLear, 1991). They also suggest that successful relationships should be characterized by the matching and timing of the cycles of relational partners, and there is evidence that this is the case (VanLear, 1991). In addition, VanLear (1991) found that stable relationships tended to have smaller (flatter) amplitudes, whereas relationships that were changing tended to have much higher amplitudes of openness/closedness cycling. VanLear (1991) also found short cycles within conversations embedded within longer cycles that developed across conversations. Other chapters discuss dissipation of cycles and modeling communication as systematic variation in cyclical behavior.

It is important to distinguish between regular cycles and the stochastic process of "drifting" (McCleary & Hay, 1980). It is possible for a stochastic process to drift above and/or below the mean value for periods of time in a "random walk" that can look like an irregular trend or cycle, but the fact that variable values return to previous levels is happenstance, not a cycle.

Spirals

Spirals have been conceptualized in several ways in the literature. Werner and Baxter (1994) seem to imply that a spiral is simply an irregular cycle that never repeats itself exactly.

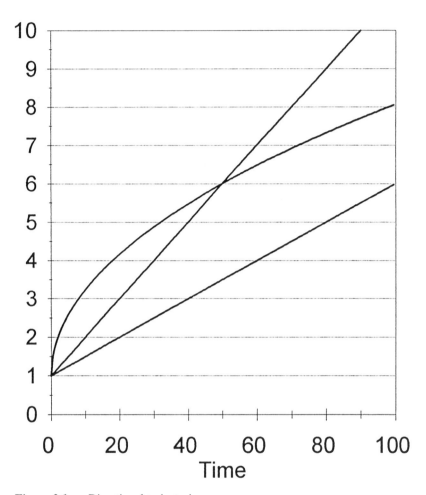

Figure 2.1a. Directional trajectories.

In another approach, it is recognized that human beings are not bound by the present but can retrospectively examine the past through memory (and even reinterpret it). They can also plan for and anticipate the future. The future and the past are therefore "layered" upon the present so that the human experience of time is not completely linear (Kolaja, 1969).

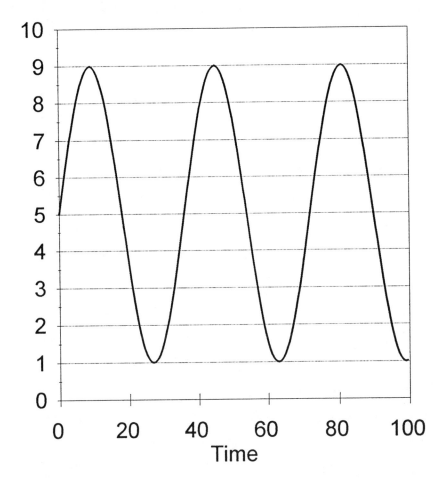

Figure 2.1b. Simple stable cycle.

This human ability to go backward and forward in time can be thought of as a spiral.[7]

One can also think of a spiral as a three-dimensional cycle or helix. As a process progresses through time, values vary in multidimensional space so that the past is only repeated when the same configuration of all values repeats itself.

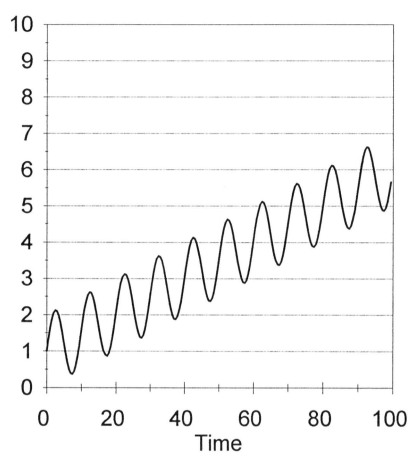

Figure 2.1c.   A cycle plus linear trend.

Nonlinear Dynamical Systems and Chaos

Dynamical systems theory differs from the open systems theory discussed previously in that it assumes a deterministic universe such that the initial states of a system do determine the later states. There are two parts to a dynamical system: "a state (the essential information about a system) and a dynamic (a rule that describes how the state evolves with time)" (Crutchfield, Farmer, Packard, & Shaw, 1986,

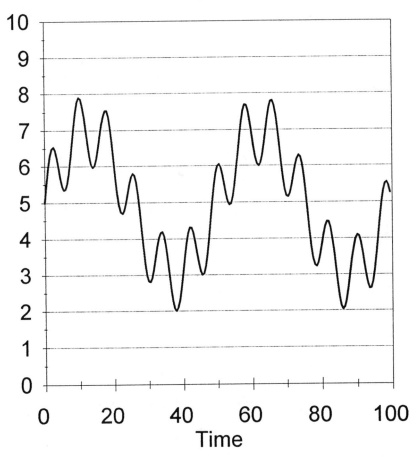

Figure 2.1d. Embedded cycles.

p. 49). Evolution of the system can be geometrically represented as movement through a "state space" (Crutchfield, et al., 1986) or "phase space" that is "a mathematical space with orthogonal coordinate directions representing each of the variables needed to specify the instantaneous state of the system" (Baker & Gollub, 1990, p. 7). For example, the state space of a pendulum can be defined by its velocity and position.

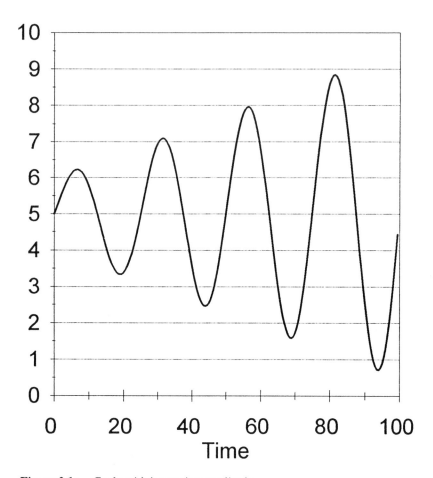

Figure 2.1e.   Cycle with increasing amplitude.

The usefulness of the concept state space is that it allows a geometrical representation of the temporal evolution of a system. Such a representation is useful for discovering the "attractors" of the system. An attractor is the behavior that the system "prefers" or "is attracted to." Given friction and no motive power, a pendulum will eventually come to rest at a given point called a "fixed point attractor." This would be geometrically represented as a spiraling orbit in two-dimensional

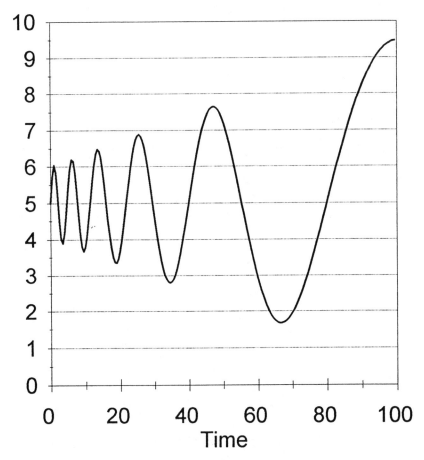

Figure 2.1f. Cycle with increasing period and amplitude.

state space. Theories that hold that the initial match of two people's personalities will lead them to gravitate toward a specific level of attraction might be analogous to a "point attractor" theory.

A second, and more complex, kind of attractor is a "limit cycle" in which the system does not come to rest but cycles periodically through a series of states and is represented geometrically as a closed loop in state space. Several models already discussed offer obvious examples.

The third most complicated attractor is a "torus." A torus attractor is the result of two (or more) independent oscillators. In state space, the geometry of a torus attractor would resemble a donut. A system may have several types of attractors such that different initial conditions result in evolution to different attractors. All three of these types of attractors have the advantage of making the system predictable.

One of the major contributions of nonlinear dynamical systems has been the discovery of "chaotic" or "strange" attractors. Poincaré (1946) noted that very small changes in the present can cause much larger effects in the future. Likewise, small uncertainties (errors) can grow exponentially into extremely large uncertainties over time, and this can happen even in very simple systems. Therefore, even a relatively simple deterministic system can display apparently random behavior, and this implies new fundamental limits on the ability to predict such systems. This means of generating apparent randomness is called "chaos." Lorenz (1963) was first to discover a chaotic attractor.

In a chaotic system, two orbits that begin nearby each other diverge exponentially fast. Yet because attractors have a finite size they cannot diverge forever and so must "fold" over onto themselves. This "stretching and folding" "shuffles," the orbits resulting in random evolution. "Chaotic systems generate randomness on their own without the need for any external random inputs" (Crutchfield et al., 1986, p. 53). Chaotic attractors demonstrate that even random behavior may have an underlying geometric form. The necessary (but not sufficient) conditions for chaos are (a) at least three dynamical variables and (b) that the "equations of motion" must contain a nonlinear term that couples several of the variables. This allows divergent trajectories, confinement of motion to a finite region of the phase space, and unique trajectories (Baker & Gollub, 1990). Some communication scholars have suggested that communication processes may be chaotic systems (e.g., Baron, Amazeen, & Beer, 1994; West & Biocca, this volume).

Although chaos has been heralded by some as the new scientific paradigm, even some of its supporters admit to its limitations. First, randomness can be generated by extremely complicated systems with many inputs (i.e., an open system) as well as by chaotic systems. Second, the evidence for chaos, especially in communication systems, is often only indirect. Third, even if we know a system is chaotic, that alone does not tell us much: It does not lead to long-term prediction. Fourth, even its advocates refer to chaos mathematics as "intractable." This may make it inaccessible to many communication students and limit its benefits as an explanation. Stochastic statistical methods can usually deal with the randomness of the system without considering chaos. Nonlinear dynamical systems may have promise as a paradigm for communication processes, but the range of application and its utility for explanation have yet to be determined (or perhaps it has been determined but its chaotic properties just make it unpredictable).

Assumptions of a
Process Model of Communication

> The theory of relativity put an end to the idea of absolute time! . . . We must accept that time is not completely separate from and independent of space, but is combined with it to form an object called space-time. . . . Thus time became a more personal concept, relative to the observer who measured it.
>
> —Stephen Hawking (1988, pp. 21, 23, 143)

Communication is a multiparadigmatic discipline, and this is nothing to be ashamed of. Since Heisenberg (1930), philosophers of science have largely rejected the positivist ideal of a single knowable true representation of reality (Feyerabend, 1963; Kuhn, 1970; Suppe, 1974). According to Hawking (1988),

> A theory is just a model of the universe, or a restricted part of it, and a set of rules that relate quantities in the model to observations that we make. It exists only in our minds and does not have any other reality (whatever that might mean). . . . You can never prove it. (pp. 9-10)

Feyerabend (1963, 1965, 1970) goes so far as to argue that the greatest advances in sciences come not from a Kuhnian revolution in which one dominant paradigm is exchanged for another but from the parallel development of competing incommensurable scientific theories, each of which is "factually adequate" within its own frame of reference and "partially overlapping." One theory cannot be critiqued with the concepts and criteria from another frame of reference because all that such an "argument from synonymy" demonstrates is the incommensurability of theories, not the superiority of one or another (Feyerabend, 1963).

This is not to say that all theories are equal, only that they cannot be evaluated by their commensurability with other theories. Neither is it necessary to reject empirical tests of evidence just because we can never have absolute positive proof of a single truth. Theory and research are a process of persuasive argument with data and results used as evidence and the theoretical explanation as the warrant (Anderson, 1987). What follows is not a model of communication but a set of conclusions and assumptions about communication processes that provide the beginnings of a perspective from which to build communication process models.

Relative Stability and Change
of Communication Processes

1. The degree of stability or change evidenced by a communication process depends upon the variables observed, the level of analysis, the temporal scope or horizon of the study or model, and the punctuation of the continuous temporal stream.

We have been told that "the more things change, the more they remain the same." Yet we have also heard that "the only constant is change." Communication processes evidence both stability and change. People need a degree of predictability in their social world, and organized patterns provide such stability. Yet people also need variation, change, and novelty. Too much stability breeds stagnation and boredom. People want progress, growth, and change.

It seems rather obvious that the degree of stability or change observed depends on the variables considered. Communication satisfaction will likely change more quickly than marital satisfaction. Not only the variables but the level of abstraction at which they are assessed affect the degree of change observed. For example, self-disclosure, measured as coded statements in a conversation, is likely to vary more frequently than global impressions of openness.

This realization leads to the following conclusion:

1a. Communication processes (especially complex multidimensional processes) are likely to exhibit stability and change contemporaneously.

For example, VanLear (1992) found that approaches to communication in marriage evidenced *both* continuity *and* change from one generation to the next. Children tended (under certain conditions) to learn and replicate certain aspects of their parents' marital style and to rebel against other aspects.

Of course, in one sense multidimensional representation of a process means that a process is less likely to recur because all dimensions must realign to a previous configuration periodically, not just a single variable value.

There are also differences in levels of process analysis. Texts devoted to time series analysis in the "time domain" (McCleary & Hay, 1980) point out that a time series may be systematically "nonstationary" in several ways. It can be "nonstationary in terms of level," indicating that it drifts or trends. A series can also be "nonstationary in terms of process," meaning that the nature of the interrelationships among variables changes over time.

1b. The degree of systematic change in communication processes can be assessed at the level of changes in variable levels (first-order change), or at the level of variable relationships (second-order change).

For example, relationships may develop by engaging in increased breadth and depth of exchange (Altman & Taylor, 1973)—first-order change, yet a degree of predictability may be maintained if they continue to exchange increasingly intimate disclosures according to the "norm of reciprocity." It may be that it is not when just the level of disclosure changes but the processes that govern the exchange changes (second-order change) that a more fundamental shift in the quality of the relationship occurs (immediate reciprocity is replaced by confidences exchanged unconditionally) (VanLear, 1987). The corollary is:

1c. The stability of a process can be represented by lack of variance in variable values over time or by a regular periodic pattern of variation that can range in its degree of complexity from a simple sinusoidal wave to periodically recurring variations in frequency, phase, amplitude, or multidimensional variable relationships.

Whether a communication process is judged to be changing or stable is also a function of the temporal scope or horizon of the study and the way the process is punctuated. Arundale (this volume) provides technical guidelines for detection of cycles and communication patterns. What looks like a linear trend may turn out to be part of a quadratic function when extended further in time, and what looks like a quadratic function may be the first of a recurring series of cycles. Cycles may appear to undergo changes in frequency and/or amplitude over time, yet the changes in the cycles may repeat themselves with time. A process may evidence stability for a considerable period of time but then change its functioning due to a major situational disruption. The observer's temporal horizon or punctuation of the sequence of events effects whether a process is identified as stable or changing.[8] We impose pattern on the world as well as detect it.

1d. The degree of stability or change in a communication process is a matter of perspective as well as detectable redundancy.

We usually treat stability and change as incompatible opposites, and we are used to thinking of them as objectively determined. This perspective asks us to think of stability and change as relative and a matter of perspective. Of course, in a given study, with an appropriate set of variables, operationalized in an appropriate way, over a specified period of time, the issue of the degree of stability or change is a potentially interesting *empirical* question.

Relative Homogeneity of Communication Processes

2. *The degree of homogeneity of a communication process depends on the variables observed, their level of abstraction and level of analysis, and the uniformity of the process across situations and cases.*

This assumption closely parallels the first assumption. Just as there can be stationarity at one level of analysis and nonstationarity at another (first- vs. second-order change), so too there can be homogeneity at one level and heterogeneity at another. For example, different dyads might display similar trends over time for self-disclosure and different patterns of exchange across dyads (VanLear, 1987). The heterogeneity, and therefore the generality, of communication processes may depend on the level of analysis on which the model is based.

Communication processes may be similar across cases when the analysis is based on one set of variables and different when it is based on another set. To some extent, the choice between a uniphasic model and a multiple-sequence model is an empirical question. There are, after all, various ways of testing for the homogeneity or heterogeneity of variable changes (VanLear, 1983). Yet at the lowest levels of abstraction, every relationship, every decision, every confrontation episode is unique. At an extremely high level of abstraction, generalizations may be easy to see (although at that level of abstraction the generalization may be trivial). It is when variables are operationalized at a level of abstraction between these two extremes that the homogeneity of communication processes becomes a theoretically interesting *empirical* question.

> *2a. Communication processes may be heterogeneous in some respects and homogeneous in others.*

The debate between a uniphasic and a multiple-sequence model has direct implications for another issue. That is the distinction between "development" and "evolution" as a model or metaphor for change. A developmental model implies a well-defined ideal end state that is the result of a maturation process. That maturation process is itself relatively systematic and uniform from case to case. Major variations are examples of arrested development, or abnormalities (even pathologies). For example, a group decision that does not go through the final phase of development (reinforcement) would be "immature" because it might lack the necessary commitment and backing by group members to see it implemented. Likewise, in a developmental model, a "casual friendship" is seen as a less mature or less developed form of relationship than a "close friendship." However, a group that skips the "conflict" phase of decision emergence is likely to suffer the pathology of "groupthink" in which ideas are not critically evaluated, so bad ideas are not eliminated and potential problems are overlooked (Fisher, 1980). Likewise, a developmental model of mate selection holds that it is efficacious that people become acquainted *before* they commit to marriage.

An evolutionary model is less likely to focus on a single ultimate end state but to see each state in the process as a temporary transition to the next state. Even when an evolutionary model identifies an "end state" (e.g., a group decision, marriage, or divorce), the focus is likely to be on alternative routes to that destination and the "end state" is not viewed as final in an absolute way. There are many potential "turning points" along the way, and a variety of situational and exogenous factors interact to produce a particular evolutionary course. This is not to say that any and all evolutionary courses are equally probable. Just as with the principle of "natural selection" in biological evolution, certain courses will be more efficacious, and we might expect these to become part of culturally sanctioned patterns. Not only might individuals repeat patterns of behavior that were effective for them in the past, but they can be socialized into adopting patterns of behavior that others have found effective. What began as evolutionary adaptation can repeat itself across cases, becoming a developmental process analogous to the developmental biology maxim "ontology recapitulates philology." Both developmental and evolutionary models are progressive in that they focus on change. However, if a developmental sequence is repeated over time it may form the basis of a cyclical pattern (e.g., the family life cycle; McGoldrick & Carter, 1980).

Evolution is clearly the more general of the two models and may be capable of encompassing development (as it does in the biological theory of evolution). Likewise, a developmental sequence may represent a prototype or template from which deviations can be observed.

Relative Determinism and Stochastic Processes

3. *Communication processes can be modeled as deterministic processes or as stochastic processes or both.*

Time series texts often distinguish between deterministic and stochastic processes. The term deterministic is sure to raise the hackles of any self-respecting humanist (a volitional rather than a conditioned response, I'm sure). Those who criticized the mechanistic model for its "linear determinism" are unlikely to be mollified by the alternative of cyclical determinism (or even chaotic determinism). However, in this context, deterministic simply means that the future states of a system are the result of the past. Usually, this implies that knowledge of the pattern of variable values temporally distant provides a good prediction of some future value, whereas for nondeterministic processes "our ability to predict an event is best nearest the event and worsens as we recede from it" (Gottman, 1981, p. 102). (As we have seen, the exception to this is a chaotic system that is both deterministic and unpredictable.) In fact, "the distinction between deterministic and nondeterministic is more of a dimension than a strict dichotomy" (Gottman, 1981, p. 82). Although it may seem like an oxymoron, it is usually more appropriate or useful to refer to the *relative* determinism of a process. There are many general and regular patterns of behavior that persist for a reasonably long period of time. Such processes can be modeled as relatively deterministic.

Relative determinism, as used here, does not imply a particular source of regularity (predictability) or irregularity. Regularity and predictability may be due to natural causal laws or conformity to rules and norms. Irregularity and unpredictability may be due to measurement error, unmeasured causal variables, chaotic determinism, or even free will. The goal of most models of communication processes is to extract the pattern from the noise and use it to explain the process. This can be done in either the "frequency domain" or the "time domain" using either "deterministic" or "stochastic" techniques (see VanLear & Watt, this volume).

One can choose to model communication as a deterministic process. Trend analysis, Fourier analysis, and chaos are three examples of deterministic models. For example, *any* time series can be modeled as an additive set of sinusoidal functions. If there is any pattern in the data (whether cyclical or not, whether the cycles are regular or irregular), it can be represented by a Fourier transformation (VanLear & Watt, this volume). The simpler and more regular the pattern, the more parsimonious the mathematical model. The more complex and the more irregular the pattern, the more complex the model necessary to adequately reconstruct the series.

One can choose to model communication as a stochastic process. Prediction is always probabilistic (whether because of unmeasured causal variables, measurement error, chaotic processes, or free will). In a stochastic analysis, the ability to predict an event is best the closer in time the prediction is to the predicted event (McCleary & Hay, 1980). Markov chain models and ARIMA models are examples of stochastic methods frequently used to model communication processes. Deterministic patterns like trends and seasonal cycles, as well as the stochastic drifting of a "random walk" process, can be detected with stochastic methods like ARIMA by the pattern of autocorrelations. Stochastic models have been the statistical methods of "choice" for those who believe that behavior is volitional and only partially constrained by rules and norms. Yet use of stochastic methods does not always imply rejection of determinism.

Communication Processes as Coordinated Social Evolution

3a. Human communication processes involve both "programmed" or "scheduled" patterns and sequences and unscheduled adaptations.

A time series can be modeled as the sum of a trend, plus deterministic cycles, plus a stationary stochastic process (Gottman, 1981). In one sense, this is a specific application of the "Wold decomposition theorem," which shows that "any discrete-time stationary process can be written as the sum of two independent processes, one of which is deterministic and one of which is nondeterministic" (Gottman, 1981, pp. 102-103).

Consider the weather as an analogy. The seasons of the year form a deterministic cycle that allows prediction of the weather at levels far better than chance. (It's almost always colder in the winter than in the summer.) Nested within this cycle is a shorter day/night cycle that also allows further prediction. (It's almost always colder at night than during the day.) Yet within each season there is a wide variance in the weather that is not predictable purely on the basis of these deterministic cycles. Using complex computer models, meteorologists attempt to make more precise predictions, but the models' ability to predict the weather on a given day improves the nearer they are in time to the predicted event, and the prediction is always a probability.[9]

There are relatively regular cycles of human behavior. Buder (this volume) and Warner (this volume) both discuss the cycles of behavior created by physiological rhythms. Likewise, conversations have beginnings, middles, and endings, with certain functions associated with each (Knapp, 1978). These conversations are often entrained to a daily or weekly cycle (Duck et al., 1991). The result is a series of embedded cycles within and across conversations (VanLear, 1991). Such cycles can be modeled as relatively deterministic functions. Yet we are constantly making "on the spot" adaptations to our behavior based on unpredictable situational occurrences (or at least I am). Such adaptations can be modeled by a stochastic function.[10]

The principles of equifinality and multifinality hold that the initial characteristics of the components of an open system do not alone predict the outcome of the system. Nonprocess differences can account for differences in deterministic (developmental) trajectories to the extent that they can account for differences in "programming," scheduling, or plans. Nonprocess individual differences (initial conditions) can account for variations in stochastic processes or outcomes if they interact with situational or process variables (VanLear & Zietlow, 1990) or if the apparently stochastic process is really generated by chaotic determinism.

3b. Developmental processes are best modeled as deterministic trajectories, whereas evolutionary models may be modeled as stochastic processes or possibly as chaotic systems.

Given the number of planets in the universe potentially like our own in most critical respects, we might expect some form of life to evolve on some other planet. But we would not expect an exactly parallel pattern of development (old *Star Trek* episodes notwithstanding). There are simply too many random or unpredictable events that have affected the course of evolution. Yet we do not find it strange that, at least at a high level of abstraction, "normal" human beings all go through a similar set of developmental stages.

A developmental sequence is "programmed" or scheduled (whether by genetics, or conditioning, or by rules, plans, scripts, or schemata), whereas an evolutionary sequence is the result of creative or "on the spot" adaptations to situations or a chaotic system.

4. Human communication requires coordination. Communicators coordinate their behaviors both by matching and timing their deterministic patterns and by stochastic adaptation to the behavior of other communicators.

There are two ways in which people coordinate their communicative behaviors. One way is to program or schedule their behavioral cycles or patterns so that they coincide at specific times. The second way is to make "on the spot" adaptations to the behavior of others. In other words, we can match and time two relatively deterministic patterns until they coincide in frequency and phase (or antiphase), or we can react to the immediate behavior of the other person (e.g., through reciprocity or compensation) and thereby produce a coordinated system.

Programmed or Scheduled Coordination

One's body has a natural circadian rhythm of sleeping and waking (a deterministic cycle) such that one can predict at any point in time whether someone will be sleeping or waking with a fairly high degree of accuracy. However, if one crosses to another time zone, or is forced to work another shift, or switches to daylight savings time, that natural rhythm must be entrained to the new schedule so that one's behaviors can be coordinated with others and the requirements of the new situation.

Linear or phasic processes also allow people to coordinate their behaviors. Knapp (1978) argues that following a normative phasic sequence of relationship development allows participants to know the status of their relationship and to know where it might go from that point so that development can be mutually coordinated.

These are examples of programmed or scheduled coordination. Programmed coordination can be modeled as entrainment of relatively deterministic patterns because it capitalizes on relatively ordered, predictable patterns of behavior that are programmed well in advance to facilitate the coordination of behaviors between communicators.[11]

Stochastic Adaptation

It is my contention that programmed or deterministic coordination is not the only way that communicators coordinate their behaviors. If two musicians are given the same score of music to record and neither could hear the other but both have something marking the *exact* same beat, it is possible to splice the two parts together into a coordinated whole. However, if professional musicians can hear each other, coordination can also be achieved, including improvisation and ad-libbing without a score or conductor.

Regular predetermined patterns can be used to facilitate coordination, yet coordination can also be accomplished if communicators can monitor each other's behavior and make ongoing adjustments to their own behavior as required by the situation and the other communicator (Cappella, this volume). Yet even stochastic adaptations are based on some principle of coordination.

The chapters in this volume by Warner and Buder relate primarily to coordination of relatively deterministic cycles. Cappella's chapter models stochastic adaptation of turn-taking cues. A process model of communication should account for both deterministic patterns and stochastic adaptations.

4a. Human communication systems can be either tightly coupled or loosely coupled, and neither is inherently superior to the other under all conditions.

By definition, a communication system must exhibit some degree of organization and coordination between communicators. Yet theory and research indicate the danger of systems that are too tightly coupled (Gottman, 1981; Rogers & Bagarozzi, 1983; VanLear & Zietlow, 1990; Weick, 1979). Research might explore when and how much coordination is desirable under what situations.

4b. Adaptation can be either symmetrical (mutual) or asymmetrical.
Asymmetrical adaptation or entrainment is thought to indicate dominance by one party (Gottman, 1979b). The type, degree, and symmetry of interpersonal coordination are issues of major theoretical importance.

Enacted Versus a Priori Constraints

5. *Patterns of communication are a function of both a priori physical factors and socially enacted symbolic constraints.*
Communication involves physical activity and therefore is constrained by biophysics, the physical environment, the availability of current technology, and so forth. Communication is also, in part, a symbolic process, and so people participate in creating their own constraints and enacting their own social structures.

Gibsonian psychology (Gibson, 1977) holds that there are aspects of the environment that match the capabilities of organisms (affordances) and therefore make certain adaptations efficacious and more probable. The environment offers both opportunities and constraints, and adaptations that can capitalize on the opportunities and function within the constraints are most likely to survive and be effective. Yet people do pattern their behavior according to social rules and structures that are created and re-created by participation in the very social activities that they regulate. These two sets of constraints (a priori and enacted) together form the communication environment.

For example, my communication with my sister is constrained by the fact that we live over 1,000 miles apart. Availability of technology and resources as well as the laws of physics limit our communication. Yet our communication is also constrained by social rules (e.g., it's not polite to call someone at 3 a.m. except in emergency or to drop in for a week-long visit unexpectedly) and the unique rules of our relationship (e.g., we call each other at least once a month). The combination of the physical and socially enacted constraints produce somewhat predicable patterns of communication. But these patterns are subject to continuous adaptations.

Not only do we participate in enacting the constraints that shape our communication patterns, but the meaning of a given configuration is a function of the history that brought it into being (Monge & Kalman, this volume). For example, the definition of a relationship is not just a configuration of variable values (e.g., trust, attraction, control) at any point in time. Rather, the nature of a relationship is found in the processes of relating: the processes that allow two people to coordinate with, adapt to, and affect each other (Rogers, 1993). To a very large extent, the entire history of that process of relating is constitutive of the nature of that relationship. Unhappily married couples tend to interpret the seemingly benign behaviors of their spouse more negatively than outsiders because of the history of negativity (Gottman, 1979b). Likewise, an unhappy marriage may be all the more painful to the participants when they reflect upon the joy and optimism that they experienced in the beginning. However, a couple who has successfully worked their way through many conflicts and problems in the past may feel their relationship less threatened by a current conflict. A self-disclosure that may appear quite revealing in the early stages of a relationship may appear mundane or even restrained in a well developed relationship after many disclosures. It is through communication that we create and define our relationships (in families, work groups, and organizations), and the nature of those relationships provides the interpretive framework that provides definition and meaning to our communicative behaviors.

5a. *The communication history creates the interpretative context for communication behavior, and that history is punctuated into events and episodes by both participants and observers.*

Conclusions

This chapter, or even this volume, cannot pretend to review all the process models of communication. Most notable, I did not address the "interpretive approach" to communication research, although Smith (1972) argued that interpretive methods are well suited to studying communication as a process. The choice to exclude this approach was an attempt to narrow the focus of this chapter to make it more manageable. It is not intended as a rejection of the validity of that approach. All methods are in some ways "interpretive." Likewise, this chapter has only dealt briefly with "the psychology of time" (McGrath, 1988), even though this is of obvious relevance to communication processes.

The concept of process has evolved over the past 40 years and will probably go on evolving. Hopefully, the social selection process will weed out the less useful ideas and retain the more useful. The perspective of this chapter rejects a strict positivism and embraces the validity of multiple perspectives. However, it does not reject empirical tests of evidence or contend that any interpretation of data is equally valid given the impossibility of complete objectivity. The goal of this perspective is to provide a starting point and set of heuristic concepts for generating process models of human communication. Given an appropriate set of variables, operationalized at an appropriate level of abstraction and precision, observed over an appropriate span of time across a representative group of cases, and analyzed in an appropriate way, these issues (stability and change, heterogeneity, the regularity of communication processes, and dynamic coordination) become important and testable empirical questions. However, the answers to these questions are applicable only within the frame of reference of their testing.

Notes

1. Hawking (1988) points out that general relativity and quantum mechanics are still inconsistent with each other, given our present state of knowledge.

2. At one level, communication is a physical activity (see Buder, this volume), and therefore a mechanistic metaphor may be appropriate. Further, mechanistic metaphors are often used because they are easier to visualize. Third, we often use mechanistic analogs because the mathematical models for them have known properties (see Kaplowitz & Fink, this volume) that are heuristic for modeling communication processes. Of course, not all mechanistic metaphors are necessarily linear or Newtonian. Finally, if an entity's "being" is wholly constituted by its "becoming," as Whitehead (1929) contends, then one could argue that we have simply substituted an interpretive determinism for causal determinism.

3. Werner and Baxter's (1994) discussion of process follows Altman and Rogoff's (1987) discussion of philosophy of science in the behavioral sciences. However, systems approaches do not fit neatly into any one of their approaches to philosophy of science because (a) they are highly abstract in their assumptions and (b) there are so many different versions of systems. Some supposed systems approaches are actually quite mechanistic, many are "organismic," probably owing to the influence of von Bertalanffy (1968) the biologist, and still others have elements of "transactional" or even "dialectical" perspectives. The unifying assumption of all true systems approaches is "holism," although how that is conceived may vary.

4. Not everyone who uses stochastic methods or advocates open systems rejects causal determinism for the epistemology of constraint, but stochastic methods are consistent with such a perspective.

5. Hawes's approach was criticized by Grossberg and O'Keefe (1975), but his response (Hawes, 1975), in my opinion, adequately answered the objections.

6. The approach jointly advocated by Fisher and Hawes (1971) was known as the "interact systems model." Although that approach has been criticized (Hewes, 1979), most of those concerns are not directly relevant to the present discussion, and those that are are considered at other points in this chapter.

7. In Scheidel and Crowell's (1964) spiral model of idea development groups reach agreement on issues that become "anchor points" that they reflect back on as precedents for future decisions in a process they call "reach testing."

8. Hawking (1988) argues that, at the cosmic level, time progresses in a directional manner based on the three "arrows of time." The "thermodynamic arrow of time" is based on the law that systems move toward entropy. The "psychological arrow of time," which Hawking thinks results from the thermodynamic arrow, is based on the observation that we remember the past but not the future and therefore generally perceive time as directional. Finally, the "cosmological arrow of time" is based on the theory that the universe appears to be expanding. Hawking allows that there may have been other big bangs in the past followed by big crunches. However, because a big crunch would create a singularity in which the laws of physics would not exist as we know them, Hawking defines the big bang as the beginning of the universe and the big crunch as its end, thus punctuating the temporal horizon of physics.

9. Actually, Lorenz (1963) has shown that weather can be modeled as a chaotic deterministic system.

10. The localized autocorrelation function (Nass & Moon, this volume) may be particularly helpful at this stage. I prefer to first use a combination of "frequency domain" techniques to assess "scheduled" deterministic patterns and then "time domain" techniques to assess the stochastic adaptations.

11. Buder (this volume) discusses the use of bivariate cross-spectral analysis in which the frequencies and phase angles of one person's spectrum are correlated to the frequencies and phase angles of their conversational partner. VanLear (1991) fit the dominant frequencies of each person's time series to the concurrent time series of their conversational partner. Both of these methods can be used to examine the extent to which the regular deterministic cycles are coordinated between communicators.

Sequentiality, Simultaneity, and Synchronicity in Human Communication

PETER R. MONGE
MICHAEL E. KALMAN

Few scholars would dispute the claim that human communication is a dynamic, unfolding process. Originally articulated by Wilbur Schramm (1954) more than 40 years ago and subsequently elaborated by Berlo (1960, 1977) and Smith (1972), this claim has been widely accepted in the communication discipline (see Johnson & Proctor, 1992, for an exception). However, *what it means* to view communication as a process has been a matter of extensive debate for years, as a review of Ellis (1979), Fisher (1978a, 1978b), Hewes (1975) and VanLear (1987, 1991) amply shows. A number of the commentaries on this topic have tended to explore the problem that our research strategies and analytic techniques often fail to capture these dynamic properties (see, e.g., Hewes, 1980; Monge, Farace, Eisenberg, Miller, & White, 1984). In fact, considerable progress has been made in dealing with the problems of design and analysis associated with studying processes, as the various chapters

We wish to express our appreciation to Arthur VanLear and James Watt for their helpful comments and insightful suggestions on various drafts of this chapter.

in this volume amply demonstrate (see also Monge, 1990). Yet considerable work still remains to be done to critically examine the *concept* of process, to more fully specify its alternative meanings, and to identify the various implications of those alternatives for our understanding of human communication. This chapter seeks to contribute to these tasks. In it we develop a framework, including a set of terms and definitions, that describes various aspects of process. This framework should assist us in describing, theorizing, and researching the processes of human communication.

The commonplace notion that communication is a process has an intuitive appeal. Most of the communication events that people experience seem to unfold over time. Stories have beginnings, middles, and endings. Decisions begin with uncertainty and ambiguity, move toward the exploration of one or more choices, and lead eventually to resolution. We sense that news stories, sports events, and movies all take allotted amounts of time. And we experience cycles in many communication events, whether daily news programs, weekly religious services, annual holiday rituals, or quadrennial sports events such as the Olympics or the World Cup. Finally, our individual lives, filled as they are with communication events, move inexorably from birth toward death. The passing of time is so integral to communication, a facet of living experience always so ready at hand, that it tends to escape scrutiny in its own right as a dimension of analysis.

As these examples might suggest, a variety of different conceptions of process exist in our daily lives as well as in communication theory and research. Process appears in trajectories and cycles, change and continuity, causation and emergence. One of the most important factors underlying these different conceptions of process is the perception and understanding of time. McTaggart (1927) contends that there are two essentially different ways to view time. In the first perspective, which McTaggart terms the *A-series*, the observer of events is always anchored in the present, in between a receding past and an approaching future. In McTaggart's second perspective, the *B-series*, the observer instead views events in a sequence of earlier and later relations and regards the sequence as a whole. Any choice of a single moment to serve as a reference point in the B-series is arbitrary, which contrasts sharply with the A-series' principal focus on the present.

In the B-series, the content of human activities is distributed across time so that each event has exactly one location. The association of events follows more from their proximity of occurrence (e.g., the events of a given day) or patterned recurrence (e.g., the first day of each month) than from their relevance to each other (e.g., actions and their reasons). Moments stretch out before an observer like beads on a string. It can be argued that McTaggart's B-series has been a much more prominent perspective in modern society than the A-series. For one thing, the B-series represents the practical standard throughout much of the physical sciences. Its great utility as a framework for scientific observation has been repeatedly demonstrated since the early discoveries of Newtonian physics. In more recent years, researchers in the dynamics of communication (including many in this volume) have similarly shown the utility of the B-series perspective. Another factor contributing to the prominence of the B-series is the fact that so much of modern life is scheduled by the clock and calendar. Mumford (1934), writing prior to the advent of the electronic computer, even regards the clock as the key machine of the modern age.

The endless variety, richness, and beauty of human communication, however, relies on both perspectives of time. Jaques (1982) extends McTaggart's duality to describe the perspectives as separate dimensions in a five-dimensional continuum of social time and space. One time dimension, anchored in the present, underscores the flux of existence and is deeply intentional. The other time dimension highlights predictable succession, continuity, and the conscious explanation of experience. According to Jaques, each time dimension forms a context for the other; neither alone is sufficient. Mead (1932) goes so far as to identify the present as the locus of reality. This followed the influence of Bergson's earlier contrast between *durée* and *temps*, the emergent and the temporal, which roughly parallel the A-series and B-series, respectively (for an extended discussion, see Adam, 1990).

A Set of Key Terms

A number of key terms serve in building a framework and vocabulary for the discussion of communication processes. First, processes are built out of combinations of *entities* as they unfold over time. The term entities refers to any conceptually distinct units chosen for study: *objects*, their various *attributes*, the *relations* among the objects, and the *activities* in which they engage. Communication typically deals with objects such as people, words, messages, media, stories, meanings, technologies, and networks. Attributes of communication objects include characteristics such as the level of individual communicator competence (Spitzberg, 1988), the ambiguity of messages (Eisenberg, 1984), the richness of the medium chosen for message transmission (Trevino, Daft, & Lengel, 1990), and emergent qualities of a communication network, such as centrality (Monge & Contractor, 1988). Relations describe the connections between objects. Some communication relations include "talks with," "reports to," and "seeks information from" (Monge, 1987), measures of proximity, and relations of causation. Activities consist of the things the objects (such as people) do, dynamic patterns in the way they behave. Space and time serve as the contexts in which all these communication entities exist and unfold. Collectively, entities comprise how we interpret and understand the world of communication.

A *structure* is a particular arrangement out of all possible arrangements for a given set of entities. We distinguish between two types of structure in the context of time: (a) a *configuration*, which is the structure at a moment (i.e., across a negligible time period), and (b) a *process*, which is a sequence of configurations. Studies of communication employ many different conceptions of structure (e.g., Conville, 1994). Structure usually serves to identify a pattern of relative stability over time, similarities across numerous instances of the same phenomenon, or both (cf. Sorokin, 1957, pp. 53-65). We will use the term *typical structure* to refer to the generalization across instances when it is not clear from the context whether structure refers to a particular instance or to a generalization. For example, a traditional news story has a structure known as the inverted pyramid: The story begins with the most general statements and proceeds to the most detailed. The type of structure in this case is a process, as the story consists of a sequence of statements. Further, it is evident from the context that this process typifies a great many particular stories. Their structure accords with the customary activities of writers and editors who compose the stories and of the newspaper readers who skim for the main ideas. Alternatively, an examination of news stories over a number of years would reveal changes in the typical structure of stories due to stylistic trends and the evolving relationship between news writers and their readership (see VanLear, this volume, regarding second-order, or structural, change in processes).

Three additional concepts are central to our efforts to understand the process of human communication: *sequentiality, simultaneity,* and *synchronicity.* These concepts capture the elements of process but reveal a variety of tensions between what constitutes occurrence in a moment versus an unfolding across time. These concepts are elemental to discussing different perspectives of time and process. They also provide the foundation for exploring the various characteristics of process such as duration, recurrence, cycles, and irreversibility or direction.

Sequentiality

Sequentiality refers to a succession of entities over time.[1] Entities that succeed themselves may change (e.g., objects change in their attributes and relations) or remain unchanged. One entity also may succeed another, altering substantially the content of a process from one configuration to the next. A common metaphor for sequentiality is the motion picture. From one perspective, the motion picture appears like a single object to the human eye and constitutes a continuous unfolding over time. The projected image succeeds itself and either will vary in its attributes, as the picture "moves," or will remain the same during a "still shot." From a different perspective, each frame of the motion picture film succeeds the frame preceding it in a definite sequence. An example of sequentiality in interpersonal communication is the conversation. The interactants in a conversation succeed themselves from one moment to the next. During this time the attributes of their joint behavior, such as the rate of interaction and the relative amounts of conversational talk and silence, may vary (Cappella & Planalp, 1981). Qualitatively distinct entities (e.g., words, gestures) succeed one another to create substantial variation in the conversation's content. To sort out these shifting perspectives on process, we turn to another metaphor, one of windows and panes.

Time Windows

A *time window* is the period of time required to "contain" the communication phenomena under study. The sequentiality of a window is that it lies between two moments, one succeeding the other, which serve to bracket or define the window. *Moments* are typically considered to be instantaneous. The interval between moments bracketing a window is a measurable length of time, its start and finish serving as the time boundaries for any contained process. A complete process of interest may be composed of many sequential configuration changes. Common communication time windows are the television sound bite, the 30-minute evening newscast, and the 50-minute college class period. Any time window will include some communication phenomena but exclude others. Entities necessarily excluded are those that occur only before or after the window or are too lengthy to fit within it. For example, a 50-minute class period cannot contain a 3-hour examination.

Windows contain *panes*, smaller regions of time that comprise windows. One way to create panes is to divide a window into mutually exclusive time periods. This creates a hierarchically organized set of time periods, panes on one level of the hierarchy comprising a window at the next higher level. The relationship of panes to one another is strictly sequential, in the manner of the B-series time perspective. A second, nonhierarchical way to create panes in a window more oriented toward an A-series time perspective is discussed later in the section on simultaneity.

When windows and panes are to be selected at the discretion of a researcher, the characteristics of the phenomena can serve as a guide. The number of panes in a window determines the resolution of measurement available to reveal the sequential structure of a process. One configuration of entities occupies each pane, so a window must at least have two panes in order to reveal any process. The most efficient size of panes is calculable from the expected rates of change in the phenomena (see Arundale, this volume, for the minimum sampling rate required for capturing continuous processes). For example, Buder (this volume) reviews studies of speech dynamics conducted across a range of time scales (i.e., windows) and measured at suitable levels of precision (i.e., panes). Windows and panes cannot necessarily be selected at will, however. In some cases, they are imposed by the limitations of instruments to observe at rates as high or over time periods as long as desired by the researcher.

Besides the formal time windows employed by researchers, some time windows emerge in common experience as people seek to make sense of their world. Some of these windows emerge in coordination with natural cycles. The earth's rotation and orbit cause day to follow night and the seasons to change. The human body also undergoes natural cycles, the most obvious being periods of wakefulness and sleep. These cycles form natural windows for the activities that typically fall within one period.

The concept of the *frame* helps in discussing still other time windows sustained through social interaction. Bateson (1972) discussed some ways that the frame concept illuminates the interpretation of interaction within social and behavioral contexts. Bateson observed monkeys engaged in playful behavior that looked like fighting. He described in terms of the frame how the monkeys' use of signals, mood signs, and messages influences the meaning of their actions toward one another. During activities framed by certain signs, the monkeys would regard each other's apparently aggressive behavior as playful. Goffman (1974) later used the concept of framing to specify segments of behavior that constitute meaningful wholes. One instance is the theatrical frame, marked temporally by devices such as the raising and lowering of the stage curtain and the actors' playing *as if* they do not know how the action will turn out. The theatrical frame encourages even an audience member already familiar with the script to follow along in the make-believe world of the play for the duration of a performance. Generally recognized bracketing events—introduction and conclusion, overture and finale, hello and good-bye—coordinate the experiences of individuals by framing social processes into shared units of windows and panes. In the event of ambiguous framing, by contrast, individuals can differ markedly in the ways they punctuate, or frame, continuous social processes into meaningful units resulting in different interpretations of their own and others' activities (Watzlawick et al., 1967).

Imposing a time window onto events can produce powerful persuasive effects. One fairly blatant instance is the sound bite. The audience to a short segment edited from a public speech hears nothing else and will likely suppose the bite to be representative of the whole speech. Someone hearing the complete speech might not consider the same segment to be a meaningful unit, let alone a representative sample. Iyengar (e.g., Iyengar & Kinder, 1987) has examined the impact of more subtle contextual frames on the interpretation of news. Newscasts convey implicit messages by their depiction of events or social groups. For example, a news report would frame the problem of unemployment in terms of individual rather than societal responsibilities if it took the approach of interviewing unemployed persons rather than reporting on factory closings and industrial trends. Although one salient difference between the two approaches is the social scope of the problem depicted by the coverage, another difference is the time scale of causes and effects framing the story. The time window suggested by an individual's plight is too short to accommodate an explanation in terms of, say, a structural shift in the nation's industrial economy.

Levels of Windows and the Structure of Process

Windows and panes provide only limited understanding of sequentiality until the hierarchical organization of time is developed more fully. Still higher and lower levels of sequentiality also may be of interest. At each level, configurations exhibit patterns of *duration* and *recurrence*.

Duration

The duration of an entity that succeeds itself in a window is equal to the number of adjacent panes it occupies. A window and its panes also may be said to have a duration, depending on the conception of time in use. Newton contended that time exists independent of any substantive content, whereas Leibniz insisted that time exists only as a sequencing of events (Whitrow, 1972). In the case of an independent, Newtonian conception of time, often called clock time, the duration of a window or pane equals the amount of time it spans. Otherwise, the configuration(s) that a window or pane contains will alone constitute the duration, often called event-based time or event time (see also Arundale, VanLear, this volume).

Recurrence

An entity recurs if it appears discontinuously across the sequential panes of a window. That is, recurrence is the second, third, and so forth separate appearance of an entity in a window. To discriminate between durations and recurrences, the panes in a window must be of short enough duration to identify discontinuity (cf. Arundale, this volume). When an entire configuration recurs, it means that the content of an earlier pane reappears in a later pane after an interval of one or more panes. The familiar "déjà vu" refers to the subjective experience of reappearing configurations.

Hierarchical Windows

The discussion up to this point has largely concerned *zero-level* windows and panes. At the zero level, a time window contains a single iteration of the process that is taken as the unit of analysis, a *unit process*. Zero-level panes each contain one configuration of the unit process. Examples of common unit processes are a conversation, a relationship trajectory, and a persuasion attempt. Corresponding configurations could include, respectively, a speech act in a conversation, one stage in a relationship, and an affective response to persuasion.

A window at the *first level up* contains numerous iterations of a unit process instead of only one. Each iteration of the process occupies one pane, such that a window at the zero level is equivalent to only one pane in a window at the first level up. At the first level up, the unit process example consisting of a persuasion attempt would instead be viewed as a sequence of separate persuasion attempts. A window that includes a sufficient number of process iterations enables the observer to arrive at a reliable characterization of the typical structure of the unit process. If the process unfolds continuously, one iteration occupies every pane in the window. In the case of a recurrent process, iterations appear discontinuously across the panes.

A window at the *first level down* is equivalent to one pane at the zero level. Panes at the first level down, in turn, subdivide a configuration of the unit process into still smaller time segments. An alternative to analysis at the first level down is to bring out increasing detail by reducing the size of zero-level panes. However, this alternative might be undesirable if each of the unit processes' configurations at the zero level is itself a meaningful unit. The creation of another set of windows and panes at the first level down preserves the zero-level organization of time into meaningful units.

To illustrate the analysis of process at multiple levels, consider the activities of a traffic cop signaling cars through a busy intersection. Take as the unit process the cop's activities over a complete work shift. The unit process consists of numerous actions in sequence, including hand gestures, blowing a whistle, and calling out verbally to certain drivers. Further suppose that each zero-level pane contains one of the cop's actions. On the one hand, analysis could shift to the first level up so as to compare the traffic cop's activities over a number of days. On the other hand, the structure of each of the cop's actions is itself an activity stretching over time: Hand gestures involve motion, the whistle's pitch can be inflected, and verbalizations consist of words in a sequence. These actions would be detailed by windows at the first level down. We could even redefine the unit of analysis so as to study the typical structure of just one of these actions (e.g., hand gestures) in a new zero-level window. Doing so then shifts the levels of all the windows up by one. Overall, the process of directing traffic is an activity composed of lesser activities and can be examined at multiple levels of analysis.

Sometimes, meaningful units emerge in a process only through lengthy observation. Previously unidentified cycles commonly appear in this manner. The unfolding process initially occupies a zero-level window. The sampling rate determines its division into panes and constitutes the only a priori structure over time. As patterns of duration and recurrence appear across the observed configurations, it eventually becomes possible to organize the process into higher level units of process. These new units—the emergent structure of the overall process —might then occupy a newly defined set of zero-level windows. The overall period of observation, previously the zero-level window, would then be redefined as a window at the first level up.

Cycles

A cycle is a process that succeeds itself. In the early stages of identifying the structure of a process, even a single recurrent configuration might suggest the presence of a cycle. But, as with the identification of any unit process, repeated observation tends to confirm whether any given recurrence is significant. Usually at least a few iterations must be observed to create confidence that the cyclic process exists. A minimum of two panes per cycle are required to establish the existence of cycles within a window. In other words, time windows that initially reveal the presence of cycles contain at least twice the number of panes as cycles.

Panes that organize a process into cycles are commonly chosen so as to punctuate the process at the moment of a recurring configuration. In the case of a smoothly oscillating function, because all of its configurations recur from one cycle to the next, the panes can be placed wherever convenient so long as their spacing matches the oscillatory period. For instance, the nadir of the oscillating trajectory might be a convenient place to start and finish each cycle. By contrast, a process could make unpredictable excursions across iterations, yet always return to a particular configuration. Punctuation at the point of recurrence brings forth a cyclic appearance. The fact that any unit process begins and ends in the same configuration suggests the existence of a cycle.

Cycles and Other Processes

Some judgment enters into making the distinction between cycles and other processes. Either periodicity or circular causation can contribute to the interpretation of a process as cyclic. Periodicity is so evident in smooth oscillation that a cyclic interpretation seems obvious. Conversely, a process that recurs at random intervals, embedded in an otherwise random sequence of events, appears more like a recurrent process than like a cycle. Even if the random events are eliminated from consideration (e.g., filtered out as noise), the process would appear more cyclic if the proximities were greater and the spacings more regular between its ends and subsequent beginnings. Proximity highlights the association between ends and beginnings, whereas regular spacing implies periodicity, or rhythm.

Another case for cyclicality exists where every configuration in a process is causally related to those before and after, continuing full around in a circle of causes. Such a process has no definite beginning and end; moreover, it tends to sustain itself in a cyclic manner. Circular causation provides a basis in event time for identifying a cycle even when periodicity in clock time is unstable. Conversational turn taking is one example because each interactant's behavior prompts the other's. Another example is found in the cycle of life where one generation gives birth to the next.

Given the many cycles of nature, both periodic and causal, it is not surprising that "most civilizations, prior to our own of the last two or three hundred years, have tended to regard time as essentially cyclic in nature" (Whitrow, 1972, p. 7). For example, the Mayans expected history to repeat itself in a grand cycle every 260 years. In such a deeply cyclic view, lasting change seems unreal because attention is focused on the typical structure of the cycle, each iteration occupying the very same (zero-level) window. Giddens (1984) follows Lévi-Strauss in viewing recurrent social practices in light of this "reversible time" that continually loops back to its origin (cf. Giddens, 1979). In this view, the enactment of rituals, the retelling of mythic stories (e.g., Bormann,

1983), and even mundane habits that contribute to the ongoing reproduction of social structure result not in similar experiences across time
but the *same* experience lived over and over again. Belief in eternal
reincarnation holds out cyclicality as the ultimate trace of existence. It
stands in contrast to the more linear view of time found in Christian
beliefs so integral to traditional Western culture (e.g., creation, final
judgment, and heaven or hell forever thereafter). Adam (1990) recommends thinking about even the most repetitive, ritualized social practices in terms of *recurrence with variation.* Time does not reverse
direction even when experience appears to recur. Emphasizing variation
as Adam does, cycles are seen to stretch across panes at the first level
up. Sufficient attention to the variation across cycles continually brings
out the emergent qualities of the present iteration.

Clock Time and Event Time

Transformations between clock time and event time can influence the
appearance of cyclicality in a process. Choosing clock time means using
some standard such as ticks of a clock, calendar days, or years to mark
the moments that bracket windows and panes. Choosing event time
means instead using the content of a process to mark its division into
windows and panes. Event time is a commonplace heuristic for simpli-
fying the complexities of processes, although it often glosses certain
details that clock time can make explicit. For example, measuring a
process in clock time can reveal varied rates of process, changing
intervals between recurrences, or structural asymmetries that we might
then seek to explain. Even the time scale attached to certain segments
of clock time, especially actions and their *intended* consequences, often
come tacitly bracketed by preconceptions of meaningful events. Clock
time can help to break through those preconceptions. In the example of
conversation, where turn taking suggests one basis in event time for
bracketing units of the process, researchers are finding other, periodic
cycles by imposing clock time (e.g., see chapters by Buder, Cappella,
and Warner, this volume). As more sophisticated techniques from nonlinear dynamics come into use, the potential increases for analytically
describing higher levels of process complexity (see Contractor, this
volume).

Transformation from clock time to event time can prompt questions
of a different sort. Because event time refers to the substance of expe-

rience, it often comes more naturally to us than clock time. However, much of our lives are regulated and framed by windows of clock time that get taken for granted (e.g., workdays, project schedules, fiscal years; see Zerubavel, 1981). Under transformation to event time, events that appeared irregularly spaced might turn out to appear not only cyclic but periodic. Event time tends to filter out the dead time separating meaningful events. We might then start to ask how the beginnings of apparently discrete processes are related to the ends of those preceding them. Is there a causal, even if unintended, relation? Does one occurrence of the process contribute to the structuration of the next occurrence? Clark (1985) further observes that event time helps reveal the crucial role of timekeepers and other temporal interrelationships across social systems ranging from organizations to societies.

Simultaneity

Simultaneity refers to two or more entities that exist together at the same moment. A common metaphor for the concept of simultaneity is the photograph or freeze frame, a pictorial representation frozen in time that captures entities as they coexist at a moment and not at any time before or after. Just as the content of the photograph is whatever the photographer chooses to shoot, in communication theory and research the content of a configuration is whatever entities a researcher chooses conceptually to include for consideration.

Insofar as entities are simultaneous, they comprise a configuration that constitutes the moment. In practice, however, the apparent simultaneity of two entities can depend on a number of factors—physical, conceptual, and psychological. Physical factors concern those time delays between the occurrence and measurement of events that limit the observer's ability to determine the sequential structure of interest. Such measurement issues are familiar to any researcher. For example, consider a telephone survey intended to track daily changes in voter sentiments prior to an election. If the responses to the survey instrument must be processed within one day or so, a mail-in survey would not suffice due to time delays that are entirely under the control of the respondents. Instead, the use of the telephone can reliably narrow the time spread of responses down to within a day or even a few hours.

The conceptual and psychological factors that influence the constitution of a moment represent more challenging and, in some ways, less familiar considerations to communication researchers. The section on sequentiality discussed how researchers observe the emergent structure of a process. However, it was never acknowledged that research participants also interpret the processes in which they take part. A researcher who seeks to include participants' interpretations into a strictly hierarchical framework of windows and panes will run into serious difficulties. On the one hand, a hierarchical framework reduces all phenomena to a succession of mutually exclusive configurations. On the other hand, an interpretation is a type of entity that incorporates aspects of other entities; it is partly constituted by what it interprets. An interpretation that reflects the structure of past configurations would therefore need to (a) occupy the one pane matching the time when it was measured and yet (b) extend across the sequence of panes whose emergent structure it seeks to explain. The hierarchical level of the interpretation would be, at best, ambiguously defined. The hierarchical framework of windows and panes cannot accommodate the interpretation of a process by its own participants.

Researchers interested in the phenomenal qualities of communication (e.g., interpretation, intersubjectivity) have elsewhere discussed some of the problems related to a strictly sequential (i.e., hierarchical) conception of process. For example, Duck (1993) challenges such common metaphors as the "trajectory" to describe the development of interpersonal relationships. The trajectory metaphor harks back to ballistics (i.e., Newtonian physics), where the equations of motion permit processes, in principle, to proceed forward or backward in time. Yet relationship partners together develop their own unique ways of speaking and thinking, which conditions their future interactions (e.g., Baxter, 1987; Bell & Healey, 1992; Hopper, Knapp, & Scott, 1981). Over time, they forge identities, make irrevocable commitments, and take actions (Calhoun, 1991). Relationship "growth and decline cannot simply be the reverse of one another," says Berger (1993), "because it is not possible for individuals' conceptualizations of their relationship to return to some earlier point." Considerations such as these indicate that the reduction of interpersonal relationships to a sequence of state variables (e.g., level of intimacy, liking) misses a self-constituting, irreversible quality of relationships that can be of great interest to communication researchers.

Nonhierarchical Windows and Panes

Nonhierarchical windows contain *cumulative panes*, overlapping regions of time that comprise the window.[2] Each pane contains all the panes preceding it in the window, plus one additional increment of time. The latest pane in the window has the same duration as the window itself. For instance, a window whose duration totals three time increments would contain three panes. All the panes would extend back in time to the same moment, the beginning moment of the window, but the durations of the panes would be one, two, and three time increments, in that order.

Cumulative panes capture several key qualities of communication process. First, even when certain entities recur or cycle predictably across configurations, a participant normally accumulates a memory of their history. The configuration that contains a participant's memory is therefore constituted by certain aspects of past configurations, something that is possible only with cumulative panes. Second, participants typically lack perfect, a priori knowledge of a process and its structure so they cannot envision the process in full detail from only a B-series perspective. Instead, imperfect knowledge of the structure of a process results in occasional failures to adequately predict events. Those failures, in turn, situate a participant in the unfolding present, the A-series perspective, and an experience of *emergence*. Emergence is a sense that the past cannot be made to contain the present (Mead, 1932). Emergence tends to prompt a reinterpretation of the past so as to better understand the genesis of the present and to increase confidence in the predictability of the future. Reinterpretation concludes with a revised conception of the structure of the process.

Works of art that unfold over time (e.g., literature, music) provide vivid illustrations of the emergent experience. Undoubtedly, this is one of the reasons for their appeal. For instance, a murder mystery generally provides clues for solving the crime. Some of the clues will suggest emergent structures (i.e., who committed the crime and how), only to be later proved wrong. The vital clues are meanwhile easily overlooked because they appear as unimportant details. Yet once the plot finally twists to a conclusion, the solution is presented and the same details leap out as critical events, reconfiguring the structure of the story as a whole.

People are at certain times less, and at other time more, psychologically open to experiencing the emergent (Klapp, 1986). Psychological closure suggests one explanation for the experience of "reversible time," discussed earlier, in connection with ritual enactments. At the opposite extreme, people sometimes open themselves up to adventure and pursue unprogrammed, novel, and even risky activities that crowd their experience with moments of emergence. The normal situation between these two extremes is a feeling that the present moment has a duration, a "now" that extends over some moderate period of time. The duration of the present likely derives from whatever familiar units of process (e.g., actions, events) are salient in the situation, that is, in the window of the present.

Windows Onto the Present

A nonhierarchical window contains the present in two ways. One experience of the present is found in emergence. The emergent is not an entity that any window or pane singles out: It lies in the *difference* between one cumulative pane and the panes preceding it.

A second way that a window contains the present is in bracketing all the past, present, and future moments being *simultaneously* taken into consideration. The present fills the window as a whole. Writers from St. Augustine to T. S. Eliot have described what Jaques (1982) says is the

all-at-onceness of the past, the present, and the future . . . these experiences of living, of striving to achieve in the future by mobilizing one's past experience and one's present abilities in a composite of activity . . . [which] blend in perfect fusion to make up the field of one's real and current flow of psychological existence. (p. 6)

Out of all the memories, perceptions, intentions, and expectations that the present window could contain, a host of cognitive and motivational processes influence its actual content (for a review, see Johnson & Sherman, 1990). Also, the symbolic practices of individuals serve to enrich the present window's content by moderating its discontinuities. For example, individuals part with statements such as "I'll see you tomorrow" to bridge the time they will spend away from each other, and they symbolize enduring relationships by exchanging rings and carrying photos of the other person to underscore their sense that they remain together even while bodily separated (Sigman, 1991). Finally, individuals differ in the overall time spans they tend to take into consideration, the typical breadth of their present windows (Jaques, 1982).

Nonhierarchical windows represent a necessary complement to hierarchical windows and form at least a context for any piece of research. First, they characterize everyday communication, which is both irreversible and self-reflexive. Second, every researcher, even one who never includes the interpretations of "participants," unavoidably participates in and interprets processes by bringing them under study (Krippendorff, 1993). Parallel concerns in the natural sciences have helped reshape the philosophy of time dramatically during the 20th century. Foremost among these developments, relativity theory redefined simultaneity relative to the observer's situation, breaking with the objectivity of Newtonian and Cartesian traditions; and natural evolution was joined by thermodynamic entropy to establish irreversibility in a post-Newtonian world (e.g., Adam, 1990; Bailey, 1990; Einstein, 1916/1961; Jaques, 1982; McGrath & Kelly, 1986; Mead, 1932; Whitrow, 1972; Wiener, 1961). The next step is to look beyond the dualities of time discussed so far—A-series and B-series, emergent and temporal, non-hierarchical and hierarchical—toward the dynamic combination of multiple processes, perspectives, and levels in time, that is, synchronicity.

Simultaneity, Sequentiality, and Synchronicity

Structure was earlier defined as one arrangement out of all possible arrangements for a given set of entities. From the standpoint of simultaneity, configurations among entities represent the structures of moments. For sequentiality, the pattern of activities that comprise a sequence is also a structure, the structure of the process (Monge, 1987, p. 248). Further, as Giddens (1984) argues, as processes unfold they constitute (i.e., reproduce and/or transform) structures. For example, emergent communication networks are created by the patterns of communication among people that occur over time (Monge & Eisenberg, 1987). When people communicate with each other, linkages are created, and the activity of communicating creates a network structure representing the relations among communicators.

Synchronicity

Simultaneity represents the freezing of single processes over time; sequentiality represents their unfolding. *Synchronicity* refers to two or more processes that unfold together over the same or similar time windows. These are parallel or related processes that occur together but may or may not be precisely synchronized, part by part, across multiple recurrences. It represents a "simultaneous sequentiality" between two or more processes. In the presentation of a conference paper, the speaker may choose to present slides via an overhead projector. The visual presentation of the overheads is simultaneous with the verbal presentation at any moment but synchronous as it unfolds over time. Insofar as the presentation fails to come off exactly as planned (e.g., the projector malfunctions or the audience asks unanticipated questions), the speaker's expectations and the actual unfolding of events will run synchronously and will mutually influence each other. The speaker could alternate many times between A-series, or emergent, and B-series perspectives while making adjustments to the plan or presentation. Meanwhile, the audience's listening and watching is essentially synchronous with the speaker's presentation, although slightly lagged in time.

Levels in Time

Bateson (1972) argued that "human verbal communication can operate and always does operate at many contrasting levels of abstraction" (pp. 177-178). In Bateson's example, adding the metacommunicative dimension to the metalinguistic dimension of communication adds new levels of abstraction. Applied in the present context, increasingly abstract structures can occur when multiple entities are specified. Greater abstraction, and complexity, occurs when the entities within a configuration are organized into subgroups or when the entities in a configuration are themselves distinct processes or cycles. Hierarchical windows and panes can be extended to as many levels as are required, and portions of the overall process can be embedded in nonhierarchical windows (i.e., cumulative panes) wherever the process reflexively constitutes itself across time.

Communication scholars are accustomed to thinking about levels of analysis. Most often, this term refers to the number of people or aggregated units involved in the process, as in the well-worn distinction between intrapersonal, interpersonal, group, organizational, and mass communication (Reardon & Rogers, 1988). But we have seen that communication processes also occupy a multiplicity of time levels. Some occur very quickly, such as the length of time it takes to utter a word. Other processes encompass years, perhaps even decades or centuries. Yet too seldom do communication scholars specify the time windows for the processes they examine. Perhaps this happens because we tend to think of communication in universalistic terms.

Think again for a moment about a common communication phenomenon: presenting a paper at a communication conference. As with other meetings, this one has specific activities that are expected to occur within an allotted time that we tend to use in defining the communication processes. Yet we can look at communication processes that occur within multiple time levels, both within the window of the meeting and outside it. These levels might include the words that constitute a meaningful unit of thought, or they could refer to the unfolding of claims, evidence, and arguments within papers. Alternatively, we could examine the unfolding of the entire meeting as the chair orchestrates the sequence and timing of the various communication events from opening remarks to the close of the meeting. Beyond the window of this particular meeting, we could examine it in the context of the other meetings occurring in this conference, or we could examine the unfolding of this meeting in the history of thought about communication processes and cycles, relating it to prior meetings, conferences, and writings on this topic. It is quite possible that a single individual will entertain thoughts in many of these levels during the presentation of one conference paper and that they will influence each other across levels (cf. Adam, 1990, pp. 161-165).

Forecasting Future Processes

A forecast is an attempt to predict the future based on past and present knowledge of processes. Forecasting can focus on a single process or on two or more synchronous processes. Further, forecasting can focus on predicting the entire trajectory of the unfolding process for some period into the future or simply attempt to predict selected entities of the process at some specified future moment.

Single Processes

An example of attempting to forecast selected entities in a process at a single time in the future is election modeling, where forecasters attempt to predict the outcome of votes on election day. Using models of voter preferences, past voting profiles, and recent poll trends, forecasters attempt to predict outcomes given current trajectories and to recommend strategies to their candidates. Other examples of predicting the future state at a particular point in time occur in decision making (see Poole, 1983a, 1983b)

Predicting the course of the time trajectory into the future is represented by research on the dynamics of organizational proximity. Monge, Rothman, Eisenberg, Miller, and Kirste (1985) measured the extent to which people in an organization were in the same physical location at the same time during the day where face-to-face communication was expected or likely. A single measure of organizational proximity was computed across all individuals and ranged from no one in the same physical location (a value of zero) to everyone in the same location, such as the company auditorium (a value of 1). Data were collected in 10-minute intervals and fluctuated throughout the day. Data for four days revealed a consistent daily pattern of high and low proximities, enough to permit a forecast of the fifth day, Friday. The forecast, done in 10-minute intervals for the entire day, was 84% accurate when compared with the actual data.

Synchronous Processes
and Granger Causality

As defined earlier, two or more synchronous processes may unfold together over the same period of time. Because both change through the same time window, it is impossible to determine which precedes the other. And, without the ability to establish sequential order, one of Mills's three canons for establishing causality is missing.[3]

Granger (1969, 1980) provided a solution to the problem of causality in dynamic processes that has come to be known as Granger causality. He observed that in order to establish one processual variable as a cause of another it was necessary to control for the past history or influence of the past values of "the caused" variable on its present value. Consequently, he defined causality to be the influence of one variable on another after removing the influence of the caused variable on itself. In multivariate time series analysis, this is typically accomplished by the statistical technique known as "prewhitening" the dependent variable (see also the chapters by Cappella and VanLear & Watt, this volume).

An example of this procedure is provided in Monge, Cozzens, and Contractor (1992), who examined communication and motivational predictors of organizational innovation. Data were collected on six variables in 12 organizations on a weekly basis for more than a year. To test the causal influence of communication and motivation on innovation, the innovation variable was first prewhitened. The time series analysis that was then used lagged the values of communication and motivation to account for the current values of innovation. The results showed that communication was a much more significant cause of organizational innovation than motivation. The test of Granger causality in this study illustrates just one of the ways that dynamic analysis can reveal the causal structure of synchronous processes.

Conclusion

This chapter has developed a framework for theorizing about and designing research on communication processes. Illustrating the metaphor of windows and panes at three levels of analysis, we have shown how to specify the process dimensions for any theory. Three concepts capture different but equally important aspects of process. Sequentiality captures the unfolding of a process across time. Simultaneity captures the configuration of the moment and, in a self-reflexive sense, the experience of the present. And synchronicity captures the parallel unfolding of multiple processes through time. Because structure is an equally fundamental concept, we have shown that processes contain and/or create structures sequentially, simultaneously, and synchronously.

It is one thing to construct a framework and quite another to actually use it. Although we have illustrated various aspects of the framework with a number of communication examples, we have yet to develop a processual communication theory that encapsulates the framework. Of course, we are not alone in this shortcoming as virtually no processual theories exist in the field of communication. That, then, remains the challenge ahead for all of us. Hopefully, the tools provided in this and the other chapters in this book should make that formidable task considerably easier.

Notes

1. The sole focus here is succession over time, although for other purposes the term sequentiality could apply to the extension of entities across space.

2. This conceptualization owes much to McTaggart's (1927) discussion of the time-independent *C-series*, said to underlie all existence. He contrasts the C-series against the temporal A-series and B-series. The value of these conceptions remains significant in spite of McTaggart's problematic argument that time itself is only an illusion (see Jaques, 1982).

3. The other two canons require establishing covariation and ruling out spurious association.

PART

Some Tools for Time

We are always acting on what has just finished happening. It happened at least 1/30th of a second ago. We think we're in the present, but we aren't. The present we know is only a movie of the past.

—Tom Wolfe, *The Electric Kool-Aid Acid Test* (1968)

A truer image of the world, I think, is obtained by picturing things as entering into the stream of time from an eternal world outside, than from a view which regards time as the devouring tyrant of all that is.

—Bertrand Russell, *A Free Man's Worship and Other Essays* (1976)

The geometry of landscape and situation seems to create its own systems of time, the sense of a dynamic element which is cinematising the events of the canvas, translating a posture or ceremony into dynamic terms.

—J. G. Ballard, "The Thousand Wounds and Flowers," in *New Worlds,* No. 191 (1969)

Indexing Pattern Over Time

Criteria for Studying Communication as a Dynamic Process

ROBERT B. ARUNDALE

It would be an interesting project to trace the historical development of theory and research on dynamic patterns in communication processes that has led to this volume. It would also be a difficult project, in that the scholar attempting such a task would face two important sampling problems, one a matter of "space" and one a matter of "time." Constructing a representative sample of articles from the "space" of the human communication research literature would be difficult because works on dynamic patterns are spread sparsely across a fairly broad "area," although procedures for such sampling are well known. But constructing a sample of articles that also represented the historical development of theory and research across "time" would be quite a bit more difficult because works on dynamic patterns are distributed unevenly across

An earlier version of this chapter was presented at the Seminar on Communication and Society, Inter-University Centre of Postgraduate Studies, Dubrovnik, Yugoslavia, May 25-31, 1987, and published as "Measuring Communication Effects Over Time" in M. Plenkovic and B. Cavaton (Eds.), *Informatologia Yugoslavica*, Special Issue 7, 1988, pp. 129-137. Portions of that chapter are reproduced by permission here. Dr. John Olson, Geophysical Institute, University of Alaska Fairbanks, offered important insights and resources in the preparation of both chapters.

time, and procedures for such sampling are little known in the social sciences. For this particular project, the total time span for sampling would be easy to determine, reaching back from the present to early work in the discipline, perhaps to Berlo's (1960) discussion of change over time as one among several aspects of the broad concept of "process." However, establishing just when and how often to sample within this historical span would be very difficult, although at the same time central to the project, because this decision on sampling across time would determine the extent to which the sample of works was representative of the dynamic pattern that constitutes the historical development. This chapter focuses on sampling across time in ways that generate data that adequately represent or index dynamic patterns.

Generating Data on Pattern Over Time

Drawing on Coombs's 1964 theory of data, Krippendorff (1970) described four steps leading from observation to interpretation in scientific inquiry: A scientist (1) decides what *observations* of what events are relevant to the research problem; (2) performs operations like labeling, ordering, and measuring that formalize the observations or translate them into *data;* (3) applies analytic procedures to detect relationships in the data, resulting in *evidence* of structures in the data; and (4) develops a theoretical *interpretation* by assigning meanings to these structures.

Krippendorff made three important points about this description of scientific inquiry. First, scientists make choices at Step 1, and at each subsequent step, that are influenced strongly by their theoretical and value commitments, research objectives, and research tools. The data that result from Step 2 therefore cannot be "objective" in the ordinary sense. Second, the observations performed in Steps 1 and 2 define or delimit the information that the data contain about the events under study. That information determines in turn both which analytic techniques are appropriate for producing evidence in Step 3 and what interpretations of that evidence are warranted in Step 4. Third, as scientists proceed with their research, they may well develop additional theoretical interpretations directly from their observations of events, inadvertently bypassing both the data generation and analysis steps. The consequence is that scientists may at times propose theoretical interpretations of their data without recognizing that part or all of these interpretations are warranted not by evidence derived from the data but simply by personal observation. In other words, scientists may at times make interpretations without recognizing that the data they had generated do not contain the information required to produce the type of evidence needed to warrant their interpretations.

Building on this discussion of the process of generating data, Krippendorff (1970) developed criteria specifying the information that data must contain to be capable of providing evidence warranting theoretical interpretations in terms of the concept of "communication." He noted that "there is no upper limit as to the informational richness that communication data may exhibit. But there is a lower limit below which data remain meaningless as far as communication constructs are concerned" (p. 246). Specifically, Krippendorff argued that data capable of warranting theoretical interpretations regarding processes of communication must contain, among several other components, adequate information on the succession of states over time in the phenomena observed. But data that contain adequate information on succession, change, or pattern over time in communication phenomena must also meet specific criteria to be capable of providing evidence that warrants theoretical interpretations in those terms. With the exception of the research programs represented in this volume, comparatively few studies of communication phenomena have generated data containing adequate information on change over time, so that most existing theoretical interpretations in terms of pattern over time in human communication are warranted only by personal observation. In other words, they lack the warrant of evidence derived from data.

It is evident from Krippendorff's discussion that the way time is conceptualized influences the decisions and operations performed in generating data regarding it. Kelly and McGrath (1988), McGrath and Kelly (1986), and Warner (1991) have examined the myriad ways time has been conceptualized in research on human behavior. As a fundamental dimension of the phenomena that are the focus of inquiry in the social sciences, time is normally conceptualized either as an "explanatory factor" or as a "reference variable." Kline (1977) indicated that, as an explanatory factor, time may be conceptualized, for example, as an expendable resource, as in studies of time allocation, and as an "object" to which individuals attach meanings, as in attitudes toward the past or in the significance attached to priority. In this chapter, time is conceptualized solely as a reference variable, that is, as a dimension of events to which one may link other variables that have explanatory significance. Processes like diffusion and growth, for example, are described with reference to time, but they are not explained by it. Other events such as media contact or cell division constitute the explanatory factors.

As a reference variable, time is measured just as any other variable in scientific inquiry. That is, if the operations performed to formalize one's observations of events in time are capable of discriminating the events of interest from other events but are not capable of identifying their order, then the operations produce *nominal data*. A particular configuration of events in time is simply named, as in "the Industrial Revolution." If the operations used to formalize the observations are capable of arraying the events in successive order, the result is *ordinal data*, as in "pretest" and "posttest" or "Trials 1, 2 and 3." Operations that generate magnitudes for the time distances between the events, in addition to their order, produce *interval data*. Finally, operations that produce not only order but also time distances from a single reference or "zero" point generate *ratio data*. Unlike many other variables in social scientific inquiry, time is readily measured on both interval scales (the message was broadcast at hour intervals) and ratio scales (person A took twice as long as person B). Recognizing both that nominal measurement of time is of very limited value when time is treated as a reference variable and that ordinal time measurement is the minimum requirement for imputing cause-effect relationships, it will be convenient in what follows to collapse this four-level distinction into a two-level distinction between discrete measurement of time or "sequential" time (ordinal data) and continuous measurement of time (interval and ratio data).

Given this conceptualization of time as a reference variable, it is evident that data that contain adequate information on pattern over time have an added complexity, for as Coleman (1968) noted, "observations of differences in time have always to run alongside the observations of differences in the state for which change is of interest" (p. 429). More formally, each datum on pattern over time must consist at minimum of a pair of values: one value representing the state of the variable having explanatory significance and one value representing the measurement of time as a reference variable. An additional variable with explanatory significance requires a trio of values and so on unless the added variable has a different time scale, in which case a separate pair of values is needed. To simplify the discussion of generating adequate data on pattern over time, what follows will refer only to values of a single variable having explanatory significance (the "variable," for short) paired with corresponding values of time as a reference variable (or simply "time").

Unlike the case for time as a reference variable, it is frequently the case that variables having explanatory significance are limited by their theoretical conceptualizations to operations that produce only one type of data. That is, whereas "attitude" has been conceptualized in ways that have permitted measurement on nominal, ordinal, interval, and ratio scales, other variables like "content category" and "order of presentation" are restricted, by definition, to measurement on nominal and ordinal scales, respectively. Here too, it will be convenient to collapse the four levels of measurement into a two-level distinction between discrete measurement of explanatory variables (nominal and ordinal) and continuous measurement (interval and ratio). Combining the two-level distinction for explanatory variables with the two-level distinction for time produces a four-part classification of data on pattern over time:

- Continuous variable indexed over continuous time
- Continuous variable indexed over discrete (or sequential) time
- Discrete variable indexed over continuous time
- Discrete variable indexed over discrete (or sequential) time

Note that this classification may be applied to data as they are (a) conceptualized in theory, (b) generated in measurement operations, and (c) characterized by analytic techniques. That is, one may *conceptualize* an attitude and the data on it as a continuous variable changing over continuous time; one may *generate* data on that attitude using a continuous scale like a semantic differential, yet in discrete or sequential time (e.g., before and after a message), and one may *analyze* the resulting data using a technique that characterizes the attitude as discrete (e.g., "for" and "against") and in discrete time.

There is one final, central issue in conceptualizing data on pattern over time, and considering it requires introducing an additional distinction not normally employed in the literature cited here. Any continuous or discrete variable, including time, may be recorded in analog or digital form. Analog recording creates a physical analogy for the indexed variation in another medium, whereas digital recording transforms the indexed variation into a set of verbal or numerical values. Note that "digital" in this usage stands in opposition to "analog" and does *not* mean "binary coding," nor does it imply measurement or analysis by digital computer. For example, the familiar trace of an electrocardiogram on the moving paper tape of a chart recorder involves analog recording of a continuous variable (i.e., the continuous vertical movement of the trace) over continuous time (i.e., the horizontal movement of the paper). With suitable adjustments, the same chart recorder could make an analog recording of a discrete variable over continuous time (i.e., vertical movement of the trace only for the presence or absence of a nominal category, or corresponding to the shift among different values of ordinal data). And if the movement of the paper tape were started and stopped in conjunction, say, with the presence or absence of observed events, the chart recorder would be making an analog recording over discrete or sequential time (i.e., ordinal time). With suitable instrumentation, every one of these analog recording operations could also be performed by digital recording, resulting in a set of paired values (one for the variable and one for time), as opposed to the chart recorder's pairing of two physical analogs of the values.

If one reflects on this distinction between analog and digital recording, it should be obvious that much data generation in the natural sciences and most of that in the social sciences employs digital recording. Furthermore, much data analysis in the natural sciences and virtually all that in the social sciences requires that the data be in digital form, for to analyze data in analog form requires specialized equipment and procedures for analog computation (e.g., an analog speech spectrograph or some type of analog computer). Hence, values originally recorded in analog form are normally transformed into digital form before analysis. Digital recording over time requires the observer or the recording device to identify (and to record) the specific points in time at which the variable of interest was indexed so as to construct the required set of paired values. This operation is usually referred to as sampling across time and may occur either in the initial data-generating step or in a subsequent step that transforms the data from analog to digital form prior to analysis. Note that in terms of the distinction introduced above, sampling over time *only* converts analog data into digital data. Although much of the literature cited here (except Freeman, 1965, p. 3) uses the term "discrete" rather loosely to characterize both time-sampled data and the analytic techniques applicable to them, sampling across time *does not* transform continuous time data into discrete or sequential time data unless the sampling operation ignores the length of time between sampling points.

Given the conceptualization of data on pattern over time developed here, it is evident that data recorded and analyzed entirely by analog means always contain adequate information on pattern over time in the variable of interest. It is also evident that the operation of sampling across time either omits information about a variable when data are recorded initially in analog form or imposes limits on the information one can obtain about a variable when data are gathered initially in digital form. Because it is the norm in the social sciences to both record and analyze data in digital form, researchers studying pattern over time must be cognizant of this central issue: *Only data generated by appropriate sampling across time will contain adequate information for producing evidence that warrants theoretical interpretations in terms of pattern over time.* Data that fail to meet the criteria for appropriate sampling across time developed below do not contain adequate information on time and so fail to represent fully the pattern over time in the variable under study. Interpretations of such data in terms of pattern over time involve only the warrant of personal observation, not the warrant of evidence produced from data.

Criteria for Indexing Pattern Over Time

Continuous Variable Indexed
Over Continuous Time

The criteria for generating adequate data by sampling across time when the variable under study is conceptualized as continuous and as changing over continuous time are based on the principles of Fourier analysis and particularly on the Sampling Theorem (see Cherry, 1957, pp. 140-143; Freeman, 1965, pp. 73-77). Fourier analysis is one approach among a large class of approaches for decomposing variance into a set of orthogonal components. In the case of Fourier analysis, the components are a set of sinusoidal functions, each having a specific frequency, magnitude, and phase relationship and together having the properties that, first, the sum of the component variances equals the total variance and, second, that the sum of the component sinusoidal waveforms creates a complex nonsinusoidal waveform whose magnitude equals the value of the variable under study at each sampling time point (see VanLear & Watt, this volume).[1]

Because the analytic objectives of decomposing the variance of a time referenced variable can be achieved, albeit less conveniently, using classes of orthogonal functions other than sinusoidal functions (Gabor, 1946, pp. 439), it should be evident that the use of Fourier analysis in decomposing variance does not imply or assume that the variable under study is actually generated by such periodic processes, nor does it require that the results be interpreted in terms of cyclic properties, although that is one option. This point would not deserve emphasis were it not often misunderstood in the social sciences (cf. Arundale, 1980, pp. 234, 237). That alternative approaches are possible was evident as early as 1946 in Gabor's decomposition of time varying signals into orthogonal "wavelet" functions, each of which represented an elementary signal or "quantum of information" he termed a "logon." His distinct and more general analysis confirmed both Nyquist's (1928) results regarding sampling rate, and related determinations of the minimum number of statistically independent values or data points necessary to specify any given stationary, band-limited signal of finite length (cf. Freeman, 1965, p. 76). The two criteria for generating adequate data developed below have been framed in terms of Fourier analysis only because it is a more convenient and better known decomposition technique. The existence of alternative approaches indicates that the criteria could be formulated in terms of other techniques for decomposition, although at the cost of clarity and familiarity.

Among the set of sinusoidal components that result from Fourier decomposition of a complex waveform, four have relevance for generating adequate data on continuous variables indexed over continuous time: the component with the lowest frequency, *or* the two components whose frequencies are closest to one another, *and* the component with the highest frequency. Both criteria below have been developed in detail elsewhere, with supporting evidence (Arundale, 1980, pp. 233-237; cf. Arundale, 1971).[2] The first criterion answers the question "How long must measurement continue?" and assures that enough data are gathered to obtain adequate discrimination of detail and to capture long-term changes. The second independent criterion answers the question "How frequently must measurements be made?" and assures that the data gathered will capture the shortest-term changes. Appropriate sampling across time from a continuous variable in continuous time requires *both* (1) measurement over a total time span, T, greater than or equal to the *longer* of *either*

$$T = \frac{1}{\Delta f},$$

where Δf is the smallest difference between component frequencies (Jenkins & Watts, 1968, pp. 48-50), *or*

$$T = \frac{1}{f_0},$$

where f_0 is the frequency of the lowest frequency component in cycles per unit time; *and* (2) measurement within T at intervals, Δt, where

$$\Delta t \leq \frac{1}{2f_n},$$

and f_n is the frequency of the highest frequency component in cycles per unit time (Nyquist, 1928; often referred to as the "Nyquist criterion").[3]

Data generated in accord with both criteria will contain adequate information on the pattern of change over time in the variable under study, in that the criteria jointly specify the number of statistically independent values necessary to specify a stationary pattern of variation over time. Nonstationary patterns of variation require more data for adequate specification, as do patterns that are embedded in or contain noise. Particular analysis techniques used to produce evidence from data may well also require a longer measurement span or a shorter interval than identified by the criteria. An analysis technique requiring fewer data points would produce evidence incapable of supporting theoretical interpretations in terms of pattern over time because the data would not contain adequate information on the pattern. And although most analysis techniques that might be applied to such data assume that the sampling points are spaced at equal intervals, the criteria themselves assume only a regular distribution across the measurement span (Freeman, 1965, pp. 77-89). Benedetto (1992) and Marquardt and Acuff (1982) have referenced a number of theoretical and analytical approaches employing unequal sampling intervals.

Several of the research programs presented in this volume have sampled continuous variables over continuous time. Barnett and Cho used Nielsen data collected by sampling households using television in order to identify and predict cycles in television viewing. Buder sampled vocal fundamental frequency and intensity as part of a study of dynamic coordination between interactants. In studying the dynamics of attitude formation, Kaplowitz and Fink sampled attitude oscillations on a ratio scale as subjects formulated decisions. Meadowcroft conceptualized attention in terms of reaction time and indexed this variable over time in studying attention cycles during television viewing. Finally, Warner describes a study involving two stages of sampling. First, she sampled vocal amplitude to construct dichotomous data on presence or absence of talk. Second, she summed the number of points at which talk was present over a 10-second interval to create an index of percentage talk. Warner used this derived index together with parallel measurements of blood pressure in studying cycles in face-to-face interaction. Each of these research programs are considered in more detail below in examining how the criteria are applied in designing and assessing research.

Continuous Variable Indexed
Over Discrete or Sequential Time

Given that time is so readily measured on both interval and ratio scales, it is perhaps puzzling at first why anyone would choose *purposefully* to study pattern over time in a continuous variable, yet at the same time conceptualize and measure time as discrete, or ordinal. But when one realizes that ordinal time encompasses "pretest-posttest" and "Times 1, 2, and 3," it is evident that a very large portion of social science research falls precisely into this category. Indeed, most researchers probably have not chosen purposefully to study pattern over time in this way: Some researchers have undoubtedly entirely ignored time as a dimension of communication events, and most have probably assumed that ordinal measurement of time (i.e., treating time simply as a sequence of events) was sufficient to index pattern over time. A brief review of the research designs most prevalent in the study of communication today should establish these assertions.

"Point designs," or designs that measure a variable at a single point in time, have value for many research questions, although the data they generate contain no information on pattern over time. The same is true for single point, cross-sectional studies of several age cohorts. Such data appear to show a pattern of development over time but do not contain the information needed to support this interpretation. Like all point designs, these studies parallel isolated photographs, even if they do picture persons of different ages. Measuring a variable at two points in time allows one to identify differences in the value of the variable over ordinal time, as do "before and after" photographs. These "difference designs" are also of considerable value in research but generate only the most basic data on pattern over time. Specifically, the two values of the variable define a straight line, but the data contain no information on any other possible pattern of variation between the two points in time.

Apart from the research programs referenced in this volume, relatively few studies have included measurement of a variable at three or more points, even though it is evident that each added point in time moves a design closer to the ideal "pattern over time design," that is, a design in which the sampling across time omits no significant information on the pattern of change in the variable under study. Note that pattern-over-time designs can be constructed to parallel not only the successive frames of a motion picture, which implies continuous measurement of time as in the first category, but also the sequence of photographs that document each key event in some process (e.g., completing the foundation, the framing, the roof, etc., of a new house), which implies discrete or sequential time measurement, as in this second category. As VanLear and Watt (this volume) note, the choice between continuous or discrete measurement of time is one best made in view of the observed or theoretical properties of the variable or process being examined.

The only cases in which one could gather adequate information on change in a continuous variable over discrete time but sample at fewer points than Criteria 1 and 2 specify are those in which one has specific a priori knowledge about the pattern of variation. For example, if one knows the variable takes on only fixed, continuous values like 0, 1.5, 3.0, 4.5, and so on, one could generate adequate data using the third criterion, below, for discrete variables. Alternatively, if one knows the rates of change and points of inflection for the variable, or that it is monotonic and increasing, or that it follows, for example, a cumulative normal curve, one could sample at fewer points and still generate data containing the information needed to produce evidence on pattern over time. Note, however, that each of these cases involves a great deal of advance knowledge about the variable, or requires very strong assumptions, or both (as in Coleman, 1968; cf. Kelly & McGrath, 1988, pp. 23-28).

Discrete Variable Indexed
Over Continuous Time

The single criterion for generating adequate data by sampling across time when the variable under study is conceptualized as discrete and as changing over continuous time also stems from the Sampling Theorem mentioned earlier. Again, the appropriate sampling interval for a continuous variable indexed over continuous time is

$$\Delta t \le \frac{1}{2f_n},$$

where f_n is the highest frequency. Because the "period," or length of one cycle of a sinusoid is

$$p = \frac{1}{f},$$

one can rewrite the sampling interval as

$$\Delta t \le \frac{p_n}{2},$$

or half the cycle period of the component with the highest frequency. For a discrete variable with two possible states, say x and z, a cycle is a time period that begins as the variable enters state x, continues as it remains in state x, moves to and remains in state z, and ends as the variable exits state z. If the variable were continuous, the appropriate sampling interval would be half of this cycle, but because a discrete variable often has one state in which it resides for intervals shorter than those for any other state, one must set the sampling interval equal to this shortest time interval. Accordingly, appropriate sampling across time from a discrete variable indexed over continuous time requires (3) measurement at intervals equal to (or shorter than) the shortest interval for which the variable under study can remain in any one of its states.

This third criterion answers the question "How frequently must measurements be made?" and is developed in detail elsewhere, with supporting evidence (Arundale, 1978, pp. 259-261).[4] The answer to the related question "How long must the measurement continue?" depends for discrete variables on the observed or theoretical properties of the variable under study. Because it cannot be derived from a formal property of the variable, the answer is not presented as a separate formal criterion. Briefly, the total measurement span, T, for a discrete variable indexed over continuous time must be sufficient to encompass long-term changes in the phenomenon under study (see Arundale, 1978, p. 278).

If one considers the third criterion carefully, it appears almost "intuitively obvious" that data generated using such a sampling interval will contain adequate information on all details of the pattern over time in the variable. But it is much less obvious that, given a specific sampling interval, Δt, the data generated cannot provide adequate information on *any* state in which the variable resides for shorter periods. Theoretical interpretations based on evidence regarding such states would be unwarranted because the data lack complete information. Unlike the earlier second criterion for continuous variables, this third criterion for discrete variables does assume that the sampling points are spaced equally across the measurement span. One can relax this assumption and generate adequate data with fewer sampling points only if one has the ability to record both the value of the variable *and* the time point at which the variable moves from state to state (in effect, a procedure for unequal interval sampling in continuous time). The advantage of equal interval sampling is ease of analysis, as for example in using the relatively straightforward discrete-time Markov chain to model a continuous time analysis. Unequal intervals would, in principle, require use of the less tractable continuous-time Markov model, although Hewes, Planalp, and Streibel (1980) have developed a modification of the discrete-time semi-Markov chain model that accommodates unequal intervals.[5]

One study presented in this volume involves sampling of discrete variables over continuous time. Much like Warner's study, Cappella's investigation of the dynamics of coordination of vocal and kinesic behavior in dyadic interaction employed two stages of sampling. Cappella began by sampling vocal amplitude to construct dichotomous talk-silence data and then summed these data over a 3-second interval to produce an ordinal measure of the extent to which each individual held the floor. Unlike Warner, he also sampled both gesturing and smiling and combined all three measures in a broader index of turn holding. Cappella's sampling procedures are examined in depth below in considering how the criteria are applied.

Discrete Variable Indexed Over
Discrete or Sequential Time

Studying pattern over time in a discrete variable while conceptualizing time as discrete (i.e., as ordinal or sequential) is a reasonably common occurrence in the social sciences and is typically grounded in a theoretical rationale or observational system. Most coding systems in use in the social sciences include definitions of the "events" to which the discrete categories apply. An "event" could be an observational unit like a "trial" or a theoretical unit like an "utterance." When one generates data by recording a category code at each time and only when one of the defined events occurs one constructs an *event sequence* sample in discrete time, as opposed to a *clock time* sample constructed in continuous time (see Arundale, 1978, pp. 265-266). Because the units that are sampled across time are defined by the measurement procedure, the data generated by event sequence sampling always contain adequate information on change over time in the variable. Indeed, unlike the case for conceptualizing continuous time in terms of clock time, one's ability to conceptualize time as discrete in a research context is tied closely to the theoretical or observational framework that defines the time units. If these units can be observed reliably, an event sequence sample will generate data containing adequate time information.

Why, then, shouldn't researchers always conceptualize and measure time as discrete or sequential? First, because the power and variety of analytic techniques available for producing evidence from discrete time data are rather limited compared to the power and variety available for continuous time data. And second, because to be consistent with the warrant provided by the evidence derived from the data, theoretical interpretations involving discrete time must be carefully circumscribed, treating time strictly as sequence and not as progressing in measured units. Although we do not always treat time as continuous in our daily affairs, the ease with which we can do so if required suggests that researchers need to take care to limit theoretical interpretations of evidence from discrete time data only to implications regarding order or sequence and to avoid interpretations in terms of clock time.

Having considered criteria for appropriate sampling across time for all four classifications of data on pattern over time, it is important to note several general issues and to return to the broader implications of this analysis for communication research. The criteria developed here constitute the necessary conditions for generating data containing adequate information on pattern over time, although they may not be sufficient conditions if noise or nonstationarity are involved. A number of authors have discussed the issues of appropriate sampling intervals for discrete variables and have provided informal and untested criteria, ranging from suggestions that the interval is arbitrary to a suggestion consistent with the third criterion (Arundale, 1978, p. 277). Parallel discussions of sampling intervals for continuous variables have generally been consistent with the second criterion because they have been guided by the Sampling Theorem but include uncritical suggestions for gathering up to five times more data than needed and normally ignore the first criterion on overall span of measurement (Arundale, 1980, p. 238). Although data in excess of those specified by the criteria generally provide redundant information that may benefit subsequent analyses, in some analytic techniques, such as the discrete-time Markov chain, having excess data produces evidence that may be as misleading as having too few data (Arundale, 1978, pp. 257, 277-278, 280).

These criteria make evident that the operation of generating digitally recorded data on pattern over time (i.e., of sampling across time) must be "tuned" carefully to the pattern of variation under study not only to achieve adequate resolution but also to avoid either under- or over-resolving it. Overresolution is preferable to underresolution not only because it is always possible to use fewer data in subsequent analyses but also because underresolution overlooks fine detail. In the case of continuous variables, underresolution transforms partially resolved details into spurious information termed "aliases" that are impossible to avoid, except by processing before sampling or by sampling at unequal intervals (Arundale, 1980, p. 244). In fact, unless such steps are taken, equal interval sampling will transform any form of noise or random variation in an observed variable into aliased information. Again, as indicated earlier, these complex problems in obtaining adequate resolution of pattern over time arise *not* from techniques employed in analysis but *solely* from the operation of sampling over time.

Implications for Designing New
Research and Assessing Past Research

The criteria are perhaps most valuable in designing new studies of dynamic processes. Used prospectively, they provide standards for choosing values for the sampling interval and for the measurement span that are appropriate to the way in which pattern over time is conceptualized in the research question and in the underlying theory. There is no single, universally applicable method for determining the appropriate sampling interval and measurement span, but there are several general approaches that draw upon existing theory or research results. Because these approaches have been developed in more detail elsewhere (Arundale, 1978, pp. 278-279; 1980, pp. 251-257), they are characterized here only briefly. Choosing an appropriate sampling interval for a continuous variable involves determining by some means the period of the sinusoidal component with the highest frequency and dividing that by 2. For a discrete variable, one must determine the shortest time that the variable can reside in any one of its states. Choosing an appropriate measurement span for a continuous variable requires finding the period of the lowest-frequency sinusoidal component or the closest two frequencies to be distinguished from one another. For a discrete variable, one must establish the longest span of change that is of interest or that is likely to be found in the data.

Previous research in communication or in other disciplines often provides data on periods or cycles, as for example on attention span (cf. Meadowcroft, this volume), on vocalization patterns (cf. Buder, this volume), or on a number of other dynamic communication phenomena, as examined in the research programs described in this volume. If data on the shortest likely period are not available, subtracting 2 or 3 standard deviations from a mean period can provide the basis for establishing an appropriate sampling interval (i.e., one that would index most of the shortest occurrences). Other research has provided time spans for "saturating" an audience with information, on diffusing information to a population, and so on that could inform decisions on overall measurement spans. Information on periods or frequencies can also be derived from data on rate of transfer over a communication channel or on its bandwidth (as in Cherry, 1957). Should existing studies provide either actual data on pattern over time in closely related variables or the means of simulating such data from a descriptive or generative model (e.g., growth or decay curves or the diffusion curve), then time series techniques (Box & Jenkins, 1976; Gregson, 1983) together with spectral analysis (Birkenfeld, 1977; Jenkins & Watts, 1968; Marple, 1987) can provide valuable information for use in choosing sampling intervals or overall measurement spans.

But whether any of the values resulting from this short list of approaches could serve as an appropriate sampling interval or measurement span can be decided only in the context of specific research objectives and in view of the theoretical context in which they are framed. Indeed, the objectives and the theory may themselves define the most appropriate interval and measurement span, as in studying conversations using "utterances" as the sampling event or in studying political attitude change over the duration of a campaign. Failing all of these approaches, one may have to conduct pilot studies to provide basic information like "What is the shortest time required for an individual (or a population) to change an attitude?" (cf. Kaplowitz & Fink, this volume).

Cappella's (this volume) study of coordination of vocal and kinesic behavior in interaction serves as an excellent example of applying the criteria prospectively in designing research. Although he does not develop the rationale for his first-stage sampling in his chapter, Cappella chose the 0.3-second interval based on considerable prior research on talk-silence sequences in dyadic interaction. In particular, Jaffe and Feldstein (1970) found that the shortest mean length among the four discrete talk-silence states they studied was 0.413 seconds ($SD = 0.055$) for simultaneous talk. Subtracting 2 standard deviations from this mean indicates that a sampling interval of 0.303 seconds should index at least 96% of these shortest states. Cappella's choice of a first-stage sampling interval is thus fully consistent with the third criterion.

To construct an ordinal measure suitable for the analyses he had planned, Cappella took the additional step of summing the first-stage, dichotomous data on talk-silence across 3-second intervals, creating ordinal scores for amount of talk that ranged from 0 to 10. He then combined these scores with similarly constructed scores on gesturing and on smiling to create a more complex index of turn holding. This second stage in data processing created a new "sampling" across time with characteristics distinct from the first-stage sampling, the primary difference stemming again from the third criterion: a 3-second sampling interval cannot provide complete information on states of turn holding that are shorter than 3 seconds, despite the procedure used to construct the index. Cappella's discussion of the implications of choosing the 3-second interval and of choosing an overall time span of 30 minutes serves as a model for the careful consideration (and trade-offs) needed in making these two key decisions in designing research on pattern over time. His discussion makes evident not only that these decisions influence the nature of the data that are collected and the types of analyses that may be conducted but also that these decisions depend directly on the theoretical framework that guides the research.

The study of cycles in dyadic interaction that Warner (this volume) describes also involved two stages of sampling, beginning much as Cappella did by sampling vocal amplitude at 0.25-second intervals to produce dichotomous talk-silence data but then summing across 10-second intervals to create a continuous percentage index of amount of talk. Following the second criterion, Warner's second-stage data do not contain adequate information on any cycle in amount of talk with a period less than 20 seconds (i.e., "two observations" in her terms, or $2\Delta t$, as above). Following the first criterion, the 30-minute measurement cannot provide adequate information on cycles with periods longer than 30 minutes (i.e., the measurement span, T). Given that the literature most relevant to Warner's interests describes cycles in communication behaviors and physiological patterns with periods on the order of 30 seconds to 20 minutes, the choices of interval and of overall span in her research design appear appropriate.

In his study of dynamic coordination in vocal interaction, Buder (this volume) employed instrumentation that provided values for vocal intensity and fundamental frequency at 1/30-second intervals. (Note that unless this instrumentation was analog, the instrumentation itself employed a prior sampling stage that must be taken into account, as Buder suggested briefly.) The second criterion indicates that Buder's data adequately indexed variations with periods at or above 0.067 seconds, which appears appropriate given his theoretical rationale for examining prosodic variables in time domains down to 0.1 second. The second condition of the first criterion indicates that the total data span of 22 seconds that Buder analyzed in his example is also appropriate for studying these short time domains, but the first condition of the first criterion points to a different issue that may well be important in this example and in other research on pattern over time.

Specifically, the overall span of measurement also establishes the smallest difference in frequencies among the Fourier components of variation that can be resolved adequately using a given data set. Buder's 22-second span does not allow discrimination between any two components of variation whose frequencies differ by less than

$$\Delta f = \frac{1}{T},$$

or by less than 0.045 cycles per second (cps). Given that the lowest frequency component his sampling can index has a frequency of

$$f_0 = \frac{1}{T},$$

or 0.045 cps, that the highest frequency is

$$f_n = \frac{1}{2\Delta t},$$

or 15 cps, and that Buder is interested in patterns over time in the range of 0.1 seconds, the fact that the data do not contain adequate information on components any closer in frequency than 0.045 cps may well be a factor to consider in the research design and/or in the interpretation of evidence produced in analysis (see Arundale, 1980, pp. 234-235, 245-251, for further discussion).

Barnett and Cho's (this volume) use of a 15-minute sampling interval was dictated by the format of the Nielsen data on "households using television" which they employed in identifying and predicting cycles in television use. But the interval is also highly appropriate on theoretical grounds. That is, although the Nielsen data are a continuous measure of households using television, they are an index of use across an entire market that is constructed by sampling usage in individual households. Because the great bulk of television programming available to each household has a "minimum state time" of 30 minutes, it is evident on theoretical grounds from the third criterion that the 15-minute sampling interval provides not only an adequate but also a conservative index of household usage. Clearly, the overall measurement span of 365 days was also theoretically appropriate given Barnett and Cho's interest in incorporating an annual cycle in their predictive model.

By contrast, Kaplowitz and Fink (this volume) had only indirect theoretical and observational guidance in choosing a sampling interval for indexing patterns in attitude change during decision making. Their own carefully developed theory predicted oscillations in attitude but not the time scale of those oscillations. In retrospect, their choice of an 18ms interval appears to have been conservative, as few if any "cycles" in their data appear to have frequencies even close to the maximum 28 cps their data can index adequately. In their case, the overall measurement span is set, theoretically, by the respondent's indication that he or she has reached a decision. As these scholars indicate clearly, much additional basic research is needed, and it is that research that will determine whether the trajectories of attitude change they have discovered contain important frequency components that approach the highest frequencies their design can index. If not, then future designs can employ a longer sampling interval.

Finally, Meadowcroft (this volume) was able to draw on past theory and research that pointed to different cyclical components of attention span to design a study that allowed her to distinguish among these components as they appeared while participants watched television. Meadowcroft defined attention in terms of reaction time, which she indexed at random, unequal intervals. She then used a linear interpolation across the unequally spaced time points as the basis for reconstructing a sample having equal 8.16-second intervals. This approach may have introduced noise or error in the data, which might well have appeared in the analyses as spurious cycles or aliases. Both of these potential problems could have been avoided by using the admittedly more complex approaches to handling unequal interval samples that were noted in discussing the first criterion.

The 8.16-second sampling interval that resulted from Meadowcroft's interpolation means that her data did not index adequately any components of attention span with periods shorter than 16.3 seconds. Given that the shortest period component she found was 58.8 seconds, the sampling interval appears appropriate, although research that rules out components with periods shorter that 16 seconds would be valuable in developing a complete, multicomponent theory of attention span. In Meadowcroft's research, the overall span of measurement was set by the length of the television program that was the research stimulus. Because at least one component she discovered cycled with a period nearly half of the 700+-second overall span, research that examines the possibility of much longer cycles would also be valuable, especially with regard to the "attention inertia" component that appeared in her data as a non-stationary linear trend.

Each of the above examples of current research on pattern over time illustrates a different aspect of using the criteria prospectively. Determining appropriate values for the sampling interval and for the overall measurement span is a necessary step in designing studies of pattern over time, and the criteria presented here generally require more frequent sampling over a longer span than is normally found in research in the social sciences. But if the required interval or measurement span cannot be attained (because of limitations in measurement, high cost, magnitude of the task, and so on), then the research objectives should be reformulated. There is no point in proceeding if the data that result lack the information needed to produce evidence that will warrant the theoretical interpretations one hopes to make. As Kline (1977) noted, "Choosing the next time class meets, the next election, or when the money for experimental manipulations will run out, are not conceptually appropriate ways of defining when the t_1, or t_2, or t_n measures are to be taken" (p. 203).

As is also evident from these six examples, the criteria are valuable in assessing past research. Employed retrospectively, the criteria allow one to establish the limits on the interpretation of pattern over time that were imposed on the data by the researcher's decisions on sampling interval and measurement span. A given sampling interval defines the highest-frequency component and the shortest period that can be resolved adequately for a continuous variable as well as the shortest time interval that can be resolved adequately in any of the states of a discrete variable. Likewise, for a continuous variable, a given span of measurement defines the lowest component frequency or longest period that can be indexed as well as the finest discrimination or resolution between component frequencies that can be achieved. For discrete variables, the measurement span defines the longest-term change that can be observed adequately. Examples of retrospective use of the criteria appear elsewhere (Arundale, 1978, pp. 257, 277, 279-281; 1980, pp. 231-232, 257-258).

In making clear the limits both on the information on pattern over time contained in the data and hence on the evidence that can be derived from them, the criteria allow one to distinguish between those theoretical interpretations that are warranted by evidence and those that stem from the researcher's personal observations of the phenomena. Clearly, there is nothing wrong with basing theoretical interpretations of pattern over time on careful personal observation. One need only be aware that the interpretations are warranted by that source and not by evidence derived from adequate data.

What are the payoffs for devoting the extra time and effort required to design and conduct a study capable of generating adequate data on a pattern over time in communication phenomena? Two stand out. First, by increasing the accuracy with which we describe pattern over time we enlarge our ability to explain the processes of human communication. If we desire, for example, to understand fully the complex, dynamic interplay of influences that lead individuals or groups to change their attitudes, we need data that reveal in detail both how and when those influences come into play. Indeed, as Kaplowitz and Fink (this volume) point out, because past theories did not predict short-term change in individual's attitudes, such change was not accurately indexed and has appeared in attitude measurement as error. Second, in choosing to study pattern over time in communication, we avail ourselves of a broad range of modeling tools, research designs, and analytic techniques not open to us if we ignore time. Many of these tools, designs, and techniques are complex but at the same time more powerful and/or more subtle than those commonly in use.

A brief suggestion of possibilities must suffice. Beyond the designs and techniques noted above, presented in the contributions to this volume, or described elsewhere (Arundale, 1978, pp. 228-229, 260), studying pattern over time creates the possibility for dynamic modeling of communication processes, as in Aoki (1987), Huckfeldt, Kohfeld, and Likens (1982), Sandefur (1993), and Woelfel and Fink (1980). A direct extension of dynamic modeling is systems modeling as in Cortes, Przeworski, and Sprague (1974). Lewis-Beck (1986), Menard (1991), and Nesselroade and Baltes (1979) have examined issues and designs in longitudinal research, which are extended in Kratochwill's (1978) volume to designs for studying single individuals. Gottman (1981) has also extended the possibilities for using experimental and quasi-experimental time series designs and at the same time provided an excellent introduction to time series analysis, as have Gregson (1983) and Priestly (1988). But it is within the broad range of techniques for analyzing pattern over time that some of the more powerful and subtle tools have been developed. The *Journal of Time Series Analysis* is a central source for current theoretical developments across a range of analytic techniques. Bakeman and Gottman (1986) and Gottman and Roy (1990) have surveyed the broad class of sequential analysis techniques. The spectral analysis techniques noted above have been refined considerably, as in Marple (1987) and Priestly (1981). Closely related (and anticipated by Gabor in 1946) is the recent development of "wavelet"-based analytic techniques discussed in Chui (1992) and Meyer (1993), and described together with a wide range of other signal processing techniques in Therrien (1992). Wavelet techniques, in particular, address many of the well-known shortcomings of Fourier approaches to analysis. All of these modeling tools, research designs, and analytic techniques assume adequate data on pattern over time.

Must all research in communication generate adequate data on pattern over time? Certainly not. There are a great many issues to be examined in studying communication phenomena for which pattern over time is irrelevant. Still, we cannot continue to virtually ignore gathering adequate data on pattern over time, for to do so is to limit our understanding of communication phenomena by overlooking the fundamental dimension of time across which those phenomena unfold. Research that falls short of the criteria for generating data on pattern over time is not thereby invalid or useless, but in such research we must always take care in our theoretical conclusions, recognizing that interpretations in terms of pattern over time will not be warranted by evidence derived from appropriate data.

Notes

1. To accomplish this matching with zero error would require up to $N-1$ sinusoids for N time points. With fewer components some error will be involved (see VanLear & Watt, this volume). Note that because the digital recording involved in sampling over time does not capture all the information that might be captured by analog recording of a variable, this complex waveform only approximates the values of the variable (in its analog form) at times between the sampling time points. This approximation can be improved only by increasing the rate of sampling, with instantaneous sampling becoming analog recording and requiring analog computation in data analysis to avoid further sampling.

2. Because I was not furnished a page proof of this article (Arundale, 1971) prior to printing, there are three confusing errors on page 240. At the close of the first paragraph, $4F_n$ should be $4f_n$, and the two equations in parentheses at the bottom of the page should read

$$(\Delta t = \frac{1}{2f_n})$$

and

$$(T = \frac{1}{f_0}) .$$

There is one typographical error on that page and four others in the article as a whole. A fourth confusing error appears on page 236, nine lines from the bottom, where the correct equation is

$$\Delta t \leq \frac{p_n}{2} .$$

3. Frequencies (*f*) are expressed here in cycles per unit time because this format is generally more familiar. The literature on pattern over time often expresses frequencies in radians per unit time (ω) because this format is mathematically more convenient, where $\omega = 2\pi f$.

4. Because I was not furnished a page proof of that article (Arundale, 1978) prior to printing, one important error appears in the references on page 284: The Anderson and Goodman article is dated 1957, not 1959. Three other typographical errors appear elsewhere in the article.

5. In an earlier article (Arundale, 1978), I suggested at two points (pp. 267, 281) that the semi-Markov chain model is continuous time, which is not correct. I also indicated (p. 268) that unequal intervals precluded using a discrete time technique to model a continuous time analysis. Hewes, Planalp, and Streibel (1980) showed that it is possible to employ the discrete-time semi-Markov chain to model a continuous time analysis, thereby allowing one to retain a conceptualization of time as continuous, as had been suggested earlier by Singer and Spilerman (1974). Although it is not the only approach to retaining a conceptualization of time as continuous, the semi-Markov chain model is more tractable.

Dynamic Systems in Continuous Audience Response Measures

MARK DOUGLAS WEST
FRANK A. BIOCCA

Television viewing is, in many ways, an activity that is difficult to measure, quantify, and study. Unlike the events studied using the traditional pencil-and-paper surveys that have, until recently, served as the basis for much if not most sociological and psychological research, television is a continuous event taking place in real time in a variety of settings. In the case of television, the *process* of viewing—the processing of a continuous stream of visual and auditory impressions—is of as much interest as the *outcomes* of viewing—changes in attitudes and behavioral intentions.

Meaning in a television message is a complex entity, contained in a continuous stream of sensory stimuli arranged in patterns; both images and their ordering convey crucial information. A significant body of research attests to the fact that these streams of sensory impressions lead to significant and long-lasting changes in behaviors and attitudes. Less frequently studied are short-term changes in cognitive states associated

The authors would like to thank Allan Combs for his kind assistance in the formulation of the dynamical systems analysis presented here.

with television viewing. Do patterns of change in these streams of visual and auditory stimuli cause similar patterns of change in cognitive states? Are there cyclical or chaotic patterns of change in cognitive states that vary with changes in television stimuli? Are there cyclical patterns in cognitive states that are independent of the content of the television programming being viewed, cyclical patterns that arise from the act of viewing television in and of itself? Are there chaotic or cyclical patterns of cognitive states that are totally independent of television viewing, arising from fundamental neurological or psychological processes? And, for all the above questions, questions of individual or group differences arise, as do questions concerning the effect of content, aesthetic and stylistic issues, and the like upon such short- and long-term cycles.

Such questions are fundamental to an understanding of the effects of television on viewers and have been a subject of inquiry since the earliest studies of television and radio effects. Yet the development of techniques of measuring and analyzing fine-grain responses to television has lagged far behind the need for such measures. Thorson and Lang (1992) have isolated four primary paradigms for the continuous fine-grain measure of audience responses to television: visual orienting studies (Thorson & Zhao, 1988), secondary task completion research (Meadowcroft & Reeves, 1989), self-reporting of emotional or affective peaks (Alwitt, 1985; Aaker, Stayman, & Hagerty, 1986), and physiological studies including electrodermal responses (Fletcher, 1985), heart rate (Lang, 1990), and electroencephalogram (EEG) tracings (Rothschild, Thorson, Reeves, Hirsch, & Goldstein, 1986).

The research presented here falls into the third category. We discuss a technique for the self-reporting of affective states and then examine data generated by such a system during three U.S. presidential debates for cyclical and dynamical characteristics. The measurement technique is continuous response measurement (Biocca, David, & West, 1994), a system for measuring moment-to-moment responses to television that is at once sufficiently fine-grained to answer the sorts of research questions posed above and flexible enough to serve to measure a variety of affective, behavioral, and cognitive questions. Handset-based measuring systems for audience response have existed for decades (Upton, 1969) but were little used due to the complexities of data collection and analysis. With recent developments in the theory of information processing, which led to a reconsideration of the measure in terms of what is known about the fine-grain processing of meaningful stimuli, including television (e.g., Biocca, 1991a, 1991b; Biocca, Neuwirth, Oshagan, Zhongdang, & Richards, 1987; Reeves, Rothschild, & Thorson, 1983; Reeves, Thorson, & Schleuder, 1984; Thorson & Reeves, 1985; Thorson, Reeves, Schleuder, Lang, & Rothschild, 1985), and the development of statistical techniques capable of dealing with cyclical, chaotic, and highly autocorrelated causal data (see Biocca et al., 1994; West & Biocca, 1992), the measure is emerging as a powerful, real-time technique for the indirect examination of the cognitive processes associated with continuous stimuli.

The Implementation and Use of Continuous Audience Response Measures

The Technology of Continuous Measurement

The present generation of audience response systems is composed of a set of electronic components designed to measure momentary shifts in cognition during message processing. Today's systems are generally microcomputer based, using some sort of simple, continually signaling device that is manually operated by a viewer. Dial-based units are generally capable of measuring audience response on some one dimension, whereas "joystick" units can measure two dimensions at once and button-based units can measure any number of attributes but only in a binary ("push-no push") manner. Whatever its form, the input device allows the audience member to continuously signal changes in some mental state using a predetermined scale.

Respondents' reports of their mental states are collected and recorded by a central-processing unit and a mass-storage device. In most portable systems, the handsets are connected to a data acquisition unit, which polls the handsets at various intervals, usually every 2 seconds. This information is recorded by the computer on a fixed disk, with custom software storing not only each handset's state at each polling interval but also continuously calculating and storing mean and standard deviation information for predefined subgroups of interest. At the end of each session, the data can be converted into ASCII format for further analysis. Most systems are also connected to VCRs and video overlay systems that allow the researcher to visually display the data as the message (stimulus) is in progress, with summary information usually superim-

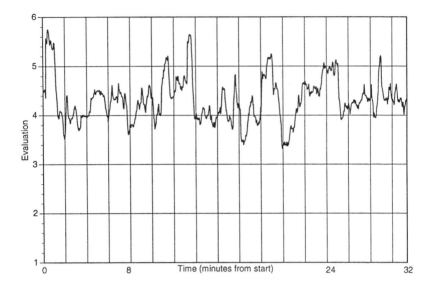

Figure 5.1.   Moment-by-moment evaluations of 1988 Omaha debate
(first 30 minutes).

posed on the stimulus image. Additionally, in the case of interactive
productions, the video overlay can be used to signal performers or pro-
ducers to take certain actions.

An example of continuous audience response data is shown in Figure 5.1.

Applications of the Measures

CRM systems are the electronic form of the pencil-and-paper questionnaire. As in most behavioral research, respondents introspect about
their reactions to the message stimulus and then signal perceived
changes in mental states. In contrast to the traditional post hoc focus of
behavioral research, the addition of electronics has led to a significant
qualitative change in that these close-ended self-reports can now be
continuous and in real time. Continuous response measurement systems
collect, in real time, discrete or continuous introspective self-reports,
evaluations, or opinions in response to any stimulus for any duration

along any discrete or continuous scale. With pencil-and-paper methods, changes in cognitive states are determined by measuring respondents' reports before and after the presentation of the stimulus. Computerized audience response systems, however, collect self-reports continuously across time, enabling researchers to analyze changing attitudes, moods, and semantic judgments. With CRM measures, changes in mental states can be modeled as a continuous process using data that are dynamically sensitive to the subtle effects of the stimulus. Also, any scale that can be answered in real time can be used in continuous response measurement; these might include affective questions on a like-dislike scale; behavioral questions, such as "How much do you want to purchase this product?"; and bipolar attraction questions, where respondents would report which of two options they prefer at any given moment.

Much of the extant CRM research has used traditional quasi-experimental designs. The continuous self-report measure is then treated as an extension of the self-report questionnaire (Millard, 1989; Rust, 1985). In the context of survey designs and quasi-experimental designs, the measure has been used in the study of political television (Biocca & David, 1990; Biocca, David, & West, 1990; West & Biocca, 1992; West, Biocca, & David, 1991), in "formative research" studying the effectiveness of educational television (Baggaley, 1986a, 1987), public information campaigns (Baggaley, 1986b, 1988), commercial television advertising research (Millard, 1989), and so-called qualitative ratings research (Beville, 1985; Philport, 1980).

Continuous response measures have also been used for content analyses of television programs and speeches. This may include the behaviors of participants or characters, structural variables of a message, or their interaction. For example, continuous response systems can be used to code such variables as camera distance, the presence of violent acts, and various interpersonal behaviors (Biocca & David, 1990; Palmer & Cunningham, 1987).

Continuous response measurement systems have also been used in focus group applications, with group evaluation profiles provided to probe group members' memory of their thoughts at critical points (Corporation for Public Broadcasting, 1981; Krueger, 1988; Morgan, 1988).

Thus, these continuous response measurement techniques are useful in a broad range of social science settings. Many of the traditional scales used in the social and behavioral sciences can be readily adapted for use with continuous response measurement systems. These adapted scales can offer new opportunities to the researcher to extend avenues of inquiry from cross-sectional studies to dynamic studies.

An Application of Continuous Audience Response Measures: Investigating the Effects of Presidential Debates

The remainder of this chapter illustrates methods of analyzing the cyclical, chaotic, and causal structures that are sometimes found in audience response data. The examples used here are drawn from a series of studies made of the effect on audiences in a variety of naturalistic settings of viewing U.S. presidential debates. The 1988 debates in Omaha, Nebraska, Los Angeles, and Winston-Salem, North Carolina, were analyzed. In each debate, the evaluations of viewers during the debate were collected using a continuous on-line audience response measurement system (Biocca et al., 1994). Each respondent received an input handset with a 7-point dial. After a 10-minute training session immediately prior to the debate, a series of questions dealing with audience demographics and initial opinions concerning the candidates were asked, and audience responses were collected by an IBM microcomputer connected to the handsets. Respondents were then instructed to continuously rate what they saw during the debate on a 7-point semantic differential scale based on the bipolar adjectives "like" and "dislike," where a dial setting of 1 indicated that respondents strongly disliked what they saw and a dial setting of 7 indicated that respondents liked very much what they were hearing or seeing.[1]

Viewers' evaluations were sampled every 2 seconds by an IBM microcomputer system, which stored the information of each of the 100 respondents' dial position on disk along with a time code. Simultaneously, a video overlay system superimposed a continuous graph for the frequency distribution and mean of the audience's evaluations on a videotape of the debate, thus allowing for accurate second-by-second registration of evaluations to the corresponding moments of the debate.

Following the debate, the questions concerning viewers' evaluations of the candidates were repeated, with responses again recorded by the handsets.

For each debate, respondents were selected from registered, undecided voters in the city where the debate was held. Because the measurement method demanded that all respondents be present in one location during the debate, a national representative sample of voters who were undecided at the time of the presidential debate was not feasible. Approximately 150 respondents were recruited for the task, with 100 selected by lot from those who actually arrived at the research site. Approximately 2,000 observations were gathered per debate per respondent, resulting in a data set of 200,000 observations.

The data collected in this manner were subject to three different sorts of analyses designed to evaluate different dynamic components of the communication process. The first, a repeated measures analysis, examines the detailed dynamics of the effect of a verbal "one-liner" during a debate on previously defined subgroups of the viewing population. The second, a Fourier analysis, examines the cyclical patterns of overall affective responses to a debate, and the third analysis investigates the chaotic properties of the affective responses of viewers to a debate. In each case, the goal is to investigate the dynamic properties of responses to a televised stimulus (in this case, presidential debates).

The overall implication of our analyses, we contend, is that continuous audience response systems are capable of generating data that are useful in examining a wide variety of hypotheses concerning dynamic audience responses to programming stimuli. More specifically, each analysis, we suggest, demonstrates that different sorts of dynamic response mechanisms are taking place simultaneously during the process of viewing. The repeated measures analysis indicates that affective responses vary after significant stimuli in programming and that these responses attenuate over time in predictable manners. The Fourier analysis indicates that cyclical patterns of change in affective responses to television programming take place, apparently cued by structural elements of programming. The chaos analysis offers support for the contention that causal mechanisms with complex outcomes are operating in viewer responses to televised stimuli. In sum, we contend that these findings indicate that the television viewer is not the passive, gullible consumer so often portrayed in writings about television. Rather, this research indicates that the television viewer is an active participant in the creation of meanings, apparently engaging in several distinct cognitive processes during viewing. The television viewer may still be a "black box," but using techniques such as those presented here and in the other chapters of this book may enable researchers to at last pry open this "black box."

Analyzing Discrete Events in
Continuous Audience Response Data

Given the nature of the data produced by continuous response measurement systems, almost all research designs using CRM will be time based. Time series experimental designs involve a number of repeated observations of some outcome variable measured across time. In studies of single, discrete events, one or more interventions are introduced at some point, with the expectation that the intervention(s) will alter the series in some measurable way.[2] In studies of the overall dynamics of television viewing, the entire data series, or some longer subset of it, is examined. Here, we first deal with the time-based analysis of discrete events, using an autoregressive least squares repeated measures designs. We then discuss the analysis of communication events as wholes, using traditional Fourier methods and complex dynamical systems models.

Theory and Method of
Repeated-Measures Designs

A standard method for dealing with data where measurements are made repeatedly is a variant of the traditional analysis of variance, repeated measures ANOVA (Winer, 1971). Conceptually, in such designs, each study participant is administered all the treatments, and responses are measured after each administration. Such designs are clearly applicable to continuous response data, with one proviso. The effect of the stimulus should be expected to have a more or less linear response curve over time because the repeated measures design is based on the derivation of a linear equation that models the response. In the case of audience response data, however, the continuous stream of stimuli implies that the effect of any one stimulus, no matter how great, would gradually attenuate with time. Hence, use of the repeated measures design is limited to the analysis of single events that are of interest.

Repeated measures designs have an advantage, however, in that factorial designs are possible in which one or more covariates or grouping variables are measured. One might, for example, model the responses of men and women to a scene in an advertisement, modeling not only the effects of the advertisement on the group as a whole but comparing the effects on men and women. Such designs are referred to as mixed designs (Myers, 1990) or as factorial designs with repeated measures (Winer, 1971).

Autoregressive Maximum-Likelihood
Repeated Measures Designs

Traditional repeated measures techniques, however, require that the observations be independent; that is to say, the researcher must reasonably be able to assume that the effects of previous stimuli have no effect on the current measurement (Dunn & Clark, 1990; Winer, 1971). Hence, standard repeated measures analyses are, in general, inappropriate for use with CRM data, where relatively brief intervals between measurements suggest that some residual effect from the stimulus at t_n is likely to exist at t_{n+1}. Violation of this requirement leads to inflated estimations of the significance of models (Greenhouse & Geisser, 1959).

Restrictive maximum-likelihood methods allow the specification of models containing first-order, general, or unstructured autoregressive parameters (Dixon, 1990). Using such techniques, models which specify residual effects of stimuli lasting for several seconds could readily be specified and parameters estimated using iterative maximum-likelihood methods. Such analytic methods, although computationally very intensive and limited to small numbers of data points, are readily applied to CRM data for the analysis of the dynamic effects of single events.

An Application of a Repeated
Measures Design: "What If Your Wife
Were Murdered, Governor Dukakis?"

A general autoregressive model has been used in a study of reactions to a verbal gaffe in the 1988 presidential debate (West & Biocca, 1992); here, prior voting intention was observed to influence audience responses to what newspapers had called the "knock-down punch" of the debates.

This most celebrated moment of the 1988 debates between Michael Dukakis and George Bush came only a few seconds into the October 18 debate, when Bernard Shaw of Cable News Network (CNN) asked Governor Dukakis if he would favor the death penalty for the imagined murderer of his wife. The governor's curiously cold and unemotional response played into images of Dukakis as an emotionless technocrat; postdebate commentary lambasted Dukakis for his response, and editorials (e.g., "Minus a Dukakis 'Home Run,' " 1988) described him as needing to seek another venue for winning the election.

In the popular press, debates are in general portrayed as crucial events in the campaign season, as "make or break" opportunities for candidates to deal a "knock-out" punch to their opponent (Robinson & Sheehan, 1983). In the scholarly literature, conversely, debates are portrayed as having little or no effect on audiences (Kraus & Smith, 1962; Lang & Lang, 1961). Using a one-factor repeated measures design, continuous response measures can be used to examine the effect of this putative "knock-out punch" on audience perceptions of Dukakis in real time; simultaneously, a mixed-design model can be employed to determine the effects of prior attitudes concerning the candidates on the effect of the Dukakis gaffe. In this debate, 1,767 observations were collected on 100 respondents; the time series of the 30 seconds during and following Bernard Shaw's question about the hypothetical rape and murder of Kitty Dukakis was extracted from the main data set. Analyses were then conducted using a repeated measures analysis of covariance on a subset of the data representing only the time of Dukakis's response using BMDP program 5R, specifying a general autoregressive covariance structure.[3]

A visual inspection of the audience response data suggests that the audience as a whole did not appear to evaluate Dukakis's response well; after a 2-second surge upward when the camera shifted to Dukakis, evaluations plunged to approximately 3.5, one of the lowest points of the debate, as shown in Figure 5.2. As Dukakis shifted the discussion to the war on drugs, his evaluations became more positive, moving to about 4.7 after an additional 20 seconds, when Bush began to speak.

The repeated measures analysis (see Table 5.1) confirms the hypothesis that audience members' evaluation of what they were seeing during Dukakis's response was increasingly negative by time, with significant changes in evaluation occurring across time.

Respondents were then divided into three groups on the basis of their predebate candidate preferences. The debate evaluation of these three groups—Dukakis supporters, Bush supporters, and those who described themselves as neutral—were analyzed in a mixed repeated measures model, shown in Figure 5.3.

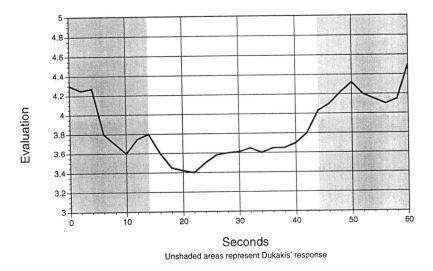

Figure 5.2. Overall evaluations of Dukakis "gaffe."

TABLE 5.1 Repeated Measures Analysis, Dukakis Evaluations, by Prior Candidate Inclinations

Overall Goodness-of-Fit Estimations			
Type	SE	z-score	p
Variance parameter	.228	12.10	< .01
Covariance parameter	.047	9.73	< .01

Wald Tests of Effect Significance			
Parameter	df	χ^2	p
Candidate inclination	2	49.25	< .01
Time	3	28.12	< .01
Inclination × Time interaction	6	90.20	< .01

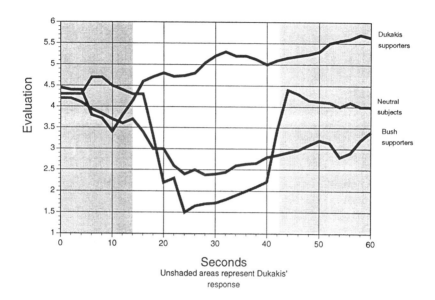

Figure 5.3.   Responses by prior inclination of Dukakis "gaffe."

Overall, the model of responses to the Dukakis remark—where time, grouping, and grouping across time are hypothesized to predict evaluations of Dukakis' response to the Shaw question—fits the data well, as shown in the significant values of the Wald tests of the variance/covariance matrices.[4]

Thus, the repeated measures analysis suggests that the autoregressive model, where prior evaluation of candidates was used as a predictor of viewer evaluation of Dukakis's response, appears to fit the observed data well.

Graphically, it appears that Dukakis's supporters evaluated his response to the Shaw question positively, with the mean evaluation of this group going from 3.4 to approximately 5.1 by the end of his response to the murder query and reaching almost 6.0 by the end of his statements about the war on drugs.

As might be expected, those subjects whose previous candidate inclination was favorable toward Bush rated Dukakis's response to the Shaw question less favorably. The evaluation of Bush supporters at the beginning of the question was approximately 3.6; for the bulk of Dukakis response, Bush supporters were rating what they saw as unfavorable 2.6. This low rating continued until Dukakis began to speak about the war on drugs, when his evaluation by Bush supporters slowly increased to about 4.0.

The surprise comes on examination of the responses of those who described themselves as neutral. These respondents appeared to have fairly neutral evaluations of the Shaw question, with evaluations staying between 4.3 and 4.6 during the course of it. But during Dukakis's response, their evaluation plummeted to 1.6, one of the lowest evaluations of the entire debate. Dukakis's evaluation during his response stayed below 2.0 until he began to talk about the war on drugs; respondent evaluation then increased to approximately 4.3, about where it was during Shaw's question. With these critical undecided and uninclined voters, Dukakis's response to the Shaw question appears to have been an unmitigated disaster, with uninclined respondents rating it even less favorably than did Bush supporters.

The repeated measures analysis of variance demonstrates that the differences between these three groups on their evaluation of Dukakis's response to the Shaw question was statistically significant, with the effect of prior candidate evaluation significant at the .05 level on overall evaluation.

Also, the repeated measures analysis suggests that the changes over time in the evaluation of the three groups significantly differed. Not only did respondents' evaluations of what they were seeing change significantly over time, and the evaluation of the three groups were significantly different, but the evaluation of the three groups changed significantly relative to one another over time. This interaction between prior candidate inclination and over-time evaluation was also significant at the .01 level.

Analyzing Trends and Cycles
in Continuous Audience Response

Questions such as those asked above examine only discrete events occupying short spans of time. As always, the assumption in such research is that the subjects are continually bombarded with stimuli, and hence the effect of any one stimulus upon audience responses decays quickly with time, being swamped, so to speak, with the effects of the next moment's stimulus. Repeated measures designs can examine the effects of stimuli over only short periods of time.

There are, however, numerous research questions of interest that deal with viewers' responses to stimuli over a longer time frame. The researcher might, for example, be interested in whether or not audience affective responses, audience attention, audience persuasion, or audience physical responses to television programming have periodic components.

Such cycles might be triggered by a number of attributes of the television stimulus. Snow (1987) lists several types of periodicities that might arise. These include narrative structures, such as acts, rising and falling action, and narrative cues, such as the "plot points" of the "well-crafted" Hollywood narrative. Another source of periodicity might be programming cues such as commercials, which appear in most programs at regular intervals. The more basic symbols of the "media language," items such as the duration of shots and other editing cues, might give rise to periodicities; a final potential source includes such extradiegetic cues as music. These cues are not trivial; almost all viewers are able to notice shots that are "too long" or music whose tempo does not agree with visual cues. As Snow (1987) suggests, "The audience becomes accustomed to a syntax that provides order and predictability in the same manner as the rhythm of a clock or a symphony" (p. 231).

Researchers have isolated numerous instances of cyclical patterns in audience responses to communication; these range from a 13½-second cycle of attitude change observed by Kaplowitz, Fink, and Bauer (1983) to an 8.5-week cycle of advertising sales (Davis & Lee, 1980). Barnett, Chang, Fink, and Richards (1991) isolated a yearly cycle in which television viewing was inversely correlated with mean temperature and with hours of daylight (see also Barnett and Cho, this volume). Similarly, researchers have found significant periodicities in interpersonal communication, with cycles involving both amounts of speech, durations of speech, and physiological measures (Warner, 1988). Most of this research deals with amounts of speech, with cycles of about 100 seconds of speech, followed by 100 seconds of silence, predominating (Warner, 1979).

Chapple (1970) has suggested a link between cycles in interpersonal communication and internal physiological rhythms. For dyadic communication to function, Chapple posits that speakers would coordinate their vocal activity both with the activity of the other and with a variety of physiological rhythms; successful communication involved a synchronization that limited silences or simultaneous speech. Warner

(1992a; see also Warner, this volume) has found that the proportion of variance in amounts of speech in adult conversations that is explained by cyclical models increases as conversations continue, indicating that partners entrain one another in maintaining appropriate rhythms in discourse.

A similar link might be posited between affective responses to mass communication and internal physiological rhythms. The orienting response has been suggested as the means by which television structures influence short-term attention (Reeves et al., 1985; Singer, 1980). Lang (1990) found that heart-rate measures of the orienting response were influenced both by structural elements of television and by the emotional content of programming; the influence of emotional conflict was thought to be through arousal (Lang, 1984, 1985). Physiological responses have been shown to be related to hedonic responses (Grings & Dawson, 1978); thus, if televised stimuli occur in rhythmic patterns, we could reasonably expect to see cyclic patterns in both physiological and affective responses to television programming.

Whatever their cause, such cyclical patterns of alteration in viewer response could be of significant interest not only to researchers but to programmers. The isolation of cyclical patterns of affective response of brief cyclicity (say, a minute or less) could be evidence for naturally occurring somatic cycles of attention. The isolation of longer patterns could have significant implications for the structuring of programming for maximum effect.

In the example of the examination of affective responses to the presidential debate, we might expect to see cyclical patterns of audience affective response corresponding to the programming cues of the debate. Ceteris paribus, we would expect to see a pattern of change in audience response corresponding to the length of time each candidate was permitted to speak to the audience—in this case, 3 minutes. We would expect a similar pattern at the length of time permitted for responses to the statements of other candidates. We might also posit a cyclicity at the average amount of length of time devoted to a single camera angle (Biocca & David, 1991). Other cyclicities isolated might be indicative of somatic or psychological cycles of interest.

Theory and Method of Spectral Analysis

Processes that repeat themselves in regular patterns are cyclical phenomena. Examples of such patterns range from simple and readily modeled systems such as sine waves to extremely complex phenomena such as nonlinear dynamical systems ("chaos") where modeling is difficult if not computationally intractable.

Spectral analyses, the decomposition of cyclical data into finite sets of cosine waves, differ from the more common time domain analyses performed on time series data in that they are performed in the frequency domain. Whereas Box-Jenkins models attempt to account for a time series through the examination of the autocorrelations of the data (Cook & Campbell, 1979), spectral analyses attempt to account for a time series by decomposing the time series into a series of processes that can be represented as sine and cosine functions (Rovine & von Eye, 1991; for a further discussion of Fourier analysis, see VanLear and Watt, this volume; Watt, this volume).

An Application of Spectral Analysis:
The 1988 Winston-Salem Debates

The remainder of this section discusses the application of the above tests to data gathered during the 1988 presidential debates in Winston-Salem, North Carolina. For this debate, 486 potential respondents were selected from a list of likely voters in Forsythe County, site of the debate. Of these, 121 were contacted and agreed to participate in the study. On the night of the debate, 100 of those who arrived were selected by lot, given a brief training session, and then watched the debates while operating the handsets in the manner described above. To analyze the 284,000 data points collected, the mean data series (Biocca et al., 1994) was employed, after detrending through first differencing.

A periodogram was then constructed, using the SERIES module of the program SYSTAT. Frequencies of length from 2 seconds to 5 minutes were examined. As can be seen from Figure 5.4, one frequency was isolated whose local maxima was significant at the .01 level. This was located at 3 minutes, 8 seconds; this length corresponds with the 2-minute response allowed for each candidate and the 1-minute rebuttal from the other candidate allotted during the debate. From this, we might conclude that affective responses to the debate were, as expected, stimulated by the question-and-answer exchange rather than by other structural features such as changes of camera angle and the like.

Because the frequency indicated by the method as significant cyclical phenomena of the debate corresponds to a structural feature of the

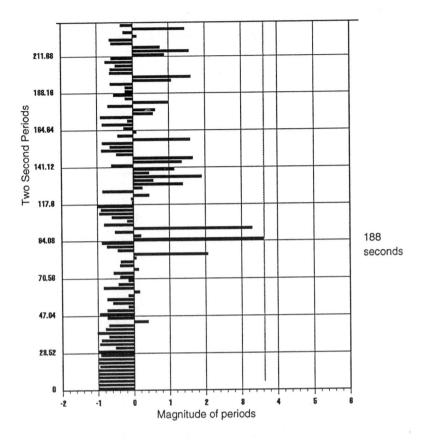

Figure 5.4. Periodogram of Winston-Salem debate (significant periodicities indicated at right).

debate, it seems reasonable to conclude that continuous response measurement data of affective responses to television can provide useful information about cyclic phenomena connected with televised stimuli. As suggested earlier, there are numerous aspects of television programming that might be posited to give rise to cyclicities of audience response. Studies might, for example, focus on the role of camera angles (e.g., Biocca & David, 1990), with measurements of the most likely lengths of camera shots being compared to cyclicities in the audience response data. And, as mentioned earlier, continuous audience response methods are not limited to the measurement of affective responses; attention, for example, might be measured, or the handsets might be used to signal "boundaries" of some sort—the presence or absence of characters, changes in extradiegetic cues such as music or "laugh tracks," and the like. More complex designs might split respondents into groups, with one group coding content and a second group recording affective responses. In such a case, cross-spectral analyses might be used to compare the spectra of affective responses and of programming elements.

Theory and Methods of Nonlinear Dynamical Systems ("Chaos")

The study of "chaos," or nonlinear dynamical systems, has garnered a significant amount of attention in the past five years, much motivated by the contention that chaos represents a paradigm for the modern era in much the same way that Newtonian physics served as a paradigm for the nascent Industrial Age. Whether or not this contention is accurate (see Lewin, 1992, for a discussion of chaos as a harbinger of a paradigm change in the postmodern era), the metaphysical inclination of many of the discussions of chaos, on the one hand, and the complexity of the mathematics, on the other, have obscured the conceptual simplicity and utility of the study of nonlinear dynamical systems.

There is little agreement on precisely how to define chaos; in general, however, most researchers agree that, to display chaos, systems must display highly disordered behavior that appears to be random. Chaotic systems are all highly dependent on the initial starting values of the systems; nevertheless, truly chaotic systems are deterministic, with outcomes that are determined (Kloeden, Deakin, & Tirkel, 1976; Rapp, 1993).

In general, most of the published research on chaotic systems has consisted of the examination of systems in which the equations defining the system were known and the object of inquiry was the output of the system. This is because the study of nonlinear dynamical systems began with the observation that simple systems of equations that were nonlinear in their parameters were extremely sensitive to their starting conditions. Later research suggested that solutions to a significant proportion of "real world" systems of equations led to solutions that appeared to be chaotic, with such sensitivity to initial or previous conditions that the outcomes were, in a significant sense, unpredictable. Models of fluid dynamics, for example, are often chaotic, leading to unpredictable oscillations in populations (Sandefur, 1990), as are a significant number of biological or ecological models (West, 1980). The mathematics required to predict future values of the variables under consideration were intractable to analysis, or the accuracy of measurement required for accurate prediction of future values was beyond the sensitivity of measuring instruments (e.g., Rapp, 1993).

In particular, interest in chaos was stimulated by the realization that many processes whose outcome was thought to be random were in fact deterministic, caused by simple processes with seemingly random outcomes. The hope of the use of chaos theory in the analysis of data series is to find indications that a series is indeed "chaotic," which implies a relatively simple causal process that causes the outcomes. The analysis presented here, as in most data analysis of systems that are putatively chaotic, does not seek to statistically model the laws that determine affective responses to television. Rather, the emphasis is on collecting evidence that the system displays chaotic qualities—hence suggesting that such a statistical model could, in principle, be developed. Given the current state of statistical understanding of complex processes, the assurance that a causal process might be at work—even though that process might be difficult, if not impossible, to model—is often the best that can be hoped for in the study of complex processes whose underlying dynamics are ill understood.

The analysis of chaotic data is, in many ways, as suffused with disagreement as is the definition of chaos. As Rapp (1993; see also Rosser, 1991) suggests, the field of chaos data analysis has been dominated by the calculation of two measures, the correlation dimension (Grassberger & Procaccia, 1983) and the Lyapunov exponent (Sano & Sawada, 1985). The phase space of chaotic data involves attractors that are stable yet nonperiodic; the trajectories of data through phase space hence do not repeat, having a complex structure that is invariant at whatever scale it is examined (Gleick, 1987). Unlike random data that have no structure, periodic data have a structure that varies across scales, being more evident at some scaling parameters and less visible at others.

The measures discussed here both take advantage of this fractal structure of chaotic data by examining the clustering of data points at various scales (Rosser, 1991); the Lyapunov exponent examines the "stretching" of the system at various scales (Rosser, 1991), whereas the correlation dimension involves the construction of a series of hyperspheres of varying sizes at each data point; the measure is then constructed from a plot of the log of the number of other data points lying within the sphere against the log of the radius (Sprott & Rowlands, 1993). For the Lyapunov dimension, a positive value indicates that the data under consideration may be chaotic, while the correlation dimension for chaotic data should be less than 5 (Sprott & Rowlands, 1993). Ideally, the Lyapunov dimension will be small but positive; noise data series can have infinite or large Lyapunov exponents. Also, all the measures of the fractal dimension should be nonintegral; integer fractal dimensions indicate periodic systems ("Measuring the Dimension," 1992).

Considerable disagreement surrounds the appropriateness of these tests of chaotic structure in data. Eckmann and Ruelle (1985) contend that Lyapunov exponents are a necessary test, whereas Takens (1980) recommends entropy measures; Grassberger and Procaccia (1983) support the correlation dimension. Beyond the selection of tests of chaotic properties, it appears that all the fractal tests discussed here suffer from Type I biases with small samples of data (Ramsey, Sayers, & Rothman, 1988), with 2,000 data points being a useful bottom limit (Smith, 1988). Also, the statistical properties on all the estimators of the fractal dimension are not well known; as the editor of *Social Dynamicist* suggests, "Dimension is a very new and active area of chaos research, so *caveat emptor!*" ("Measuring the Dimension," 1992, p. 5).

In analyses of putatively chaotic data, Combs (1993) suggests that both the Lyapunov exponent and the correlation dimension be calculated along with the capacity dimension (a measure similar in many respects to the correlation dimension but less difficult to calculate) (Sprott & Rowlands, 1993). The correlation dimension should not be an integer (Combs, 1993). Also, Combs (1993) suggests a "Monte Carlo" analysis, in which the time series data are reordered randomly. If the original data set does not show a higher correlation dimension than the randomly ordered data, then the contention that the data set shows a chaotic structure is problematic, even if a positive Lyapunov exponent and a small correlation dimension are obtained. In the best case, the capacity and correlation dimension would be smaller than the embedding dimension, a positive but small Lyapunov exponent would be observed, and the correlation dimension of the random data set would be larger than the correlation dimension of the time series ordered data.

Television as a Dissipative System

It is clear from an examination of a plot of the time series audience response data that there is some reason to think that these data might be chaotic. An examination of the entire data series, when compared with an enlarged view of a 10th of the data, suggests a level of scalar invariance that is compatible with chaotic data. On a theoretical level, we posit that audiences do indeed affectively respond to television and that those responses are cognitively mediated, at least in the case of presidential debates. This "active" audience (Biocca, 1988) is processing its perceptions of the events of debate according to a set of rules. Viewers' responses to what they see are formed by those rules; hence, we would assume that there is a causal relationship between what viewers see and how they respond. We would thus assume that these responses are not random, and the repeated measures analysis presented earlier suggests that, at least in the short term, it is possible to create models that adequately represent these processes.

On the large scale, however, the impact of events during the debates, or during any televised programming, is much more difficult to model. Television viewing, as discussed earlier, is a serial process, with noteworthy stimulus following noteworthy stimulus. Hence, the impact of all but the most overwhelming and powerful images and events fades with time, its effect dissipating as it is superseded by novel stimuli.

This notion of television viewing as a dissipative system is of critical importance to the notion of affective responses to television displaying chaotic characteristics. Dissipation has been posited as the cause of the folding of the phase space that creates fractal structures (Gleick, 1987); Nicolis and Prigogine (1977) and Prigogine and Stengers (1984) have suggested that this dissipation is the hallmark of the complexly ordered system. If we posit that television viewing is such a dissipative system—one in which energy, in the form of information, is introduced at varying intervals and then dissipated by the formation of transient affects—then it is reasonable to hypothesize that affective responses to television viewing can take the form of dynamical systems. Thus, if current conceptions of how chaos functions are correct in their emphasis on dissipative structures and our understanding of the way in which television is perceived is correct, then we might reasonably expect that the resultant time series data have chaotic characteristics.

An Application of Nonlinear Dynamical
Systems Theory: The 1988 Omaha Debate

The remainder of this section discusses the application of the above tests to data gathered during the 1988 presidential debate in Omaha, Nebraska. For this debate, 480 potential respondents were selected from a list of likely voters in the greater Omaha area. Of these, 132 were contacted and agreed to participate in the study. On the night of the debate, 100 of those who arrived were selected by lot, given a brief training session, and then watched the debates while operating the handsets in the manner described above. There were 281,400 data points collected for analysis. As in the previous example, the mean data series (Biocca et al., 1994) was employed, after being detrended by taking the first difference. The data were also smoothed, using a simple averaging method.[5] A phase plot of the debate responses is presented in Figure 5.5.

Correlation, Capacity,
and Lyapunov Dimension

Table 5.2 presents the correlation and capacity dimensions for the Omaha data set, along with its largest Lyapunov exponent. The largest Lyapunov exponent is .529, which, being small but positive, is consistent with the contention that the data series is chaotic. The estimate of the capacity dimension is 1.441, again consistent with chaos.

Monte Carlo Test

In the Monte Carlo test, the time series data were randomized and then differenced and smoothed in the same manner as were the ordered data. Correlation dimensions were calculated for both the new randomized data set and the original ordered data. These results are also presented in Table 5.2.

The ordered data have a correlation dimension of 2.417, whereas the correlation dimension of the randomized data is about 3.048. This offers support for the contention that the data are structured; if the data series were effectively random or if the smoothing were introducing an artifactual correlation dimension, the correlation dimensions for the randomized and the ordered data should be approximately the same.

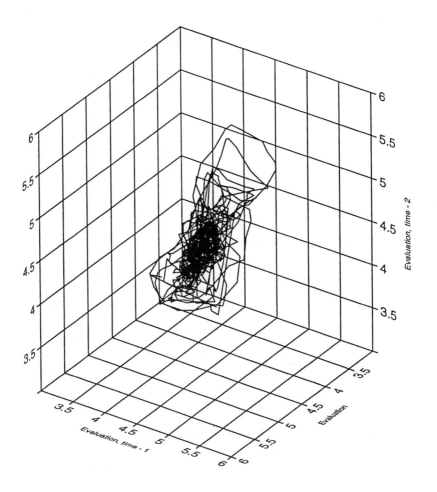

Figure 5.5. Phase plot: Omaha debate evaluations.

Conclusions About Chaos

The notion that the audience response data gathered during the Omaha debate are chaotic is supported by these analyses. They are, of course, by no means conclusive; the best that a researcher can hope for is the accumulation of positive evidence.

TABLE 5.2   Omaha Debate, Correlation, Capacity, and Lyapunov
Dimension; Reordered Data, Capacity Dimension

Debate		
Lyapunov	.529	+/– .045
Capacity	1.441	+/– .190
Correlation	2.417	
Dominant frequency	.015	
Reordered		
Capacity	3.048	

If, however, such data are found to appear to be chaotic in other studies, using the same and other analytic methods, it could have significant implications for the study of television viewing. As discussed earlier, the notion that television viewing is a dissipative system has implications for how we think about the process of watching television. If television viewing is indeed a dissipative system, then viewers are rescued from the doldrums of passivity into which many modern researchers have placed them. The viewer is constantly creating structures and order and then constantly revising them according to rules we have yet to understand—but are, in principle, fathomable, and may be, in practice, quite simple. The notion of the viewer as a "black box" for which we have no key (Biocca et al., 1990) may have outlived its usefulness; the study of chaos, with its suggestion that there are laws that determine audience response, with all its complexity, may provide the key.

Yet it may be the case that the advent of dynamical systems studies on mass communication research will not be an unmitigated blessing; the study of chaos in the economic sciences, for example, has had a curious impact on that field. On the one hand, the finding that the distributions of income and prices are Lévy stable (see Mandelbrot, 1983, p. 422) indicates that those and other economic entities may be chaotic (Mirowski, 1990); the possibility exists of using such methods for profit (see, e.g., Peters, 1991). But, as Mandelbrot (1963) pointed out, this implies that long-term prediction of economic time series is unlikely because of the difficulty of achieving sufficient accuracy of measurement when considering the extreme sensitivity to starting conditions found in chaotic time series. One author has gone so far as to suggest that "chaos models would render orthodox [economic] theory meaningless" (Mirowski, 1990, p. 305). This implies that, although chaos may enable us to suggest that there is indeed some form of order in many time series data sets of communication events, we may find it difficult to predict a priori what the outcomes of communication events will be. It may be that chaos theory will at once hold out the promise that there exist causal rules for audience response while simultaneously suggesting that those rules could never be used to predict the outcome of communication events (see Rosser, 1991, for a discussion of these notions in the economic realm). It will be interesting to examine the successes of the firms seeking to predict stock prices; their success or failure may be a harbinger of the success or failure of chaos theory to provide a tool for predicting the effects and processes of communication.

Conclusions: On Predicting and Understanding Trends and Cycles in Continuous Audience Response Data

The examples presented here suggest that the analysis of dynamic and cyclical processes in continuous response measurement data can offer means to examine questions of interest about the responses of subjects to television. The analysis of short-term impacts of stimuli can be examined through repeated measures analyses; spectral analysis can be used to investigate questions about cyclical phenomena, whereas dynamical systems analyses can examine questions about the complex but deterministic aspects of responses to television viewing.

As new, telephone-based systems for continuous response measurement systems are perfected, the method will offer a means for more naturalistic studies of responses to television viewing. As our understanding of chaos and dynamical systems increases, more powerful techniques for studying such data will undoubtedly appear. The coupling of these dynamic methods of analysis with the versatility of continuous response methods of data collection presents a potent tool for investigating how people watch television.

For the past 40 years, most research into the responses of television viewers has been static in its nature. In general, research either was conducted via experiment in artificial laboratory settings and used aggregate data that removed the dynamic element from a dynamic process or was conducted via person-to-person or telephone surveys. Although these techniques have clearly increased our knowledge of the effects of television viewing, they are incapable of dealing with the dynamic aspect of what is without doubt a dynamic process. With new techniques of continuous audience measurement and with the development of new and powerful techniques for the examination of the data generated by such measurement technologies, the dynamic aspect of television viewing—and of a host of related psychological and sociological processes—is likely to become a major topic of future research and inquiry.

Notes

1. For further details on the measurement system, see Biocca, David, and West (1994).

2. The time series design may also result from unplanned interventions such as a change in public opinion after a governmental reform or new legislation. Whereas post hoc analysis is appropriate for economics and macrolevel public opinion, planned experiments are more appropriate for behavioral sciences.

3. In general, continuous on-line audience response methods generate time series data that are highly autocorrelated; that is to say, the outcome at t is highly dependent on the outcome at $t - 1$. This is particularly true in studies such as this, where respondent polling takes place at such short intervals. Consequently, application of the traditional standards of repeated measures analysis to the independence of observations is inappropriate, calling for the use of statistical measures that deal with serial autocorrelation. Here, a maximum-likelihood iterative estimation procedure was used that posited a covariance and variance structure with autocorrelation.

4. In maximum-likelihood repeated measures analyses with autocorrelated observations, traditional statistical tests that depend on the assumption of sphericity of errors and no significant autocorrelation are not useful. Here, as in other sorts of complex covariance structure modeling (LISREL models and nonlinear regression analyses), goodness of fit is determined by the magnitude of the difference between observed and predicted variance and covariance matrices. Specification, then, of the sort of variance/covariance matrix expected becomes a critical although seldom addressed concern. In this instance, due to the frequency of measurement, a general autoregressive variance/covariance matrix was assumed. See Dixon (1990) for further discussion of autoregressive repeated measures designs.

5. The results presented here were generated by *Chaos Data Analyzer*, by Julien C. Sprott and George Rowlands. This software, which runs on an IBM PC, is capable of performing sophisticated analysis of putatively chaotic data. Other programs exist for the IBM PC, notably *Dynamical Software* and *NLF* by Dynamical Systems, Inc. One distributor of such software is Media Magic, located in Nicasio, California.

Localized Autocorrelation
Diagnostic Statistic (*LADS*)
for Time-Series Models

Conceptualization, Computation, and Utilization

CLIFFORD NASS
YOUNGME MOON

In regression analysis of time-series data, one can use the underlying temporal structure of the data to identify systematic relationships among the residuals (termed *autocorrelation*) that affect the quality of the model. Traditionally, analyses of temporal autocorrelation assume that the pattern among error terms is relatively consistent across the entire range of the data (Cryer, 1986; Pindyck & Rubinfeld, 1981; Tuma & Hannan, 1984). If only a small portion of the data set exhibits patterned residuals, these statistics do not provide relevant information for model adjustment.

Identifying and addressing unusual sets of residuals is the domain of regression diagnostics (Belsley, 1991; Belsley, Kuh, & Welsch, 1980; Cook & Weisberg, 1982). Methods have been developed to identify both

This chapter benefited from the helpful suggestions of Luc Anselin, Steven Chaffee, Kenneth Land, and James Watt. David Garfinkle provided key insights into the derivations.

single points and sets of points that are poorly fitted by or exert undue influence on a regression model (Belsley, 1991; Kempthorne, 1989).

In this chapter, we suggest a regression diagnostic for autocorrelation that identifies and treats the presence of consecutive time points among only the most extreme residuals. *Localized autocorrelation*, the existence of such a time period, can be a generative tool for exploration (Tukey, 1977), providing post hoc guidance in identifying important omitted variables and the source of heteroskedasticity.

To determine whether the presence of a time period among the most extreme residuals is worthy of further investigation, this chapter introduces the *localized autocorrelation diagnostic statistic (LADS)*. Given a set of the most extreme, same-signed E residuals from a model with T cases, the *LADS(T, E, C)* for a given C is the probability that residuals associated with C or more consecutive time points from a set of E residuals would arise by chance arrangement of the E residuals on the T time points. The localized autocorrelation diagnostic statistic is therefore used to determine whether the limited time period defined by the most poorly fitting cases is particularly unusual rather than whether the entire set of residuals is consistently related, as in traditional analyses of autocorrelation. If the probability of finding such a time period, as determined by the *LADS*, is smaller than a previously established critical level (reasonable critical levels are .10 and .05), the units of the unusual time period can suggest a new variable or variables to enhance model development. Thus, like other regression diagnostics, the *LADS* approach identifies unusual patterns relative to the entire data set. Conversely, like autocorrelation statistics and unlike other regression diagnostics, the technique is based on an exogenous characteristic of the data (sequence in time) rather than solely on results of the model.

As is demonstrated in the appendix, one can compute the *LADS* via the following formulae (PASCAL programs that implement the *LADS* are available from the first author):

Result 1. For $C \le E < 2C$ (the most common cases) and no global autocorrelation,

$$LADS(T, E, C) = (T + 1 - E) \left[\frac{\left[\binom{T - C}{E - C} \right]}{\binom{T}{E}} \right]. \qquad [6\text{-}1]$$

Of course, $LADS(T, E, C) = 0$ when $(E < C)$ or $(T < E)$.

Result 2. For all $E \geq C$ and no global autocorrelation,

$$LADS(T,E,C) = \left[\frac{1}{\binom{T}{E}} \right] n(T, E, C) -$$

$$\frac{1}{\binom{T}{E}} \left[\sum_{s=C}^{E-C} \sum_{p=1}^{T-E} n(T - (s + p), E - s, C) + \right.$$

$$\left. \sum_{s=C}^{E-(C+1)} \sum_{m=1}^{E-(s+c)} \sum_{p=m+2}^{T-(E-m)} n(T - (p + s), E - (s + m), C)[1 - LADS(p - 2, m, C)] \binom{p-2}{m} \right],$$

$$\text{where } n(G, H, I) = (G + 1 - H)\binom{G-I}{H-I}. \qquad [6\text{-}2]$$

In the following sections, we first provide an example of the use of the *LADS* and then give additional guidance on the choice of C and E. We next provide a general description of the interpretation and use of a significant *LADS* statistic, compare localized autocorrelation to related techniques for the assessment of data clustering and propose a parametric formulation of *LADS*, and conclude by summarizing the arguments for the utility of the concept of localized autocorrelation and of the *LADS*.

Example of the Use of *LADS*

Before providing the details of the use of *LADS*, consider the following example. The first column of Table 6.1 provides the adoption/disadoption model of weekly movie attendance per household between 1922 and 1977 (DeFleur & Ball-Rokeach, 1982). The 27 time points do not represent equal intervals of time, making analyses of global autocorrelation virtually impossible; however, because localized autocorrelation is based on ordinal relationships, it becomes possible to test for localized autocorrelation.

TABLE 6.1   Regression Models of Movie Attendance ($N = 27$)

Variable	Initial	Model Suggested by LADS
Intercept	2.1***	2.1***
(Year-1921)	.021	.029
(Year-1921)^2	−.0011**	−.0012***
Rate of diffusion of television	—	−4.2**
R^2	.82***	.88***

*$p < .05$; **$p < .01$; ***$p < .001$.

Table 6.2 presents the most extreme residuals from the model. (For convenience, we number the time points in ascending order from 1 to 27). To use *LADS* to evaluate these residuals, we visually inspect the residuals to see if the extreme values cluster in a single time period. We notice that four of the five most negative residuals represent a single time period (the 16th through 19th time points) between 1954 and 1965 (the seventh most negative residual is also a part of this block). Therefore, we set $C = 4$ and $E = 5$ (of course, $T = 27$) and calculate *LADS*. The probability of at least this large a contiguity pattern happening by chance is .0066:

$$LADS(27, 5, 4) = \frac{(27 + 1 - 5)(27 - 4)! \, 5!}{27!(5 - 4)!} = .0066.$$

This is a highly unlikely occurrence.

Given the extremely low value of *LADS*, we suspect there is a variable that (a) has extreme values for the period between 1954 and 1965 and (b) might be related to the dependent variable. One possible variable is the rate of diffusion of televisions, which was extremely high in the mid-1950s to the mid-1960s and which could suppress movie attendance via novelty effects (DeFleur & Ball-Rokeach, 1981). Because the residuals are negative and the rate of diffusion of television sets is large and positive during these years, we expect a negative and significant relationship between diffusion rate and movie attendance.

For the positive residuals, the most noteworthy relationship is that two of the five residuals form a block. The probability of at least this level of contiguity happening by chance is very high (*LADS(27, 5, 2)* = .583). Therefore, we do not explore this block of residuals.

TABLE 6.2 Most Extreme Residuals From Initial Model of Movie Attendance

	Attendance				
Negative Residuals			Positive Residuals		
Time Point	Year	Residual	Time Point	Year	Residual
18	1960	−0.70	5	1930	0.82
17	1958	−0.57	8	1936	0.56
16	1954	−0.54	27	1977	0.46
1	1922	−0.54	13	1946	0.45
19	1965	−0.51	9	1938	0.40

The new model, with rate of diffusion of televisions (measured by annual change in televisions per household; DeFleur and Ball-Rokeach, 1981) included as a linear term, is presented in the second column of Table 6.1. As suggested by *LADS*, the rate of diffusion is significantly and negatively related to movie attendance (the $B = -4.2$, $p < .01$). The increment to R^2 is also clearly significant, $F(1, 23) = 11.5$, $p < .01$.

The omitted variable, rate of diffusion of televisions, came to the attention of the researcher only *after* the initial model had been estimated. The researcher does not need to know why growth rates were particularly high during the key years. Instead, the researcher need only theorize about the direct relationship between the newly discovered independent variable and the already chosen dependent variable. Thus, the localized autocorrelation diagnostic statistic suggested a substantively interesting new variable that was omitted from the original model.

The present volume provides other types of studies for which the use of *LADS* would have been helpful. For example, Barnett and Cho (this volume) examined residuals to determine the influence of "special events" such as holidays and NFL football games on their television-viewing model. Because they did not take advantage of the underlying connectivity pattern in the residuals, they were unable to systematically examine the contiguous set of negative residuals occurring in the 17 days before Christmas. The application of *LADS* would have given a priori evidence that this was a special time period.

The *LADS* approach can also provide useful information in analysis of continuous audience response measures of the type outlined in the West and Biocca chapter in this volume. They describe how CRM was used to study reactions to a 1988 presidential debate. In one example, the analysis was conducted as follows: (a) a priori specification of the portion of the debate of interest, (b) extraction of the subset of relevant response data from the entire data set, and (c) examination of this subset using a repeated measures design. An alternative method would have been to use *LADS* to determine whether this subset of data points was, in fact, significantly different from the rest of the data set, that is, whether audience responses to one portion of the debate were significantly negative relative to responses during the rest of the debate. Notice that in cases such as these, *LADS* can be applied to raw data rather than just residuals.

West and Biocca also describe how cyclical models can be used to examine rhythmic patterns in responses to television stimuli. *LADS* complements this method by providing an efficient means of examining extreme, localized deviations from the cyclical pattern. By identifying which of these deviations are statistically significant and worthy of investigation, *LADS* directs the researcher to specific portions of the television stimulus to look for omitted variables.

Choice of *C* and *E*

The general localized autocorrelation diagnostic statistic, *LADS(T, E, C)*, is based on a given number of cases and a focus on the most positive or most negative residuals. For a given model with a given data set, one must choose the value of either *C* or *E* because given one of these two parameters the other can be set. For a given *C*, *E* is positively related to *LADS*. Therefore, one should choose the minimum number of *E* extreme residuals that contain a contiguous block of size *C* (the smaller the value of *LADS*, the more likely the researcher is to identify an omitted relationship). Conversely, for a given *E*, *C* is negatively related to *LADS*. Therefore, one should choose the maximum value of *C* contained within the set of *E* residuals. (It is simple to determine the maximum size of *C* among a set of *E* prespecified residuals—one simply sorts the extreme residuals by time.)

There are two approaches to the selection of *C* and *E*, one of which leads to a simple but liberal estimate and one of which is somewhat more cumbersome and more conservative. The liberal approach is to examine the residual pattern and set the value of C and E based on the observed pattern. Because this builds in information about uninteresting as well as interesting residual patterns without a statistical penalty, this approach provides a smaller value of *LADS* than is technically accurate. However, there is no means for taking account of visual inspection. Of course, if one tests *LADS* for both positive and negative residuals, one should first divide the critical level by 2. Thus, for example, if one sets the critical probability for examining a connected set to be .05 and one intends to examine both the most positive and most negative residuals, than the critical level of *LADS* should be approximately .025.

The more cumbersome approach is to choose, based on the data set but *not* on a prior examination of the residuals, a range of values of C. The range should be bounded by the minimum number of connected residuals which might suggest a new variable, and by the maximum size which is likely to lead to a value of *LADS* below the critical value. One then chooses either the most extreme positive or negative residuals, picks one of the permitted values of C, and determines whether that value of C (and the associated value of E) leads to a value of *LADS* for the actual residual pattern that is below the critical value. When one finds a set of C residuals that indicate a *LADS* below the critical value, one stops the search and attempts to identify the omitted variable. For t tests of *LADS*, with an initial critical value of p_{init}, the critical value should be made smaller via the Bonferroni adjustment

$$P_{adjusted} = 1 - (1 - p_{init})^{\frac{1}{t}}. \qquad [6\text{-}3]$$

When the researcher uses visual inspection to determine E, there is no clear way to adjust the critical probability; the researcher should be aware that *LADS* is susceptible to Type II error in this case.

As presently constituted, *LADS* does not take into account the ordering of the C residuals within the E time points (although the parametric formulation does). That is, if we denote the C contiguous points with c and the noncontiguous E points with e, *LADS* gives the same probability for the patterns *ececec* and *eeeccc*, for example. If one felt that the second case is more indicative of a localized pattern of autocorrelation than the first case, one can deflate *LADS* by computing the Wald-Wolfowitz runs statistic (Siegel, 1956) for the two groups of size C and E and scaling *LADS* by the result. This deflation would be appropriate if one wished to see whether the block of size C was unique with respect to the E residuals as well as the nonextreme residuals. In general, however, this procedure provides too optimistic estimates for *LADS*.

Interpretation and Use of *LADS*

Assume that C of the E most extreme positive or extreme negative residuals from a model using time series data with T units are associated with a set of C or more consecutive time points (i.e., a block of size C or greater). Assume further that *LADS(T, E, C)* indicates that the pattern is unlikely to have occurred by chance (i.e., *LADS* is below the previously specified critical level). How should one proceed?

As in the earlier section's example, the first step is to consider a variable not in the initial model that has similar, extreme values for the entire time period and that might covary with the dependent variable. (If one cannot find such a variable, one should examine the model for heteroskedasticity, as discussed below.) One looks for extreme values because only such variables can explain extreme residuals. For ratio, interval, or ordinal variables, extreme values are the largest or smallest values; for nominal variables, extreme values are the most uncommon category or categories.

There are two important considerations in choosing the variable. First, because the most extreme units are associated by time, the researcher need only consider those variables that tend to covary with time period. However, the researcher need not consider the historical processes that lead to this covariation. Second, the variable should be chosen so that the chosen variable and the dependent variable are expected to be related across time rather than in only the small subset of time identified initially. Thus, for example, one generally should not choose a dummy variable that is 1 for the time period with extreme residuals and 0 otherwise, as this formulation will have limited theoretical utility.

Having identified the variable, the researcher can decide whether the variable should be included in a model that incorporates all time points or whether the variable suggests a distinct regime that necessitates a unique model. If the variable is not expected to interact with the initial independent variables, the most common situation, one should reestimate the model with the new independent variable included; this new variable is likely to be significant not just because it explains the worst-fitting cases in the model but because it is hypothesized to be related to the dependent variable across time. Therefore, it should improve *many or all* of the residuals, not just the most extreme residuals. The inclusion of the new variable can also improve the parameter estimates of the model. After using the new variable and reestimating the model, the researcher can again check for localized autocorrelation.

If, conversely, the identified variable is expected to interact with one or more of the initial independent variables, then the researcher should create a new regime based on *all* the temporal units that have the unusual value or values for the omitted variable, not just those units that led to the identification of the omitted variable. The researcher will then run two models, one for the segregated units and one for the other units. The two models should have different parameter estimates, and both models will fit their cases better than the initial model. Of course, the researcher should then check both models for localized autocorrelation.

One can extend the uses of *LADS* by taking the absolute values of the residuals before examining the most extreme cases. A sufficiently small *LADS* in this instance, especially if it clearly exceeds the critical level for the most extreme positive or most extreme negative residuals, identifies time periods with unusually high error variance; that is, *LADS* can be used to identify heteroskedasticity (this is in the spirit of the Wald-Wolfowitz runs test; see Siegel, 1956, pp. 136-145). *LADS* is much more flexible than traditional approaches to the determination of heteroskedasticity, which require the researcher to make an a priori specification of the variable that is the source of the heteroskedasticity (Pindyck & Rubinfeld, 1981, chap. 6). Using *LADS*, one can deduce the source of the heteroskedasticity by identifying the variable in the model that has extreme values for the identified residuals. One can then decide whether to adjust the residuals in the initial model (Pindyck & Rubinfeld, 1981) or whether to use the identified variable to create distinct regimes. The use of *LADS* is not impeded by adjustments for global temporal autocorrelation. The researcher can first perform the requisite global autocorrelation diagnostics and adjustments, thereby identifying the most appropriate base model and residuals, and then use *LADS*. Of course, *LADS* can also be used in cases for which global autocorrelation adjustments are impossible (e.g., nonuniform time intervals).

Localized Autocorrelation
and Related Approaches

The present conceptualization and measurement of *LADS* essentially creates two groups of data: the E points with the most extreme residuals and the $T - E$ remaining points. These two groups are treated quite differently, as the group with E points is examined for a set of C or more contiguous points, whereas the only important characteristic of the group with $T - E$ points is its size.

The *LADS* approach is quite different from traditional approaches to the clustering of ordered data. Runs tests, such as the Wald-Wolfowitz runs test (see Siegel, 1956, for a general discussion of runs tests), begin with two or more groups and adopt the null hypothesis that each point of each group can take on any value (appear in any position in the sequence). That is, the groups are treated identically and symmetrically. In contrast, under the *LADS* framework, the null hypothesis cannot be that each point can appear anywhere in the sequence because we have constrained the location of each of the groups. This contention (and the remainder of the paragraph) holds whether one thinks in terms of the aforesaid groups of E and $T - E$ points or whether one considers groups of $T - C$ and C or groups of C, $E - C$, and $T - E$. (Of course, the location of points *within* a group is equiprobable, but this is an assumption rather than a potentially disprovable part of the null hypothesis.) Furthermore, *LADS* does not treat the groups identically: The group with E residuals is analyzed with respect to the fact that the E points come

From a sequence of time points; the structure of the remaining $T - E$ points is ignored.

Similarly, the localized autocorrelation approach is quite different from traditional tests for autocorrelation. This is best illustrated via the specification of a test of localized autocorrelation treating the residuals as interval rather than ordinal. It is important to note that this treatment of the residuals is presented solely for its utility in understanding the underlying mathematics of *LADS* and should only be used in those very rare occasions for which the magnitude of the residuals is considered key. This parametric approach is very tedious to compute and it is unlikely to provide relevant information beyond that provided by the nonparametric (i.e., ordinal) *LADS*.

To calculate the parametric form of *LADS* for a given set of E extreme residuals, one partitions the residuals into B distinct contiguous blocks, C_k, with each block of size $1 \leq C_k \leq E$. One can then compute a variant of Moran's I (Anselin, 1988; Cliff & Ord, 1973, 1980), a generalized autocorrelation statistic, as follows:

$$I' = \max \left\{ [1 \leq k \leq B] \left[\frac{E}{2\binom{C_k}{2}} \sum_{i \in c_k} \sum_{\substack{j \in c_k \\ i \neq j}} \left(\frac{z_i z_j}{\sum_{h \in c_k} z_h^2} \right) \right] \right\}, \qquad [6\text{-}4]$$

where z_g is the z-score (based on the mean and standard deviation of the E residuals) of the gth most extreme of the E residuals. Like I, I' has the classical structure of autocorrelation; namely, the numerator term is similar to a measure of covariance among the residuals in each block, and the denominator term is similar to a measure of the variance (Cliff & Ord, 1973). (The numerator and denominator are not true variance and covariance measures for the block because the mean is based on E residuals rather than just the residuals in the block.)

There are two key differences between I' and I (as well as other autocorrelation statistics) that make the former consistent with the localized autocorrelation approach. First, I' ranges over only E points rather than over all T points. Second, I' uses a maximum rather than a sum, highlighting the idea that I' is based on the most unlikely (largest value) subset of a subset of points rather than on the complete set of points.

To determine whether I' is significant, we use a randomization procedure in which the placement of the E residuals is permuted over the T time points and determine where the observed value of I' is located in the resulting pseudosampling distribution (a similar approach is used in testing the significance of Geary's, 1954, autocorrelation statistic, c; see Burridge, 1988). A one-tailed test is appropriate because *LADS* is based on positive autocorrelation.

Because of the regularity of the contiguity patterns in time series data, the derivation of the sampling distribution requires a great deal fewer computations than the $T!$ computations associated with all possible permutations of the T time points. Assign the T time points to the E residuals of interest and the remaining $T - E$ residuals. Each of the $T!$ possible assignments of residuals partitions the E residuals of interest into one or more contiguous blocks; patterns associated with the other $T - E$ residuals are not relevant. If one defines $P_M(N)$ as the number of partitions of N points such that each contiguous block in each partition is of size M or greater, the number of distinct partitions of E points into blocks (ignoring the ordering of the blocks) is $P_1(E)$, where

$$P_M(N) = \begin{cases} 0 & \text{if } n = 0 \text{ or } N < M \\ 1 + \sum_{k=M}^{N} P_k(N-k) & \text{if } N \geq M \end{cases} . \qquad [6\text{-}5]$$

For each partition, the assignment of time points to the E residuals creates a temporal ordering of the B_i contiguous blocks among the E residuals. The number of distinct temporal orderings of the blocks in partition i is

$$\frac{B_i!}{\prod_{s=1}^{E} m_{i,s}!} ,$$

where B_i is the number of contiguous blocks in partition i, and $m_{i, s}$ is the number of blocks of size s in partition i. Therefore, the number of distinct I's that must be computed is

$$\sum_{i=1}^{P_{1(E)}} \frac{B_i !}{\prod_{S=1}^{E} m_{i,s} !} ,$$

The computation of the I's is not particularly burdensome because the number of computations is a slow-growing function of E (much slower than $E!$) rather than the $T!$ analogous computations required for I or Geary's c.

To compute the probability of a particular temporal ordering of a particular partition i, list the sizes of the blocks, $s_{i, j}$, in temporal order. If one lets t_k be the time point associated with the beginning of the kth block, the probability is then

$$\sum_{t_1 = 1}^{a(0)} \cdots \sum_{t_k = t_{k-1} + (s_i, k-1 + 1)}^{a(k-1)} \cdots \sum_{t_{B_i} = t_{B_i - 1} + (s_i, B_i - 1 + 1)}^{a(B_i - 1)} \frac{(T-E)!}{T!} , \text{ where}$$

$$a(N) = (T + 1 - (E + B_i - 1)) + \sum_{h=1}^{N} (s_{i,h} + 1) . \qquad [6\text{-}6]$$

Given these probabilities and the values of I' for each temporal ordering of each partition, one can compute the pseudosampling distribution (that is, for a given value of I', sum the probabilities of all of the configurations with values of I' less than the given value) and determine the probability of obtaining a value of I' greater than or equal to the initially measured value.

Summary and Discussion

The underlying structure of time series data provides an opportunity for a diagnostic analysis of residuals based on the notion of localized temporal autocorrelation, which blends traditional approaches to temporal autocorrelation and regression diagnostics. Localized autocorrelation treats extreme errors correlated over time as an indicator of interesting, ignored relationships. A high level of localized autocorrelation can suggest variables to be included in a model, variables that identify distinct regimes necessitating separate models, and variables that lead to heteroskedasticity.

This chapter provides an exact formula for the computation of the localized autocorrelation diagnostic statistic, *LADS(T, E, C)*, the probability that, given a dataset with T time points, a consecutive set of size C or more among the E most extreme, same-signed residuals occurred by chance. It also suggests a parametric statistic for localized autocorrelation, I' (based on Moran's I) and the pseudosampling distribution for determining the probability of obtaining a value greater than or equal to the measured value of the statistic.

Unlike other approaches to the clustering of data, such as runs analysis and traditional approaches to autocorrelation, the localized autocorrelation approach differentiates the analysis of extreme residuals from the analysis of other residuals. *LADS* is concerned with the distribution of a subset of points within the context of a larger subset of points, as opposed to the distribution of two or more subsets of points that comprise the entire data set.

In sum, the localized autocorrelation diagnostic statistic represents a unique approach to residuals from time series data that serves as an invitation and guide to enhanced model development.

Appendix:
Derivation of Results 1 and 2

The localized autocorrelation diagnostic statistic can be computed as the probability that for a given time series of T units, a randomly selected subset of size E contains a set of consecutive years (a "block") of size C or larger. To derive for temporal data, we first determine the number of different possible ways to arrange the E residuals on the T time points. We then find the number of these arrangements that results in at least one block of size C or larger. $LADS(T, E, C)$ is then the ratio of the second count over the first.

We derive the denominator first. Time series data with T units can be seen as equivalent to sites or positions on a line numbered from 1 to T. The number of different possible arrangements of the most extreme E residuals is then the number of ways of placing E points into the T sites. This is simply

$$\binom{T}{E}.$$

To derive the numerator, one first counts the number of configurations of the E most extreme residuals that results in a block of size C or greater, but one overcounts such that if B distinct blocks of size C or greater are contained among the E residuals, one counts the configuration B times. One then derives the formula for the overcount and subtracts the overcount from the initial total.

Consider configurations with at least one block of size C or larger among the E points. Let p be the position of the leftmost time point of one of the blocks. If $p = 1$, then C of the points must be distributed in the first C sites. The number of configurations of this type are the distinct ways of distributing the remaining $E - C$ points into the remaining $T - C$ sites, that is, assigning times to the remaining $E - C$ residuals. The number of ways of doing this is

$$\binom{T - C}{E - C}.$$

Now consider the case in which the position of the leftmost point of one of the blocks is not the first site (i.e., $p > 1$). C of the points must be distributed in the sites p through $p + C - 1$. The remaining $E - C$ points can be distributed in any of the remaining sites *except* for the site $p - 1$ because a point at the $p - 1$ site would mean that p is not the leftmost site of the block. Thus, the ways to make distinct configurations with a given $p > 1$ are the ways to distribute $E - C$ points in $T - (CH)$ sites. For a given $p > 1$, the number of ways is

$$\binom{T-(C+1)}{E-C} = \binom{T-E}{T-C}\binom{T-C}{E-C}.$$

If one sums across all possible values of p ($1 \leq p \leq (T+1-C)$), a configuration with B blocks will be counted B times, the correct formulation for the first half of the numerator. Because p does not enter into the equations for the number of configurations and because there are $T - C$ possible values of p for $p > 1$, the net number of blocks of size C or greater, $n(T, E, C)$, is

$$n(T, E, C) = \binom{T-C}{E-C} + (T-C)\frac{T-E}{T-C}\binom{T-C}{E-C} = (T+1-E)\binom{T-C}{E-C}.$$

If $C \leq E < 2C$, a given configuration of E residuals can contain at most one block of size C or greater; that is, each configuration with a block of size C or greater is counted once and only once. Therefore, if $C \leq E < 2C$, one can compute $LADS(T, E, C)$ simply by dividing $n(T, E, C)$ by the total number of ways one can place E residuals given T time points,

$$\binom{T}{E};$$

giving Result 1:

$$LADS(T, E, C) = \frac{n(T, E, C)}{\binom{T}{E}} = (T+1-E)\frac{\binom{T-C}{E-C}}{\binom{T}{E}}.$$

When $E \geq 2C$, $n(T, E, C)$ counts those configurations with $B > 1$ distinct blocks of size C or greater among the E time points B times. To adjust the numerator of $LADS(T, E, C)$, one must subtract from $n(T, E, C)$ an adjustment that counts each configuration with $B \geq 1$ distinct blocks $B - 1$ times.

Consider those configurations with $B > 1$ distinct blocks of size C or greater. Assume that the first (earliest in time) block is of size s; $C \leq s \leq (E - C)$ (because there is more than one block of size C or greater). Let the leftmost position of this first block be p.

The first block divides the remaining $E - s$ residuals into two sets—those to the left of the block (if any) and those to the right. Consider configurations for which the remaining $E - s$ residuals are all located to the right of the first block. As there are $T - (s + p)$ sites to place the remaining $E - s$ residuals (none of the residuals can be placed immediately to the right of the time period), the number of blocks encompassed by all such configurations (not including the first block) is then $n(T - (s + p), E - s, C)$. Because all the E residuals must be at or to the right of position p and there must be a space between the first block of size s and the remaining residuals, $1 \le p \le (T - E)$. If one sums across s and p, those configurations with $B > 1$ blocks for which the remaining $E - s$ residuals are all to the right of the first block will be counted $B - 1$ times, the desired result. Thus, the first half of the overcount is

$$\sum_{s=C}^{E-C} \sum_{p=1}^{T-E} n(T - (s + p), E - s, C) .$$

Now assume that only $r < (E - s)$ residuals are to the right of the first block. Then $m = (E - (s + r))$ of the residuals are to the left of the first block. The only permissible configurations with $m \ge 1$ residuals to the left of the first block are those that *do not* have a time period of at least size C or greater among the m residuals (if a block of size C or greater did exist among the m residuals, the stated first block would not be first). As there are $p - 2$ sites available for the m residuals (none of the m residuals can be immediately to the left of the first block), the number of permissible configurations is the total number of configurations,

$$\binom{p-2}{m},$$

multiplied by the proportion of configurations that do not have at least one contiguous block of at least size C, $(1 - LADS \, (p - 2, m, C))$. Therefore, the total number of possible configurations to the left of the block is

$$\binom{p-2}{m}(1 - LADS(p - 2, m, C)) .$$

For each of these possible configurations to the left, there are $n(T - (p + s)$, $r, C) = n(T - (p + s), E - (s + m), C)$ (overcounted) configurations to the right of the first block. To derive the total number of (overcounted) configurations, one must sum across all permissible values of s, m, and p: $C \le s \le (E - (C + 1))$ (because at least one of the E residuals is not part of a block); $1 \le m \le (E - (s + C))$ (because there must be at least C residuals to the right of the first block); $p \ge (m + 2)$ (there must be an empty time point between the residuals to the left of the block and the block); and $p \le (T - (s + r)) = (T - (E - m))$ (there must be an empty time point between the block and the residuals to the right of the block).

Thus, the overcount when there is at least one residual to the left of the first block is

$$\sum_{s=C}^{E-(C+1)} \sum_{m=1}^{E-(s+C)} \sum_{p=m+2}^{T-(E-m)} n(T-(p+s), r, C)\binom{p-2}{m}(1 - LADS(p-2, m, C)).$$

Thus, configurations with $B > 1$ blocks with at least one of the E residuals to the left of the first block will be counted $B - 1$ times, the other part of the overcount.

Removing the two parts of the overcount from the initial count, $n(T, E, C)$, and dividing by the possible sets of E residuals given T time points,

$$\binom{T}{E},$$

one finds Result 2.

When $E < 2C$, the adjustment term is 0 (the first term of the adjustment is 0 because $(E - C) < C$, and the second term of the adjustment is 0 because $(E - (s + C)) < 1$). In these cases,

$$LADS(T, E, C) = \frac{n(T, E, C)}{\binom{T}{E}},$$

consistent with Result 1.

Analyzing Cyclical Effects in Experimental Designs

JAMES H. WATT

In several chapters in this volume (e.g., those by Barnett & Cho, Warner), researchers describe the process of relating nominal variables that are presumed to be causes to time-sequenced effect variables. In these studies, the nominal independent variables such as gender, makeup of conversational dyads, or availability of special event television programming are not manipulated. The analyses used tend to be descriptive within, and comparative across, nominal groups, as is usually the case with observational research designs. In this kind of design, the analysis of time-sequenced data often stresses discovery and description of models of the data rather than testing formal hypotheses that involve partitioning the effects of a set of independent variables.

By contrast, in experimental research designs, the levels of the independent variables are systematically manipulated so that their effects on the dependent variable can be isolated and examined with less ambiguity. Unfortunately, very little use of time series analysis is made in experimental settings. This is not the result of any limitation in the analytical techniques. Although time series analysis has traditionally been used for exploratory and descriptive studies, it can also be used to great advantage in the verification of formal theory.

The chapter by Meadowcroft in this volume describes a full experimental design in which nominal independent variables are manipulated in a factorial design that has a time-sequenced dependent variable (reaction time as an operationalization of attention level). In this analysis, the effects of the independent variables are partitioned into independent sources of influence on the dependent time series so as to test formal hypotheses that concern the production of cyclic effects by the independent variables. This design is the exemplar for the discussion of analytical techniques contained in this chapter.

In both observational and experimental research, the use of a time-sequenced variable as dependent variable raises many analytical difficulties. Traditional analysis of variance procedures, illustrated below, are simply not well suited to extracting concise and easily interpretable results that describe some of the important ways in which independent variables can affect a dependent variable. Analysis of variance statistics are designed primarily to test unsequenced "level hypotheses" (i.e., differences among group means), even when there are repeated measurements of the dependent variable made over a number of time points. Repeated measures ANOVA can provide some information about difference in levels of the dependent variable at differing time points, but these are aimed at finding mean differences at discrete time points, not extracting the functional nature of the variation of the dependent variable over time (see Watt, 1994, for a more extensive discussion). But it is the dynamic functional description of effects, such as trends and cycles, that often contain the most important theoretical findings.

The essential difference between the studies mentioned above along with other studies that fall in this class (cf. Barnett et al., 1991; VanLear, 1991) and traditional studies of single-time-point effects lies in the search for dynamic effects that go beyond simple differences in mean levels. However, the analytical tools for detecting nonlinear trends and cycles are often poorly understood by behavioral and social researchers. As a result, hypothesis tests are frequently based on a somewhat qualitative interpretation of statistics that may not be directly suited for such formal tests. For example, sometimes, functional relationships are inferred by searching for perceived similarities among several univariate analyses. In a typical analysis, univariate ARIMA models of two groups may be constructed and contrasted. Finding similar models leads to the inference of a common factor operating in both groups; conversely, finding differing models leads to the conclusion that some unique factor or factors are operating in one of the groups. Similarly, conclusions are often drawn by examining individual spectral analyses of two groups, as Warner (this volume) notes. Although these procedures are not incorrect, they do not provide the basis for a fully confident assertion about the effect of one variable on another.

In all cases where simple comparisons are used, there is a serious problem in eliminating spurious relationships between each of the time series being examined and any external variable or variables. The individual models of the two groups, or the two spectra, may be similar simply because the time series from both groups are affected in a similar way by some unknown external factor(s) (see VanLear & Watt, this volume).

More sophisticated analyses like multivariate ARIMA models and coherency analysis may introduce some statistical control into the analysis. These can be used to distinguish real covariances from possible spurious covariances but only to the extent that all confounding variables are included in the analysis. This is the standard limitation of an observational design.

Unfortunately, statistical control in observational studies is made difficult by the limitations of the statistical tools that are available to analyze multivariate time series. In the case of cross-spectral analysis, two variables are frequently the maximum that the analytical tools support. The resulting statistics are the analog of bivariate correlations, and they share with zero-order correlations the problem of lack of control of additional outside confounding variables. Spurious covariation may still obscure the true relationships.

The classic experimental design was developed to attack this problem by systematically manipulating independent variables while assuring that all confounding variables exert no systematic effect on the dependent variable (Campbell & Stanley, 1966). Experimental designs introduce control that allows elimination of most spurious covariance. But there are very few examples of either univariate or multivariate time series techniques being employed to analyze data obtained from controlled experimental conditions. When time-sequenced measures of the dependent variable in experiments are made, they are typically subjected to analysis with standard ANOVA and MANOVA tools that are not well suited to the task.

This chapter illustrates some relatively simple procedures that use standard analytical techniques for univariate time series to partition the variance produced by independent variables in a simple factorial design that may result from either observational or experimental research. This approach differs from a standard ANOVA by the fact that the variance in the dependent variable is the result of a (possibly nonlinear) functional relationship between the independent and dependent variables, not a deviation from a grand mean. The resulting partitioned variance is an analog of simple factorial ANOVA, but unlike ANOVA, the dependent variable variance is produced by some nonlinear relationship, not deviations from a single constant value (the grand mean).

The procedures described here can be extended to multiple factors and to multiple levels of each factor. However, for the sake of simplicity in this introduction, the simple 2×2 factorial design is used. This is one of the most frequently used designs in experimental studies.

A Simulation of a 2×2 Experiment
to Detect Cyclic Effects

The Data

To develop and illustrate techniques for applying the logic of factorial experimental design to situations where the dependent variable measurements produce a time series, a computer program was constructed to produce data from simulated subjects. The mean of each cell in the design was specified, as was the total variance in each cell. The cell variance is split into two parts: (a) variance due to some effect of the independent variables and (b) random error variance. In this simulated experiment, the effect of the independent variables is assumed to produce cycles of differing periods. The experimental design and the periodic effects are similar to those described by Meadowcroft in this volume.

Table 7.1 summarizes the experimental design and the data generated by the simulation program. The design is a simple 2×2 factorial design with two independent between-subjects variables (X_1 and X_2), each of which has two levels: None and Present. One cell (Cell 00) is thus a control group in which both X_1 and X_2 are absent.

In the simulation data, the presence of X_1 produces a cycle in the dependent variable that has a period of 20 time units. This cycle has an amplitude of 5. The presence of X_2 produces cycles with a period of 7 time units and an amplitude of 2.5. Thus, the variance in Cell 00, where

TABLE 7.1 Data for Simulated Experiment

		X_1	
		None	*Present*
X_2	*None*	**Cell 00** Control group $N = 20$ 80 time points Mean = 20.00 $SD = 4.96$	**Cell 01** Period = 20 Amplitude = 5 $N = 20$ 80 time points Mean = 20.07 $SD = 4.98$
	Present	**Cell 10** Period = 7 Amplitude = 2.5 $N = 20$ 80 time points Mean = 19.99 $SD = 5.06$	**Cell 11** Period = 7 and 20 Amplitudes = 2.5 and 5 $N = 20$ 80 time points Mean = 20.10 $SD = 5.07$

neither X_1 nor X_2 is present, is only random error variance; the variance in Cell 01 is a combination of the effect of X_1 (a cycle with period = 20 and amplitude = 5) and error variance; Cell 10 contains the combination of the effect of X_2 (a cycle with period = 7 and amplitude = 2.5) and random error variance; in Cell 11, the total variance is made up of the effects of the two cycles produced by X_1 and X_2, plus random error variance.

The data were defined as very well behaved: The means of each cell were set to 20 units of the dependent variable, and the variance of each was set to 25 (standard deviation, or $SD = 5$). The combination of relatively large effect sizes for each of the independent variables and relatively small total error variance permits clear visualization of the data at each analytical step.

The simulation data contains only cyclical effects for each of the experimental independent variables. In practice, this will not always be the case. Linear and nonlinear trends may be present as well as noncyclical processes. Watt (1994) describes a process for detecting, modeling, and separating multiple effects. Here, however, we will limit the discussion to the simpler case of detecting cycles and estimating the unconfounded main effect of each independent variable in producing the cycles.

The dependent variable was constructed at 80 time points for each simulated subject in the experiment. Twenty simulated subjects were placed in each of the four cells. The resulting data are summarized in Table 7.1. Actual means for the 6,400 data points (80 simulated subjects × 80 time points for each subject) ranged from 19.99 to 20.10, with actual SDs ranging from 4.96 to 5.07. This simulated data set is used in all analyses. The first analysis demonstrates the limitations of traditional repeated measures ANOVA when the dependent variable consists of a time series whose values cycle.

Repeated Measures Analysis of Variance With the Simulation Data

The first problem that surfaces in analyzing the data lies in the number of error degrees of freedom available. Because repeated measures ANOVA constructs contrasts among pairs of time points in the time series, the total number of subjects (each of whom introduces an error degree of freedom, or df) must exceed the number of measurement points by at least one. When between-subjects factors are introduced, the number of subjects must again be increased to provide error df larger than the effects df.

In the simulation data, there are too few error df (number of individual subjects) to fully analyze the data. Either the number of subjects per cell must be increased or the number of time points analyzed must be decreased. In a real situation, the former is expensive and the latter takes the chance of missing effects that persist for long periods (if the time series is truncated) or of missing rapidly changing effects (if every nth observation for the whole series is deleted—see Arundale, this volume). However, as we already know that the longest effect in the simulation data has a period of 20, the series was truncated at 40 time points for this ANOVA analysis.

Table 7.2 shows the results of an SPSS MANOVA repeated measurement analysis. In the first part of the table, the between-subject effects of the experimental independent variables on the dependent variable are tested. Because this analysis uses differences in the means among cells as the indicator of an effect of an independent variable, the tests are all

TABLE 7.2 Repeated Measures MANOVA Analysis of the Simulated Experiment

Tests of Between-Subjects Effects

Source of Variation	SS	df	MS	F	Signif. of F
WITHIN + RESIDUAL	979.44	76	12.89		
X_1	12.43	1	12.43	.96	.329
X_2	4.77	1	4.77	.37	.545
X_1 by X_2	10.31	1	10.31	.80	.374

Tests involving TIME Within-Subject Effect

Mauchly sphericity test	=	.00000257
Chi-square approximation	=	953.32486 with 779 *df*
Significance	=	.000

Multivariate Tests of Significance

EFFECT . . X_1 by Time

Test Name	Value	Exact F	Hypoth df	Error df	Signif. of F
Pillais	.95244	19.51119	39	38	.000
Hotellings	20.02465	19.51119	39	38	.000
Wilks	.04756	19.51119	39	38	.000
Roys	.95244				

EFFECT . . X_2 by Time

Test Name	Value	Exact F	Hypoth df	Error df	Signif. of F
Pillais	.88953	7.84608	39	38	.000
Hotellings	8.05255	7.84608	39	38	.000
Wilks	.11047	7.84608	39	38	.000
Roys	.88953				

Univariate (Mixed-Model) Approach

Source of Variation	SS	df	MS	F	Signif. of F
WITHIN + RESIDUAL	51459.29	2964	17.36		
Time	12460.76	39	319.51	18.40	.000
X_1 by Time	10886.57	39	279.14	16.08	.000
X_2 by Time	3762.25	39	96.47	5.56	.000
X_1 by X_2 by Time	857.51	39	21.99	1.27	.125

predictably null, as all the cells have nearly the same mean. This ANOVA tests only level (mean differences) hypotheses and is not sensitive to other patterns of difference among the time points of the dependent variable series. It thus misses the presence of the cycles produced by the independent variables.

In the second part of Table 7.2, the repeated measurement factor, called "Time," is tested for within-subjects effects. Here the dynamic effects of the independent variables do appear in a limited form. But problems immediately surface: The Mauchly sphericity test is highly significant, indicating that the variances of the contrasts among time points are not equal and/or there are covariances among the contrasts. The covariance will result from the nonindependence of the time series observations (see West & Biocca, this volume, for further discussion of problems of repeated measures in time series). Because some of the cells contain cyclical components and others do not, this homogeneity of variance violation will occur when the dependent variable cycles over time in some cells and not in others (i.e., when a control group is present). Normally, both these problems would minimally constrain the researcher to using multivariate tests in which each time point is treated as a separate, covarying variable rather than multiple observations of the same variable. These are less statistically powerful tests (Norusis, 1993, p. 116).

However, the multivariate tests for the effects of X_1 and X_2 are indeed significant. The effects in the simulation data are sufficiently strong that the less powerful test can still detect them. In addition, the univariate test, even with the violation of sphericity, indicates that X_1 and X_2 are related to the level of the dependent time series over time.

This is the correct finding, but it is not too informative. Although we can correctly conclude that there is some dynamic relationship between the independent variables and the dependent variable within subjects, we cannot see the nature of the relationship. The longer-period, higher-amplitude cycle produced by X_1 is not distinguishable from the shorter-period, less intense cycle produced by X_2. Both are non-null, and that is the extent of the information that repeated measures ANOVA can provide.

A Harmonic Modeling Approach

It is clear that some other approach is needed to adequately convey the information in these data. The analytical tool should describe the periodic nature of the effects of the independent variables as well as test the significance of the effects of independent variables against the null hypothesis.

ARIMA models might be used to describe periodicities, but they are somewhat difficult to apply in this situation. ARIMA models are fundamentally descriptive models of a single time series, and they are not well suited to the task of partitioning variances in multiple time series. Variance partitioning is critical to making formal hypothesis tests.

A simple and informative procedure for isolating the cyclical effects of independent variables does exist, however. It is based on constructing different harmonic models that summarize periodicities within groups of cells ("collapsed cells") that represent the main effects and interaction effects of the independent variables and then mathematically contrasting the models to detect each of the independent effects.

Isolating Main Effects

The logic of partitioning the effects of the independent variables is identical to that used in ordinary factorial ANOVA. By contrasting groups of cells in which the main effect is expected to be present (or high) from those in which it is not expected (or expected to be lower), the effect of differing levels of the independent variable can be estimated.

Looking at Table 7.1, it is evident that Cells 01 and 11 contain the effect of X_1 (the cycle with period = 20), whereas Cells 10 and 11 contain the effects of X_2 (the cycle with period = 7). If Cells 00 and 10 are collapsed into a single time series, that series will not contain any cycles of period = 20. If Cells 01 and 11 are collapsed into a similar time series, that series will contain a strong periodicity with period = 20. Both collapsed series will contain a cycle with period = 7, however.

If the first collapsed series is contrasted with the second collapsed series, they will differ only by the presence of a cycle with period = 20 in the second series. This is precisely the main effect of the independent variable X_1.

Likewise, contrasting a series made by collapsing Cells 00 and 01 with another series consisting of Cells 10 and 11 will produce differences only in the presence of a cycle with period = 7 in the second series. Both collapsed series will contain a cycle with period = 20. The difference between the two series thus represents the main effect of X_2.

To contrast the cyclical components, one must first detect them and model them so that their relative contribution to the explanation of the variance of the dependent variable can be expressed quantitatively. Modeling the data within experimental cells introduces some general issues that must be considered.

Modeling Subjects' Means Versus
Modeling Subjects' Dynamic Responses

The first difference between the harmonic modeling approach and the repeated measures ANOVA approach lies in moving from analyzing the individual responses of subjects to analyzing the time series that is made up by averaging subjects' responses at each time point. This procedure reduces the data analyzed in each cell from 20 series (one per subject) of 80 time points to a single 80 time point series made up of the means for all subjects within the cell.

This reduction essentially removes between-subject variation within each cell. The series of means has less total variation as a result. Figure 7.1 illustrates the difference between the two types of data series. The points of the series made up of the means at each time point deviate much less from the cell mean of 20 than does the typical individual subject's data values. The means series also shows a smoother variation that more clearly indicates the underlying cycles present in that cell.

Within-cell variation due to subject differences is normally treated as error. In essence, averaging responses at each time point arbitrarily sets this error to zero. This strong assumption implies homogeneity of process (VanLear & Watt, this volume). If there are only a few subjects per cell, making this assumption may produce serious errors. To apply the harmonic modeling approach, one must have sufficient observations in each cell to confidently assume that the sampling error of the means at each time point is small. If this assumption can be made, using the mean to represent the response of all subjects at a particular time point produces accurate models of the theoretical process. Unfortunately, because between-subject error never appears in the error term any F-ratio (as it would if one were modeling individual subjects' responses), this critical assumption is hidden from direct scrutiny. The best way to examine validity of the assumption is to look at descriptive statistics for each time point in the series in each cell. The ideal situation occurs when each time point has a relatively small standard error of the mean and no significant skew. This is the case in the simulation data.

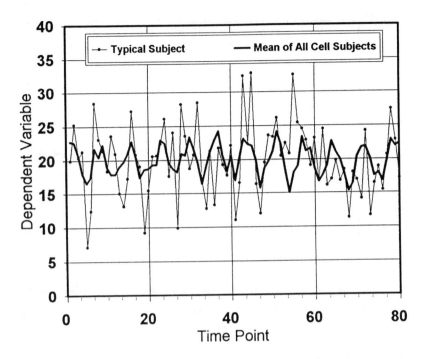

Figure 7.1. Typical data in an experimental cell containing a cycle.

To isolate the periodic effects of each of the independent variables in the simulation data, the mean of subjects' responses at each time point were constructed in each cell. The result in the simulation data is four series (one for each cell), each consisting of 80 time points. Figures 7.2a-d show the series.

The means series for each of the collapsed cells that are used to detect main effects are constructed in a similar fashion by averaging the subjects' responses within each combination of cells. For example, the data from all 40 subjects in Cells 00 and 10 are averaged into a single 80-time-point series to provide a series that represents the "None" level of X_1. This series will be contrasted with the 80-time-point averaged data from the 40 subjects in Cells 01 and 11 (representing the "Present" level of X_1) to detect main effects of X_1. The grand mean series for all subjects in all cells is shown in Figure 7.3.

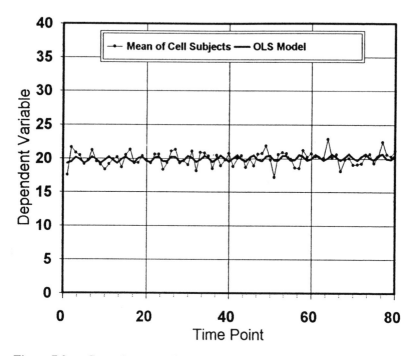

Figure 7.2a. Control group cell, no cycles (Cell 00).

The key to detecting cyclical main effects lies in detecting simple periodicities that appear in one collapsed cell but do not appear in another. To do this, we must find a simple mathematical representation for the cycles. Using the ANOVA analogy, this is the equivalent of the formula for computing cell means.

OLS Modeling of Cycles

Any pure sinusoidal cycle in the data can be represented by

$$x_t = \mu + R\cos(\omega t + \phi) + e_t, \qquad [7\text{-}1]$$

where x_t is any data point in the series, μ is the mean of the stationary series, R is the maximum amplitude, ω is the frequency in radians per unit time, ϕ is the phase angle in radians, t is time units, and e_t is residual error.

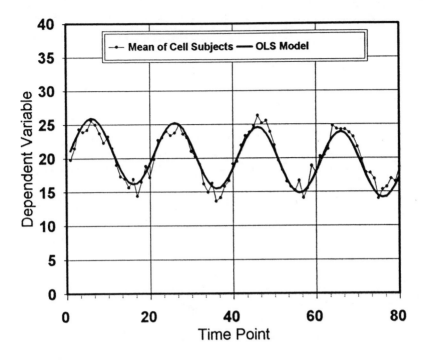

Figure 7.2b. Cell with period = 20 cycle (Cell 01).

This can be rewritten by trigonometric identity (Bloomfield, 1976) as

$$x_t = \mu + A\cos(\omega t) + B\cos(\omega t) + e_t. \quad\quad [7\text{-}2]$$

The constants A and B are called the cosine weight and the sine weight, respectively, and are computed by

$$A = R\cos(\phi) ; \quad\quad [7\text{-}3]$$

$$B = R\sin(\phi) .$$

Periodicities more complex than a single sinusoid can be modeled as a series of additive sinusoidal components, as outlined in VanLear and Watt (this volume). Any periodic function of any shape can be repre-

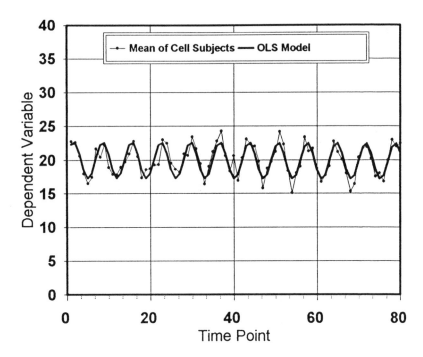

Figure 7.2c.   Cell with period = 7 cycle (Cell 10).

sented as the summation of a set of sinusoidal components (Wylie, 1960, p. 248). This procedure is thus not limited to cycles but can be used to model any nonlinear effect.

To minimize the squared error between a set of m sinusoidal functions and the observed data points, optimal values for the frequency, phase, and amplitude for all the sinusoidal components in the additive set must be found. This involves selecting A_k, B_k, and ω_k to minimize Function 7-4 below (Bloomfield, 1976, p. 23).

$$\sum_{t=0}^{n-1} \left\{ X_t - \mu - \sum_{\substack{j=1 \\ j \neq k}}^{m} \left(A_j \cos(\omega_j t) + B_j \sin(\omega_j t) \right) \right. \left. - A_k \cos(\omega_k t) - B_k \sin(\omega_k t) \right\}^2 \qquad [7\text{-}4]$$

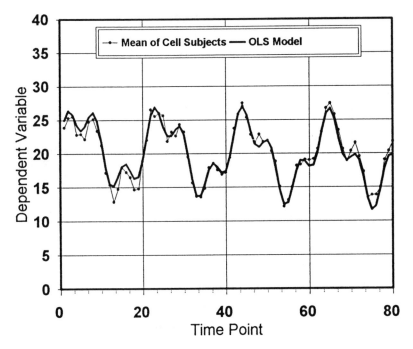

Figure 7.2d.　Cell with both period = 7 and period = 20 cycles (Cell 11).

The derivatives of this function are nonlinear and have many zeros, so an analytical solution is not possible. Because of the number of zeros, numerical solutions will also converge to local minima for the sums of squared residuals.

Numerical methods such as Newton's (cf. Conte, 1965) can be used to compute a local solution to the function. OLS optimization can be done with a nonlinear regression procedure, such as the NLR procedure in SPSS, or the cyclic descent method used by Bloomfield (1976) and modified by Watt (1979, 1988) in the FATS (Fourier analysis of time series) program.

As noted above, none of these methods will produce a global maximum for the parameters across the full range of the parameters. Solutions will converge to different local maxima, depending on the initial values of the parameters.

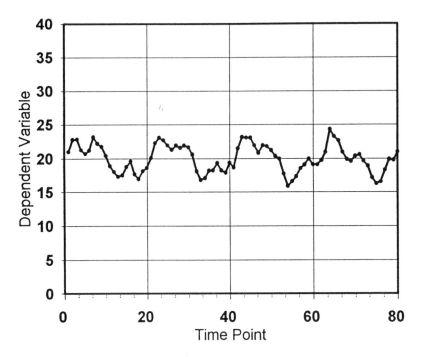

Figure 7.3.   Mean series for all simulated subjects.

To obtain accurate parameter estimates, it is critical to provide initial values that are in the near neighborhood of the optimal values as the starting points for the numerical solutions. To get these initial values, a Fourier transform of the data is first obtained.

As discussed in VanLear and Watt (this volume), the Fourier transform consists of a series of sinusoids that, when added together, produce a smooth curve that passes through each point in a time series. If the time series is made up of a finite number of observations equally spaced in time, the transform is called the discrete Fourier transform (DFT). DFTs are normally used with experimental or observational data sampled at a number of time points. The simulation data are one example of this type of data, as are the data described by Buder, Warner, Meadowcroft, and Barnett and Cho (all in this volume).

Strong periodicities in the time series data produce large amplitudes in nearby DFT sinusoidal components. By examining the amplitude of cycles at the Fourier frequencies (i.e., examining the spectrum), the neighborhood of the strongest periodic components can be identified.

But the Fourier frequencies used to construct the spectrum are chosen for their orthogonal properties, not to maximize fit with the time series data points. Further adjustment of the frequency of the periodicity is necessary to get the optimal estimate of the actual periodicity. This can be done with the nonlinear estimation procedures in NLR or FATS.

To fit nonsinusoidal periodicities or any general nonlinear function or to identify cycles produced by two or more independent processes, more than one sinusoidal component must be fitted to the time series. To do this, a sequential process similar to stepwise regression is used, as described in VanLear and Watt (this volume).

Modeling Main Effects

The DFT for the grand mean series shown in Figure 7.3 was constructed and is shown as a periodogram in Figure 7.4. The large amplitude of the Fourier components in the neighborhood of period = 7 and period = 20 confirms the presence of these cycles in the simulation data. But this analysis does not relate these cycles to the presence or absence of the independent variables.

To investigate the effect of the independent variable X_1, periodograms for collapsed Cells 00 and 10 (cells in which X_1 effects are absent) and for collapsed Cells 01 and 11 (cells in which X_1 effects should be present) were prepared. Figure 7.5 shows the periodogram with X_1 absent, and Figure 7.6 shows the periodogram with X_1 present. There is a clear visual difference between these periodograms, with Figure 7.6 showing a strong amplitude in the region of period = 20.

This difference is shown more clearly in the difference periodogram of Figure 7.7. This periodogram is constructed by simply subtracting each amplitude squared value shown in Figure 7.6 (X_1 present) from its corresponding value in Figure 7.5 (X_1 absent). Nonzero values in the difference periodogram thus show cycles that are present in one set of collapsed cells but not in the other. This is precisely what we need to isolate the effect of X_1 from the effect of X_2 or any other confounding

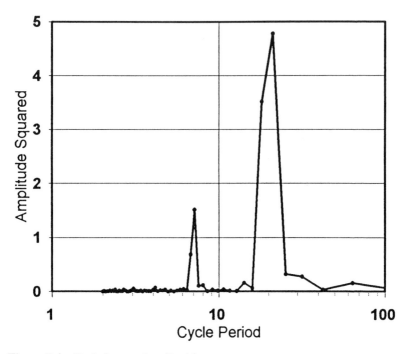

Figure 7.4. Periodogram for all subjects.

variable whose effect is presumably present in both sets of collapsed cells.

Figure 7.7 indicates only one area in which there is a major difference between the two sets of collapsed cells. At period = 21.333, the difference of the squared values is 17.9, whereas at period = 18.29, the difference is 14.5.

Squared values are typically used in periodograms to emphasize strong components. Squared values are also used to make the comparison insensitive to differences in phase angles between the components in the two series. This is important in comparing two series because the orientation of the series starting point with the time origin is usually less important than the simple presence of a periodic component of some frequency in one series and not in the other.

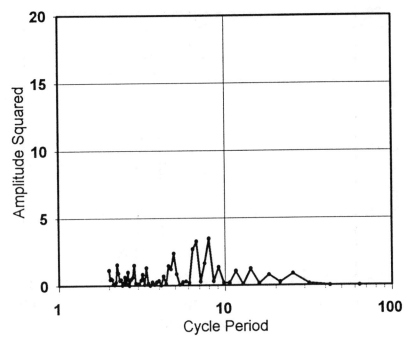

Figure 7.5. Periodogram for Cells 00 and 10 (X_1 is absent).

For example, suppose two series with the same mean μ are compared, both having components of frequency ω and amplitude of R but with a phase difference of $\phi = \pi$ radians (180°). This is the maximum difference that can occur between two series with the same frequency component, as the first series has its maximum at the same time point that the second has its minimum. From Equation 7-3, with the first series as the reference for comparison ($\phi = 0$), $A_1 = R \cos(0) = R$ and $B_1 = -R \sin(0)$ = 0. The second series weights are then $A_2 = R \cos(\pi) = -R$ and $B_2 = -R \sin(\pi) = 0$. Simply subtracting the sine and cosine weights gives the result

$$A_{\text{diff}} = A_1 - A_2 = R - (-R) = 2R,$$

$$B_{\text{diff}} = 0 - 0 = 0.$$

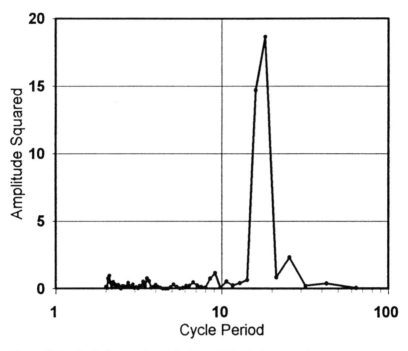

Figure 7.6. Periodogram for Cells 01 and 11 (X_1 is present).

Although both series have the same frequency component at the same amplitude, the difference between the A (and B) weights can vary from 0 to $2R$ in value, with differences in the phase angle. However, the following shows how squaring removes the phase dependency:

$$A^2 + B^2 = [R \cos (\phi)]^2 + [^-R \sin (\phi)]^2$$

$$= R^2 \cos^2 (\phi) + R^2 \sin^2 (\phi) = R^2 [\cos^2 (\phi) + \sin^2 (\phi)]$$

$$= R^2 [1] = R^2 .$$

The amplitude squared of the frequency is thus the sum of the squared cosine and sine weights, regardless of the phase angle ϕ. This means

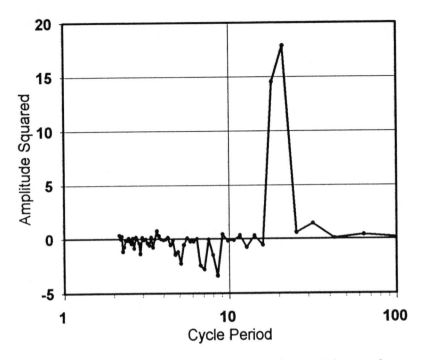

Figure 7.7. Difference periodogram for X_1 main effect (periodogram of Cells 01 and 11 minus periodogram of Cells 00 and 10).

that subtracting the squared amplitude values of one series from that of another is independent of the phase angle between the two series. This gives the contrast necessary for determining whether a periodic component is present in one series and absent in another.

In the difference periodogram shown in Figure 7.7, the difference between the squared amplitude of the components is positive, meaning the amplitude of the cycle at period = 21.33 is larger in collapsed Cells 01 and 11 (X_1 present) than in collapsed Cells 00 and 10 (X_1 absent). All other squared differences between the two collapsed cells are less than 5 units. As the effect of the presence of X_1 is to produce a cyclical effect in the dependent variable with period = 20, it is evident that this procedure has correctly detected a periodicity in the neighborhood of that produced by X_1.

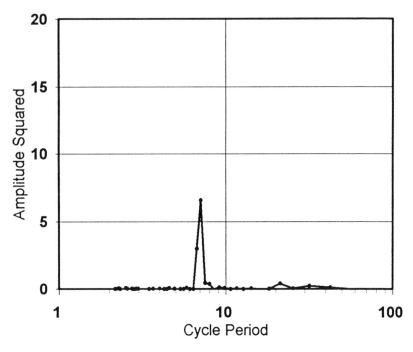

Figure 7.8. Difference periodogram for X_2 main effect (periodogram of Cells 10 and 11 minus periodogram of Cells 00 and 01).

A similar analysis with the other two collapsed cells, shown in Figure 7.8, shows that collapsed Cells 10 and 11 (X_2 present) have a much stronger periodicity at period = 7.11 than do collapsed Cells 00 and 01 (X_2 absent). Again, the effect of the independent variable X_2 is clearly shown.

The next step is to more precisely describe the frequency and amplitude of the cyclical effect. This is done by OLS modeling. Table 7.3 summarizes this modeling for each collapsed cell. The FATS program (Watt, 1988) was used in this case to fit a single periodic component. The starting period of the X_1 and X_2 effects was taken from the difference periodograms.

In the cells in which X_1 is present, the OLS fit indicates a strong component with amplitude = 4.75 and period = 19.99. This is very close

TABLE 7.3   OLS Models for Main and Interaction Effects

Effect	Cells	Start Period	Fitted Period	Amplitude of Cycle	Explained Variance	F-Ratio (df)
Main effects						
X_1 present	00 and 11	21.33	19.99	4.75	.85	431.6
X_1 absent	00 and 10	19.99	.29	.03		(1; 78)
X_2 present	01 and 11	7.11	7.02	2.63	.49	75.4
X_2 absent	00 and 01	7.02	.10	.00		(1; 78)
Interaction effects						
Interaction-A	00 and 11	2.67	2.67	.15	.00	1.54
Interaction-B	01 and 10	2.67	2.67	.38	.02	(1; 78)

to the population values of 5.00 and 20. This strong component explains 85% of the variance in the series in these cells. The component with this period represents the effect of X_1.

To verify that this component is significant, it is contrasted with the same component in the cells in which X_1 is absent. The OLS fit at the same frequency finds a weak component with amplitude = .29 in these collapsed cells. This component explains only 3% of the series variance in these cells.

A similar computation for X_2 gives a cycle with an OLS period of 7.02 and amplitude of 2.63 for the collapsed cells in which X_2 is present (explained variance 49%). The amplitude of the same component is .10 in the cells in which X_2 is absent (explained variance less than 1%).

The common inferential question based on the null hypotheses follows: Is the difference in explained variance due to the independent variables larger than chance alone might produce? An appropriate way to approach this question is to use the model based on the collapsed cells in which the independent variable is absent as a representation of the null hypothesis. The model based on the collapsed cells in which the independent variable is present thus represents the alternative hypothesis. The inferential question then is transformed into this: Is the variance explained by the model based on cells in which the independent variable is present sufficiently larger than the variation explained by the corresponding null model so that chance may be ruled out as a reasonable explanation? If so, we may reject the null hypothesis.

A simple incremental F-ratio (Cohen & Cohen, 1983) will answer this question. The computation of this ratio for the two main effects is shown below:

$$F_{inc-X_1} = \frac{MS_{explained}}{MS_{null\ model}}$$

$$= \frac{[Var.\ explained_{X_1\ present} - Var.\ explained_{X_1\ Absent}]/df_{X_1}}{(1 - Var.\ explained_{X_1\ Present})/(N - df_{X_1} - 1)}$$

$$= \frac{(.85 - .03)/1}{(1 - .85)/(N - 2)} = \frac{.82}{(.15/78)} = \frac{.82}{.0019}$$

$$= 431.6\ ;$$

$$F_{inc-X_2} = \frac{MS_{explained}}{MS_{null\ model}}$$

$$= \frac{[Var.\ explained_{X_2\ present} - Var.\ explained_{X_2\ Absent}]/df_{X_2}}{(1 - Var.\ explained_{X_2\ Present})/(N - df_{X_2} - 1)}$$

$$= \frac{(.49 - .00)/1}{(1 - .49)/(N - 2)} = \frac{.49}{(.51/78)} = \frac{.49}{.0065}$$

$$= 75.4.$$

The degrees of freedom for explained variation in X_1 (numerator df) is 1. X_1 has two levels ($L = 2$), which gives $L - 1$, or 1 df. The error degrees of freedom (denominator df) is the simple error term for unexplained variation in the series. As X_2 also has two levels, its F-ratio has the same degrees of freedom.

Because the F-ratios for both main effects are well beyond the critical F of 3.98 (with 1 and 78 df), we can conclude that there is a significant main effect for both X_1 and X_2. This duplicates the findings of the repeated measures ANOVA. But importantly, the OLS model of each main effect in the harmonic modeling approach adds a description of both the period of the effect and its amplitude. This is valuable information for interpretation of the results, as illustrated in the Meadowcroft chapter in this volume.

Taking the ANOVA analogy a step further, it is also possible to test for interaction effects due to the joint action of X_1 and X_2. To do this, one must contrast the pooled means of the diagonal cells (see Watt & van den Berg, 1995); that is, Cells 00 and 11 must be collapsed into a single series and then contrasted with collapsed Cells 01 and 10.

The logic of this approach can be seen by examining Table 7-1. Collapsed Cells 00 and 11 will contain both period = 7 and period = 20 components (Cell 00 has neither; Cell 11 has both). Collapsed Cells 01 and 10 will also have both components (Cell 01 has period = 20; Cell 10 has period = 7). Subtracting the periodograms of the two collapsed cells will cancel any common components, including the main effects. Only components that are present disproportionately will be strong in the difference periodogram.

This will detect interaction effects at the same frequencies as the main effects (e.g., multiplicative effects of the independent variables), and it will also detect new periodic or nonlinear components associated with particular combinations of the independent variable. Detecting cyclical interactions at the same frequencies as the main effects is the analog of the ANOVA interaction effect. But detection of interaction at differing frequencies is beyond the ability of ANOVA. Finding interaction effects at differing frequencies represents the detection of a new functional response of the dependent variable as a result of the joint combination of the independent variables.

As an example of a multiplicative effect, suppose the joint presence of X_1 and X_2 increased the amplitude of the resultant cycles by 10%. The peak amplitudes in each of the cells would be as follows:

Cell 00: $R_7 = 0$; $R_{20} = 0$

Cell 01: $R_7 = 0$; $R_{20} = 5$

Cell 10: $R_7 = 2.5$; $R_{20} = 0$

Cell 11: $R_7 = 2.5 + .25 = 2.75$; $R_{20} = 5 + .50 = 5.50$

Collapsed Cells 00 and 11: $R_7 = 0 + 2.75 = 2.75$; $R_{20} = 0 + 5.50 = 5.50$

Collapsed Cells 01 and 10: $Rv_7 = 0 + 2.5 = 2.5$; $R_{20} = 5 + 0 = 5$

Difference between collapsed cells: $R_7 = .25$; $R_{20} = .50$

In a similar vein, suppose the joint presence of X_1 and X_2 produce a new cyclical effect with an amplitude of 3 and a period of 10. The contrasted peak amplitudes would then be as follows:

Cell 00: $R_7 = 0$; $R_{20} = 0$; $R_{10} = 0$

Cell 01: $R_7 = 0$; $R_{20} = 5$; $R_{10} = 0$

Cell 10: $R_7 = 2.5$; $R_{20} = 0$; $R_{10} = 0$

Cell 11: $R_7 = 2.5$; $R_{20} = 5$; $R_{10} = 3$

Collapsed Cells 00 and 11: $R_7 = 0 + 2.5$; $R_{20} = 0 + 5$; $R_{10} = 0 + 3$

Collapsed Cells 01 and 10: $R_7 = 0 + 2.5$; $R_{20} = 5 + 0$; $R_{10} = 0 + 0$

Difference between collapsed cells: $R_{10} = 3$

Here the interaction difference is the new component produced by the interaction effect.

To test interactions in the simulation data, the classical ANOVA approach is used, in which the variance due to the main effects is removed before testing for interaction effects (sometimes referred to as "adjusting the cell means for the main effects"). In the case of cyclical main effects, this is done by replacing the original subjects' mean values in the cells with the residual between that value and the OLS model of the main effects:

$$x'_t = x_t - \{[A_1 \cos(\omega_1 t) + B_1 \sin(\omega_1 t)]$$

$$+ [A_2 \cos(\omega_2 t) + B_2 \sin(\omega_2 t)]\}. \quad [7\text{-}5]$$

This removes the two main effects from all cells. The procedures for creating the collapsed cells' data, based on x'_t, the difference periodogram, and the collapsed cell models are identical to those used for testing the main effects.

Figure 7.9 shows the difference periodogram between the two sets of collapsed cells. The strongest component (larger in Cells 01 and 10, so it is shown as a negative peak in the periodogram) is at period = 2.6667. This component was fitted, using FATS, to the x'_t data in each cell. The model for Cells 00 and 10 explained less than 1% of the variance; the model for Cells 01 and 10 explained 2%. The F-ratio for the interaction effect is thus:

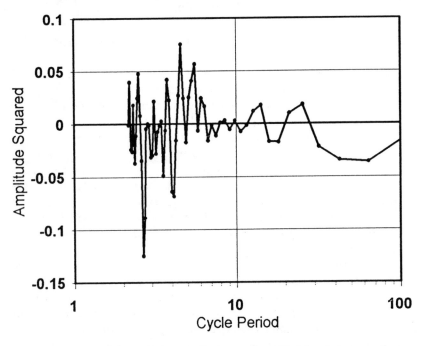

Figure 7.9. Difference periodogram for interaction effect (periodogram of Cells 00 and 11 minus periodogram of Cells 01 and 10).

$$F_{Inc. - Interaction} =$$

$$\frac{[Var.\ explained\ by\ model\ A - Var.\ explained\ by\ model\ B)/1}{(1 - Var.\ explained\ by\ model\ B)/(N-2)}$$

$$= \frac{(.02-.00)/1}{(1-.02)/78} = \frac{.02}{.013} = 1.54$$

This F-ratio again has 1 and 78 degrees of freedom. It is lower than the critical value, correctly indicating that no $X_1 \times X_2$ interaction is present in the data.

Conclusion

The procedures illustrated in this chapter provide a guide for analyzing nonlinear periodic effects in a simple experimental design. These procedures can be extended to handle more than two independent variables and/or more than two levels of any independent variable. For example, a $2 \times 2 \times 2$ design can be analyzed with the same procedures by simply constructing the correct collapsed cells for the contrasts.

Multiple levels of the independent variables, such as a 3×3 design, can also be analyzed, but the variance for each main effect and the interaction effect will be produced by a set of contrasts and a set of OLS harmonic models rather than by a single contrast and model. Reference to a standard text such as Cohen and Cohen (1983) for the logic of coding the effects of nominal independent variables will show the correct procedure for constructing the collapsed cell contrasts and the incremental F-ratios.

Although the effect in the simulation data was a simple cycle, the procedure can be used with any linear or nonlinear effect (with respect to time). This is somewhat more complicated than the simple cycle case, as a single functional relationship may be represented by a number of simple sinusoidal components. In the procedures illustrated above, each OLS model would have several frequency components rather than a single one. The procedures are thus quite general and quite powerful.

Cellular Automata as Models
of Unintended Consequences
# of Organizational Communication

STEVEN R. CORMAN

The thing that really piqued my interest in cellular automata was the following easy illustration. Take a piece of graph paper and color in two or three randomly selected cells on the top line. Each of the remaining lines is generated by applying a rule to the cells of the line immediately above. To get the second line, for example, start with the second cell. If on line 1 either cell 1 or cell 3 is colored in *but not both*, color cell 2 of line 2. Now apply the same rule for cell 3: If one or the other of its neighboring cells on line 1 is colored in but not both, then color cell 3 on line 2. Apply this procedure for all the remaining cells, "wrapping" the ends of the line (i.e., the last cell is the left neighbor for the first cell and the first cell is the right neighbor for the last cell).

When you repeat this process for a few successive lines, an interesting pattern of triangles begins to develop. As the generations go on past a

---

I would like to thank Noshir Contractor, Arthur VanLear, and James Watt for their very helpful comments on an earlier draft. An earlier version of this chapter was presented at the Arizona State University conference "Organizational Communication: Perspectives for the 90's," held in Tempe.

Figure 8.1. Automaton described in introductory example, iterated several hundred times (grid = 640 columns wide × 480 rows long).

few lines the complexity increases to a rather startling level: Triangles of all different sizes appear. Some are embedded in larger triangles, and those are occasionally embedded in even higher-order triangles (see Figure 8.1).[1] This is an impressive demonstration. Very complex structure results from the application of a simple rule, and the rule is applied by individuals based on their local circumstances. Other than the fact that all individuals are following the same rule, there is no need to posit any kind of collective coordination or intent to explain the resulting complex structure. This simple rule that causes complicated structure has interesting implications for organizational communication, as it suggests that the complexity we observe therein may not necessarily result from teleological behavior of the collective.

In this chapter I argue that cellular automation (CA) models represent a promising technique for modeling organizational communication phenomena of this kind. I begin by reviewing the history of CA models, some of their more important formal characteristics and varieties, and their application in other areas of science. Next, I argue that they are especially good models for unintended consequences of organizational communication and offer a reductionist baseline for building explanations of communicative emergence or "assembly." I give illustrations of both these uses. Finally, I discuss two approaches to the validation of CA models.

History of CA Models

Cellular automata were first proposed as models of complex, self-reproducing systems by von Neumann (1966) and were popularized by Wolfram (1983, 1984, 1986). At base they consist of a *domain* of discrete areas of space, referred to as *cells*. Each cell can assume some finite number of *states*, where the state of individual cells is determined in *discrete time steps* according to some *transition rule* applied by all cells depending on some *neighborhood* of surrounding cells:

$$x_i^t = \varphi[x_{i-r}^{t-1}, x_{i-r+1}^{t-1}, \ldots, x_{i+r}^{t-1} = 1] \qquad [8\text{-}1]$$

where x_i represents a cell that can take on any of k states, k represents some discrete period of time, r is an interval or radius defining the neighborhood of x_i, and φ represents the transition rule. For the above "triangles" example $k = 2$, $r = 1$, and

$$\varphi = set\ x_i^t \begin{Bmatrix} 1\ if\ [\ x_{i-1}^{t-1} = 1 \vee x_{i+1}^{t-1} = 1] \\ 0\ otherwise \end{Bmatrix}. \qquad [8\text{-}2]$$

Whereas many approaches described in this book rely on the notion of *clock time*, cellular automata are *event time* models (see VanLear and Watt, this volume), in which time "happens" in discrete units.

Many varieties of automata have been developed, varying in terms of dimensionality, determinism, and neighborhood restrictions. Regarding *dimensionality*, the cells in an automaton occupy space, and space can be conceptualized on more than the one dimension represented in the above model. A well-known example of a two-dimensional automaton is the game of LIFE (see Berlekamp, Conway, & Guy, 1982), which is widely available on computer networks.[2] LIFE simulates a population of living organisms that live or die based on their number of living neighbors. Rather than producing triangles, the algorithm generates clusters of cells that expand, contract, die out, take over other clusters, and even oscillate periodically, depending on starting conditions and thresholds set in the transition rule. Two-dimensional automata are often used to model pattern recognition processes (Broggi, d'Andrea, & Destri, 1993) and biological phenomena that occur on surfaces such as that of the earth (Colasanti & Grime, 1993; Deadman, Brown, & Gimblett, 1993). Automata of even higher dimension are also used, especially in studies of fluid dynamics (e.g., Kohring, 1992).

CA models also vary in terms of their assumptions of determinism. Many CA models use deterministic transition rules, such as that in Equation 8-2 above, because they model physical laws assumed to be time-reversal invariant (Gutowitz, 1991). However, in social systems, time-reversal invariance is not normally assumed, and totally "uniform patterns are rarely seen to exist. Moreover, such systems have many parameters that vary randomly. It seems reasonable, therefore, to require that the state of such systems at step $t + 1$ be determined not only by the state at step t, but also by parameters that are essentially random in nature" (Bhargava, Kumar, & Mukherjee, 1993, p. 90). *Stochastic cellular automata*, then, rely on transition probabilities or apply decision rules as constraints on random behavior. Such models describe innovation diffusion processes (Bhargava et al., 1993), population migration patterns (White & Engelen, 1993), and social behavior in insects (Millonas, 1993).

Finally, CA models vary in terms of *constraints on the neighborhood* of the cells. Many of the examples cited above assume that the effects being modeled depend critically on spatial proximity, and the transition rule thus operates on the past states of one or two radii of neighboring cells. However, this restriction is not necessary for CA models. The neighborhood of a CA model may include any number of surrounding cells, up to and including all the other cells in the domain of the automaton. In neural networks (see Woelfel, 1993), which are special cases of cellular automata (Reitman, 1989), connections are often quite widespread.

Cellular automata are interesting models that are being fruitfully applied in many areas of science. While any of the foregoing kinds of automata have potential application to the study of dynamic patterns in organizational communication, three generalizations seem warranted regarding which are most likely to bear fruit. First, deterministic automata do not seem well suited for modeling communication phenomena. There is widespread agreement that human communication is not governed by laws. At best, it is subject to rules. Even functionalist theorists hold that such rules are mediated by volition of communicators (see Cushman, King, & Smith, 1990), and stochastic automata are better suited for modeling such cases.

The second generalization has to do with the effects of space on communication in organizations. There is a fair amount of evidence that space in organizations and other large social collectives is functionally discrete (Corman, 1990; Hatch, 1987; Rice, 1993) and delimited by barriers. Members of subgroups of these collectives may be separated by some measurable distance (e.g., in a shared office or work area), but especially if they are insulated from the larger organization by a barrier, that distance may not place any significant *practical* restrictions on communication within the group. When this is true, one need not hypothesize multidimensional automata with neighborhood restrictions. Only one dimension is necessary to represent members as discrete corporeal elements in an automaton, and unlimited-neighborhood automata will often be appropriate where there is a lack of effective spatial constraint on action.

Of course, higher-dimensional space and space-limitation of action are important in some theoretical formulations. In these cases the dimensionality and neighborhood size of the automaton would need to reflect these effects. One notable application of CA models to the study of communication in groups is Latané's (in press) dynamic social impact model. He uses distance as an indicator of the influence that one person is likely to have on another. He concludes that "impact decreases as a function of the distance squared ($d/d^2 = 1/d$). Social influence thus seems to be very much a local phenomenon, even for academic social psychologists whose disciplinary interests often correspond most with those of people located at great distance" (Latané, in press, p. 13; see also Latané & Nowak, in press).[3] Thus, I do not mean to imply that multidimensionality and restricted neighborhoods are never necessary in CA models of communication, only that they are not always necessary.

Finally, Gutowitz (1991) distinguishes two broad uses of CA models in physics: "The forward problem is: Given a cellular automaton rule, determine (predict) its properties. The inverse problem is: Given a description of some properties, find a rule, or set of rules, which have these properties" (p. vii). Although both tacks may have application in communication research, the inverse problem is the most exigent because it asks whether human communication systems can even be represented as automata.

What Can CA Models Do
for Communication Research?

To date, cellular automata have mainly been applied to the study of physical and biological phenomena, and to a lesser extent to modeling social behavior of living organisms. The hazards of generalizing too quickly from the natural to the social domain are well known, and CA models have barely been explored as possibilities for the study of human communication. It is a truism, then, that the full potential of CA models can only be known as we develop more experience applying them. Nonetheless, I believe that existing use of CA models suggests two especially "good bets" for their application in communication research.

Unintended Consequences
of Collective Communication

First, CA models seem especially well suited to studying the unintended consequences of collective communication behavior. Unintended consequences have traditionally interested social scientists, especially sociologists. Merton's (1936) concept of unanticipated consequences and discussions of manifest versus latent functions (Merton, 1963) of action are well known. More recently, unintended consequences have assumed a central role in Giddens's (1984) structuration theory, and it is on his ideas that I focus here.

Giddens (1984) holds that the study of the unintended consequences of action is "fundamental to the sociological enterprise" (p. 12). The effects of situated action constitute conditions *of* further situated action, providing an institutional mechanism through which the consequences of an act can "stretch" across time and space away from the situation of copresence where it occurs. Giddens offers an interesting example of how unintended consequences of action might result in a social problem familiar to us all:

A pattern of ethnic segregation might develop, without any of those involved intending this to happen, in the following way. . . . Imagine a chessboard which has a set of five-pence pieces and a set of ten-pence pieces. These are distributed randomly on the board, as individuals might be in an urban area. It is presumed that, while they feel no hostility to the other group, the members of each group do not want to live in a neighborhood where they are ethnically a minority. On the chessboard each piece is moved around until it is in a position such that at least 50 percent of the adjoining pieces are of the same type. The result is a pattern of extreme segregation. The ten-cent pieces end up as a sort of ghetto in the midst of the five-cent ones. The "composition effect" is an outcome of an aggregate of acts . . . each of which was intentionally carried out. But the eventual outcome is neither intended nor desired by anyone. It is, as it were, everyone's doing and no one's. (p. 10)

In this example, the intent of the individuals is very consistent with the idea of *integration;* anyone would be happy living where 50% of their neighbors are like them. However, the collective result of applying this intent is extreme *segregation,* an outcome that can be described as both unintended and perverse.

Giddens (1984) is not at all specific about how the "rearranging" process that moves pieces around the chess board would work, and this is indeed where things get more complicated.[4] To avoid digressing too much I will leave interested readers to think out that problem more fully. But Giddens's example demonstrates a mode of analysis where "a definite 'end result' is taken as the phenomenon to be explained, and that end result is shown to derive as an unintended consequence from an aggregate of courses of intentional conduct" (p. 13).[5] His illustration contains the hallmarks of a process of cellular automation. A *domain* of discrete sites (chessboard/city) is specified, and these are *cells* (coins/people). The states of the cells are distributed in a *random start.* Each cell obeys a simple *transition rule,* which is *applied locally* based on attributes of its *neighborhood* (if half or more of your neighbors are like you, then stay put, otherwise move).

CA models of unintended consequences are promising because they can challenge commonly held teleological assumptions. It is normal for social theorists to assume that collective phenomena are intentional, as illustrated by the fact that they single out unintended consequences as a special topic. Communication scholars share this bias too. Some attention has been paid to the issue of mindlessness in interpersonal communication (Langer, 1978) and group communication (Hewes, 1985), but mostly we treat verbal communication as intentional action. An organization is a collection of these intentionally communicating individuals, so there is a natural tendency to assume intent at the collective level also. This is perhaps most evident in critical-theoretic approaches, which attribute social ills to the coordinated, intentional, discursive actions of powerful groups. For example, Ranson, Hinings, and Greenwood (1980) argue that the "structural framework [of an organization] is not some abstract chart but one of the crucial instruments by which groups perpetuate their power and control in organizations" (p. 8). Another example of assumed collective intentionality is dystopian criticism of information technology. For example, Winner (1992) argues that computer systems are exquisite instruments of control, which management will impose with gusto so that "workers' motions can be ubiquitously monitored in units calculable to the nearest microsecond. . . . Here is an electronic equivalent of Jeremy Bentham's Panopticon" (pp. 57-59).

CA models offer an alternative to this assumption of collective intent, because they show that very complex collective behavior can result from the application of simple rules by individuals acting based on local conditions. Whereas a structural Marxist might explain segregation as the outcome of oppression by a dominant group, a CA model might show that it is only a perverse result of people avoiding social isolation, as in the illustration by Giddens above. Where Winner might explain the diffusion of information technology as a move by management to more thoroughly exploit workers, a CA model might show that it is a process of peer-to-peer propagation of attitudes through a communication network (see Contractor and Grant, this volume).

CA models cannot "falsify" critical explanations in the Popperian sense: It is not clear how one could formulate the competing explanations in similar terms such that a competitive empirical test would be possible. However, there are at least two reasons why one might favor a CA explanation in the absence of a definitive test. First, CA models are more parsimonious than explanations that assume collective intent. Hanneman (1988) notes that the complexity of a system depends on four factors: (a) the elements in its *state space*, that is, the number of elements in the system and the number of values they can take on; (b) the interconnection of the elements in the state space; (c) the order of functional forms connecting the states to one another; and (d) the order of the over-time relations between the states. By these criteria, any explanation that assumes intentional collective control of a group is more complex than a CA model of the same phenomenon, as long as it does not preclude action and interaction on the individual level.[6] This is because in addition to acting and interacting individuals, its state space must include a coordinating entity. The coordinating entity must have connections to the elements it coordinates and has a complex structure itself. Moreover, its control mechanisms are almost certainly more complex than the simple rules applied to local conditions that are characteristic of CA models.

A second and related advantage of CA models is that they contain a definite generative mechanism for collective structure. Where critical approaches attribute collective structure to vaguely defined processes of, for example, "hegemony" or "domination," CA models offer explicit rules that govern the individual actions that lead to structure. For example, a CA model of my own design, called POWERPLAY (Corman, 1990), shows how a dominance hierarchy could develop from the application of simple behavioral rules by individuals.

Assume for the purposes of the model that time is unitized according to conflict episodes, so that we are modeling a system of constant conflict within a group of individuals, represented as a set of cells. Assume further that these members are an interacting, face-to-face, small group, with no effective spatial constraints on their conflict behavior. As such, they may be modeled as a one-dimensional stochastic automaton with an unlimited neighborhood. Each member (cell) has the goal of winning every conflict in which it engages. Furthermore, each member stores information about its *power*, defined as its percentage of wins in the most recent 20 conflicts. It also stores information about the *revenge factor* for all the other members, defined as the proportion of past conflicts where each of the others has attacked the member.

The simulation begins with zero history and each member having equal power. In each round, the transition rules are applied such that all members select targets for a conflict episode; then all the conflicts are resolved simultaneously. A given member selects a target only if one or more cells have lower power than itself. If one of the others has the least power, then it is made the target, but if there are ties, then those members are ordered according to their revenge factor. If one of these members has the highest revenge factor, it is targeted. Otherwise, a random choice is made between the remaining members.[7] Once all members have selected targets, the targeted members are engaged, and the conflicts are resolved through a random draw weighted by the power of the cell being

TABLE 8.1   Pseudocode Representation of the POWERPLAY Algorithm

```
while no person has complete power:
    for each cell determine target
        select all cells with power ≤ your power
        set n to number of cells selected
        conditions
            when n is 0
                set target to null
            when n is 1
                set target to selected cell
            when n > 1
                order selected cells according to their power
                if only one cell has the least power then
                    set target to that cell
                otherwise
                    order cells according to need-for-revenge
                    if only one cell has highest need-for-revenge
                        set target to that cell
                    otherwise
                        choose target randomly from tied cells
                    end if
                end if
        end conditions
    end for
    for each cell initiate conflict with target
        if target is not null
            set x to random number between 1 and 100*  Recall that power is expressed
                                                        as a percentage of wins
                                                        in the last 20 conflicts
            if x > power of target
                register a loss for target
                register a win for self
            otherwise
                register a win for target
                register a loss for self
            end if
        end if
    end for
end while
```

engaged.[8] Finally, the revenge factors and power values for the members are updated. Rounds continue until one cell remains with all the power. Table 8.1 gives a pseudocode representation of the POWERPLAY algorithm.

TABLE 8.2 Statistics From an Example Run of POWERPLAY

Player	Round Out	Conflicts	Wins	Batting Average
C	15	57	15	0.26
E	32	149	37	0.25
F	76	270	70	0.26
I	116	300	99	0.33
H	136	205	108	0.53
G	159	246	135	0.55
A	263	509	246	0.48
J	320	462	247	0.53
B	390	415	307	0.59
D	Winner	415	307	0.74

After a few rounds, one can stop this simulation at any point and order the cells according to how much power they have, defining a power hierarchy. Under the set of rules given above, members often "gang up" on the weakest member until he or she is out, behavior consistent with that of a coalition. After more play, some cells lose all their power and drop out of the action (as eventually do all of the cells but one). If one is willing to equate dropping out with being dominated, the length of time a member stays in can be used to locate it in a structure of domination (see Table 8.2). It is not hard to imagine how such a process like this playing in a real organization might result in an employee getting "stuck," assigned to an undesirable job because he or she lost out early in an extended conflict process. Yet there is no active collective coordination. Individuals are simply following their interests in winning conflicts and getting revenge for past attacks. Although a dominance hierarchy emerges, no individual in the simulation intends for this to happen.

In summary, one thing that CA models do for communication research is offer a new method of challenging explanations of communication that assume collective intent. Cellular automata can generate complex collective behavior through application of simple rules by individuals based on local conditions, and such structure may therefore be regarded as unintended. If CA models can account for observed structure in collective communication, it becomes questionable why more complex postulates of collective-level intent are necessary.

This is not to say that the models allow for no collective coordination on any level, however. Taken in isolation, CA models beg the question of how it is that all cells come to follow the same transition rules. Sometimes, it may be plausible to argue that human cells act in ways that are instinctual, as in competing and seeking revenge in POWER-PLAY. But once we allow that the rules might be normative or otherwise socially learned, collective level coordination becomes an issue again. It might be, for example, that a collective-level process causes cells to obey norms or rules that promote the automatic development of particular kinds of structure. Mumby (1987), for example, favors the view that shared narratives in organizations promote common accounts of organizing, which we could view as interpretive rules. The idea that collective interaction processes might create rules that guide automatic behavior is an intriguing one, suggestive of Giddens's (1984) distinction between *system* (interaction between agents in circumstances of copresence), which would be represented by the automaton, and *structure* (rules and resources produced and reproduced in interaction), which would be represented by the transition rules. So CA models are hardly the death knell of theories assuming collective coordination at any level. They do, however, suggest a very different picture of the way collective coordination might operate. If Giddens's segregation automaton from above were developed and validated, it would imply that *integrationist* ideologies are most responsible for observed patterns of segregation!

Reductionist Baseline for Model Building

The second promising use of CA models is as reductionist baselines for building explanations of communicative emergence. Here an automaton is used to generate a critical foil or "expected value" for collective communication under given transition rules. Its outputs can be compared, either formally or interpretively, to actual communication to identify points of similarity and contrast. The CA model might then be tuned in an attempt to better account for the phenomenon. It could also serve to highlight what is *un*automatic about collective communication, suggesting fruitful areas for theoretical development.

An example of this kind of application comes from an old but unresolved debate about whether juries, when deliberating, do anything more than combine prediscussion preferences according to simple rules. Davis (1973) argues that jury deliberation is more or less just a formality. Jurors are simply enacting a decision predetermined by social decision schemes applied to their prediscussion preferences. Poole, McPhee, and Seibold (1982), using interaction analysis and modeling techniques, argue that communication is more than *pro forma*, that group discourse does, at least sometimes, cause decisions to emerge that differ from those predicted by social decision schemes.

Both sides have published results supporting their positions. Rather than joining this debate directly, I intend to show how CA models offer an additional and interesting approach to the same issue. An implication of Davis's (1973) position is that juries' deliberations are automatic. When juries "make" a decision they behave according to rules that operate on prediscussion preferences. Members engage in seemingly organized interaction where they and other jury members express their preferences, but they do not influence one another, and no changes in individual preference result. One way of assessing the reasonableness of a social decision schemes explanation, then, would be to attempt to create an automatic jury to see if and how their deliberations could not be distinguished from those of an actual jury.

Hewes's (1986) notion of socioegocentric group communication suggests a way to approach this task. He argues that decision interaction might result from nothing more than individual members' intentional efforts to solve the problem in their own minds while appearing to communicatively engage other group members. He points out that group theorists usually begin from the premise that decision-making communication "makes a difference" in producing group outcomes. Their emphasis, therefore, is on using communication behavior to explain how a group earns (or fails to earn) an advantage over a noninteracting collection of individuals. Hewes (1986) argues that we might just as easily assume that "much, if not all, small group communication is epiphenominal—that is, identifiable noninteractive factors can explain group communication, and it is these noninteractive inputs that produce decision outputs" (p. 278), a theme that resonates with that of Davis (1973). Specifically, Hewes says, *intra*personal decision making, a cognitively demanding task, may simply be played out in a context of social norms regarding turn taking and conversation management:

> The conversants are unable to manage their attention so as to meet at least two goals at the same time—formulating their own thoughts while attempting to manage the flow of conversation with full consideration of the other's contributions to it. . . . Interactants appear to act so as to minimize their own deficiencies by employing a structural norm of conversation (turn-taking) and a cosmetic bid toward meaningful extension of the conversation (vacuous acknowledgments). (pp. 279-280)

In Davis's view, juries apply social decision schemes without influencing one another or changing their preference. However, juries do at least *seem* to deliberate. The SEM is therefore a good basis for an automatic jury because it suggests a way they could seem to interact without really communicating or influencing one another. In the socioegocentric automaton, jurors are represented by cells in a limited spatial domain acting in discrete time. They express their unchanging opinions on guilt or innocence, take turns doing so, and use vacuous acknowledgments to give the illusion of interaction.

I used interaction data from mock jury deliberations to construct a socioegocentric automaton of this kind. Mock juries, composed of students from basic psychology classes at a midwestern university, were formed for another study (see Davis, Nagao, Spitzer, & Stasser, 1981, for a full description of the methods). Each jury viewed a videotape of a fictitious murder trial where testimony and evidence for the prosecution and defense were presented by actors. They then went on to deliberations where their task was to render a guilty or not-guilt verdict. The deliberations were taped.

Tapes from the deliberations of four 4-person juries were used for this example. The tapes were transcribed and analyzed to yield lists of reasons for and against a guilty verdict.[9] Applying the analysis across the four mock juries, I compiled lists of 35 reasons for a guilty verdict and 47 reasons for a not-guilty verdict.

Hewes's (1985) work does not address the subject of how acknowledgments should be accounted for in a socioegocentric model. In the mock jury transcripts, many acknowledgments were evident, always at the beginning of a turn. Examples included "right," "that's true," "exactly," and "yeah, you're right." There were also what might be called negative acknowledgments, such as "but," "wait, wait," and "well, I don't know." The kind of acknowledgment used by the group members consistently varied according to the valence of the preceding member's comment. Hence, separate lists of eight agree-acknowledgments and eight disagree-acknowledgments were developed from the transcripts, and other logical possibilities were added arbitrarily. Finally, members sometimes gave two reasons in a row for their positions, separated by connecting phrases; a list of five such connective phrases was developed from the transcripts to allow for this behavior.

Using this database of guilty and not-guilty reasons, vacuous acknowledgments for agreements/disagreements, and connectives, a four-cell stochastic CA with an unrestricted neighborhood was implemented. The starting assumptions were that (a) members are either for a guilty or not-guilty verdict and this preference does not change over the course discussion, (b) members always express reasons that are consistent with their preferences and choose these from a set of possible reasons held in common by all members with the same preference, (c) members always precede their reasons with a vacuous agree-acknowledgment or disagree-acknowledgment, depending on their preference and the valence of the immediately preceding statement, (d) each member bids for the floor every turn, and (e) bids are resolved randomly.

A brief example of output from this automaton is shown in Table 8.3. Readers can judge for themselves the plausibility of the interaction shown in the transcript, but it seems unsettlingly plausible to me. The comments follow themes, for example in the first five turns, although they are chosen randomly. And even when Mark, in Statement 8, makes an ambiguous reference ("he came in with that") it is easy enough to fill in the blanks (especially, one could imagine, for the other "jurors").

At the same time, there are differences between this transcript and the actual transcripts that are worth noting. First, the CA algorithm adds an acknowledgment every turn. In the actual transcripts, only 1/4 to 1/3 of the statements contained acknowledgments. The overabundance of acknowledgments makes the interaction seem unnatural, as if differences of opinion and agreements between members are being overemphasized.

Second, members follow themselves more than seems natural. In the actual transcript, members sometimes expound on reasons at some length. They give more detail about why they hold a particular position but rarely give more than one substantively different reason in a row. This happens twice in the brief example shown in Table 8.3.

Finally, although space considerations prevent me from showing this, more extended runs of the above algorithm show reasons being reused, sometimes repeatedly. This kind of repetition is unlike the interacting groups, who tend not to revisit topics so much. Nothing in the algorithm prevents a cell from obtaining the floor twice in a row and giving the same randomly chosen reason both times, and this sort of thing occasionally crops up in longer runs.

Any good model-building effort involves refinement of the model to make it more consistent with observed phenomena, and this one could be improved. Acknowledgments could be added not every turn, but at

TABLE 8.3   Sample Interaction Produced by the Socioegocentric
Automaton

Mark: I don't think he's guilty. if you go by proof and by what the, as far as what the lawyers say, how they present their stories and everything, um, there really was no witnesses to say that beyond a reasonable doubt . . . the only thing that's holding me back is this reasonable doubt stuff.

Rick: Wait a minute. What it is, is that I don't believe in the law, but still by the law I believe he's guilty.

Scot: I don't know about that. He was riled up.

Dave: But you have to admit, it's still attempted murder and they'll put him away for a long time, y'know.

Rick: Yeah it doesn't even have to be premeditated, if you heard the second part of the judge's thing. it just has to be doing it and causing and injury that could kill.

Mark: But on the other hand, the one guy was probably a little drunk, and the other guy, the waitress said he was upset when he came in, so those two things it could really go out of hand.

Rick: Wait a minute. There was something else too. The first guy . . . um said that . . . he said that like a glass flew or something and that broke, but he didn't say anything about a bottle.

Mark: I don't know about that. He stabbed him in the side. He didn't necessarily stab him in the chest or something . plus its, it doesn't seem like he came in with really with that . . . y'know what I mean.

Rick: Yeah, but I really think that he did go after him with the glass.

Mark: Well that may be, but he could have done this in a fit of rage. Not to even hurt the guy just because he was mad.

Rick: Wait a minute. I think they proved beyond a reasonable doubt that Adams did go after . . . after. and not only that, but the only reason I wouldn't say its attempted murder is because, first of all they have no witnesses. I mean the girl, the waitress, she just walked in there and stuff. And so they really have no witnesses.

Dave: I see what you mean. See they were probably both drunk and could've come from another bar too.

Scot: Well that may be, but see I would know that if I stabbed a person in the side, if I wanted to . . . ok if I wanted to stab a person with the intent to kill a person I would stab, I would not stab him in the side. I would more like if anything go for the back or the front or, I mean anything.

---

random with a lower probability (say, .25) to provide a more realistic usage rate. This would amount to an important substantive change from the point of view of the SEM: Group members neither have random number generators in their heads nor flip coins to formulate comments, so a full account would have to posit some cognitive process that is responsible for regulating members' use of acknowledgments. This may seem like a small cognitive load compared to full-blown discursive involvement, but we must consider that the above algorithm already gives members more cognitive credit than the SEM, in that it assumes members adapt their acknowledgments to the valence of the preceding statement. Problems 2 and 3 could be reduced, although not eliminated, by using larger databases of reasons. They might also be solved by using more complex turn-taking mechanisms, but again these would need to operate via some plausible cognitive mechanism operating in group members.

It is an open question whether this automaton can be improved to the point where its interaction could not be distinguished from a deliberating jury. If it can, then we would have an explanation for how juries can sound like they are deliberating in earnest when they are in fact just automatically applying social decision schemes. To the extent that it falls short it will reveal important ways the deliberation process differs from automatic speech.

Validation of CA Models

In closing, I discuss the validation of CA models in general terms. There are two approaches to this problem. In the *formal approach*, one tests the behavior of an automaton to see whether it conforms to some theoretical expectation or corresponds in some particular way with structure in a human system of communication. All one needs is the ability to quantitatively measure the states or aggregate structure of the automaton, then practically any modeling method can be applied to analyze these measurements.

For example, one might argue that some transition rule produces a characteristic progression toward differentiation. To test this argument, measures of differentiation could be made at each time step while running the CA model, and the resulting time series could be analyzed to determine whether it conforms to the predicted pattern. Automata hypothesized to produce abrupt structural transitions could be studied using interrupted time series experiments, or alternatively, with tests of stationarity.

The real and the simulated can be compared too. One way of testing the socioegocentric automaton proposed above would be to compare the sequential structure of its deliberations to those of a "live" jury using Markov or semi-Markov analysis and a suitable coding system (see Hewes, 1979). For example, one might test whether the marginal distribution of interacts in the jury are (or are not) significantly different from those expected under the automatic model. Interactional organization in jury deliberations might be demonstrated at the second- or third-order process, with interaction organized around groups of sequential utterances. This would show that the socioegocentric automaton, which is based on a first-order transition rule, could not adequately account for the group interaction. One critique I made of the model above, that members follow themselves more than seems natural, can also be conceptualized in terms of waiting time and holding time in semi-Markov analysis. Here again, the observed parameters of the automaton could be formally compared to those of deliberating juries.

Although it is possible to formally test CA models, it would be a mistake to assume that this is their only proper use. Complex adaptive systems are

> hard to analyze with standard mathematics. Most of the conventional techniques like calculus or linear analysis are very well suited to describe unchanging particles moving in a fixed environment. But to get a really deep understanding of . . . complex systems in general, what you need are mathematics and computer simulation techniques that emphasize internal models, the emergence of new building blocks, and the rich web of interaction between multiple agents. (Waldrop, 1992, p. 147, citing John H. Holland)

A CA model, then, can be thought of as an act of interpretation cast in semimathmatical theoretical language (see Hanneman, 1988, pp. 20-27). Thus, the *interpretive approach* to validating CA models relies on qualitative judgments of the modelers and other observers to assess the fit of the simulation to complex behavior of collectives being modeled. Here one asks, does the automaton look, sound, and/or behave like the phenomenon in question?

This was the approach I took above in discussing the socioegocentric automaton. Another illustration I will use in closing is Reynolds's (1987) model of flying "boids." His model is not a cellular automaton but a kissing cousin based on assumptions of continuous time and continuous space. It is a dramatic example of how well automatic models can work and how they are often both developed and validated using an interpretive approach.

Reynolds (1987) proposes that flocking birds are like particle systems.[10] Birds are conceptualized as moving particles, "boids," that pursue a goal while engaging in rule-based interactions with other boids. Flocking, for example, can be explained as group movement toward a perch governed by three rules. *Collision avoidance* means that a boid tries to avoid collisions with other boids nearby. *Velocity matching* means that a boid tries to match its flying speed with that of nearby flockmates. *Centering* stipulates that a boid tries to stay as close as possible to most other boids.

Interested readers can see the original article for a complete description of the model. The point here is that when Reynolds's simulation is run, it *looks like* flocking birds. Unfortunately, I cannot show this in a book chapter. As a substitute, I offer Figure 8.2, a few still frames from a boids simulation of a flock flying around columns. If the boids were more anatomically realistic, one could easily mistake Figure 8.2 for freeze-frame images of a flock of pigeons flying through columns fronting a city building.

The boids simulation therefore seems a good interpretation of the flocking behavior of birds. Reynolds did not formally test this model against the flocking behavior of real birds. He could have, perhaps by placing the simulated columns to model a real building and comparing the spatial dispersion of both the boids and real birds with respect to these at several points in time. But in a sense there is no need for this kind of testing because it is obvious to most observers that the boids do behave like birds. In an interpretive sense, the simulation validates the assumption underlying the model that to coordinate their behavior birds need only avoid collisions, match velocity, and seek the center of the flock.

Whether human communication behavior can be reduced to something so simple as a three-rule automaton remains to be seen. However, communication scholars should not make the mistake of putting CA models completely under the stricture of traditional, formal statistics. CA models are amenable to testing, but the interpretation of social processes as automata, and the intuitive comparison of automatic to actual communication, are equally worthwhile for communication researchers.

Figure 8.2.   A flock of "boids" flying around simulated columns.
SOURCE: Reprinted with permission of Craig Reynolds (1987).

Conclusion

In this chapter I have described the formal characteristics and parameters of cellular automation models and shown that they are widely used in many scientific areas to explain collective behavior as the result of individuals applying simple transition rules based on local conditions. Cellular automata seem especially promising as models of unintended consequences of collective communication and for explaining how interaction is coordinated in groups. The models support both formal and interpretive validation methods, which promotes their application in many different areas of communication inquiry.

Notes

1. In fact, this simple automaton is self-similar at any scale. According to Wolfram (1984), this and other related "patterns are characterised by a fractal dimension; the value $\log_2 3 \approx 59$ is the most common" (p. 419).

2. Readers with INTERNET access can probably download a free copy of a LIFE program and other CA simulations by running a network search (e.g., using VERONICA, Lycos, Web Crawler, Yahoo, etc.) on the keywords "cellular automata."

3. These results apply to a spatially distributed group. They do not preclude my argument above that within a *local* group spatial constraint may not be so consequential.

4. There is more than one possible way to implement the moving-staying algorithm, and choices made here would influence the external validity of a CA model of urban ethnic segregation. One problem is how individual actions are to be located in time. Cellular automata operate in discrete time steps where a new set of states for the cells is computed and states are changed en masse. Yet it is not clear that people in cities make moves simultaneously—as if they were standing up and exchanging houses.

5. I should note here that this definition represents only one of three forms of research on unintended consequences distinguished by Giddens (1984), the one illustrated by his segregation example. The other two forms of research are much more concerned with micro- and macrolevel phenomena, respectively. CA models may be appropriate for these (especially the macro level), but in this chapter I limit my concern to the domain between individual action large-scale social institutions, which is the domain traditionally of interest in studies of organizational communication.

6. That is, a collective coordination model could be more parsimonious than a CA model if it assumed complete control of components by a central authority. However, such extreme structural determinism is rarely proposed to explain human social behavior.

7. These rules could be formalized à la Equation 8.2; however, it would be a nightmarish affair with little practical benefit given that we are not interested in formal symbolic manipulation of the rules.

8. Because power is represented as a percentage, a random number between 1 and 100 is drawn. If the number is greater than the power of the target, the attacker wins; otherwise, the attacker loses.

9. A reason was operationalized as a statement of fact used to support an assertion of innocence or guilt or to support an assertion of agreement or disagreement with a preceding statement by another speaker. Where conjunctions or disfluencies occurred in a single floor turn, these were taken as possible markers of a new reason, and if the factual content indeed seemed to change, these were unitized as separate reasons.

10. "Boids" is not exactly like a particle system; see Reynolds (1987) for an explanation of the difference.

PART

Some Exemplary Uses of Time

Here or henceforward it is all the same to me, I accept Time absolutely.

—Walt Whitman, *Leaves of Grass,*
"Song of Myself," sect. 23 (1855)

We should not say that one man's hour is worth another man's hour, but rather that one man during an hour is worth just as much as another man during an hour. Time is everything, man is nothing: he is at the most time's carcass.

—Karl Marx, *The Poverty of Philosophy* (1847)

The Emergence of Shared Interpretations in Organizations

A Self-Organizing Systems Perspective

NOSHIR S. CONTRACTOR
SUSAN J. GRANT

The past decade has seen the emergence of an enduring interest in the study of organizational communication from an interpretive perspective. In a comprehensive critique, Putnam (1983) notes that past functionalist research treated "social phenomena as concrete, materialistic, entities—types of social facts" (p. 34) and "organizational charts as fixed, concrete structures that determine authority and task relationships" (p. 35). Functionalist research tended to "reify social processes by ignoring the creation of structures, by recasting individual actions into fixed properties as levels, departments, and boundaries, and by treating organizations as containers or entities" (p. 35). It assumed a "unitary view of organizations; that is, organizations [were] treated as cooperative systems in pursuit of common interests and goals" (p. 36). There was also a tendency for functionalist research to pursue "universal laws, that is, explanatory theories that apply to a wide range of circum-

The research reported in this manuscript was supported by a grant from the National Science Foundation (NSF-ECS-9422730).

stances" (p. 40)—laws that were premised on a "unilateral and linear" (p. 42) conception of causality.

This chapter begins with the premise that the interpretive critique of past functionalist research, including research that claimed to be inspired by traditional systems theory, is fair in many cases. However, unlike most interpretive scholars, we argue that the response to this critique does not entail abandoning the quantitative approaches accompanying this research tradition. Instead, the critique offers a constructive opportunity to revise and redirect the focus of systems theorizing and research. This chapter presents recent developments in the field of self-organizing systems theory that are well-suited to complement and extend our understanding of social systems from an interpretive perspective. The chapter concludes with a simple, yet novel, self-organizing systems model to illustrate the emergence of shared interpretations in organizations.

Interpretive Critique of
Traditional Functionalist Research

During the past two decades, several organizational communication scholars have questioned the utility of functionalist research (Hawes, 1974; Putnam, 1983; Weick, 1979). Their concerns can be broadly classified into three categories:

• Longitudinal inference from cross-sectional research
• A focus on objectively measured explanatory variables
• Predominance of linear analytic models

First, even though scholars have had a long-standing interest in theorizing about communication processes (Berlo, 1960), the overwhelming body of empirical research was cross-sectional in design (Monge et al., 1984). Less obvious, but perhaps more significant, the knowledge claims made on the basis of this cross-sectional research implicitly assumed that the systems being studied were static in character (Abell, 1971). That is, they claimed to be taking a snapshot of a still picture. Hence, there was a growing chasm between the verbal articulation of processes in communication theory and the cross-sectional empirical research that purported to test these theories. The token acknowledgment at the end of cross-sectional research articles calling for "future longitudinal research" has worn thin.

Second, in its enthusiasm for measurement precision, reliability and validity, traditional functionalist research, had privileged objective phenomena in organizations. This in turn led to the theoretical reification of certain material aspects of organizations that failed to recognize the fact that organizations can also be usefully conceptualized as products of their members' visions, ideas, norms, and beliefs (Pondy & Mitroff, 1979). As a result, although there was a growing intellectual movement conceptualizing organizations as cultures and meaning systems (Eisenberg & Riley, 1988; Putnam & Pacanowsky, 1983), its influence on functionalist theories and research was virtually nonexistent.

Third, although methodological advances in functionalist research were making substantial strides (Monge & Cappella, 1980), these advances were primarily concerned with the estimation of linear, unidirectional causal analysis of covariance structures. Critics (e.g., Abbott, 1988; Weick, 1983) noted that these techniques were ill equipped to capture the contemporary intellectual conceptualizations of social systems. Scholars were theorizing about communication process in terms best captured by systems' concepts such as nonlinearity, historicity, mutual causality, causal loops, time irreversibility, discontinuity, and deviation amplifying feedback (for details, see Contractor, 1994). However, with a few notable exceptions (e.g., Monge, 1977, 1982), these concepts were not in the discursive mainstream of organizational communication research. Even research that claimed to be based on a system perspective would often deploy the terminology in a ceremonial way while eschewing the precise articulation embodied by such a perspective (Berlinksi, 1976).

Disillusionment with functionalist research and, by unfair but understandable association, systems perspectives in the three areas discussed above were largely responsible for the rise of the interpretive paradigm in organizational communication research. In an attempt to organize the intellectual domains, scholars (e.g., Putnam, 1983) distinguished between the two paradigms in terms of their different ontological and epistemological assumptions (Burrell & Morgan, 1979). Functionalist research was invested with an objective ontological stance in contrast to interpretive research's interest in the subjective. Epistemologically, functionalist research sought generalizable, ordered knowledge claims, whereas interpretive research was more concerned with understanding the particular (Putnam, 1983).

Having made these distinctions, the 1980s witnessed an uneasy coexistence between scholars within these two paradigms. An examination of publications and conference papers indicate a normative wall separating functionalist research, with quantitative methods on one side and interpretive research using qualitative methods on the other side.

Extending the Interpretive Perspective

In the past few years, a few scholars (Barnett, 1988a, 1988b; Monge & Eisenberg, 1987; Poole, 1990, 1994) have advocated, and attempted to demonstrate, the utility of applying the quantitative techniques of functionalist research to interpretive questions. In their review of organizational communication networks, Monge and Eisenberg (1987) propose the operationalization of networks from a cultural tradition. They note that past functionalist research on communication networks had been justly criticized for ignoring the content of communication networks (Richards, 1985; Rogers & Kincaid, 1981). Rogers and Kincaid (1981) summarized this deficiency:

> We need to combine the research method of content analysis of communication messages with the technique of network analysis to better understand how individuals give meaning to information that is exchanged through the communication process. (p. 77)

Monge and Eisenberg (1987) proposed the use of the coorientation model (McLeod & Chaffee, 1976) to operationalize a new genre of networks—semantic networks—in which the dyadic link measures the extent to which communicators share common interpretations.

Unlike traditional communication networks that measure the amount (or duration) of communication between individuals, semantic networks tap into the shared interpretation systems by asking individuals to provide their interpretations of key terms, slogans, stories, or rituals in the workplace. A semantic network link measures the degree of overlap (or lack thereof) of organizational members' interpretations. Further, mapping the configuration of individuals in a semantic network makes it possible to deploy the techniques of network analysis to further our systemic understanding of a collective of individuals as an interpretation system. For instance, whereas communication network density indicates the extent to which a group of individuals communicate with one another, semantic network density indicates the extent to which a group of individuals share their interpretations. Likewise, whereas communication network heterogeneity indicates the extent to which some individuals communicate with others who do not communicate with one another, semantic network heterogeneity measures the extent to which some individuals hold multiple interpretations that they share with others who do not have shared interpretations.

The operationalization of semantic networks is an example of the judicious application of quantitative research techniques to address questions that are central to an interpretive conceptualization of organizational communication. Monge and Eisenberg (1987) note that

semantic network analysis can be used to examine the assumption held by some researchers that organizations are made up of individuals with highly similar core values and beliefs. Organizations could be compared empirically to assess the degree of homogeneity of interpretations or core values. Subcultures could be identified around semantic . . . cliques. (p. 334)

As such, semantic network analysis has the potential for advancing our understanding of organizations as shared interpretation systems beyond what is capable by purely qualitative analysis. Many of the central concepts in interpretive-critical research are richly evocative verbal descriptions that are highly inadequate both in operationalizing the concepts and articulating their interrelationships. Poole (1990, 1994) describes these inadequacies as the interpretive version of the reductionist problem associated with some functionalist research.

Although the operationalization of semantic networks is a first attempt at incorporating quantitative methods to the study of interpretations, it does not directly address a central focus of interpretive researchers: "Interpretivist research extends beyond disclosing subjective meanings to an examination of why and how shared meanings exist" (Putnam, 1983, p. 41). That is, the interpretive perspective conceptualizes the emergence of shared interpretation as a circular causal chain relating, on the one hand, the manner in which interpretations are created and altered through interaction and, on the other hand, the manner in which shared interpretations shape interaction among individuals. Typically, interpretivists describe this relationship in a verbal narrative in the context of a particular study. They prefer this ideographic explanation and dismiss functionalists' search for a nomothetic explanation

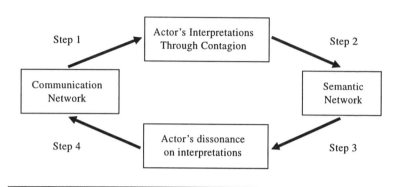

Figure 9.1.   Self-organizing model for the emergence of shared interpretations.

(i.e., a universal law) that would predict the same emergent process in all organizations. The next section discusses a reconceptualization of the emergence of shared interpretations from a self-organizing systems perspective. Although this perspective offers the precision associated with functionalist research, it is also based on the premise that the observed emergence processes can vary considerably.

A Self-Organizing Model of the Emergence of Shared Interpretations

Broadly speaking, self-organizing systems theory seeks to explain the emergence of patterned behavior in systems that are initially in a state of disorganization or in a different state of organization. From the start of this century, researchers in many of the physical and life sciences had observed that systems initially in a state of disorganization (high entropy) would under certain conditions spontaneously demonstrate patterned behavior (Nicolis & Prigogine, 1977; Prigogine, 1980). Further, these systems under certain specifiable conditions would spontaneously change to a different state of organization. The theoretical requirements of self-organizing systems are described in Contractor (1994) and Contractor and Seibold (1993). The generative mechanisms, describing the dynamic interrelationship among the elements of a self-organizing system, must include a feedback loop.

In the past decade, there have been calls for the application of self-organizing perspectives in management (Malik & Probst, 1984; von Foerster, 1984), organizational change (Ford & Backoff, 1988; Gersick, 1991; Goldstein, 1988), the appropriation of new communication technologies (Contractor & Seibold, 1993), communication and societal development (Krippendorff, 1987), communication and cultural evolution (Kincaid, 1987), and mass communication technologies and society (Batra, 1990). Cellular automata models (a class of self-organizing models) have also been used to study the unintended consequences of organizational communication (see Corman, this volume).

In this chapter we offer a simplified, but illustrative, self-organizing systems model of the process by which shared interpretations emerge among organizational members. That is, we attempt to model the process by which a group of individuals who start out with some initial communication and semantic network configurations self-organize their subsequent levels of interactions (i.e., communication networks) and interpretations (i.e., semantic networks).

Figure 9.1 depicts the four generative mechanisms in this self-organizing model. The four mechanisms are labeled Steps 1 through 4. Let C_{ijt} denote the communication link between individuals i and j at time t. In addition, let I_{it} and I_{jt} indicate individuals i's and j's agreement (on a scale from 0 to 12) with a particular interpretation at time t.

In Step 1, an individual i's interpretations are given by Equation 9-1:

$$I_{it+1} = b_p I_{it} + b_s \sum_{i \neq j} C_{ijt} I_{jt} + random\ noise, \qquad [9\text{-}1]$$

where the autocorrelation parameter b_p indicates the individual's interpretation inertia (i.e., the disposition for an individual to retain the same interpretation from one point in time to the next); the parameter b_s indicates the extent to which the individual is vulnerable to social influence from the communication network. The parameters b_p and b_s are scaled to sum to 1.

Equation 9-1 states that the interpretation held by individual i at time $t + 1$ is in part based on the individual's interpretation at the previous point in time, t. It is also based in part on the interpretations held by all other individuals in the network weighted by the extent to which individual i communicates with each of these other individuals. Finally, the effects of unaccounted variables on an individual's interpretation are assumed to vary in a nonsystematic manner and are characterized in

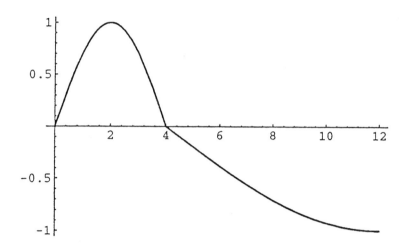

Figure 9.2. Change in communication as a function of differences in interpretations. *X*-axis reflects difference in interpretations; *Y*-axis reflects change in communication.

the equation by a random noise component. This equation has been described by Burt (1982) as the contagion model for network effects.

Step 2 describes the configuration of a semantic network based on individuals' interpretations. A semantic link, S_{ijt+1}, between two individuals i and j is given by:

$$S_{ijt+1} = 12 - |I_{it} - I_{jt}|$$ [9-2]

Equation 9-2 states that the semantic link between two individuals will be strongest (i.e., 12) if the two individuals have no disagreement in their interpretations. It will have a minimum value of 0 if the two individuals are in complete disagreement about the interpretation.

Step 3 maps the dissonance created as a result of differences in interpretations. Newcomb (1956) notes that differences in opinion among individuals has a curvilinear effect on their propensity to communicate. That is, in cases where there are modest differences in opinion between individuals, their need for balance (Heider, 1958) will motivate them to increase their communication with one another in order to reach agreement. However, there comes a point where substantial differences in opinion will result in individuals withdrawing their communication with one another. Figure 9.2 maps ΔC_{ijt+1}, the change in communication between individuals i and j, as a function of $|I_{it+1} - I_{jt+1}|$, the absolute difference in their interpretations. This function is represented by the equation:

$$\Delta C_{ijt+1} = \sin\left[\frac{\pi|I_{it+1} - I_{jt+1}|}{4}\right] \quad \text{if } |I_{it+1} - I_{jt+1}| \leq 4$$

$$\Delta C_{ijt+1} = \sin\left[\frac{\pi(4 - |I_{it+1} - _{jt+1})|}{16}\right] \quad \text{if } |I_{it+1} - I_{jt+1}| > 4$$

[9-3]

Equation 9-3 states that if two individuals share a common interpretation there will be no change in their level of communication. If their disagreement is less than or equal to 4, they will increase their communication. If their disagreement is greater than 4, they will decrease their communication. The number 4 was used as a cutoff value because it is the expected value of the absolute difference $|I_{it+1} - I_{jt+1}|$ if I_{it+1} and I_{jt+1} are allowed to vary randomly between 0 and 12.

Finally, Step 4 describes C_{ijt+1}, the new communication link between individuals i and j, as a function of C_{ijt}, the previous level of communication ΔC_{ijt+1}, the change in communication between individuals i and j, described above, and random noise. Hence:

$$C_{ijt+1} = C_{ijt} + \Delta C_{ijt+1} + random \; noise \qquad [9-4]$$

As the cycle repeats itself through several iterations, the communication and semantic networks can self-organize into stable configurations. The self-organizing process modeled above offers a simple, yet novel, approach to understanding the emergence of shared interpretations. In the model specified above, the process by which shared interpretations emerge will depend on the characteristics of the initial communication and semantic networks, the extent to which individuals' interpretations are susceptible to network influence (i.e., the relative value of b_s as compared to b_p), and random noise. Even if these parameters are fixed at certain values, it is not possible for the human intellect to construe mentally the emergent process by inspecting the four dynamic equations. Hanneman (1988) advocates the use of computer simulations to gain insights into the long-term implications of a dynamic model.

Traditional Research Process	SOST Research Process
• Theory	• Theory
• Verbally deduce hypotheses	• Formulate logics of emergence
• Empirical validation	• Run dynamic simulations
	• Deduce hypotheses from simulation data
	• Empirical validation

Figure 9.3. Comparison of traditional and proposed research process.

Carley and Prietula (1994) suggest the emergence of a new field, Computational Organizational Theory, to signal the growing interest in the construction of computational models to augment theory building. It is important to emphasize that the results of a computer simulation are not a surrogate for empirical data. Rather, they indicate the emergent process implied by the model proposed above. As such, simulation data provide the researcher with an opportunity to deduce hypotheses (that are implied but not immediately obvious) about differences in the emergence of shared interpretations in varied contexts. The distinctions between traditional and proposed research process are summarized in Figure 9.3. The next section describes the deduction of hypotheses based on a series of computer simulations executed on the model described above.

Deducing Hypotheses About the Emergence of Shared Interpretations

Research Questions

As discussed above, there are several potential influences on the emergent process specified by the self-organizing model. In this chapter we report the extent to which the emergent process is influenced by one initial communication network characteristic, communication network heterogeneity, and one initial interpretation characteristic, the initial variance in interpretations among the individuals.

Communication network heterogeneity is defined as the variation in the level of prominence among individuals in the network. An individual i is prominent to the extent that he or she receives links from other prominent individuals. The prominence, P_i, of individual i, is given by

$$P_i = \sum_{j=1}^{N} P_j \, C_{ij} \qquad \forall i \neq j \qquad [9\text{-}5]$$

where C_{ij} represents a communication network link between individuals i and j. Computationally, the prominence of individuals is the first eigenvector of the normalized communication network (Knoke & Kuklinski, 1982).

In a heterogeneous network, a few individuals will be very prominent while others would have low prominence. Conversely, a network in which all individuals are equally prominent is homogeneous. Knoke and Burt (1983) proposed the following information-theoretic measure as an operational definition of *network heterogeneity, H,*

$$H = \frac{\sum_{j=1}^{N} \left[\left(\frac{P_j}{P_m} \right) In \left(\frac{P_j}{P_m} \right) \right]}{N \, ln(N)} \qquad [9\text{-}6]$$

where P_j is the prominence of individual j, P_m is the mean prominence of all individuals in the network, N is the number of individuals in the network, and ln is the natural logarithm. Network heterogeneity, as operationalized here, is analogous to Freeman's (1979) operationalization of network centralization.

The goal of running the computer simulations is to deduce hypotheses in response to the following two research questions:

RQ1: According to the self-organizing model for the emergence of shared interpretations described above, to what extent does the initial level of communication network heterogeneity influence, in the short and long term, the subsequent communication and semantic network densities among the individuals? That is, will the emergence of shared interpretations in groups where some members start out being much more prominent in the communication network than their peers differ significantly from the emergence process in groups where all members are equally prominent in the communication network?

RQ2: According to the self-organizing model for the emergence of shared interpretations described above, to what extent does the initial level of variance in individuals' interpretations influence, in the short and long term, the subsequent communication and semantic network densities among the individuals? That is, will the emergence of shared interpretations in groups where members vary greatly in their initial interpretations differ significantly from the emergence process in groups where all members do not vary greatly in their initial interpretations?

Data Generation

The self-organizing model described above requires initial values for the communication network and individuals' initial interpretations.

Initial Communication Network Structure

The initial communication network structure was operationalized as a binary asymmetric communication network of 6 individuals. One hundred such networks were generated using Monte Carlo techniques (Burt, 1991). All 100 networks were specified to have a density of 0.2. That is, in each network the total number of communication links were 6, one-fifth of the total number of possible 30 links. In 50 of the networks generated, the communication network heterogeneity was specified to be high (*mean* = .61, *SE* < .001). In these networks, some members were significantly more prominent than others. In the remaining 50 networks, communication network heterogeneity was specified to be low (*mean* = .23, *SE* < .001). There was not much variation in individuals' prominence scores in these networks.

Individuals' Initial Interpretation

Individuals' initial interpretations were operationalized as a 6 × 1 vector. Forty vectors were generated, with each vector containing the interpretation scores for each individual in a group of 6 individuals. Each individual's interpretation was allowed to vary between 0 (no agreement) and 12 (high agreement). For each of the 40 vectors, the mean interest among the individuals was held constant at 6.0. In 20 of the vectors generated, the variance among the individuals' interpretations was held constant at a high value (*mean* = 4.0, *SE* < .01); for the remaining 20 vectors, the variance among individuals' interpretations was restricted to a low value (*mean* = 1.00, *SE* < .005).

The parameters b_p and b_s were fixed at 0.4 and 0.6, respectively, and were held constant through the simulation.

TABLE 9.1 Correlation Coefficients of Communication Network Densities at Each Time Period (T1 through T10), With Initial (T0) Communication Network Heterogeneity and Interpretation Variance ($N = 4,000$)

	T1	*T2*	*T3*	*T4*	*T5*	*T6*	*T7*	*T8*	*T9*	*T10*
Initial communication heterogeneity	0.002	0.002	0.003	0.002	0.001	0.002	0.003	0.002	0.001	0.001
Initial interpretation variance	0.003	0.012	0.027	0.078	0.087	0.122	0.187	0.226	0.226	0.226

Design of the Simulation

The initial communication network matrices and initial individual interpretation vectors generated were used to examine the emergence of shared interpretations as implied by the self-organizing model described above. Combinations of the 50 communication network matrices and 20 interpretation vectors in each of the four conditions (high/low initial communication network heterogeneity, high/low variance in initial interpretation) resulted in 4,000 simulations, which were executed on a supercomputer using *Mathematica* (Wolfram, 1991). An inspection of a large number of random simulation runs indicated that the self-organizing process stabilized in well under 10 iterations. Hence, each simulation was allowed to progress through 10 iterations.

Results

The data from the simulations were analyzed to deduce hypotheses based on the two research questions posed earlier in this section. In particular, at each of the 10 points in time, communication network densities and semantic network densities were computed for each of the groups. Table 9.1 reports the correlation coefficients of the communication network densities at each time period (T1 through T10) with initial (T0) communication network heterogeneity and initial (T0) interpretation variance. Table 9.2 uses the same time parameters to report the correlation coefficients of the semantic network densities.

TABLE 9.2 Correlation Coefficients of Semantic Network Densities at Each Time Period (T1 through T10), With Initial (T0) Communication Network Heterogeneity and Interpretation Variance ($N = 4,000$)

	T1	T2	T3	T4	T5	T6	T7	T8	T9	T10
Initial communication heterogeneity	0.004	0.003	0.041	0.132	0.172	0.188	0.043	0.007	0.007	0.007
Initial interpretation variance	−.781	−.657	−.637	−.174	−.135	−.056	−.008	−.003	−.003	−.003

The correlation coefficients reported in these tables suggest the following hypotheses:

H1: Initial differences in communication network heterogeneity will have no short- or long-term effect on the communication network density.

H2: A higher initial variance in individuals' interpretations will have a positive but delayed impact on communication network density.

H3: Initial differences in communication network heterogeneity will have a delayed but transient positive impact on semantic network density.

H4: A higher initial variance in individuals' interpretations will have a negative but transient impact on semantic network density.

It must be emphasized that the model presented above is intentionally simplified to serve as an illustration. A more realistic self-organizing model must remedy two serious limitations of this illustrative model. First, the above model does not permit individuals to possess multiple interpretations, some of which may be more influential than others. For instance, individual A may offer three interpretations of the organization's slogan—and may be variably committed to each of the three interpretations. Second, the above model is essentially closed, implying that communication is the only variable influencing, and being influenced by, shared interpretations. The literature on organizational socialization suggests that shared interpretations are also significantly influenced by other variables, such as similar levels in the hierarchy and tenure within the organization (Van Maanen & Schein, 1979). It must be noted that both these limitations are specific to the model illustrated above and not the self-organizing systems perspective in general. Hypotheses, deduced from a more realistic model, will be tested using longitudinal communication and semantic network data that have been collected over a six-year period among scientific research teams at a large midwestern university. Empirical support for the hypotheses would indicate that the proposed self-organizing model for the emergence of shared interpretations cannot be rejected.

Conclusion

This chapter began with a critique of traditional functionalist research. These criticisms dealt with the inappropriateness of cross-sectional validation of process theories, the reification of objective measures and concepts while shying away from more compelling but difficult to measure interpretive concepts, and the methodological primacy of linear, unidirectional causal modeling. The critical-interpretive perspectives that were launched in the wake of this dissatisfaction have offered new and useful insights into organizational communication processes. However, in their haste to dismiss and discredit the quantitative approaches associated with the traditional functionalist approaches, the interpretive perspectives have severely limited their own ability to add precision and rigor to the concepts and processes they seek to examine.

The self-organizing systems perspective described and illustrated in this chapter has accommodated three of the criticisms offered by the interpretive tradition but not its ontological and epistemological commitments. First, its explicit focus on deducing hypotheses based on the simulation of dynamic interrelationships precludes the possibility of researchers conflating cross-sectional and dynamic knowledge claims. Second, the substantive domain of the example used in this chapter—the emergence of shared interpretations in organizations—underscores the ability of a self-organizing systems model to explain phenomena in terms that are not objective, reified, and relying on material aspects of the organization. Third, our use of computer simulations as a tool to assist theory building is offered as one strategy to deal with the methodological challenges and analytic intractability of social scientific theories that describe nonlinear processes. Simulations can also facilitate precision by being used to disambiguate theories that, in their verbal description, are amenable to more than one set of generative mechanisms. For instance, Monge and Kalman (this volume) note that many theories do not adequately distinguish between generative mechanisms that are sequential, simultaneous, or synchronous.

It is important to note that the self-organizing systems perspective, while attempting to extend the interpretive perspective, does not share the latter's ontological and epistemological assumptions. First, ontologically, unlike interpretivists, a systems approach subscribes to the goal of nomothetic explanations. In a self-organizing systems perspective, the nomothetic explanations are articulated as the generative mechanisms, describing the interrelationship among the elements of a system. It must be pointed out that a nomothetic set of explanations at the level of generative mechanisms allows for the manifestation of seemingly ideographic emergent processes. Hence, it is possible that two groups in which the emergence of shared interpretations are manifestly different can be explained by the same set of generative mechanisms.

Second, epistemologically, unlike interpretivists, a systems approach subscribes to a deductive logic. In a self-organizing systems perspective, the hypotheses are not deduced directly from the theory. Instead, the theory is used to identify generative mechanisms. Hypotheses are deduced by dynamically modeling the generative mechanisms. It must be pointed out that the commitment to a deductive model of shared interpretations does not preclude a researcher from allowing the data in a specific organization to reveal the existence of interpretations that are unique to members in that setting.

Following the lead of a few pioneering scholars, this chapter has attempted to demonstrate the utility of employing recent intellectual developments in systems theory and new computational capabilities to extend our understanding of key themes within the interpretive perspective.

10

Predicting Television Viewing

Cycles, the Weather, and Social Events

GEORGE A. BARNETT

SUNG HO CHO

Television viewing is a major consumer of the leisure time, occupying over 28 hours a week per person or over 49 hours a week per household (Condry, 1989; Lodziak, 1986; Robinson, 1981). It has become a regular social habit along with sleeping, working, and various other activities (Goodhardt, Ehrenberg, & Collins, 1987).

Television constitutes a complex innovation as its adoption not only changed the everyday use of time but also culture (Barnett, 1988a). Further, its adoption has altered the communication patterns and social habits of society's members (Barnett, Chang, Fink, & Richards, 1991; Hamblin, Miller, & Saxton, 1979; Robinson, 1972). Condry (1989) divides the effect of television into indirect and direct. The direct effects result from watching *specific* program content. Indirect effects arise simply from the *adoption* of television because this leads to changes in the distribution of time in daily life. This chapter focuses on the indirect effects—how the average household uses television regardless of its specific content.

Television, as a complex innovation, has changed the use of leisure time (Robinson, 1981; Sahin & Robinson, 1980). Since its beginning, several studies have described viewing patterns and suggested several

231

models. Viewing patterns include the long-term adoption curve as well as short-term patterns that include annual (seasonal), weekly, and daily cycles. The seasonal pattern of television viewing has long been observed (Barnett, 1982; Comstock, Chaffee, Katzman, McCombs, & Roberts, 1978; Gensch & Shaman, 1980; Wunschel, 1982). Goodhardt, Ehrenberg, and Collins (1987) indicate that a seasonal pattern of television viewing also occurs in the United Kingdom. People tend to watch more television during the winter than during the summer.

Barnett et al. (1991) examined the long-term trend of television viewing with monthly data from 1950 to 1988. They developed a mathematical model to explain the diffusion of television viewing as well as the seasonal patterns in viewing. The model consisted of three components: a *simple* oscillation to account for the seasonal pattern of viewing, a *logistic* to account for the increase in viewing due to television's diffusion, and an *intercept*, the initial (1950) amount of television viewing.

$$Y_t = B_1 \cos [B_2(t + B_3)] + \frac{B_4}{1 + B_5 e^{-B_6 t}} + B_7 . \qquad [10\text{-}1]$$

The model (Equation 10-1) accurately explained over 99.8% of the variance in long-term television viewing.

In spite of the model's accuracy, it did not reflect the shrinking annual viewing cycle. The difference between the peak number of viewing hours in winter and the minimum time devoted to television in summer has decreased. In the early 1950s, it was approximately 2 hours. It was reduced to only 1 hour, 20 minutes in late 1980s (Barnett, Cho, & Choi, 1993). Barnett et al. (1993) revised the model to account for the dampened oscillation in viewing. It was composed of three components: a *dampened* oscillation term that describes the changing seasonal variation in viewing, a logistic term, and an intercept. This model (Equation 10-2) fits the data better.

$$Y_t = e^{-B_1 t} B_2 \cos [B_3(t + B_4)] + \frac{B_5}{1 + B_6 e^{-B_7 t}} + B_8 . \qquad [10\text{-}2]$$

Whereas the day, month, and year are derived from natural cycles based on the movements of the earth and moon, a week is a culturally defined cycle (Woelfel, Barnett, Pruzek, & Zimmelman, 1989; Zerubavel, 1981, 1985). Weekly and daily viewing cycles were observed by Gensch and Shaman (1980). Wunschel (1982) suggested a model to explain daily patterns of viewing. He tested the model with half-hour interval data from 28 days. The model was composed of three cycles of sine and cosines. It explained about 89% of the variance in the amount of viewing. Even though the single daily model accurately explained the pattern in viewing, the exclusion of the weekly and annual cycles may have reduced its accuracy in predicting overall viewing. One purpose of this research is to determine if a weekly cycle exists. If so, it will be incorporated in a model that describes this cycle and tests it with a long sequence of viewing data.

Television viewing competes for leisure time with other activities. Environmental factors such as the weather may influence fluctuations in viewing (Gould, Johnson, & Chapman, 1984). If the weather permits outdoor leisure activities, then television viewing will decrease. On the contrary, inclement weather may increase viewing. This phenomenon has been indirectly observed with the seasonal fluctuation of viewing behavior. Gensch and Shaman (1980) found differences in the amount of viewing in early evening hours between summer and winter. They indicated that people watch more television during the winter than the summer due to the amount of daylight. Similarly, Barnett et al. (1991) tested the relationship between television viewing and environmental factors such as daylight, temperature, and precipitation. They found these variables also have annual cycles with strong links to viewing.

Based on the above discussion, the following theoretical hypotheses may be suggested.

H1: The frequency of television viewing is composed of three significant cycles: a daily cycle, a weekly cycle, and an annual cycle.

H2: Departure from the frequency of viewing as predicted by the three cycles will be a function of weather conditions, namely, temperature and precipitation.

Programming may also determine patterns of viewing. Generally, planned programs are broadcast at a specific time (Comstock et al., 1978; Condry, 1989). For example, during the typical afternoon, soap operas are broadcast; on Saturday morning, a large proportion of the programming consists of children's programs, such as cartoons; and on Saturday and Sunday afternoon, sports are broadcast. As indicated earlier, people tend to watch more television when they have free time. Further, special programs are offered on holidays. For example, football games make up the programming on New Year's Day and Thanksgiving. This implies that people may watch more television on holidays. However, the existence of social conventions may limit viewing on religious holidays such as Christmas and Easter.

The networks spend millions of dollars attempting to attract viewers. Are they successful, or do they simply compete for an audience fixed by the cycles of nature and culture? Further, what is the impact of special events on viewing? Do they also help to determine the size of the television audience? This discussion suggests two additional hypotheses.

H3: *Departure from the frequency of viewing as predicted by the three cycles will be a function of social events such as religious and secular holidays.*

H4: *Departure from the frequency of viewing as predicted by the three cycles will be a function of special programming offered by the networks.*

The overall purpose of this study is to predict television viewing more accurately and to explain the sources of variance in viewing. It will determine the cycles that exist in viewing and then examine those cycles (daily, weekly, and annual). Because the annual cycle has been precisely described by Barnett et al. (1991, 1993), this chapter focuses on the shorter daily and weekly cycles. Mathematical models are evaluated that describe each cycle. Once the pattern of viewing is described, the impact of the weather, social events, and programming on viewing is examined.

Methods

The Data

The data for this research were the Nielsen Television Index for Chicago describing the average 15-minute interval ratings (the number of television sets turned on) per household (HUT) for the period, February 1, 1990, to January 31, 1991 (Nielsen, 1991). Some data between 2:00 a.m. and 5:45 a.m. were missing: February 26 to May 6, May 28 to July 8, July 30 to October 31, and November 19 to January 31. The missing data were estimated by applying a simple linear interpolation with existing data from February, May, July, and November

1990. For example, if the value at t_1 was missing, it was estimated by adding two values, t_0 and t_2, and dividing by 2 (value $t_1 = (t_0 + t_2) / 2$).

The total data points were 35,040. This full data set was used to examine cycles of viewing. The moving average process might bias the results by making them appear more periodic.

To test the weekly model, the daily cycle was removed from the time series by taking the mean for each day. The full data set was transformed into 365 data points, with each representing the daily average. This method was advantageous because each point corresponded to a specific date. The lowest amount of viewing occurred on July 4, Independence Day. The average rating was 27.74. The peak occurred on January 20, 1991, Super Bowl Sunday, with a rating of 41.90.

To examine the relationship between the frequency of viewing and the weather, daily weather data were taken from the *Chicago Tribune*. The available data were low and high temperatures and various symbols that indicate the day's weather conditions.[1] Even though these data were crude, they were sufficient to determine if a relationship existed between viewing and temperature and precipitation.

Average temperature was calculated by dividing the sum of the low and high temperatures by 2. The final variable was formulated by subtracting the daily average temperature from the average monthly mean temperature. It was assumed that unseasonably warm or cold weather affects viewing. The absolute temperature was taken into account by the annual cycle (Barnett et al., 1991). The average monthly temperatures were taken from the National Oceanic and Atmosphere Administration's (NOAA; 1991) publications. The various symbols that indicate the weather conditions were transformed into two conditions, precipitation (rain or snow) and no precipitation.

Football games and other special programs were determined from the Nielsen records. Social events were taken from a calendar.

Analysis Procedures

Spectral Analysis

To examine the cyclical patterns in viewing, a spectral analysis was conducted with one year of 15-minute interval data ($N = 35,040$). Spectral analysis is the appropriate method for examining whether regular patterns are presented in time series data (Davis & Lee, 1980). This technique applies a large number of sinusoidal models with different amplitudes and wavelengths to the time series. The results indicate regions of strong periodicities by using finite Fourier transforms (see VanLear & Watt, this volume).

The resulting spectral density indicates the presence of strong cycles in a series. The function peaks at frequency bands that contribute important sources of variation to the series. It is closer to zero elsewhere. In other words, the spectral density describes a peak in the frequency ranges where one expects to find cycles (Gottman, 1981). By using spectral density, one can quantify the strength of the cycles in the series. The periodogram reveals important frequencies that have peaks in a series. Both the periodogram and the spectral density identify the important frequencies in the time series.

The Daily Cycle

Nonlinear regression was used to describe the daily cycle. Following Wunschel (1982), the daily cycle should be composed of a combination of two or more sinusoidal curves. Mathematically, a simple sine function is presented as Equation 10-3:

$$Y_t = B_0 + B_1 \sin [B_2 (t + B_3)], \qquad [10\text{-}3]$$

where, Y_t is the predicted number of households viewing television at time t, B_0 is the starting value for the time-independent term, B_1 is the amplitude of the cycle, B_2 is the frequency of the cycle, expressed in radians, and B_3 is the phase shift, also expressed in radians, with its value depending on the point in time when the cycle begins (i.e., where the value of the sine = 0.0).

B_2 is the frequency of the cycle and may be determined through the application of Equation 10-4.

$$B_2 = \frac{2\pi}{\Theta}, \qquad [10\text{-}4]$$

where Θ is the number of discrete observations in one cycle.

Here, Θ equaled 96, as one cycle, the day, was composed of 96 measurement points. Applying Equation 10-4, the expected value of

B_2 was .0654. Because the daily cycle may be composed of two or more cycles as revealed by the spectral analysis, Equation 10-3 was modified by repeating the expressions that describe the oscillation for each sinusoidal, terms B_1 through B_3. For example, Equation 10-5 shows a model composed of two sine curves.

$$Y_t = B_0 + B_1 \sin [B_2 (t + B_3)] + B_4 \sin [B_5 (t + B_6)]. \qquad [10\text{-}5]$$

Weekly Models

Two possible models for the weekly cycle were tested with daily data. One model used the cosine or sine model, as the revealed cycles in spectral analysis were derived from sinusoidals. This model for the weekly cycle is similar to the daily model. It may also be represented by Equation 10-3. Following Equation 10-4, Θ equaled 7, as one cycle was composed of 7 days of a week. Thus,

$$B_2 = \frac{2\Theta}{7(.898)}.$$

B_3, the phase shift, depends on the starting day of a week.

To find the other possible model, the mean of each day of the week for one year was calculated. These are presented in Table 10.1 with their standard deviations. They indicate that weekend (Saturday and Sunday) viewing was greater and that ratings fluctuated more on weekends than on weekdays.[2] The weekdays had relatively smaller variance. The average viewing on Monday was 32.67, decreased until Wednesday (31.94), and peaked on Sunday (34.79). The weekly cycle is represented in Figure 10.1. This plot looks like a negative absolute sine cycle.[3] Thus, the second model for weekly viewing cycle was specified as the absolute value sine model shown in Equation 10-6.

$$Y_t = B_0 - B_1 |\sin [B_2 (t - B_3)]| . \qquad [10\text{-}6]$$

The difference between the models is that in the absolute value model the 7 days of a week compose a *half* cycle, whereas in the sine model, 7 days describe one *full* cycle. Thus, B_2 in the absolute value sine model equals $\pi / 7 = .449$ instead of $2\pi / 7 = .898$.

Figure 10.2 represents the two models graphically. Another difference between the models is that the sine model looks like regular sine

TABLE 10.1 Means From Monday to Sunday ($N = 365$)

Variable	N	Mean	SD
Monday	52	32.67	2.10
Tuesday	52	32.20	1.88
Wednesday	52	31.94	1.87
Thursday	52	32.00	2.02
Friday	52	31.49	2.07
Saturday	52	32.52	2.89
Sunday	52	34.79	3.69

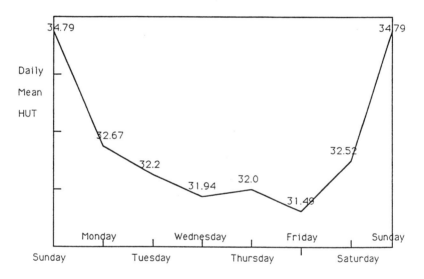

Figure 10.1. Television viewing by the day of the week.

wave, whereas the absolute value sine model has sharp peaks every cycle on Sunday.

The Annual Cycle

As will be indicated later, spectral analysis revealed three cycles of daily, weekly, and annual period. To compare the weekly models, both

Absolute Value Sine Model: $Y = -|\sin\theta|$

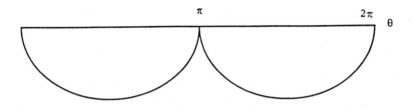

Sine Model: $Y = \sin\theta$

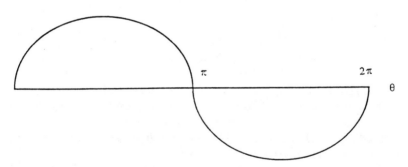

Figure 10.2. Absolute-value sine model and sine model.

were combined with the annual model because all exist in the same time series. To test the models, the daily cycle was removed from the time series by averaging. Equation 10-7 (below) was applied instead of the simple oscillation model (Barnett et al., 1991) or the dampened oscillation model (Barnett et al., 1993) because we had only a single annual cycle, not multiples. As a result, there were insufficient data to model the cycle as a sinusoidal (see Arundale, this volume). The annual model was represented as a quadratic equation. Because the data begin with February, we expected the curve to resemble a U. Therefore, the sign of B_1 should be negative (see Equation 10-7).

$$Y_t = B_0 - B_1 t + B_2 t^2 , \qquad [10\text{-}7]$$

where Y_t is the predicted frequency of viewing at time t, B_0 is the starting value for the time-independent term, and B_1 and B_2 are the values affecting the slope of curve.

Before testing the two weekly models, the annual model was fitted to the data, and then weekly models were compared using SAS linear program (SAS Institute, 1990).

Combining the Weekly and Annual Cycles

To test the weekly models, both were combined with the annual model. Equation 10-8 represents the combination of the weekly sine model and the annual model and Equation 10-9 the combination of the absolute value sine and the annual model.

$$Y_t = B_0 + B_1 \sin [B_2 (t + B_3)] + B_4 t + B_5 t^2. \qquad [10\text{-}8]$$

$$Y_t = B_0 - B_1 |\sin [B_2 (t - B_3)]| + B_4 t + B_5 t^2. \qquad [10\text{-}9]$$

In Equation 10-8, B_2 was set at .898. To match the shape of the model with the first data point, B_3 was set at 3 because the first data point began with Thursday and the data peaked on Sunday, three days away. In Equation 10-9, B_2 was set at .449. Similarly, B_3 was set at 1 because the data reached its lowest value on Friday.

To compare each model's explanatory ability, R^2 and plausibility of the derived parameters were examined. Further, the residuals of each model were examined. If the model was complete, the residuals from the regressions should have been homoskedastic, normal, and not exhibit any systematic patterns (Bauer & Fink, 1983). Results that did not satisfy these assumptions were reexamined.

TABLE 10.2 Spectral Analysis for TV Viewing (N = 35,040)

Frequency (cycles/15-minute)	Period (15-minute)	Periodogram	Spectral density
0.000179 (Annual)	35,040.0	102,448.0	5,488.22
0.009324 (Weekly)	673.8	14,833.4	685.43
0.065450 (Daily)	96.0	7,431,201.0	198,178.00

Results

Spectral Analysis

A white noise test conducted with Bartlett's Kolmogorov-Smirnov test statistic revealed cycles in the time series. If the time series did not have any significant cycles, the test statistic should have been close to 0. On the contrary, if the data had significant cycles, the test statistic would be close to one. Here, the Bartlett's Kolmogorov-Smirnov statistic was 0.916 ($p < .01$) indicating that there were significant cycles in the time series.

The results of the spectral analysis for the 15-minute interval data are presented in Table 10.2. They revealed three cycles: an annual cycle (period = 35,040.0), a weekly cycle (period = 673.8), and a daily cycle (period = 96.0).[4] Among the cycles, the daily was the strongest (spectral density = 198,178.0), followed by the annual cycle (spectral density = 5,488.2). The weekly cycle's frequency (spectral density = 685.4) was rather weak compared to the other two cycles.

The Daily Cycle

Table 10.3 gives the average values for each 15 minutes for the daily cycle. It is graphically presented in Figure 10.3. At midnight, the rating was 28.9. It declined, reaching a minimum of 8.7 at 4:45 a.m. As people

TABLE 10.3 Average 15-Minute Interval Mean Ratings for a Day

Time	Rating	Time	Rating	Time	Rating
00:00	28.9	08:00	23.2	16:00	39.6
00:15	26.6	08:15	24.4	16:15	40.5
00:30	24.4	08:30	24.7	16:30	41.4
00:45	22.6	08:45	25.5	16:45	43.1
01:00	20.8	09:00	26.9	17:00	44.3
01:15	19.3	09:15	27.7	17:15	46.0
01:30	17.6	09:30	28.0	17:30	47.4
01:45	16.4	09:45	28.2	17:45	49.1
02:00	14.9	10:00	27.7	18:00	51.0
02:15	13.9	10:15	27.7	18:15	52.6
02:30	12.9	10:30	27.6	18:30	53.9
02:45	12.2	10:45	27.9	18:45	55.6
03:00	11.5	11:00	28.5	19:00	56.6
03:15	11.0	11:15	29.1	19:15	57.8
03:30	10.4	11:30	29.7	19:30	58.6
03:45	09.9	11:45	30.8	19:45	60.0
04:00	09.5	12:00	33.0	20:00	60.9
04:15	09.1	12:15	33.8	20:15	62.0
04:30	08.8	12:30	33.5	20:30	62.4
04:45	08.7	12:45	33.6	20:45	63.6
05:00	08.9	13:00	32.4	21:00	63.7
05:15	09.3	13:15	32.4	21:15	63.9
05:30	09.6	13:30	32.1	21:30	63.7
05:45	10.1	13:45	32.3	21:45	63.5
06:00	10.5	14:00	31.9	22:00	61.2
06:15	11.9	14:15	32.3	22:15	58.7
06:30	13.9	14:30	32.4	22:30	51.5
06:45	15.3	14:45	33.8	22:45	47.4
07:00	17.1	15:00	33.8	23:00	42.5
07:15	19.0	15:15	35.4	23:15	39.5
07:30	20.5	15:30	37.3	23:30	34.8
07:45	21.8	15:45	38.9	23:45	32.0

awoke, viewing increased until 10:00 a.m. It remained relatively stable between 10:00 a.m. and 3:00 p.m., except for a slight rise between noon and 1:00 p.m. Viewing was slightly greater during the early afternoon but increased by late afternoon as children returned from school and adults from work. It continued to rise throughout prime time, peaking between 9:00 and 10:00 p.m., the last hour of prime time in Chicago. It then decreased as people went to sleep.

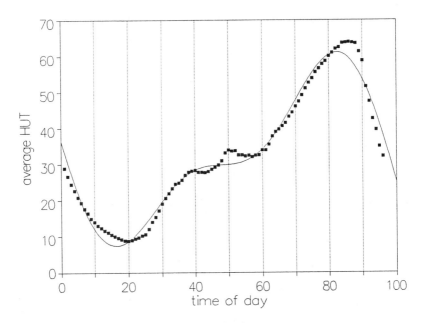

Figure 10.3. Daily cycle of television viewing.

Mathematically, the daily cycle was best described by a combination of two sinusoidal curves. This differed from Wunschel (1982), who found that a combination of three curves best explained the daily cycle. The addition of a third curve did not improve the variance explained. The results of fitting the daily cycle are presented in Table 10.4 and Figure 10.3. The predicted model is also presented in Figure 10.4. The model described by Equation 10-5 explained about 98% of the variance, $F = 716.059$, $p < .0001$. All individual terms were statistically significant and theoretically plausible. For example, B_0, the time-independent term, equaled 32.27. The mean HUT score was 32.5. B_1, the amplitude, was 25.89. Half of the difference between the maximum and the minimum values was 27.6. Empirically, B_2, the frequency, was .074. The expected value was .065. The theoretical values were estimated with only a single curve (Equation 10-2). The addition of the second sine curve would have altered these values.

TABLE 10.4   Descriptive Parameters for the Daily Cycle ($N = 96$)

		Coefficient	SE	t^*
B_0		32.267	.345	93.45
B_1		25.891	8.475	3.05
B_2		.074	.009	7.95
B_3		−13.861	7.518	−1.84
B_4		15.956	8.763	1.82
B_5		.116	.012	9.44
B_6		3,146.823	328.396	9.58
R^2	.980			
Residual analysis				
SD	2.38			
Skew	.726			
Kurtosis	.619			
Correlation of residuals with time		.000 ($p = 1.00$)		
Correlation of residuals with viewing		.020 ($p > .05$)		

*All t values are statistically significant ($p < .05$).

Although the residuals are not normally distributed (there are 54 negatives and 42 positives), they did not correlate with time ($r = .000$) or viewing ($r = .020$). Those whose probability of occurrence was less than 5% can be explained by social behavior. They happened between 9:30 and 10:15 p.m., the end of prime time, when viewership was greater than predicted and between 11:30-11:45 p.m. when fewer people were watching than predicted. The greatest percentage error for the individual estimates occurred between 3:00 and 4:00 a.m. when viewing was underestimated and between 5:45 and 6:30 a.m. when viewing was overestimated. In other words, some people retire and arise later than the model predicted.

The Annual Cycle

The results of the annual model are presented in Table 10.5. Figure 10.4 shows the best-fit curve and the plot of daily mean viewing. The seasonal pattern, with rating appearing lower during summer than during winter, can be seen. Some of the peaks between the period 230 and 350 were Sundays during football season. The two lowest ratings were Christmas Eve and Christmas Day. The annual model explained 45% of

TABLE 10.5 Descriptive Parameters for Annual Model ($N = 365$)

	Coefficient	*SE*	*t**
Initial intercept			
B_0	34.3861	0.306	112.28
Seasonal term			
B_1	−0.0475	0.004	−12.28
B_2	0.0002	0.000	14.96
R^2	0.455		
Residual analysis			
SD	1.934		
Skew	0.831		
Kurtosis	1.508		
Correlation of residuals with frequency of viewing		0.738 ($p < .0001$)	
Correlation of residuals with time		−0.000 ($p = 1.000$)	

*All *t* values are statistically significant ($p < .001$).

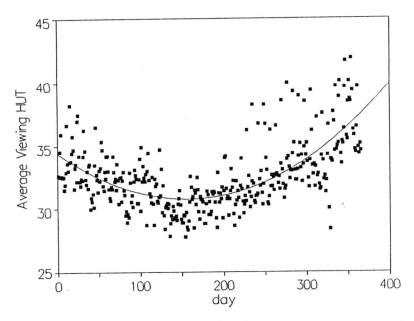

Figure 10.4. Annual cycle of television viewing.

the variance in the number of households viewing. The coefficients fit the model well with small standard errors. As predicted, B_1 was negative. All terms were statistically significant ($p < .001$). The examination of the residuals of the annual model showed that they are not normally distributed. Kolmogorov D, which is used to test the normal distribution of a sample, was 0.097 ($p < .01$). If the residuals were normal, Kolmogorov D should have been close to zero. The test results indicate that the probability of the sample's normal distribution was not over 99%. The skew was 0.991, and kurtosis was 1.015. The correlation of the residuals with the frequency of television viewing was significant ($r = .738$, $p < .0001$), whereas its correlation with time was not ($r = -0.000$, $p = 1.000$). The results for the residuals indicated that there remained an unexplained pattern in the data. It meant that viewing was not explained with only the annual model, supporting the addition of the weekly model to the annual model.

The Weekly Cycle

The results of fitting the weekly model with the annual model are presented in the Table 10.6 and Figure 10.5. Both the sine and absolute-value sine model fit the viewing data well. The sine model explained an additional 8.4% of the variance ($R^2 = 0.539$) in viewing. The absolute value sine model explained an additional 11.6% ($R^2 = 0.571$).

Inclusion of the weekly term was statistically significant for both models. In both cases, B_1, B_2, and B_3 were significant at $p < .01$. If the weekly component was not significant for the combined viewing model, the coefficients should have been zero. Because they were not, it indicated that a weekly cycle existed. Even though both models fit the data well, the absolute-value sine model was better.

The examination of the residuals of the sine model revealed that they were not normally distributed. Kolmogorov D equals 0.07 ($p < .01$). The skew was 0.405, and kurtosis was 1.230. The analysis of the residuals of the absolute-value model also revealed that they were not normally distributed. Kolmogorov D equaled 0.064 ($p < .01$). The skew was 0.218, and kurtosis was 0.925. The residuals of the absolute-value sine model were less skewed and less peaked than the sine model. The correlation between the residuals and time was not significant ($r = -.000$, $p = 0.998$ for both models). Although the relationship was not significant, there may have remained an unexplained pattern partly because the model was incomplete. The correlation of the residuals with the fre-

TABLE 10.6　Descriptive Parameters for Sine Model and Absolute Value Sine Model With the Annual Model ($N = 365$)

	Sine Model			Absolute Value Sine Model		
	Coefficient	*SE*	*t**	*Coefficient*	*SE*	*t**
Initial intercept						
B_0	34.4004	0.283	121.64	36.2213	0.333	108.70
Weekly term						
B_1	−1.0745	0.133	−8.10	2.8405	0.294	9.66
B_2	0.8980	0.001	767.50	0.4492	0.000	1028.81
B_3	0.9357	0.277	3.38	2.7336	0.209	13.08
Seasonal term						
B_4	−0.0477	0.004	−13.36	−0.0479	0.003	−13.88
B_5	0.0002	0.000	16.28	0.0002	0.000	16.91
R^2	0.539			0.571		
Residual analysis						
SD		1.778			1.711	
Skew		0.405			0.218	
Kurtosis		1.230			0.925	
Correlation of residuals with frequency of viewing						
	0.679 ($p < .0001$)			0.653　($p < .0001$)		
Correlation of residuals with time						
	−0.000 ($p = 0.998$)			−0.000　($p = 0.998$)		

*All t values are statistically significant ($p < .01$).

quency of viewing was significant for both models ($r = .679$, $p < .0001$, for the sine model; $r = .653$, $p < .0001$, for the absolute-value sine model). Even though the correlations between the residuals and frequency of television viewing need some explanation (see below), the results indicated that the absolute sine model fit better than the sine model because the correlation was lower.

Figure 10.6 shows the residuals after fitting the annual and the absolute-value weekly models. The inclusion of the weekly component to the annual model resulted in less skewed residuals. The skew in the annual model was 0.831 and in the weekly model 0.218. The correlations between the residuals and viewing in the annual model was .738 ($p < .0001$); the weekly model $r = .653$ ($p < .0001$) also decreased. These results support the inclusion of weekly cycle in the model.

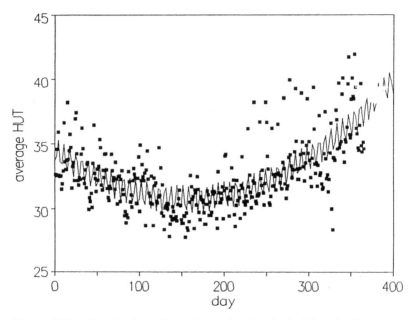

Figure 10.5. Combined weekly and annual cycle of television viewing.

Hypothesis 1: Cycles of Television Viewing

The results supported Hypothesis 1. Television viewing displayed three cycles: a daily cycle, composed of two sinusoidals that accounts for 98.0% of the daily pattern in viewing; an annual cycle, accounting for 45.5% of the annual viewing pattern after the daily cycle was removed from the data; and a weekly cycle, best described by an absolute-value sine model that accounted for an additional 11.6% of the variance in viewing.

Hypothesis 2: Television Viewing and the Weather

The correlation between the weather variables and television viewing (Table 10.7) revealed that precipitation ($r = 0.143$, $p < .006$) had a positive relationship with viewing. People watched more television

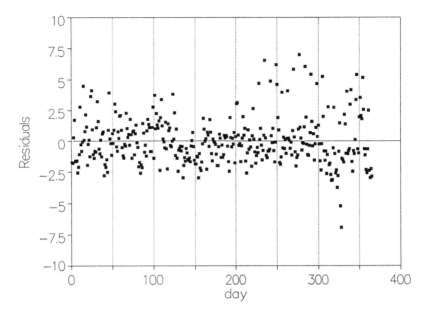

Figure 10.6. Residuals of annual and weekly model.

during rainy or snowy weather. Temperature $(r = -0.155,\ p < .003)$ had a negative relationship with viewing. People watched less television when the temperature was above the monthly average. Further, the two weather variables had no significant relationship with each other $(r = -.011,\ p = .827)$ or with the residuals.

The results of the regression of the two weather variables on the television viewing are also presented in Table 10.7. Together these variables explained an additional 7.8% of the variance in viewing left unaccounted for by the time-dependent model. The coefficients of the two weather terms were statistically significant $(p < .01)$. The interaction of temperature and precipitation did not significantly predict viewing. In other words, cold rainy days produced no greater viewing than did cold days or wet warm days. The residuals of the multiple regression were normally distributed (Kolomogorov $D = .04,\ p < .15$). The skew was 0.428, and the kurtosis was 0.472. These results supported Hypothesis 2 that weather influences television viewing.

TABLE 10.7 Relationship of Weather Variables to Viewing

Pearson Correlations (coefficient/probability)			
	TV Viewing	Precipitation	Temperature
Precipitation	0.143		
	$p = 0.006$		
Temperature	−0.155	−0.011	
	$p = 0.003$	$p = 0.827$	
Residual	0.978	0.000	0.000
	$p = 0.000$	$p = 1.000$	$p = 1.000$

Descriptive Parameters for Weather Factors ($N = 365$)				
Variable	Coefficient(b)	SE	t	Mean (SD)
Intercept	−0.031	0.109	−0.29	
Precipitation	0.577	0.179	3.22*	0.36 (0.48)
Temperature	−0.039	0.009	−4.44*	1.11 (9.68)
R^2	0.044			
Residual analysis				
SD	1.642			
Skew	−0.428			
Kurtosis	0.472			

*t values are statistically significant ($p < .01$).

Hypothesis 3: Holidays and Football

What accounted for the remaining variance? Did programming explain additional variance in viewing? An examination of the 22 residuals whose probability of occurrence were less than 5% revealed that 7 were holidays. For example, Christmas Day was the most deviant single day in viewing. People watched less television than predicted. To examine how the holidays affected viewing, all holidays were dummy coded.[5] The test results indicated that holidays explained an additional 11.7% of the variance ($p < .0001$) in viewing unexplained by time alone.

Further, regular "special" events such as NFL football games attracted large audiences. Seven of the 22 residuals were days when Chicago Bears games were broadcast. The days with Bears games were also dummy coded to examine their influence on viewing. The results revealed that the football games explained an additional 13.2% of the variance ($p < .0001$). These results support the hypothesis that departure from the frequency of viewing as predicted by the three cycles was a function of holidays and social events.

Two of the remaining eight largest residuals were attributable to an unusual social event, the Persian Gulf War. These results suggest that television viewing was not much affected by programming but rather by social, cultural, and weather factors that predisposed the audience to watch television. In other words, television viewing can be considered a cultural phenomenon, with broadcasters competing for an audience of fixed size except in those situations where special circumstances expand audience size.

Taking the analysis one step further, the residuals were again examined after the influence of Bears games and holidays were removed. There were 19 residuals whose probability of occurrence was less than 5%. Of these, three positive residuals took place at the beginning of the Persian Gulf War. Another was Super Bowl Sunday. Eight significantly negative residuals occurred during the summer on either Saturday or Sunday when social prescriptions suggest outdoor activity. One positive residual occurred in May after three days of warmer than average weather. Two others occurred in August; one on a cold wet day and another after a week of above-average temperatures. The largest negative residual occurred on December 23, the Sunday before Christmas. For the 17 days prior to Christmas, viewing was lower than expected. Clearly, "the holidays" provided alternative activities to television, such as shopping, and attending parties or family gatherings. Together the 17 days for which an attribution for deviant viewing levels can be justified accounted for 23.8% of the unexplained variance. These patterns may also be attributed to sociocultural factors, suggesting that programming has only a limited impact on audience size.

Hypothesis 4: The Sweeps

Rating service companies such as Nielsen and Arbitron conduct national surveys with large samples three times a year. During these sweep periods, networks broadcast special programs to increase ratings. The sweep dates were dummy coded to examine the effect of special programming. The sweeps explained only 1.7% of the remaining variance, suggesting that special programming has little effect on overall viewing level.

In a further attempt to look for a programming effect, three special programs that might impact audience size were examined: the Academy Awards, the NCAA basketball finals, and the Miss America Pageant. In all three cases, the residuals were not significant. Thus, programming itself seems to have little impact on viewing.

Discussion

The overall purpose of this research was to predict how many households turn on the television. This study followed step-by-step analysis instead of testing a single model or hypothesis. We began by theoretically deducing a set of a priori structural cyclical components through Fourier analysis and then detected further periodicities as we modeled this cyclic process with nonlinear regression. This approach differs from Meadowcroft's and Buder's (both this volume), who only detected a posteriori cycles.

This study examined the viewing cycles with one year of 15-minute interval data. The results of the spectral analysis revealed three cycles: daily, weekly, and annual. The daily cycle may be best described by a combination of two sinusoidals that explained 98% of the variance in viewing. Next, the daily cycle was removed by taking the daily mean, and the annual cycle was analyzed. It explained 45.5% of the variance in viewing. Two mathematical models describing the weekly cycle, the sine model and the absolute-value sine model, were tested. The absolute-value sine model explained an additional 11.6% of the variance. Together the annual and weekly cycles accounted for 57.1% of the variance in viewing.

These results suggest that television viewing is a habitual process rather than a result of programming efforts by broadcasters. People simply turn on the set depending on the time of year, the day of the week, and the hour of the day. The impact of the weather on viewing behavior was examined with the residuals. Temperature and precipitation explained an additional 7.8% of the variance. One reason why they contributed little variance is that the majority of weather's impact can be accounted for by the annual cycle (Barnett et al., 1991). In total, 64.9% of the variance in daily viewing was explained by the weekly and annual cycles and the weather.

Two important social events were also examined. Holidays and football games explained an additional 24.9% of the variance. In total, 89.8% of the variance was explained. Last, the sweeps explained an additional 1.7% of the remaining variance. The still unexplained variance in viewing may be explained by cultural processes. The overall results suggest that television viewing may be defined as a sociocultural process rather than a result of programming efforts by broadcasters, which have only a limited impact on audience size. It should be noted that Bears games, the Super Bowl, and news coverages of the Gulf War may be considered programming. Clearly, in the case of football, programming has evolved from the coverage of a game into a "media event." And although broadcasters can choose to cover events of social significance, they cannot program them into the regular broadcast schedule.

This research has some limitations in generalizability. First, the data were limited to the Chicago area. Future research needs to examine other areas with different weather and cultural patterns. Second, some of the data from 2:00 a.m. to 5:45 p.m. were estimated. Using a moving average may have produced the regular daily cycle. Third, the weather data were crude. There was only a single measure for each date. The intradaily volatility of Chicago's weather was not considered. Also, precipitation was only dummy coded. A blizzard or light flurries or a thunderstorm and all-day rain were treated identically. Thus, the data may not be precise enough to accurately describe the influence on television viewing.

Precise weather data from the NOAA (1991) may be used to examine the influence of environmental factors on viewing. Hourly data could be used, including such variables as humidity, cloud cover, daylight, and temperature. With these data, cross-spectral analysis could be conducted to examine the precise causal relationship between weather conditions and viewing patterns as well as the lag between the meteorological variables and viewing. In this way, the full extent of the weather on audience size can be determined.

Notes

1. The various symbols that indicate the weather conditions are sunny, partly sunny, partly cloudy, cloudy, rain or thunderstorm, rain or rain mixed with snow, partly sunny and snow, partly sunny and rain, partly cloudy and rain, partly cloudy and snow, cloudy and rain, cloudy and snow, and rain and snow.

2. Sunday's variance is significantly greater than Tuesday and Wednesday. It is not significantly greater than Thursday or Friday.

3. The means were calculated with 365 residual data points after fitting the seasonal model. The plot of the residual data show a pattern similar to the negative absolute sine model.

4. There were 96 data points per day (4 per hour × 24 hours), 672 per week (96 × 7), and 35,040 per year (96 × 365). These were the lengths of the three cycles.

5. The dummy-coded holidays were Washington's Birthday, Easter Sunday, Memorial Day, Independence Day, Labor Day, Columbus Day, Thanksgiving Day, Christmas Eve, Christmas Day, and New Year's Day. Because some holidays resulted in less viewing and others greater viewing, the absolute value of the residual was used in the regression analysis.

11

Attention Span Cycles

JEANNE M. MEADOWCROFT

As other authors in this book demonstrate, human behavior patterns are sometimes characterized by cycles. Warner, for example, reports cycles in social interaction patterns, and Barnett explains 89.8% of television viewing variance in Chicago households as a function of daily and weekly viewing cycles, weather conditions, and social events.

Given that human communication behaviors can generate cycles of activity, it is logical to ask if human cognition produces information processing cycles. This question is addressed here by documenting the existence of attention span cycles produced while children watch television. To make it clear that "attention span" as conceptualized in this chapter refers to a cognitive act rather than a behavior the next section offers explication of the term.

Attention Span Explication

Conceptual Meaning

When used in the literature, the term attention span most often refers to a behavior. In the child psychology literature, for example, attention span refers to the length of time a child will remain engaged in a particular task, and attention deficit studies are concerned with individuals whose attention spans are particularly short (Buchoff, 1990; Trivedi & Raghavan, 1989). A concept in the literature with similar conceptual meaning, vigilance, refers to the length of time people can remain engaged in a particular task before performance suffers or fails (Levy, 1980; Mackworth, 1950).

A very different conceptualization of attention spans is possible, however. When we think of attention to television, for example, we might think about the amount of mental effort viewers invest in processing program content from one moment to the next, and available evidence suggests that these attention levels are not constant. Instead, viewers are selective, and they allocate more mental effort to processing some kinds of information, compared to other program content (Meadowcroft & Reeves, 1989; Thorson & Lang, 1992). It is possible, then, that when plotted over time, the pattern of attention to television is defined by repeating cycles that reflect this varying attention rhythm. The shift here is from viewing attention spans as a behavior, such as the length of time a viewer remains engaged in a television-viewing task, to conceptualizing attention spans as repeating cycles of mental effort produced by allocating varied amounts of mental effort toward processing information from television.

Measuring Lower-Order Concepts

Further explication of the attention span process is difficult without first defining attention because explication is contingent upon assumptions made about the nature of attention itself. Attention is defined here as mental effort underlying all cognitive activity. Attention is inherently selective, focusing mental effort toward processing a selected subset of available information (Neisser, 1976), and selection can be directed by either salient stimulus characteristics (e.g., motion and loud noises) or by the individual's knowledge and goals (Anderson & Lorch, 1983; Lang, 1992; Lynn, 1966; Sokolov, 1963). Conceptualized this way, attention can be thought of as the fuel for cognition, the intensity of mental effort allocated to performing cognitive tasks.

Appropriate measures of attention and attention span must be consistent with these conceptual definitions (Chaffee, 1991). In the study reported here, attention is measured using a secondary task method. This method is based on Kahneman's (1973) attention allocation theory.

According to Kahneman, attending to something requires mental effort, a resource limited by total cognitive capacity. When performing simultaneous tasks, available capacity must be divided between tasks, and increased allocation of effort to one task, therefore, necessarily implies a corresponding decrease in attention allocated to a concurrent task. It is further assumed there is a direct allocation-performance trade-off, so that when much effort is allocated to one task, performance on a concurrent task suffers.

An implication of Kahneman's theory is that attention can be measured as mental effort by a secondary task method that requires individuals to perform two simultaneous tasks—an ongoing primary task and a periodic secondary task. Attention allocated to the primary task is measured by noting performance variation in the secondary task, typically measured as accuracy or reaction time (RT) variance (Kahneman, 1973; Kerr, 1973; Norman & Bobrow, 1975; Posner, 1978).

Similar assumptions are made in this study. Participants performed two simultaneous tasks: attending to television (the primary task) and pressing a button in response to periodic tones (the secondary task). It is assumed that attending to television requires mental effort and that people allocate attention resources between the two tasks. When reaction times on the secondary task are fast, it is assumed that people are not allocating much effort toward attending to television at that time. When reaction times are relatively slow, it is assumed that secondary task performance deteriorates because individuals are allocating more available capacity to the primary task, attending to television.

Given this definition of attention, attention spans are defined as recurring cycles of mental effort produced by information processing activity. As shown in Figure 11.1, each cycle can be described by three lower-order concepts: *frequency* (the number of cycles completed within a given period of time), *duration* (the time it takes to complete a given cycle, that is, the inverse of the frequency), and *intensity* (amount of mental effort within a particular cycle).

When a secondary task method is used to measure attention, Fourier terms (shown in Figure 11.2) translate nicely into measures of lower-order concepts associated with attention spans. A comparison of Figures 11.1 and 11.2 shows that the term frequency in both figures describes the speed of cycling of a sine wave, or the number of cycles completed within a given period of time. The Fourier term *amplitude* defines the vertical range (maximum positive or negative deviation

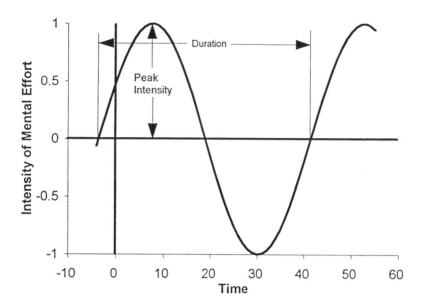

Figure 11.1.   Lower-order constructs of attention.

from zero) of the wave and indicates of the intensity of mental effort associated with the attention span cycle. Cycle duration corresponds to the Fourier term *period*, and *phase* refers to the time at which peaks occur, relative to some zero time point. Fourier analysis procedures are considered appropriate for operationalizing attention spans because Fourier terms describe cycles in ways that allow measurement of the three basic lower-order concepts associated with attention spans: cycle frequency, duration, and intensity.

At this point, attention is conceptualized as mental effort, and attention spans are defined as recurring cycles of mental effort produced by information processing activity. Further, secondary task methods are selected to measure mental effort allocated toward processing television content, and Fourier analysis is identified as a strategy offering the potential to describe the three lower-order concepts associated with attention spans: cycle frequency, duration, and intensity. Discussion now turns to the Meadowcroft and Watt (1989) multicomponent theory of attention spans that predicts that unique attention patterns will be

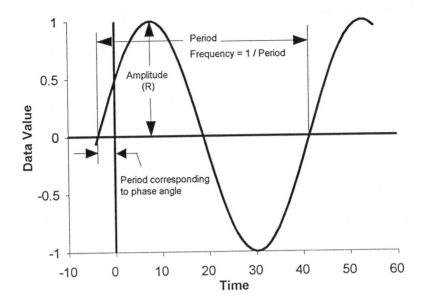

Figure 11.2. Fourier terms describing periodic wave.

produced by specific types of cognitive activities—predictions that are tested in this study.

A Multicomponent Theory
of Attention Spans

Consistent with the idea that attention underlies all information processing activity, the multicomponent theory predicts different types of cognitive tasks will produce unique attention patterns (Meadowcroft & Watt, 1989). At least four unique explanations are offered in the literature to account for attention variance: attention inertia, environmental monitoring, dramatic sampling, and story processing skills. With the exception of attention inertia, these explanations describe repetitive cognitive tasks to account for attention variance—the kinds of tasks that might logically be expected to produce attention span cycles. These explanations are briefly discussed below.

Attention Inertia

Anderson, Alwitt, Lorch, and Levin (1979) introduced the term "attention inertia." Based on visual selection patterns for a sample of 3- to 5-year-old children, they found that "a sort of behavioral 'inertia' is built up such that the child is more likely to continue looking at the TV the longer he or she has already been looking" (p. 338). If attention inertia is present in this study, a significant linear trend should be observed, indicating increased investments of mental effort with elapsed program time.

Environmental Monitoring

Several theorists have described a fundamental perceptual process related to attention that suggests that attention is always divided between monitoring the environment and performing the task at hand (Hochberg, 1968; Hochberg & Brooks, 1978; Neisser, 1976). In simplified terms, this theory states that perceptual processes are guided by an internal cognitive model of the environment that is used to direct perceptual pickup and to generate hypotheses about the environment that are tested by perceptual and sensory explorations. Information picked up modifies the initial anticipatory scheme, affecting further exploration and information pickup (Neisser, 1976). It is not unreasonable, then, to expect that a television viewer's attention must periodically shift from the screen to the surrounding environment. If so, fundamental attention span cycles produced by environmental monitoring should be observed under all viewing conditions.

Dramatic Sampling

Huston and Wright (1983) suggest that television viewers periodically sample program content to make a "quick assessment of program features and content" (p. 61). They identify three levels of formal features: program structure, including dialogue and narration; pacing, variation, and levels of action; and sensory (visual and auditory) events. If attention is influenced by dramatic sampling activities, formal features such as program structure should influence attention patterns, producing cycles of high frequency that reflect the periodic and frequent sampling predicted by Huston and Wright's theory.

Story Processing Skills

Many have suggested attention is directed by schemata, metacognitive structures that provide a framework for organizing and attending to incoming information (e.g., Anderson & Lorch, 1983; Meadowcroft & Reeves, 1989). If so, the rhythm of cognition should differ between schema-directed and non-schema-directed processing, producing distinct attention span patterns as a result. Also, because cognitive tasks associated with the use of schema are repetitive (e.g., instantiation), it is likely that the use of story schema produces attention span cycles.

It is important to note that Meadowcroft and Watt (1989) do not view the above theoretical explanations offered to account for attention span variance as competing with theirs. Instead, the multicomponent theory of attention spans predicts the coexistence of multiple attention span patterns, each produced by specific cognitive tasks. The question to address now is how one might go about detecting and describing attention span cycles, and the following discussion of Fourier and harmonic analysis procedures describes such a method.

Fourier and Harmonic Analysis Procedures

Fourier terms (amplitude, phase, and frequency) have already been introduced to show how they allow description of attention span cycles. What needs to be explained here is how Fourier and harmonic analysis procedures allow observation of coexisting, additive sources of variance. Because readers are not expected to be familiar with these analytic tools, a brief discussion follows. A more complete discussion is beyond the scope of this chapter; readers interested in more information are referred to other sources for more detail (e.g., Bloomfield, 1976; Kreyszig, 1972; VanLear & Watt, this volume; Watt, 1979).

Fourier discovered that when plotted over time, variable change can be "represented as the sum of several simple sine waves of different amplitudes, phases and frequencies" (Campbell, 1986, p. 117). In other words, the shape of an initial pattern over time is complex: It is literally defined by summing its simpler spectral component parts.

The first step in detecting those components is to construct a Fourier transform. This is accomplished by using Fourier analysis to isolate periodic components in the original time series data, if they exist, and to describe those spectrum components in terms of cycle amplitude, phase, and frequency. Adding together all Fourier components produces a complex function that reproduces the original data exactly. Although Fourier transform data provide a full description of the original data in a new (and possibly more revealing) form, the procedure does not offer the simplification and generalization useful in isolating the simple, fundamental processes that produce the data. To achieve this, an additional set of procedures loosely termed harmonic analysis is used (Bloomfield, 1976).

One of the more useful harmonic analysis tools employs least squares procedures to estimate the frequency, amplitude, and phase of a single harmonic component so that the squared error between the simple sine or cosine wave produced and the original data is minimized. This is essentially the analog of fitting a linear regression line to a set of bivariate data, and the procedure can be generalized to fit more than one harmonic component to a time series (this is the analog of multiple regression). These procedures are outlined in VanLear and Watt (this volume) and are used here to describe attention span cycles and to test for the presence of cycles predicted by the Meadowcroft and Watt (1989) multicomponent attention span theory.

Attention Span Model Validation

In this study, attention is defined as mental effort and is measured by a secondary task. Attention spans are defined as recurring cycles of mental effort, produced by cognitive activity, and Fourier analysis procedures are used to detect and to describe attention span cycles. The multicomponent theory of attention spans predicts that many different attention span cycles coexist, each produced by specific cognitive tasks. When cognitive tasks are periodic, it is predicted that, when plotted over time, the pattern of attention to television will be defined by repeating cycles that reflect the varying rhythm of attending to television that would fuel such periodic cognitive activity. The first goal in the analysis reported in this chapter is to detect attention patterns representing components in the multicomponent attention span theory—a linear attention inertia pattern and attention span cycles produced by environmental monitoring, dramatic sampling, and story processing skills.

Once the presence of attention span patterns is documented, Fourier terms are used to describe attention span cycles.

Method

Participants

Children (5 to 8 years old) were recruited from day care centers to participate in this study. Forty completed both testing sessions and are included in reported analyses.

Design and Overview of Procedures

A 2 (story schema skill) × 2(story structure) between-subjects design was used. The design required two separate testing sessions. In the first, story schema skills were assessed, as described below. In the second, children watched television while performing a secondary task to measure attention.

Measures

Story schema skills. Two unique skills were identified in the literature as related to story schema operations: seriation skills, the ability to keep a series of events in memory (Brown & French, 1976; Piaget, 1926, 1969); and the ability to distinguish central from incidental story content (Collins, 1983; Thorndyke & Yekovich, 1979). The sequencing and sorting tasks described below directly assess these skills.

Before engaging in these assessment tasks, children participated in a practice session to familiarize them with "story games." Then, they watched two stories on television, *The Three Robbers* and *Leopold, the See-Through Crumbpicker*. Immediately after viewing each story, story schema skills were assessed by the sorting and sequencing tasks.

In the sequencing task, children were given eight pictures from a story they had just viewed and were asked to put the pictures in sequence. Procedures for scoring the sequencing task are based on those described by Collins (1979): One point was given for each adjacent pair of pictures placed in correct temporal order. Maximum score was 7 points for each of the two stories (14 points total).

In the sorting task, children were asked to look at the same pictures used in the sequencing task and to select one picture that represented "the most important thing that happened in the story" by marking a large X through that picture. The process was repeated until four pictures were marked as representing central story content. Points awarded for picture selections were based on the number of adult judges who had previously identified each picture as representing central story content. Maximum score for the *Leopold* story was 34 and for *The Three Robbers* 35.

Performance on the sequencing and sorting tasks were summed to create an index of overall story schema skills. To give performance on each task equal weight in this index, all four performance scores were first converted to a 7-point scale before summing (maximum index score = 28). The mean score ($M = 16.53$, $SD = 4.39$) was used as the dividing point for assigning children to high versus low story schema skill groups.

Attention. Attention to story content was measured by the children's reaction time (RT) to auditory cues in a secondary task. Tone placement was random (average interval of 8.16 seconds), and children responded by pressing a button on a hand-held joystick. RT was measured in milliseconds (ms) and recorded by an Apple IIE computer.

Story structure. All children watched edited versions of the same television program. In the story structure condition, the program was edited to maintain the original story line and one subplot. The nonstory structure condition used some of the same episodes (placed at the exact elapsed program time as in the story structure condition), but the underlying story line was disrupted by inserting episodes from other stories in the same program series. Because entire episodes were used during editing and because characters in all episodes were from the same children's program series, the structure manipulation was subtle. Block randomization was used to assign the participant children to either story structure or nonstory structure conditions.

Analysis strategy. The experimental design for this study offered a strategy for testing predictions of the multicomponent attention span theory. The linear attention inertia and periodic environmental monitoring components, for example, should be present in all experimental cells because these processes theoretically represent universal processes that occur across all viewing conditions. Components produced by sampling dramatic structure, however, should be present in the two story structure cells but *not* in the nonstory structure cells, reflecting the presence or absence of dramatic structure in these conditions. Likewise, attention span components produced by viewer story schema skills should be present in the high-schema cells but *not* in the low-schema cells and can be detected by contrasting the data from the two high-schema cells with those from the two low-schema cells.

Data Preparation

RT probes were randomly spaced during the experiment to avoid predictability in the secondary task. Because of this, all reaction time data points were linearly interpolated onto an equally spaced grid of 8.16279 seconds (the average time between measurement points) before conducting the Fourier analysis. This was accomplished by a straight-line interpolation between all pairs of actual observation points. For each equally spaced grid point falling between the actual observation points, the equivalent reaction time was obtained from the constructed interpolation line. RTs for all participant children in a cell were then averaged to give a single 87-point time series for each of the four cells.

It should be noted that this interpolation process does not create additional data points but, rather, shifts observations to a fixed-interval time grid. Serial autocorrelation would be introduced if additional observations were created by interpolation (those linearly related to the interpolation endpoints), but this was not the case with this procedure. No additional autocorrelation was introduced, as the original observations were merely replaced with the interpolated values.

Results

Attention Inertia Component

According to theory, the attention inertia component should be present in all viewing conditions. To test for it, responses in all four treatment cells were collapsed to produce a single 87-point time series which was the grand mean of the attention measure for all participant children at each time point. Results supported the presence of an attention inertia component because linear regression showed a strong and significant positive trend (see Figure 11.3) that explained 39% of the variance

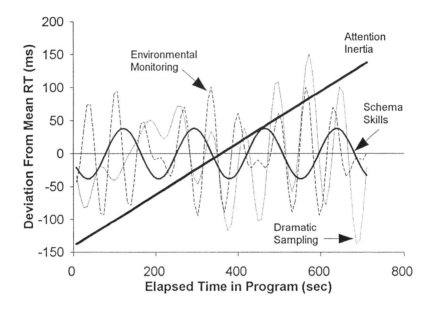

Figure 11.3. Individual attention components.

in this 87-point grand mean time series ($R = .62$), $F(1, 85) = 55.19$, $p < .0001$. To meet the assumption of stationarity of the time series, this trend was removed from the data for all subsequent analyses.

Environmental Monitoring Component

If present as theorized, the environmental monitoring component should also be observed in all experimental cells. The grand mean time series used in the previous analysis was also used in this analysis. To determine common periodic components in all cells, a cross periodogram was constructed by multiplying the Fourier periodogram component amplitudes for each of the four experimental treatment cells (see Watt, VanLear & Watt, both this volume) for descriptions of analytical methods). Only two frequencies showed commonality in every cell. These occurred at periods of 74.63 seconds (product = .95) and 58.85 seconds (product = .17). All remaining components had cross products of .02 or lower.

Using the least squares harmonic analysis procedures described earlier, these two components were used as starting points for a harmonic model. The resulting model explained 16% of the variance in the series $(R = .40)$, $F(2, 84) = 15.19$, $p < .0001$.

Each of the simple periodic cycles explained similar amounts of variance (7% and 9%). This might indicate they are *both* independent environmental monitoring attention cycles. Another interpretation, however, is just as likely: An environmental monitoring attention cycle may not be described by a simple sine or cosine wave. Figure 11.3 shows the components from each of the different attention processes. As can be seen, the fitted curve for the environmental monitoring component is cyclical but has periodic "flat spots." The addition of both sinusoids offers a model of this curve shape, so the preferred interpretation is that both represent parts of a single attention process that has repeating latent periods of constant attention level.

Dramatic Sampling Cycle

If there is an independent attention cycle being produced by story structure, it will occur in the two story structure cells but not in the nonstory structure cells. To explore this possibility, both the environmental monitoring cycle model (composed of two periodic components) and the attention inertia trend were removed from the data. The residual values for the two story structure cells were averaged with each other, as were the two nonstory structure cells. Each of the resulting 87-point time series were then Fourier transformed, and a difference periodogram was produced from the two. A difference periodogram isolates frequency components that are present in one periodogram but absent in the other (Watt, this volume).

Two large difference components were found at 74.6 seconds and 80.4 seconds and a third moderately large component at 348.2 seconds. These components were present in the story structure cells but not in the nonstory structure cells. The remaining difference components were fairly small, indicating that these frequencies were present both in cells that had story structure and in those that did not.

To model the cycles, a least squares fit with the three strong difference frequencies as starting points was constructed. This model was fitted only to the story structure cell data, as the dramatic sampling component(s) produced by story structure will be present only when the program shows normal dramatic construction.

This model explained 24% of the remaining variance (after removal of the attention inertia and environmental monitoring components) in the story structure cells ($R = .49$), $F(3,83) = 8.94$, $p < .0001$. As Figure 11.3 shows, the three-periodic-component model for the dramatic sampling component exhibits fairly low amplitudes early in the program, building intensity as time progresses.

Story Schema Skill Component

Attention effects due to story schema skills will occur in the high-story-schema cells but not in the low-story-schema cells. These data were collapsed into two time series: one containing the means for the high-schema-skills cells, and the other for the low-schema cells. Each series was Fourier analyzed, and a difference periodogram was constructed, using the same procedures described above. This analysis was conducted on data after removing variance from the attention inertia, environmental monitoring, and dramatic sampling components.

A single component at 209 seconds was the strongest in the difference periodogram. This component was fitted with least squares estimation procedures in the high-story-schema cell data. This single harmonic component is shown in Figure 11.3 and explains 11% of remaining variance in the high-story-schema cells ($R = .33$), $F(1, 85) = 10.78$, $p < .002$.

The Simultaneous Multicomponent Model

Prior analyses examined attention components individually and found evidence for the presence of each. It is possible that the processes are not independent, however, and that there may be covariance between some attention components. Further, earlier analyses give no indication of the relative strengths of each component in predicting attention variance.

To adequately test the final multicomponent model, all components present in a particular cell must be simultaneously included in the prediction of attention levels in that cell. The overall predicted value then can be compared to the observed value (multiple R), and the contribution of each component to the prediction can be assessed (beta weights). A computer program was written by Watt (see Meadowcroft & Watt, 1989) to construct the predicted attention values in each cell at each of the time points. Table 11.1 displays the multicomponent model

TABLE 11.1   Final Multicomponent Model Predictive Equation

Component	Formula
Predicted attention	$RT_{predicted} =$
Attention inertia	$710.6 + 3.203t$
Environment monitoring	$-5.52735 \cos (.6703836t) + 55.6174 \sin (.6703836t)$ $-37.7805 \cos (.8833107t) - 26.2787 \sin (.8833107t)$
Dramatic structure	$\left\{ \begin{array}{l} -35.1484 \cos (.1507940t) - 3.7801 \sin (.1507940t) \\ +48.8789 \cos (.6337572t) - 27.5968 \sin (.6337572t) \\ -47.6628 \cos (.6851071t) - 17.2552 \sin (.6851071t) \\ \text{OR} \\ 0.0 \quad \text{if a nonstory (no plot) cell} \end{array} \right\}$
Schema skills	$\left\{ \begin{array}{l} -21.3040 \cos (.2975051t) - 31.9818 \sin (.2975051t) \\ \text{OR} \\ 0.0 \text{ if a low-schema cell} \end{array} \right\}$

t = measurement point number, on equally spaced time grid, beginning with $t = 0$.

predictive formula used by this program. The coefficients in this table were developed in the single component analyses reported above.

If a cell did not have an attention model component (according to theory), it received a score of 0.0 for the component. Table 11.2 indicates that the model is most predictive in the story structure cells, explaining about 50% of the variance in attention in these cells. In the nonstory structure cells, the model (which contains fewer components) explains only 25-35% of the variance. The least explained variance is in the nonstory/low-schema cell, which has only attention inertia and environmental monitoring components as predictors.

In Figure 11.3, each of the attention components are plotted separately. In Figures 11.4a-d, the set of attention components that exists in each experimental cell are plotted (cell components are listed in Table 11.2). When added together, these components form a curve of predicted attention levels. By examining these figures in sequence, one can see the cumulative effect of the addition of each attention component to the final model. Figure 11.4a presents the experimental cell for participant children with low schema skills and who were watching the presentation with no story structure. The predicted responses for this cell, then, are

TABLE 11.2   Correlation Between Observed Attention Measure
(RT) and Value Predicted from Multicomponent
Model for Each Treatment Condition

	Low Schema	High Schema
Story		
Multiple R	*.74*	*.75*
Model components in cell	Inertia	Inertia
	Monitoring	Monitoring
	Dramatic structure	Dramatic structure
		Schema
Nonstory		
Multiple R	*.52*	*.64*
Model components in cell	Inertia	Inertia
	Monitoring	Monitoring
		Schema

All correlations significant at $p < .001$.

both attention inertia and environmental monitoring. The predicted
curve plotted in this figure is the simple addition of these two components, as seen in Figure 11.3. Figure 11.4b adds the dramatic sampling
component to the previous two, as the children in this cell saw a
presentation with a normal plot. Figure 11.4c does not contain dramatic
sampling because these children viewed the nonstory structure presentation. Instead, this figure has the schema component added to the
attention inertia and environmental sampling because children in this
cell scored high on story schema skills. The final plot, Figure 11.4d, is
the summation of all four attention components. These participant
children had high story schema skills and viewed the normally plotted
program.

The predicted curve is plotted with the observed attention levels in
each of the cells to show the correspondence of each model to the observed data and to illustrate the correlational results shown in Table 11.2.

An overall assessment of the model is shown in Table 11.3, where all
components are used to simultaneously predict attention levels in all
cells. The N for this analysis was 4 cells × 87 time points per cell, or
348 observations. The table shows that the simultaneous multicomponent model explained 26% of the variance in attention. The strongest
predictor was attention inertia and the weakest was schema skills, with

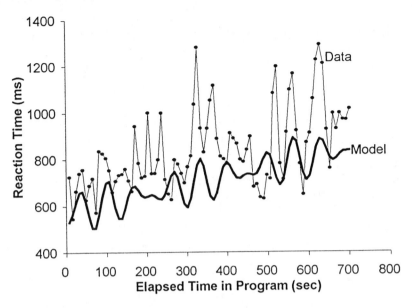

Figure 11.4a. Attention inertia plus environmental monitoring.

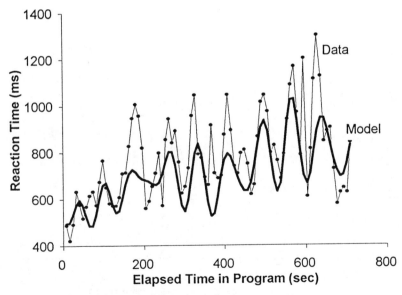

Figure 11.4b. Attention inertia, environmental monitoring, and dramatic sampling.

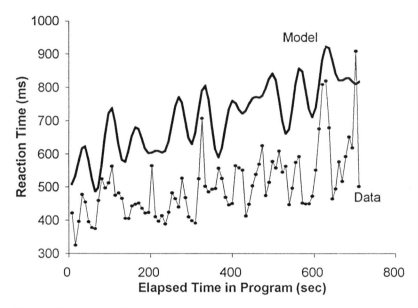

Figure 11.4c. Attention inertia, environmental monitoring, and story schema skills.

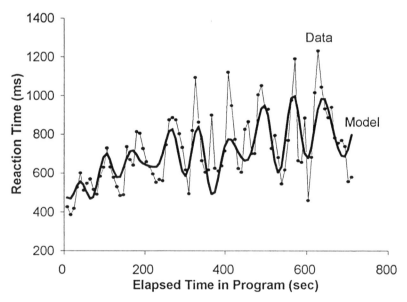

Figure 11.4d. Final model with all attention components present.

TABLE 11.3 Predictive Ability of the Full Multicomponent
Attention Model

Component	Beta	t-value	Signif. of t
Inertia	.38	8.25	< .0001
Monitoring	.20	4.14	< .0001
Dramatic structure	.23	4.74	< .0001
Schema	.10	2.11	< .05

Multiple $R = .53$, $F = 33.03$ (4; 343 df), $p < .00001$

environmental monitoring and dramatic sampling components posi-
tioned between these extremes. All components were statistically significant, indicating that all components in the final multicomponent
model operated independently of each other.

Discussion

This study offers a convincing demonstration that Fourier and harmonic
analysis procedures can be used to advance our understanding of attention spans and the fundamental processes that produce attention span
cycles. Just as important, findings support key assumptions in the
Meadowcroft and Watt (1989) multicomponent attention span theory.
First, evidence supports the notion that attention spans can be defined
not only as a behavior but also as repeating cycles of mental effort. If
this were not the case, attention span cycles would not have emerged in
the first stage of Fourier transform analysis. Findings also support the
theoretical assumptions that different cognitive tasks produce distinct
attention span rhythms and that repetitive cognitive tasks are likely to
produce attention span cycles. Finally, results support the conclusion
that attention span is not a singular concept, as often discussed. Instead,
this construct is best defined by the operation of coexisting, additive
processes. Together these cycles tell us children's attention spans are
more complex than previously thought; individually, each cycle reveals
something unique about what it means to attend to television.

Fourier description of environmental monitoring attention span cycles, for example, reveals that this process is not defined by a simple
sine or cosine wave. Instead, the two periodic components of moderate

intensity describe environmental monitoring activity. When added, as shown in Figure 11.3, these components reveal a repeating attention span pattern that begins with two to three cycles of similar frequency, intensity, and duration, followed by "flat spots," or periodic lulls in environmental monitoring activity.

Similarities between dramatic sampling and environmental monitoring rhythms were found in the analysis, although unique aspects of dramatic sampling cycles were observed and are theoretically important. A unique feature of this component, for example, is the finding that spectrum components are characterized by increasing intensity over time. This trend was present, even after removal of the positive linear attention inertia trend, and it is likely a graphic representation of increased attention that results from dramatic tension that is initially at low levels and builds throughout a television drama.

Like environmental monitoring activity, dramatic sampling was found to be defined by more than one spectrum component. One is identical in duration (1.24 minutes) to one of the environmental monitoring attention span components. Other dramatic sampling components, however, were defined by relatively long duration (1.34 minutes and 5.8 minutes).

It is interesting to note the correspondence between dramatic sampling components and theory. As stated earlier, Huston and Wright (1983) suggested that sampling of program features and content can occur at three levels: program structure, pacing, and sensory events. It is tempting, therefore, to speculate that the three dramatic sampling components reflect sampling at each of these levels. If true, it could be argued that cycle duration reflects the length of information-processing tasks and that the cycle duration of 1.24-minute duration common to both dramatic sampling and environmental monitoring attention spans might represent a fundamental rhythm for sensory-level sampling tasks—whether sampling environmental or television stimuli.

Findings also suggest some degree of coordination between attention span activity produced by environmental monitoring and dramatic sampling processes. The graph in Figure 11.3 suggests this: Attention spans produced by the two sampling activities achieved synchrony after a few minutes of program viewing. This is an intriguing finding because it suggests that children coordinate dramatic sampling and environmental monitoring cycles in a way that periodically frees up attention capacity at regular intervals so that mental effort can be allocated toward completion of other cognitive tasks. Similarly, Watt and Meadowcroft

(1990) found that older children (7 and 8 years old) are better able to coordinate attention span cycles, compared to younger children (5 and 6 years old), suggesting that adult viewers would be relatively skilled at coordinating attention span rhythms as they view television.

A potential limitation in describing cycles in this study is discussed in Arundale's chapter in this book: Because data observations used to measure attention in this study occurred, on average, every 8.16 seconds, the smallest attention span cycles detectable here are over 16 seconds in duration. It is possible, therefore, that shorter cycles exist and represent significant cycles in attention span components described in this chapter. Given that the smallest cycle detected in the analysis had a period of 58.85 seconds, however, it seems unlikely that cycles less than 16 seconds in duration would prove to be important components for cycles produced by cognitive tasks examined in this study.

Unlike other processes in the multicomponent theory, the attention inertia trend is linear and is not associated with specific cognitive operations. It is not at all clear, therefore, what cognitive processes produce attention inertia patterns, although results of this study shed some light on this process.

First, because attention inertia is associated with a linear (rather than cyclical) trend, the implication is that attention inertia patterns are produced by an information processing task that involves relatively continuous information processing activity. It is also clear that the underlying mechanism is associated with allocation of relatively intense mental effort, reflected by the greater RT values associated with the slope of the attention inertia trend, compared to intensity levels associated with attention span cycles, as shown in Figure 11.3.

One possible explanation is suggested by Geiger and Reeves (1993), who found that when an information processing task requires television viewers to maintain event sequences in memory, this task requires increasing investments of mental effort as the length of time increases between presentation of program segments that make up the event sequence (also see Burns & Anderson, 1993). Perhaps, then, the linear attention inertia pattern reflects this type of sustained integration of incoming information and the fact that with elapsed program time, incoming information becomes increasingly distant in proximity from program events presented early in the program. If so, one would expect to find a linear trend showing increased attention investments with increases in elapsed program time.

Future research is needed to confirm this suspicion. The inability to specify cognitive operations associated with this trend remains frustrating, particularly given the fact that this component explained more attention variance than any other in the multicomponent model. If the suspicion is confirmed, however, the label attention inertia would prove misleading and should be replaced by a less theoretically biased term that does not imply that cognitive activity producing this trend is passive and controlled by outside forces. For example, if event sequencing, in fact, accounts for the linear attention pattern, it might be labeled "event sequencing attention component" or some similar label that identifies the cognitive task producing this attention pattern.

An increasing linear trend in attention could possibly be attributed to fatigue effects that increase RT as the program progresses. However, Menelly, Wiegel, Yan, and Watt (1992) found no evidence of attention inertia in young adults who simply pressed a button in response to a tone. In contrast, a similar sample showed an increase in RT while viewing a program of the same duration. Although these results do not rule out fatigue in younger viewers, they do suggest that fatigue alone may not be sufficient to explain an increasing trend in RTs.

Finally, this study helps illustrate the importance of the kinds of analysis tools discussed in this book. Without them, observation of cyclical processes—in communication behaviors or in cognitive activity—would not be possible. Warner's chapter (this volume), for example, clearly demonstrates that such tools can provide important descriptions of interpersonal interactions and influential variables—insights that would likely go unnoticed without appropriate analysis tools. Similarly, Fourier and harmonic analysis enabled detection and description of attention span cycles in this study, expanding our understanding of what it means to attend to television.

12

Cybernetics of Attitudes and Decisions

STAN A. KAPLOWITZ
EDWARD L. FINK

Many of us have had the experience of changing our mind and sometimes even changing it back and forth several times. We believe that such *vacillation* or *oscillation* (our preferred term) or cycling (this volume's term) is an important phenomenon. In this chapter, we present some of the existing evidence for cognitive oscillation, present a theory that predicts it, and describe some of our own recent laboratory studies investigating cognitive oscillation.

Lorenz (1977) posited that "any self-regulating process in whose mechanisms inertia plays a role tends toward oscillation" (p. 237). As there is evidence that cognition has such an inertial principle (cf. Saltiel & Woelfel, 1975), it is reasonable to expect oscillatory dynamics for cognition. Such dynamics are relevant both to decision making and to attitude and belief change. Although the literature in these areas has generally been quite separate, these phenomena are closely related. This relationship is seen, for example, in Fishbein and Ajzen's (1975) suggestion that a major determinant of people's behavioral intentions (i.e., their behavioral *decisions*) is their *attitude* toward the relevant behav-

Portions of this chapter are based on Fink and Kaplowitz's "Oscillation in Beliefs and Cognitive Networks," which appears in G. A. Barnett and W. Richards (Eds.), *Progress in Communication Sciences* (Vol. 12, pp. 247-272), Norwood, NJ: Ablex, 1993.

ior.[1] Second, indicating one's attitude involves *deciding* the attitude to be expressed and perhaps also the attitude one actually has. As Tourangeau, Rasinski, Bradbury, and D'Andrade (1989) argue, respondents do not simply retrieve an evaluation previously stored in memory but "*generate one* based on material retrieved when the attitude question is asked" (p. 496).

With a few exceptions (e.g., Lewin, 1951), until the late 1970s the theory and research on attitudes and decisions focused on the outcome of the process rather than on its dynamics. For example, a recent review of the decision-making literature (Abelson & Levi, 1985) focused on models predicting decisions based on the probability of and utility of various outcomes.[2] In attitude research, the major emphasis has been on how source, message, and receiver characteristics influence an attitude, typically measured only once after an experimental treatment. Thus, those investigating decision making and attitude change have generally failed to measure the time course of variables associated with the underlying psychological dynamics.

However, understanding dynamics in general and cognitive oscillations in particular is critically important. First, understanding the time course of attitude and belief change may add considerably to our understanding of the forces causing this change.

Second, because beliefs are typically measured at one point in time, oscillations can introduce what appears to be unreliability into their measurement. In other words, *systematic change*, in the form of oscillation in beliefs, can be mistaken for the *random* disturbances in a measurement, which we usually think of as unreliability. Determining the time parameters of such oscillations may allow us to separate unreliability from instability in the measurement of an attitude or belief (Heise, 1969).

Finally, because oscillations appear to be associated with stressful decisions (see Janis & Mann, 1977), understanding cognitive oscillation may help us learn strategies by which people can reduce or cope with decisional stress. And this lessening of decisional stress may have the indirect effect of improving decision making.

Both attitude and decision researchers have recently begun paying more attention to process and dynamics. In the attitude area, not only have thoughts been considered an important intervening variable (e.g., Chaiken, Liberman, & Eagly, 1989; Petty & Cacioppo, 1986), but a number of studies (Liberman & Chaiken, 1991; Millar & Tesser, 1986) suggest that thinking is sufficient to bring about attitude change. Thus, McGuire

(1989) states that those who study attitudes increasingly view them as an interacting dynamic system. The decision-making literature has also shown increasing concern with the dynamics of the process (e.g., Janis & Mann, 1977; Tversky & Shafir, 1992).

Cognitive Oscillation: Indirect Evidence

Probably the greatest amount of attention to oscillation has been given by those studying postdecisional attitudes. Walster (1964) and Brehm and Brehm (1981) have found that people often regret a choice they have just made and only later reduce their postdecisional dissonance due to that choice.[3]

Reversal of beliefs without additional informational input has also been found in other studies. For example, Poole and Hunter (1979, 1980) note this reversal effect in studies involving sets of concepts that were assumed to be hierarchical, and Gilbert, Krull, and Malone (1990) show that an idea must first be entertained as true before it can be rejected as false. If correct, this would indicate that an individual's beliefs must change at least once in the process of rejecting a proposition.

Other investigators providing evidence consistent with the idea of cognitive oscillation include Latané and Darley (1970), who state that bystanders experiencing the stress of an emergency can "cycle back and forth" between beliefs like "the building's on fire, I should do something" and "I wonder if the building's really on fire" (p. 122), and Wegner (1989), who indicates that the stress of being deceptive "can promote an unstable mental state, one that oscillates between trying not to think and thinking a lot" (p. 34).[4]

How have cognitive oscillations been explained? Lewin (1951) posited that as we approach a goal both the attractive and repulsive forces associated with the goal get stronger. Further, he proposed that in an approach-avoidance conflict the repulsive forces increase more rapidly than the attracting ones. Thus, whereas at great distances the net force is attractive, as the goal is approached the net force becomes repulsive, thereby leading to oscillation (p. 264). Although not seeking direct evidence of oscillation, Houston and Sherman (1991) provide circumstantial evidence for Lewin's ideas: People in an approach-avoidance conflict take more time to make a decision than those in an approach-approach conflict.

In a similar vein, Brehm and Brehm (1981) examined the process of reactance. As a decider moves toward one choice alternative, freedom to choose another choice alternative is threatened, thereby causing the previously rejected alternative to become more attractive. This certainly could result in an oscillatory decision trajectory.

Janis and Mann (1977) predict such vacillation to occur when the conflict felt by the decision maker involves a "serious risk from the current course of action," a "serious risk from a new course of action," and when "a better solution may be found" (p. 78). Similarly, Bruss (1975) attributes "a wavering in the process of deliberation" to

> an unclear ranking of preferences or incommensurable preferences, vague or uncertain beliefs about how well an object or act will satisfy a preference, what the available alternatives are and the relative probabilities of attaining each, and unresolved notions of the risk that is warranted or tolerable if a chosen alternative fails. (pp. 557-558)

Wegner (1989) discusses circumstances in which a "thought . . . contains the seed of its opposite" (p. 113). Consistent with the findings of Gilbert et al. (1990), this process of denying or disregarding ideas involves reversal of beliefs or attitudes, which can bring about cognitive oscillation.

A Network Model of Cognitive Dynamics

The dynamics of cognitive change are presented here as part of a model of cognitive networks. In all such models, nodes represent concepts or entities, and linkages of varying strengths represent the associations between the nodes. Two distinct types of cognitive network models are presented; the primary difference between them is that one of them is based on a geometric, or spatial model, and the other is not.

The nonspatial models, called *semantic network* or *activation* models (e.g., J.R. Anderson, 1983; Higgins, 1989; Rumelhart, McClelland, & PDP Research Group, 1986; Woelfel, 1993) assume that the likelihood of concept B being thought of (activated) following activation of concept A is proportional to the strength of the A-B linkage. These linkages are assumed to grow stronger with repeated usage and to decay over time in the absence of use. Judd and Krosnick (1989) have adapted this model to study attitudes toward political objects; in their model, both the node and the linkage have strengths that may be positive or negative.

Our framework for understanding cognitive oscillations is based on a *spatial* model. This model assumes that an individual's beliefs may be represented by the location of concepts in a multidimensional space, with the distance between any two concepts representing their perceived dissimilarity (Woelfel & Fink, 1980). Moreover, the evaluation of a concept can be represented by its distance from a concept denoting positive evaluation, such as "My Preference" or "Things I Like" (Fink, Monahan, & Kaplowitz, 1989; Neuendorf, Kaplowitz, Fink, & Armstrong, 1986).

Like the semantic activation model, the spatial model assumes that there are associative linkages of various strengths between the nodes (concepts). These linkages are assumed to be springlike in that as a concept moves from its equilibrium location, the force moving it back toward equilibrium increases (see Fink & Kaplowitz, 1993; Kaplowitz & Fink, 1982, 1988, 1992; Kaplowitz, Fink, & Bauer, 1983; for earlier treatments, see Barnett & Kincaid, 1983; Kincaid, Yum, Woelfel, & Barnett, 1983; Woelfel & Fink, 1980, esp. pp. 158-159; this model also bears some resemblance to the loose link model in McGuire, 1969). Moreover, the stronger the linkage, the stronger this restoring force.

As with the activation models, these linkages are assumed to grow stronger with repeated usage and to decay over time in the absence of use. Furthermore, we expect that the stronger the linkage between two concepts, the harder it should be to change their relationship. Messages that associate two concepts may have the effect of strengthening their linkage and reducing their separation.

Linkage of Beliefs and Attitude Change

Although only a few studies have directly investigated oscillation of beliefs, attitude change research offers several theoretical underpinnings for assuming that concepts are linked.

Effect of Associating Beliefs

Studies show that *resistance* to attitude change can be increased by creating associations between beliefs (Holt, 1970; McGuire, 1964;

Nelson, 1968; Watts & Holt, 1970; see also Danes, Hunter, & Woelfel, 1978), including associations to positively valenced groups or individuals (Kelly, 1955; Tannenbaum, 1967). Scott (1968) summarized this by stating that strong attitudes are *embedded* (i.e., associated with other cognitive elements).

Linkages to beliefs associated with focal concepts within a message can also *promote* attitude change (Leippe, Greenwald, & Baumgardner, 1982; McGuire, 1981; Rokeach, 1975). The idea that change can be promoted by linking beliefs in messages is described by McGuire (1990) as follows: "Persuasion by the usual technique of communicating new information from an outside source will have specifiable *remote* effects on other, unmentioned topics in the person's thought system" (p. 512, emphasis added).

Mere Thought and Consistency

Tesser (1978) shows that thought in the absence of external messages can result in attitude polarization. He explains this by arguing that beliefs form structures, or *schemata*, that are activated by thought; the activation itself takes time. Further, thinking under the direction of such schemata induces cognitions to become "locally" evaluatively consistent. More recent studies have shown that whereas some cognitive structures become *more* polarized with thought (Millar & Tesser, 1986), other structures (those with uncorrelated dimensions or with value conflict) become *less* polarized with thought (see Chaiken & Yates, 1985; Liberman & Chaiken, 1991).

Theories that deal with consistency (e.g., Festinger, 1957; Heider, 1958) or with schemata can be translated into a network structure with concepts and linkages. This is made explicit in some formal versions of consistency theories (e.g., Cartwright & Harary, 1956). Tesser and Shaffer (1990, esp. pp. 482-489) review the recent evidence that shows how attitudes can be modeled as associative networks.

A Simple Model of Cognitive Forces

The apparent existence of cognitive oscillation suggests the existence of restoring (negative feedback) forces. Such restoring forces are built into our spatial network model with our assumption that the associative linkages between concepts are springlike. Consistent with the operation of a mechanical spring, we assume that the forces attracting one *toward* an alternative increase in strength as the individual cognitively moves *away from* that alternative.

A network of springlike linkages is by no means the only system that predicts oscillation. Indeed, some alternatives (such as an inductance-capacitance circuit) are mathematically isomorphic to a spring system. However, we find the spring imagery especially attractive for two reasons. First, we use a spatial model of cognition wherein dissimilarity is equivalent to distance. A spring system makes the forces dependent on the instantaneous distances between concepts. Second, as discussed more fully below, a spring analogy helps make sense of the *tension* people feel when experiencing opposing forces.

We first present a simple model incorporating springlike forces. This model assumes that cognitive motion proceeds in a mechanistic fashion and that conscious thought is not an independent causal factor. Next, we present more complex variants of this model, in which the independent causal effect of thought is considered.

The simple model assumes that a linkage between two concepts, A and B, creates a force satisfying the following equation:

$$F_{A, B} = K_{A, B}[d_{Eq} (A, B) - d(A, B)], \qquad [12\text{-}1]$$

where $F_{A,B}$ is the force between the concepts, $d_{Eq} (A, B)$ is the equilibrium distance of the linkage, $d(A, B)$ is the distance between those concepts in the receiver's cognitive space, and $K_{A, B}$ is the restoring coefficient of the linkage.[5] This model posits that on either side of the equilibrium location the net force is directed toward the equilibrium location.

People often see a choice alternative as consisting of both attractive and unattractive features (cf. value conflict as discussed, e.g., in Liberman & Chaiken, 1991). In this choice situation, there should be springlike linkages pulling in opposite directions. The equilibrium of the system is that point at which the opposing forces balance; the relevant restoring coefficient is the sum of the effects of all the individual linkages.

We now consider the motion of a system whose behavior is consistent with Equation 12.1. From Newton's laws of force and motion, it follows that

$$m \frac{d^2x^*}{dt^2} = Kx^*, \qquad\qquad [12\text{-}2]$$

where x^* is the distance of a concept from its equilibrium location, K is the net restoring coefficient on a concept (from all linkages), and m is the mass of a concept, defined below. If K is constant over time, this leads to a sinusoidal trajectory of undamped oscillations (i.e., with a constant amplitude and a constant period of oscillation). Moreover, the period of oscillation is a decreasing function of the restoring coefficient.

Sometimes people seem to manifest no perceptible cognitive oscillation. Furthermore, even when they do oscillate, our knowledge of both cognitive and physical systems suggests that such oscillations should die out. Just as mechanical systems have friction, which serves to damp oscillations, we suggest an analogous cognitive damping process. Letting C reflect the degree of damping and assuming that the damping force is proportional to, and in the opposite direction from, the velocity of the concept in motion yields the following:

$$m \frac{d^2x^*}{dt^2} + C \frac{dx^*}{dt} + Kx^* = 0. \qquad\qquad [12\text{-}3]$$

If $C^2 \geq 4Km$, the system is overdamped or critically damped, and this creates an S-shaped trajectory for the motion of the concept. If, however, $C^2 < 4Km$, the system is underdamped and an oscillatory trajectory is generated.

Like Lewin (1951), we see the forces on a person's decision as depending on one's cognitive distance from an alternative. Our model, however, explains Lewin's ad hoc assumption that the repulsive force increases more rapidly than the attractive force as one approaches the goal. Our model is also more precise because its explicit equations of force and motion enable us to predict the time course of change.

The Psychological Meaning of the Model

Mass

Mass formally refers to the property of an object that causes it to resist acceleration.[6] Psychologically, we assume that the mass of a concept is proportional to the number of meanings or attributes it has.

Equilibrium Length

The equilibrium length of a linkage is the distance between concepts that the linkage implicates when taken in isolation from other linkages. Thus, for most people, the linkage between *good pay* and *jobs I want* has a small equilibrium length, whereas the linkage between *long hours* and *jobs I want* has a large equilibrium length.

We extend the model to persuasion by assuming that a message linking concepts A and B establishes a linkage between them, whose equilibrium length, $d_{Eq}(A, B)$, is the dissimilarity between A and B specified in the message. Thus, the equilibrium length is the position advocated by the message.

The equilibrium predictions of our spatial linkage model are mathematically isomorphic with N. H. Anderson's (1981) information integration model of attitudes (see also Kaplowitz & Fink, 1992, pp. 353-354).[7] Anderson's model is built on the assumption that one's evaluation of an object (e.g., a possible job) is a weighted average of the evaluations of the various attributes of the object (e.g, pay, hours of work). In our model, the equilibrium length of the linkage between an attribute and an evaluative concept is analogous to the evaluation of the attribute.

Restoring Coefficient

The restoring coefficient is analogous to the *weight* of the attribute in the information integration model. Because the weight reflects the importance of the attribute in the decision calculus, attributes that are more important have greater restoring coefficients. The cognition and memory literature (e.g., J. R. Anderson, 1983) suggests that more frequent associations between concepts cause stronger linkages and that the lack of recent co-occurrence causes these linkages to weaken. Thus, we see the restoring coefficient as related to co-occurrence.[8]

Information integration models have been extended to persuasion situations by Anderson and Hovland (1957) and Saltiel and Woelfel (1975), and we have also employed such a model (see Fink, Kaplowitz, & Bauer, 1983; Kaplowitz, Fink, Armstrong, & Bauer, 1986; Kaplowitz & Fink, with Mulcrone, Atkin, & Dabil, 1991). A fundamental equation of such an information integration model is

$$\Delta P = \frac{w_A Dp}{w_0 + w_A}, \qquad [12\text{-}4]$$

where ΔP is the change in the receiver's position (opinion) toward the object, D_p is the message discrepancy (the difference between the position advocated by the message and the receiver's initial position), w_0 is the weight of the receiver's initial position, and w_A is the weight of the message position.

In this model, the relationship between attitude change and discrepancy is a function of w_0 and w_A. In particular,

$$\frac{\Delta P}{Dp} = \frac{w_A}{w_0 + w_A} . \qquad [12\text{-}5]$$

The parameter w_0 is expected to be an increasing function of premessage factors that inhibit attitude change, such as the strength of the initial attitude (or value-relevant involvement; see Johnson & Eagly, 1990). The parameter w_A is expected to be an increasing function of message factors that facilitate attitude change, such as source credibility and argument strength. Further, because the ratio

$$\frac{\Delta P}{Dp}$$

generally decreases as discrepancy increases (see, e.g., Fink et al., 1983; Kaplowitz & Fink et al., 1991) and because at extreme discrepancies attitude change sometimes decreases (see, e.g., Aronson, Turner, & Carlsmith, 1963), Equation 12-5 requires that w_A be a decreasing function of message discrepancy.

When we move to the spatial linkage model, the analogous equation is

$$\Delta P = \frac{K_{A,B} Dp}{K_R + K_{A,B}} , \qquad [12\text{-}6]$$

where $K_{A,B}$ is the linkage created by the message, and K_R is the anchoring linkage.[9] $K_{A,B}$ is the analogue of w_A and thus should be an increasing function of source credibility and of argument strength and a decreasing function of message discrepancy.

Although messages are assumed to establish springlike linkages between concepts, they do not fully determine the receiver's new view. The force created by a new message linkage is opposed by and ultimately in balance with the pre-existing forces from the network of other linkages in the receiver's cognitive system. These *anchoring* linkages, like w_0 in the information integration model, represent the strength of the receiver's initial view and are the result of prior messages.

We have stated that all linkages are assumed to decay over time (see Ebbinghaus, 1964); however, new messages or self-generated thoughts may have the effect of strengthening these linkages (see below).

Tension

People often are said to feel torn, pulled apart, or strained by conflicting demands of competing roles (see, e.g., Goode, 1960) as well as by the difficulty of making decisions. Such situations are clearly ones of great tension or stress. Our model, incorporating springlike linkages, is quite compatible with these ideas. People feel the greatest tension when a set of demands is incompatible and important; the tension (i.e., restoring forces) operating in a system of linkages is greatest under precisely those circumstances. Thus, we predict the following:

> *H1:* People will feel the greatest stress when being pulled in opposite directions by messages or thoughts (a) with strong arguments, (b) concerning strong attachments, (c) involving a credible source and a strong initial attitude, and (d) involving important and balanced attributes associated with decision alternatives.

Damping Coefficient

We have two opposing hypotheses about the damping coefficient. On the one hand, greater time pressure to make a decision may lead to greater damping. On the other hand, Janis and Mann (1977) imply that rushed decisions may lead to more regret and thus more oscillation subsequent to the decision.

Frequency and Amplitude of Oscillation

The frequency of oscillation of a spring is an increasing function of its restoring coefficient. Because the total restoring coefficient is the sum of the coefficients of the message linkage and the anchoring linkages, we can derive these interesting hypotheses.

> *H2:* Other things being equal, the frequency of oscillation is an increasing function of (a) source credibility, (b) argument strength, (c) strength of initial opinion, and (d) issue importance.

H3: Other things being equal, the frequency of oscillation is a decreasing function of message discrepancy.

We now examine determinants of the amplitude of oscillation. Our model predicts sinusoidal trajectories that are symmetric about the equilibrium location, and have amplitudes that are greatest at the start of the cognitive trajectory. Thus, we predict the following:

H4: The maximum possible amplitude of oscillation of a concept is the distance between the equilibrium location of a concept and the concept's original location.

In other words, the model predicts that the closer one is to a decisional endpoint (i.e., the less one is conflicted), the less should be the amplitude of oscillation.

This hypothesis also has some implications for many persuasion situations. Because by definition the more attitude change, the greater a concept has moved from its prior location to a new equilibrium location, we predict the following:

H4a: The greater the attitude change, the greater the amplitude of oscillation.[10]

By Hypothesis 4a, the amplitude of oscillation should be an increasing function of source credibility and argument strength and (usually) of discrepancy and a decreasing function of the strength of the receiver's initial belief. Consistent with this proposition, Kaplowitz et al. (1983), in an experiment with messages with three levels of discrepancy (high, moderate, and a control condition), found that the message with the greatest discrepancy induced the most attitude change and that this message also induced an oscillatory trajectory with the greatest amplitude.

Continuous Versus Dichotomous Decisions

Some decisions require a choice between two opposing alternatives, whereas others allow for the possibility of a "compromise" choice between them. Some decisions, in fact, allow for a nearly continuous range of possible outcomes (e.g., the amount of money to contribute to an organization). This distinction affects our predictions regarding oscillations.

Suppose that the balance of attitudinal forces causes the decider to desire a compromise and therefore to be uncomfortable with either decisional choice alternative. If the decision is continuous, this equilibrium location is a viable decision. However, if the decision is dichotomous, neither pre-existing choice alternative may be satisfactory, whereas any compromise choice is an impossibility by definition. Thus, for dichotomous decisions, for oscillations to die down it is not sufficient that they be damped. It may also be necessary that the restoring coefficients be *altered* so that one decisional endpoint can become the equilibrium location. As discussed below, how this comes about may be explained by a more complex variant of our model, one that incorporates cognitive elaboration.

The above discussion suggests that oscillations are more likely to persist for decisions and attitudes that are dichotomous than for those that are continuous; however, this prediction is not so simple. If the decider does not favor an extreme outcome but clearly leans to one side, that person may not oscillate when presented with a dichotomous decision. In contrast, if the decision were continuous, the decider might oscillate in the region of preference. Thus, the following are posited:

> *H5a:* If the decider clearly prefers one decisional endpoint to another, oscillation is more likely for a continuous decision than for a dichotomous one.
>
> *H5b:* If the decider does not clearly prefer one decisional endpoint, oscillations will last longer for dichotomous decisions than for continuous ones.

Furthermore, for a dichotomous decision, as long as the decider is being pulled to positions near both extremes of the scale, the amplitude will not decrease until the oscillation entirely stops.[11] Thus, we hypothesize the following:

> *H6:* Damping is less likely for dichotomous decisions than for continuous ones.

Conscious Thought and Cognitive Oscillation

Up to this point we have assumed that cognitive oscillation does not require conscious thoughts or reasons. There are two variants of this view. In one variant, the ongoing decision and evaluation process has no relationship at all with conscious thoughts, such as "On the one hand . . . , but on the other hand. . . ." In the other variant, although such thoughts may be associated with these oscillations, they are consequences rather than causes of the process of oscillation.

The cognitive response approach to attitude change (see, e.g., Petty & Cacioppo, 1986; Petty, Ostrom, & Brock, 1981) differs from the above model in that it proposes that thoughts are a major intervening variable between external messages and attitude change.[12] If this is true, then such thoughts should be predictive of any oscillations that occur.

The insights from the study of cognitive responses may be translated into our model by assuming that strong opposing linkages create a motivational process. This process results in people feeling uncomfortable with any decision they are moving toward. However, if the decider is engaging in what Petty and Cacioppo (1986) call *central* processing (or what Chaiken et al., 1989, call *systematic* processing), changing one's attitude may also require the individual to generate persuasive reasons for this change.[13] Thus, in this version of the model oscillations require conscious thoughts.

If the decider does provide such self-generated reasons, these, like other messages, should have a greater effect the more they provide new information (see Harkins & Petty, 1987, on the role of information in attitude change). Thus, such reasons should be persuasive if they are not simply redundant paraphrases of reasons that have already been dealt with. Moreover, such cognitive responses should, like other messages, create or strengthen linkages. This would cause the net restoring force and the equilibrium location to change as the decider thinks, resulting in two important observable effects. First, thinking should cause a person who is initially ambivalent to move to an equilibrium location that leans toward one alternative. Second, changes in the restoring forces and equilibrium location make it quite likely that there will be abrupt changes in the frequency or amplitude of oscillation; indeed, the trajectories may even be chaotic (see, e.g., Moon, 1987).

To the extent that oscillation requires cognitive elaboration, oscillation is more likely when people have the ability and motivation to elaborate (see Petty & Cacioppo, 1986). The ability to elaborate should be related to the availability and accessibility of the decider's thoughts (see Fazio, 1989; see also Tversky & Kahneman, 1974, on the availability heuristic). Thus, elaboration should be more likely when the decider has a detailed or complex schema for understanding the issue (see, e.g., Tetlock, 1983a, 1983b). The availability and accessibility of thoughts may also be greater when deciders have just been provided with a set of relevant reasons. Based on Petty and Cacioppo's (1986) elaboration likelihood model, the motivation to elaborate should also be a function of the individual's need for cognition and of the importance of the issue to the decider.

If thoughts make the kind of difference that we are considering, then the period of oscillation will be related to the time between the processing of sequential arguments. This in turn may be a function of both the difficulty of the decision task, the cognitive abilities of the decider, and the decider's concentration on the task.

This more complex model, in which cognitive responses have an independent effect, enables us to make predictions about the effect of ambivalence on the attitude trajectory. Recall that in the absence of thought, linkages are expected to decay, whereas thought is expected to maintain or strengthen the linkages. Therefore, the resolution of ambivalence about a dichotomy made by opting for one side should result in the reduction of the amplitude of oscillation. Further, making a decision should result in cessation of the thoughts relevant to the decision. This cessation can lead to the subsequent reduction in the restoring coefficients in the relevant linkages, thereby reducing the frequency of oscillation as well. Thus, we predict the following:

H7: The greater the unresolved ambivalence, the greater the amplitude and frequency of oscillation.[14]

Distraction

A number of studies (e.g., Petty, Wells, & Brock, 1976) have found that distraction results in fewer cognitive responses. This suggests that distraction reduces the number of opinion changes. If the time allotted for thinking is constant, this implies

H8: Distraction will cause oscillations to have a lower frequency.

This hypothesis can also be derived by assuming that distraction increases the damping coefficient. The equation for the frequency of a simple oscillator is

$$\omega = \frac{\sqrt{4Km - C^2}}{2m}, \qquad [12\text{-}7]$$

where ω is the frequency of oscillation, C is the degree of damping, K is the restoring coefficient, and m is the mass. Equation 12-7 shows that greater damping leads to a lower frequency; if distraction increases the damping coefficient, then it will cause the amplitude to decrease over time.

Cognition and Damping

Although the effects of distraction are consistent with a damping process, adding conscious cognition to the model offers an alternative conception of the damping process. Our simple model assumes a constant damping process and therefore an amplitude that decreases at a constant rate. Conversely, the cognitive damping process may appear only when circumstances require a decision and when thoughts are generated consistent with this requirement. In this case, the cognitive motion would stop more abruptly than in the model with a constant damping process. Gollwitzer, Heckhausen, and Steller's (1990) evidence of separate deliberative and implemental mind sets is consistent with the more complicated possibility.

Experimental Evidence About Oscillation

We have predicted the conditions affecting the likelihood of oscillation as well as its amplitude and frequency. Below, we present some of the existing evidence.

Previous Studies

The first study to test statistically a model of cognitive oscillation was Kaplowitz et al. (1983). This study used a persuasion paradigm and a continuous opinion measure (the preferred amount, in dollars, of a university health service fee). Each study participant was randomly assigned to one of three messages, of varying discrepancy, about the health service fee. In addition, participants were also randomly assigned to a period of time during which they could consider the message. By treating the views of *different* participants at different times as indicative of the time course of the view of *one* person, a model with oscillation components was found to significantly but modestly fit the data.[15] Most important for our current discussion, the message with the greatest discrepancy had both the greatest final attitude change and the greatest estimated amplitude of oscillation, consistent with Hypothesis 4a.

Fink and Kaplowitz (1993) report other studies of cognitive oscillations. In one study, participants were given a set of hypothetical decision problems (scenarios) and asked for paper-and-pencil responses to them. Consistent with Hypothesis 7, those who reported the decision to be difficult were more likely to also report having oscillated.

Another study described in Fink and Kaplowitz (1993) measured persons' decision trajectories by having them use a computer mouse to record their attitude as they made a decision. Six participants were each given two hypothetical decision scenarios. One was *dichotomous*—respondents were asked to specify the probability (see Note 11) that they would tell their father that their mother was having an affair—and one was *continuous*—how to divide $100 between two charities. Both scenarios were carefully designed to create conflict; in each one, 5 of the 6 respondents engaged in oscillation. Consistent with Hypothesis 6, when individuals are considering the continuous scenario, they display some evidence of damping; when they are considering the dichotomous decision, they do not. In the dichotomous case, respondents eventually stopped oscillating without any prior decrease of amplitude. Moreover, consistent with a model that includes the effects of cognition, the trajectories appeared chaotic rather than periodic.

Vallacher, Nowak, and Kaufman (1994) had respondents evaluate a stimulus person as they thought about that person. As in Fink and Kaplowitz (1993), these individuals used a computer mouse to record their instantaneous judgments on a continuous scale. The independent variable in the Vallacher et al. study was the valence of the information provided about the stimulus person, which was either positive, negative, or mixed (ambivalent). Although respondents in all conditions were likely to oscillate initially, the amplitude and frequency of oscillation of the positive and negative individuals declined, whereas the oscillations of the ambivalent persons did not die down. This result is consistent with Hypothesis 6, which predicts that those who are ambivalent have oscillations of greater amplitude and frequency. Vallacher et al. (1994) also confirm our model's fundamental prediction that the further the attitude is from the equilibrium location, the greater is the force of the attitude change and therefore the greater the acceleration. They found (in their Experiment 1) that persons given positive information showed more acceleration when their instantaneous attitude was relatively negative, whereas those given negative information showed more acceleration when their instantaneous attitude was relatively positive. Mixed-valence persons, who were far from their equilibrium when in either a positive or negative region, showed high levels of acceleration in both regions.

Current Research

Here we report some findings from two current studies, one involving a dichotomous decision and the other an attitude change study using a continuous scale.

A Dichotomous Decision: College Admissions

Fink, Kaplowitz, and Wang (1994) asked individuals to decide which of two fictitious applicants should be admitted to their university. The applicants were described as having very similar academic qualifications but differed in race: One applicant was black, the other white. This study had two manipulated independent variables (individuation of the black applicant and amount of distraction), and one measured variable, reflecting individual differences (need for cognition). Need for cognition was measured via the 18-question Need for Cognition Scale taken from Petty and Cacioppo (1986).

Respondents thought about the admissions decision and used a computer mouse to indicate their instantaneous opinion as to which applicant should be admitted. One end of the 0-100 scale was "definitely admit [black applicant's name]"; the other end was "definitely admit [white applicant's name]." Mouse position was recorded about every 18 milliseconds (ms). The dependent variables were measures derived from the cognitive trajectories and from cognitive responses.

Participants were 67 white students from the same university; they were randomly assigned to experimental conditions and completed the experimental procedures individually. They learned of the applicants' academic qualifications and personal characteristics by listening to an audiotape.

In the *high distraction* condition, there was distracting noise on the tape-recorded instructions and the experimenter rustled papers and snacked nearby on crunchy foods. In the *no distraction* condition, none of these things happened.

To vary the decision difficulty, the hypothetical black applicant was described in either an *individuated* (i.e., in ways less consistent with a typical black applicant) or a *stereotypical* way. Note that in neither condition were evaluatively negative terms or beliefs used to describe either applicant. The individuating and stereotyping traits were compiled from a series of pilot studies. Based on literature regarding how white Americans perceive blacks (e.g., Bobo & Kluegel, 1991; Jackman & Senter, 1983), and on the literature regarding individuation (see, e.g., Wilder, 1978, 1981), we expected the admissions decision to be more difficult when the black applicant was individuated than when he was stereotypical.

Given the pilot data, we expected that, for most respondents, the black applicant's race would create some doubts about his suitability for college. However, if he were perceived to be atypical of other blacks, this might suggest that he would be very suitable. Thus, respondents considering the individuated black applicant should be very ambivalent, whereas those who consider the stereotypical black applicant should be less ambivalent about his suitability for college. Thus, we expect a greater amplitude and a greater number of changes in direction in the decision trajectory of the individuated than in the stereotype-consistent condition.

Manipulation checks showed that the experimental independent variables were manipulated successfully: The distraction condition was rated as significantly (at $p < .001$) more difficult to hear, or concentrate, in, and more distracting than the nondistraction condition. In the individuation condition, the fictitious black applicant was viewed as significantly less like other blacks or other (predominantly black) D.C. high school students, as compared to the stereotype-consistent condition. Even more important, the individuation condition created significantly greater decision difficulty.

The most important measure of the decision trajectory was the total *number of changes of direction* the respondent made. Because small changes could reflect random motion rather than cognitive change, we established the criterion that the mouse had to move at least 5 points on the 100-point scale for it to be recorded as a change of direction.

Other measures were total *amount of time* the respondent spent deciding, the *pseudoperiod* (the number of changes of direction divided by the decision time), and the *pseudoamplitude* (half of the difference between the maximum value of the decision trajectory and the minimum).[16]

Of the 67 respondents, 59 (88%) had at least one change of direction. As predicted by our model, individuation had positive and significant (at $p < .01$) correlations with the number of direction changes within the respondent's decision trajectory ($r = .541$), decision time ($r = .460$), and pseudoamplitude ($r = .401$). The correlations with decision difficulty were less strong (perhaps because of the reliability of the decision difficulty manipulation check). Greater individuation produced more thoughts ($r = .368, p < .01$), and the number of thoughts was positively correlated ($r = .411, p < .01$) with the number of changes of direction.[17]

The results also contained some surprises. First, the Need for Cognition Scale had little correlation with either the number of thoughts ($r = -.038, ns$) or the number of changes of direction ($r = -.262, p < .05$). Second, although individuation and decision difficulty were significantly correlated with each other ($r = .372, p < .01$), neither individuation nor decision difficulty was significantly correlated with pseudoperiod (for individuation, $r = .003$; for decision difficulty, $r = .086$). Third, distraction had effects opposite to those we expected. It had a positive correlation ($r = .221, ns$) with the number of thoughts and a significant and positive correlation ($r = .420, p < .01$) with the number of changes in direction.

Thus, decisional conflict increased the tendency to change one's mind, and this made the decision process take longer. This conflict did not increase the frequency of the oscillations (the pseudoperiod). Contrary to the findings of previous studies, distraction apparently did not reduce thought production; rather, it made the thinking process take longer, and subsequent analysis of the data suggests that distraction led to thoughts that were more concrete and sequential. Perhaps the decision-making process took longer and more thoughts were produced because distraction caused dissatisfaction with the instantaneous decision that was generated.

In summary, these results provide evidence that oscillation occurs (especially for difficult decisions) and exhibits a systematic relation to theoretically relevant independent and dependent variables. The results also show the importance of including conscious cognition in any research attempting to explain decisional dynamics.

Continuous Attitudes: Criminal Sentencing and Tuition

Whereas the preceding study had respondents deal with a dichotomous decision problem, the study reported here concerned attitude change, measured on a continuous scale. For each of two issues, the respondent was given a persuasive message and then the attitudinal trajectory generated was measured using a computer mouse.

The first issue was the appropriate prison sentence for a convicted armed robber. (This was a slight modification of the scenario used in Kaplowitz & Fink et al., 1991.) The second issue was the appropriate increase in tuition at the student's university. (This was a slight modification of the scenario used in Fink et al., 1983.) These issues were expected to differ in their importance to the respondent and therefore in that person's involvement. Thus, these two issues would create linkages of different strengths and create different amounts of motivation for elaboration.

A measured independent variable in this experiment was *ambivalence* (attitude conflict). Ambivalence was measured by a questionnaire about each issue. We conceived of ambivalent respondents as those who agreed with the arguments on both sides of the issue.

The experimentally manipulated between-subject variables were *message discrepancy*, with three levels; *source credibility*, with two levels; and *order*, with two levels.

Order differentiated respondents by whether they responded to a questionnaire assessing ambivalence before or after the attitude trajectory was measured. Order was varied to determine whether the effect of ambivalence is only evident when it is primed by its being measured before the attitudinal trajectory data are gathered.

Each respondent made a decision about two issues, thus creating the within-subjects variable of *issue*. The sample consisted of 99 university students. The experimental procedure (using the computer to generate the attitudinal trajectory) was administered to each study participant individually.

As with the college admissions study, we sought to disregard motion in the trajectory that might not reflect actual cognitive change. Thus, we again set a minimum threshold for the amount of change that would be considered to reflect a true change of direction. This minimum threshold was set at 4% of the range of the scale. Thus, we disregarded changes smaller than one year for criminal sentencing and less than 1% for tuition. We also did not count spikelike changes, in which the respondents, upon reaching a position, immediately moved in the opposite direction. We interpreted such motion as unreliable and due to the respondents having overshot their "true" position, hastening to correct it.

Examining the decision trajectories for our respondents, we found that 35% changed direction at least once for the sentencing scenario, and 47% changed at least once for the tuition scenario. Both figures are considerably less than the proportion who oscillated in the college admissions study. However, the greater tendency to oscillate in the tuition scenario than in the sentencing scenario is consistent with Hypothesis 2d, which predicted more oscillation for more important issues. The assumption that the tuition scenario would be viewed as more important and thus more thought provoking was also supported by the data. The mean number of thoughts that respondents listed for the sentencing scenario was 2.91, whereas for tuition, it was 3.17, $t(96) = 1.93, p = .056$.

When we examined the effects of the between-subject variables, we found no support for our hypotheses. Although credibility was successfully manipulated, contrary to Hypothesis 2a we found essentially no effect of credibility on number of changes of direction.[18] For both scenarios the correlation between credibility and number of changes was less than .08.

From Hypothesis 3, we predicted that greater discrepancies would cause fewer changes. For the sentencing scenario, the correlation between discrepancy and number of changes was positive, $r = .19, p = .06$. For tuition, the correlation was .05 (ns). Although Hypothesis 7 predicted that ambivalence leads to more oscillation, a variety of measures of ambivalence yielded no clear support for this hypothesis. And contrary to the findings of the earlier study (Fink et al., 1994) and to our discussion on thought, the correlation between number of thoughts and number of changes of direction was less than .10 (ns) in each scenario.

Hypothesis 4a predicted that the greater the attitude change, the greater the amplitude. Using the pseudoamplitude (and counting the amplitude as missing when there were no changes in direction), we found strong support for this hypothesis only for the sentencing scenario.[19] For the criminal sentencing scenario, the correlation between amplitude and final attitude change was .45, $p < .01$. However, for the tuition scenario, the correlation between these variables was only .08.

Conclusion

Oscillations can be measured, and they occur in both decision processes and attitude change. Our simple linear spring model has the virtue of being a parsimonious model with many interesting implications. At the same time, the fact that the oscillatory trajectories are clearly not simple sinusoids suggests that we need to supplement this model with theory based on conscious cognition. The fact that data from the sentencing and tuition scenarios failed to support a number of hypotheses also requires some further thinking.[20]

Cycles in cognition can be created and dissected in the laboratory, and our increased knowledge in this area has significant methodological and theoretical implications. A cycle is one of the simplest forms of observable regularity, and the study of cyclical patterns typically appears early in the history of scientific disciplines. We believe that our study of cognitive oscillation can help us learn about and understand essential cognitive processes involved in messages and in thoughts.

Notes

1. Indeed, if one includes the beliefs and evaluations that are part of the subjective norm as attitudes (something advocated by Miniard & Cohen, 1981), then, theoretically, one's decisions may be considered to be entirely determined by attitudes.

2. A related approach, well known in both the attitude and decision-making literature, is information integration theory (see N.H. Anderson, 1981), which predicts decisions as a function of the subjective value of certain attributes and the weight of the information about them.

3. A recent book by a psychologist (Landman, 1993) also examines this issue.

4. Still other evidence of attitudinal oscillation is provided by Warner (this volume), who reports that Gottman and Levenson (1985) found cyclical patterns of affect in the interaction of marital couples. This differs somewhat from our own emphasis in that the oscillation appears to result from external feedback. By contrast, our main concern is the effect of internal feedback.

5. See, for example, Ingard and Kraushaar (1960) for a discussion of the mathematics of springs.

6. Woelfel and Fink (1980, pp. 146-150) show how the mass of concepts can be estimated in a way consistent with the physical definition of this term.

7. Our discussion applies most directly to the form of the information integration model that is applied to persuasion, but the isomorphism holds more generally.

8. Psychological co-occurrence is expected to be more important than mere physical co-occurrence. If two entities co-occur physically (e.g., if they are in the same visual field) but this is not noticed, this co-occurrence is ordinarily not expected to strengthen the cognitive linkages. However, the literature on perception without awareness (see, e.g., Bornstein & Pittman, 1992) indicates that there are circumstances under which awareness of the co-occurrence may not be a necessary condition for a linkage to be strengthened.

9. This equation is actually a special case of a more general equation proposed in Kaplowitz and Fink (1992, p. 352). The more general equation gives separate consideration to the linkages anchoring A and B.

10. A different derivation of this principle using differential equations is presented in Kaplowitz and Fink (1982).

11. This may, to some degree, be a measurement issue. If the scale asks for the probability of choosing an alternative, then any time the decider is clearly leaning toward that alternative, that person may choose an extreme value. In this case, Hypothesis 5 is likely to be supported. If, however, the scale asks how *strongly* the respondent is leaning and the midpoint is labeled *undecided*, then a clear but not strong leaning in one direction may be recorded as close to the midpoint. In this case, we would not expect Hypothesis 5 to be supported.

12. Eagly and Chaiken (1993), however, state that although cognitive responses and attitude change are correlated, it is possible that cognitive responses reflect rather than cause attitude change.

13. This suggests that oscillations may operate with less interference from conscious cognition when the attitude is based almost entirely on pure affect. However, it is not easy to think of an attitude that is not only purely affectively based but that also involves conflicting forces from the springlike linkages.

14. The absence of oscillation can be considered oscillation with a frequency and amplitude of zero.

15. We clearly prefer a methodology in which we can examine the complete trajectory for each respondent. This preferred methodology requires computer technology that we lacked for this study. We have since devised a method of data collection that allows each respondent's trajectory to be recorded. This new method has been adopted in our more recent studies, reported below.

16. These latter quantities are called "pseudo" to reflect the fact that we do not have regular sinusoidal trajectories.

17. Most of the dependent measures were transformed to meet statistical assumptions.

18. For the two scenarios, the correlation between the experimental manipulation of credibility and its manipulation check were .43 and .71, respectively, $p < .001$ for both correlations.

19. An alternative would be to consider the amplitude as zero in those cases. If this were done, the correlation between amplitude and the number of changes would exceed .80, and it would then not be possible to disentangle the effects of our predictors on amplitude and frequency.

20. We should note that there were procedural differences between the college admissions study (Fink, Kaplowitz, & Wang, 1994) and the sentencing and tuition study that may explain some of the differences in the findings. Our research in progress will help establish an optimal experimental protocol for future investigations.

13

Dynamics of Speech Processes in Dyadic Interaction

EUGENE H. BUDER

Speech data are replete with principled cycles and dynamic patterns, so much so that any speech scientist seeking meaning among them needs to be heavily guided by an understanding of the mechanisms generating the data. This understanding is also incumbent of a communication scientist wishing to investigate interpersonal aspects of speech in dyadic conversation. Physiological aspects of speech are the fundamental mechanisms of human vocal communication.

In this chapter, I sample the variety of results in the social interaction analysis of speech measures from two-speaker conversations. This is achieved in two ways: by a brief literature review and by applications of a technique for synchrony analysis. Both of these sections are developed in support of two claims that follow from the physiological basis for speech: That choice of speech parameter and temporal domain can deeply affect substantive conclusions and that a deterministic model of individual behavior may be sufficient to support measures of speech coordination. The applications include an analysis of physiologically disordered conversational speech.

AUTHOR'S NOTE: Preparation of this chapter at the University of Washington was supported in part by training grant DC-00032 from the National Institute on Deafness and other Communicative Disorders.

301

TABLE 13.1 Cycles Found in Speech

Speech Unit	Approx. Period of Cycle
1. Phoneme	0.1 second
2. Syllable	0.1-1.0 second
3. Phrase	0.4-1.0 second
4. Sentence	3.0 seconds
5. Turns, thought units	3-45 seconds
6. Topics, activity levels	3-12 minutes
7. Tendency to converse	45, 90 minutes

Speech Coordination:
Parameters and Domains

Along with more widely understood functions for verbal communication (Borden, Harris, & Raphael, 1994; Denes & Pinson, 1993; Kent & Read, 1992), dynamic speech patterns are also fundamental to the regulation of social interaction. When people speak to one another, they produce sound patterns that are richly organized at many temporal levels. For normal language, the temporal organization of speech phonemes must, in many cases, be timed to a precision of milliseconds (thousandths of seconds), and syllables often must be timed within centiseconds (hundredths of seconds) or better to be correctly perceived.

This temporal structuring extends to "larger" (longer period and lower frequency) temporal domains as well. Table 13.1 lists some potentially cyclic aspects of conversational speech. Many if not all of the items of Table 13.1 include inherently oscillatory physiological processes, such as respiration and mastication. They are *potentially* cyclic because of an underlying tendency for the physiological system that produces these units to oscillate with a natural frequency. For example, consonant-vowel alternations tend to result from an oscillation between partially closed (consonantal) and open (vocalic) vocal tract positions. Prolonging "ah" while oscillating the mandible fully to a vocal tract closure at the lips, one creates a "bahbahbah" sequence with a regular cycle (producing what many view as the prototypical speech of baby babble!).

At a more macroscopic level, both phrases and sentences (Domains 3 and 4 in Table 13.1) are driven by inherent cyclic processes of respiration and valved by laryngeal and supralaryngeal vocal tract activity. For example, simply activating the vocal cords while continuing the inherently cyclic processes of breathing will produce a rhythmic series of utterances. Prosodic (melodic and rhythmic) aspects of phrases and sentences correlate with a respiratory-based unit of production called "the breath group" (Lieberman, 1967).

At a yet higher domain of special interest to interaction researchers, turn taking in conversations is normally a cyclic alternation of vocal activity between the partners, with variable periods at least on the order of several seconds. This pattern of alternation may occur at even more macroscopic levels as well in the form of "megaturns"; an episode of activity alternations (turns) may generally favor one speaker for several minutes, followed by a similar period during which the other speaker is relatively more active (Dabbs, 1982; Warner, 1979). Warner (this volume) provides substantial information on physiological aspects of longer vocal activity cycles. It would be redundant to repeat that material from Warner's chapter here, though her extensive consideration of respiratory correlates of vocal activity behaviors is exactly to the point.

Finally, the seventh domain of Table 13.1 refers to a report by Navy-funded researchers (Hayes & Cobb, 1979) studying couples in isolation from external temporal cues (e.g., no daylight or clocks). Discussing their findings, the authors cite other "ultradian" rest-activity cycles of a 90-minute period that appear to have a neurophysiological basis (as well as harmonic relations with the yet slower circadian cycles).

There are therefore multiple temporal domains at which speech is patterned in dyadic interaction. For detecting these cycles and dynamic patterns at the more macroscopic domains, communication researchers, especially those operating in a deductive mode, have generally been satisfied to track the parameter of vocal activity (talk/silence). To extend understanding of coordination to more microscopic levels however, it is necessary to consider variation of other speech parameters such as vocal pitch, loudness, and patterning of segmental durations (*prosody*).

The physiological basis for the perceived speech properties of pitch and loudness is the process of phonation (see Borden et al., 1994, for an expanded introduction to this process). Phonation is the periodic vibration of the vocal folds by the appropriate combinations of respiratory pressures and laryngeal muscle tensions. This activity generates an acoustic signal that can neatly be analyzed for two parameters: funda-

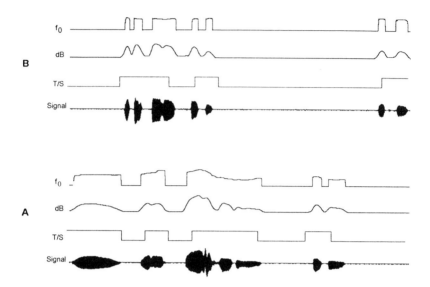

Figure 13.1.   Speech signals and extracted parameters from a conversation. See text for parameter explanations.

mental voice frequency (or f_0, measured in Hertz) and intensity (often measured in decibels, or dB). The values of these parameters tend to predict perceived pitch and loudness, respectively. Such variables are often investigated by communication scientists as "paralinguistic" or "nonverbal" channels that can participate in turn taking as well as convey attitude, affiliation, and emotion. They are included here as elements of interpersonal coordination (see Pittam, 1994, for a recent review of voice-related social interaction effects).

Introduction to Some Speech Parameters

Figure 13.1 displays about 4 seconds of speech data from a conversation between two women, partners A and B (from Buder, 1991b). The speech is displayed in four forms: the raw waveform and three extracted parameters. A and B's traces are time aligned—a turn begun by A is briefly joined by B, then A's solo speech is followed by B alone (a synchrony analysis including this section of data is provided below). In each panel, the traces are ordered from bottom to top:

1. The raw signal (from a contact microphone worn against the throat)
2. Talk/silence data taken from the signal in 300 millisecond sampling units
3. A continuous intensity trace (dB) based on the signal
4. A continuous fundamental voice frequency (f_0) trace based on the signal

The talk/silence data are derived as in Jaffe and Feldstein (1970) and Cappella (1979). The f_0 and dB traces are based on signal processing routines. In this case, intensity is derived from the raw signal by a root mean square (RMS) smoothing operation by the CSpeech analysis system (Milenkovic, 1992). Fundamental frequency is also extracted by the same program.

The physical bases of the intensity (dB) and f_0 traces may be seen more clearly in Figure 13.2, which zooms in on partner A's second utterance from Figure 13.1. The intensity trace is clearly an integration of the waveform envelope into a smooth positive contour, describing the intensity or power of vibration. This quantity will correlate with perceptions of loudness. F_0 tracks the period of the main vibration of the speech waveform, corresponding physiologically to the vibration of the vocal cords. Scanning the waveform in Figure 13.2, one can see an increase in the vibration frequency, in correspondence with the f_0 trace above it. This acoustic parameter will correlate with the perception of pitch, and its rise and fall in a phrase or sentence is sometimes called speech intonation. It is evident from Figure 13.1 that in this temporal domain the f_0 and dB parameters are more richly variable than the 300 ms talk/silence variable. Most important, within-utterance information is available in f_0 and dB but not in talk/silence.

To summarize, speech has been discussed as a physiological process with many parameters and units in many different temporal domains. The inherent cyclicity of such processes may be used to help coordinate interactive discourse. One more introductory theme needs to be highlighted before continuing with literature and applications. Because many speech units are based on cyclic processes with naturally preferred periods, such as respiration, one might anticipate that deterministic cycles could be a fundamental element of interpersonal coordination. If the personal speech dynamic has a predictable rhythm, then the simplest means for conversationalists to interpersonally coordinate

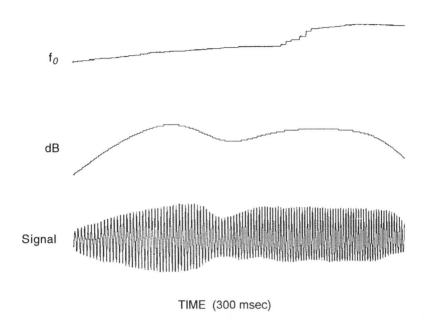

Figure 13.2.   Speech waveform, f_0, and dB traces.

their speech would be to fit these rhythms together somehow. This implies a fundamentally deterministic model.

In developing a science of speech dynamics for dyadic interaction, all basic scientists should at some point consider an important theoretical issue. In dynamic modeling, it is important to judge whether the phenomenon of interest is best modeled as a stochastic or a deterministic process. This issue gets to the very heart, or engine, of a process by asking whether it is driven by essentially random forces (a stochastic process, like the rolling of a die) or whether the process is driven by continuously constrained ballistic, inertial forces (a deterministic process, like the swinging of a pendulum).

The timing of speech processes such as those reviewed in the previous section is inextricably bound up in the dynamics of the physiological mechanisms generating them, and as discussed above, many of these mechanisms are predisposed to cyclic patterns. The pendulum concept is thus more intuitively satisfying as the basic model for speech motor control processes.

It is not a goal of this chapter to outline methods by which deterministic dynamics can be decisively demonstrated in interaction data vis-à-vis stochastic models, nor is it my goal to encompass all the conceptual difficulties that are involved even in defining terms in this area (chapters can be found in this volume that achieve these goals better; see Arundale, Cappella, VanLear & Watt, & Warner). This chapter is intended, however, to support and focus the investigation of coordinated cycles in conversational speech data by regarding speech as physiologically generated by deterministic processes with fundamentally cyclic dynamics. The following literature suggests how it is that stochastic models have nonetheless prevailed in some interaction studies. The subsequent gallery of applications will also demonstrate interactionally relevant cyclic patterns in conversational speech, including one example of conversation involving a physiologically disordered speaker.

Selected Literature

Because the literature on dyadic interaction is large, even just within the vocal modality, the themes introduced at the outset are used to focus this chapter's selective review. The primary purposes are therefore to determine which parameters and temporal domains were investigated and to discuss whether deterministic or stochastic models are used. The literature is also divided into two traditions: a deductive tradition, in which findings tend to be obtained by deducing particular quasi-experimental outcomes from general principles; and an inductive or interpretive tradition, in which findings are generalized from particular examples.

Below, Table 13.2 lists a series of studies on vocal synchrony that may be grouped as belonging to a deductive tradition. Table 13.3, presented later, lists studies under a separate tradition of study that is more inductive in nature, rooted in descriptive sciences such as linguistics and ethnography. Sets of references are organized within traditions in historical order by year of their senior authors' initial work in the area, and they are identified with a code that is referenced in a table to follow.

TABLE 13.2   Selected Literature on Vocal Synchrony:
Deductive Traditions

Author(s)	Parameter
1a	Chapple (1939, 1971)	Vocal activity
1b	Jaffe and Feldstein (1970)	Vocal activity
1c	Cobb (1973)	Vocal activity
1d	Hayes and Cobb (1979)	Vocal activity
1e	Warner (1979, 1988, 1992a, 1992b)	Vocal activity
1f	Cappella (1979, 1980, 1981)	Vocal activity
1g	Dabbs (1983)	Vocal activity
1h	Gregory (1990)	Speech sound
1i	Gregory, Webster, and Huang (1993)	Speech sound

Deductive Traditions

As shown in Table 13.2, a historical overview of the deductive tradition begins with the theorizing of anthropologist Eliot Chapple, whose 1939 monograph stated theoretical and empirical principles based on a model of social interaction as a deterministic dynamic system, with partners' speech dynamics guided by the preferred action/inaction equilibrium definitive of their interaction "personalities." Even though the descriptive domain of this work extends to all action (muscular patterns) and interaction (Chapple, 1970), from dyads to hierarchical institutions, its central tenets are typically expressed and measured empirically in terms of the talk/silence patterning of turn units. Although the early empirical results viewed the data in a probabilistic framework (Chapple, 1939), the general concept is deterministic. To Chapple, interactants are driven by internal physiological systems to oscillate with preferred rhythms, and they complement one another when these rhythms are compatible, that is, when they cycle at equal frequencies and in opposite phase to one another. In a later book chapter, Chapple (1971) extended his ideas on talk/silence based measures to speculations on how to handle vocal pitch, although he has never reported such measures.

Chapple's theoretical view of the dynamics of speech in dyadic interaction is probably the best exemplar of a deterministic "pendulum" viewpoint. He viewed human organisms as hierarchies of coupled nonlinear oscillators (Chapple, 1981) and developed equations for interaction based specifically on Van der Pol oscillator equations originally used to model cardiac rhythms (Chapple & Lui, 1976). From this viewpoint, social interaction is fundamentally a deterministic coupling of nonlinear oscillators.

In contrast, an independent program of research carried out by Jaffe and Feldstein (1970) is an exemplar of the stochastic "die rolling" perspective. They obtained results from the analysis of multiple talk-silence data sets supporting Chapple's (1970) ideas that interaction timing "could provide the behavioral data needed for a reliable assessment of personality" (p. 117). Yet Jaffe and Feldstein modeled these data as Markov processes, a stochastic model in which transitions between states (e.g., a transition from the state of partner A talking to the state of partner B talking) are stated as probabilities and not as deterministic trajectories or cycles. In a simple form of such a model, one might generate simulated data by rolling a die at set time intervals (e.g., 300 ms), marking transitions between partner states purely on the basis of the outcomes of each roll of the die (to complete the analogy, such a die would have to be specially shaped and coded to match real transition probability data). Jaffe and Feldstein (1970) concluded that such a model was adequate because of data indicating that individuals tended toward stable talk-silence state transition probabilities, a stability that was altered somewhat by adaptations to the partner.

Cobb (1973) juxtaposed the Chapple and Jaffe/Feldstein approaches, contrasting Chapple's rhythms hypothesis with "the probabilistic approach." Instead of examining aggregated action/silence ratios or transition matrices, Cobb used autocorrelation analyses to study time-series-type vocal activity data in casual conversations. He found periods ranging from 46 to 132 seconds in length in some but not all of the conversations. Cobb interpreted his results as favoring Chapple's deterministic cycles view, but it is important to recognize how certain methodological choices may have predisposed this. Along with the change in analytic approach from Markov modeling to time series analysis, Cobb also introduced a change in temporal unit by integrating talk-silence proportions within 5-second intervals. Cobb was therefore performing investigations with pseudocontinuous rather than dichotomous talk/silence data, and these investigations focused on a different temporal domain than the Jaffe and Feldstein work.

The remaining work listed in Table 13.2 extends the themes raised by these first three authors: When talk/silence data are aggregated into

TABLE 13.3   Selected Literature on Vocal Synchrony:
Interpretive Traditions

	Author(s)	Parameter
2a	Condon and Ogston (1967)	Phonetic and kinesic segments
2b	Byers (1976)	Phonetic and kinesic segments
2c	Mair (1978)	f_0, head movements
2d	Erickson and Shultz (1982)	Prosody, kinesics
2e	Scollon (1981)	Prosody
2f	Buder (1986)	f_0

longer-term units, deterministic cycles seem to predominate—as in most work by Warner (e.g., 1979, 1992a, 1992b), Hayes and Cobb (1979), and Dabbs (1982)—but when talk/silence data are investigated as moment-to-moment transitions, stochastic models seem adequate—as in the series of investigations by Cappella (1979, 1980) and Cappella and Planalp (1981). Cappella and Warner (both this volume) review these investigators' recent work and current perspectives on dyadic interaction, addressing other interpretive and methodological issues pertaining to choice of descriptive model.

Acoustic variables other than talk/silence patterning have been examined for partner adaptation effects: Gregory finds covariation between interview partners in fundamental frequency (Gregory, 1990) and convergence in voice pitch and amplitude (Gregory, Webster, & Huang, 1993). The operational definitions of pitch and amplitude in Gregory's work are nonstandard, however, and do not correspond to the concepts as generally understood by speech scientists (Hess, 1983; Kent & Read, 1992). This work is still important in suggesting that patterns of other acoustic speech variables may be important in dyadic interaction.

Inductive Tradition

Table 13.3 lists a series of studies on vocal synchrony performed within a more interpretive or inductive tradition. These studies demonstrate that cycles and dynamic patterns in speech processes are found in other parameters than just overall speech activity, and they suggest that deterministic processes may be found in microscopic as well as macroscopic temporal domains.

Some of the strongest claims regarding interpersonal synchrony have been made by Condon and his associates. The central goal of this program was articulated in Condon and Ogston (1967) as the segmentation of behavior, based on linguistic principles and measured by meticulous analysis of audiovisual records. In later work, Condon and Sander (1974) reported observing interpersonal synchrony in the body movements of 1-day-old infants in response to adult speech. Condon's microanalysis, performed with 1/24th- and 1/48th-second sampling intervals, is much finer grained than those presented in the previous section of this review; Condon claims that the strongest levels of synchrony obtain at temporal domains of word length and smaller.

In another example of the sort of extremely microscopic analysis performed within an interpretive tradition, Byers (1976) found that speech onsets and stresses in interpersonal interactions appear to occur in quanta of 0.1 seconds, an observation that he interprets in light of the 10 Hz "alpha" rhythm found in EEG traces of resting individuals. By inspection of the intensity envelope of speech, Byers found that speech onsets of respective partners are typically either 0.2, 0.3, or 0.4 seconds apart, that is, in multiples of 0.1. Byers, unlike Condon, claims that the basis for interpersonal synchrony is the presence of periodicity and is therefore more clearly making a deterministic claim.

The work of Mair (1978), an ophthalmologist with training in anthropology and neurology, has yielded some intriguing observations. Using split-screen photography, electroglottography, and 3D imaging software, Mair performed detailed analysis of episodes from casual conversations between adult partners. Although most synchrony researchers in the interpretive tradition implicate speech prosody in their claims, the measurement of fundamental voice frequency in Mair's work constitutes some of the only acoustic phonetic data on interpersonal synchrony. In particular, Mair observed many examples of a "wavelike" structure in f_0 traces. These observations support Mair's claims that interpersonal synchrony is based on the continuity of f_0 trajectories, that "speech melody is itself supra-individual" (p. 29). Describing these traces, Mair says "the term trajectory well sums up their continuity across silence, and the way that the rest of the contour is implied by the preceding form" (p. 17). This is clearly a deterministic viewpoint, supported at a relatively microscopic level by a prosodic speech parameter; this is also highly descriptive of the type of example presented in applications below.

The educational research agenda described by Erickson and Shultz (1982) was not developed specifically for the measurement of vocal synchrony, yet the observation of matching and mismatching of rhythmic conversational tempo constitutes a central focus of their study on the gatekeeping functions performed by career counselors in junior colleges. Erickson and Shultz observe these rhythms to be approximately 1 second in period and maintained by prosodic and kinesic behaviors. Although their transcription process is impressionistic, the data are used to support their observation that "the verbal and nonverbal speaking behavior of speakers maintains the underlying rhythmic interval within and across speaking turns" (p. 89). Following Erickson and Shultz's notion of discourse beat, Scollon (1981) listened to a wide variety of recorded speech samples, including traditional narratives, family breakfast table interactions, baseball announcers, and Groucho Marx. He claimed to hear a universal duple (2/4) meter in all these speech samples ranging in period from about .5 to 1 second.

Buder (1986) found some episodes in which there was demonstrable periodicity in the fluctuation of conversational f_0. Specifically, Buder documented two conversational episodes in which partners both began speaking simultaneously. Using autocorrelation analyses of the f_0 data, he found that these simultaneous onsets were preceded by cycles in the foregoing speech and appeared to occur on the "beat" of such cycles. This study thereby described prosodic rhythm as a governing factor in the timing of participants' contributions.

Temporal Domain

Table 13.4 reviews the literature surveyed in the previous two sections, organizing the references by temporal domain. Reference labels from Tables 13.2 and 13.3 are ordered by increasing temporal domain. In the final column, an attempt is made to assign reference groups to either a deterministic or a stochastic model, if clearly implied by the author(s).

Three comments on this table help synthesize the preceding "traditions," yielding a call for studies of speech prosody under a deterministic theoretical framework. First, no deductive studies of vocal activity have inspected temporal domains with periods finer than 0.6 second. Second, deductive analysis of the contingencies at the fastest temporal

TABLE 13.4 Citations Arranged by Temporal Domain and
Model Type

Temporal Domain	Studies	Model
0.1 second	2a	?
0.1 second	2b	Deterministic
0.1-3 seconds	2c	Deterministic
0.5-3 seconds	2e, 2f	Deterministic
0.6-3 seconds	1b, 1f	Stochastic
1 second	2d	Deterministic
1-3 seconds	1a	Deterministic
2-128 seconds	1g	Deterministic (?)
45-176 seconds	1c	Deterministic
3-12 minutes	1e	Deterministic
45, 90 minutes	1d	?

domains has yielded stochastic models. Third, interpretive studies on speech prosodic variables like vocal pitch and loudness have found essentially deterministic dyadic interaction models in faster time domains (down to 0.1 second).

At the outset of this chapter, I argued that we should use deterministic models in speech data because of the physiological nature of the generating mechanisms. Here, in a review of methods employed in the literature, examples have shown how choice of parameter and analytic technique can make a deterministic model seem dispensable or inadequate in certain domains. Many of those deductive studies that focused on local contingencies have arrived at stochastic models of sequential contingencies. Although occupying a narrow niche in the temporal domain chart of Table 13.4, these studies are significant in the power of their results—they are not wrong in claiming that a stochastic model is perfectly adequate for moment-to-moment vocal activity measures. But vocal activity is not the whole picture, as has been seen in the interpretive tradition. Deductive studies have only found deterministic patterns in vocal activity when it is integrated into longer-term units. Those longer-term units then prevent these researchers from detecting relatively short-term deterministic patterns in syllable, word, and sentence-length speech units domains. It is certainly of interest to see whether any aspects of phrases and sentences are also matched.

Studies performed in an inductive tradition have uncovered rich prosodic patterns in interesting contexts. However, the patterns have typically been impressionistically described, often without replicable measurement or analysis operations, and accumulated only as examples. Principles of validation using objective and replicable measures and the accumulation of numerical results amenable to inferential testing against chance baselines have therefore not been applied to deterministic short-term patterns in prosodic domains. This may have been due partly to technical limitations: Microcomputer-based speech science is now capable of accumulating far more prosody data than was generally possible in the past (Buder, 1991b; Read, Buder, & Kent, 1992).

To summarize the problem, the techniques of the deductive tradition have been applied either to short-term stochastic patterns or to long-term deterministic patterns in vocal activity data, whereas the interpretive traditions have clearly pointed to the existence of short-term deterministic synchrony patterns in prosody data. The problem can be approached with the best features of both traditions intact with analysis of the prosodic speech parameters using the appropriate tools. Although a deductive framework is not developed or applied in this chapter, the demonstrated techniques do yield quantities that could be used in such research designs.

Notes on a Synthetic View

At the risk of clouding the issues somewhat, it is necessary to acknowledge at this point that a clear discrimination between purely deterministic and stochastic processes can be blurred in at least three ways:

- A stochastic model such as the Markov transition matrix models employed by Jaffe and Feldstein (1970) can actually generate cyclic patterns that would appear to be deterministic.
- A deterministic model for dyadic interaction that produces chaos, such as the logistic equation employed by Buder (1991a), can generate patterns of data that appear to be random and therefore, to most appearances, stochastic.
- A full time series model designed to maximally account for variance will usually contain both deterministic and stochastic components (Gottman, 1981).

Rather than render deterministic/stochastic distinctions completely false, however, these observations support the claim that a deterministic model may be more fundamental in speech modeling: because both types of models can be adapted to fit data with either cyclic or noisy (random or chaotic) dynamics, the choice of model should be based not on adequacy of fit alone but, rather, on theoretical and interpretive considerations. What type of mechanism makes most sense for prosodic data from conversations?

The next section attempts to demonstrate that a model describing an underlying cyclic pattern is adequate for investigating dynamic patterns in vocal interaction in some parameters and domains. As a set of examples, it does not demonstrate that a deterministic model is superior—a stochastic modeling is not even attempted (see Cappella, this volume, for discussions of such modeling). The examples do purport to show that (a) occurrences of shared cyclic patterns can be objectively measured in an interaction analysis and (b) parameter and domain selections can have very significant effects on results. In doing so, the applications invoke many of the methodological principles enunciated by Arundale and VanLear and Watt (both this volume); these chapters are recommended as companion pieces on matters of sampling and analysis of time series data in the frequency domain.

Some Applications

Space simply does not permit a full development of all operational steps for the synchrony analysis that produces the following examples—details can be found in Buder (1991b). The following example (from Buder, 1991b) occurs about 10 minutes into an initial interaction between two college-age women who rated the quality of their interaction as quite positive on a variety of questionnaire items pertaining to overall attraction to partner, smoothness and fluency of the conversation, and a feeling that they were "on the same wavelength." As will be seen, this figurative description of synchrony is given a quite literal meaning by the technique: The example is from a very highly rated portion of a highly rated conversation and contains prosody data that does appear to cycle with wavelengths that are shared by both participants.

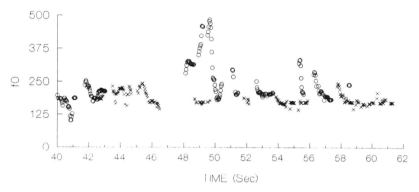

Figure 13.3.   22 seconds of f_0 data from a conversation between two women; partner A plotted with "x," partner B with "o."

Demonstration of the Technique:
High Participant-Rated Synchronous
Conversational Speech

Figure 13.3 displays a long-term series of f_0 points from conversational speech, approximately 22 seconds at 30 samples per second (sps). The data are an extended extract from the same conversation introduced in Figures 13.1 and 13.2 (Figure 13.1 occupies Seconds 48 through 52 of this plot).

Figure 13.4 charts and illustrates the three major phases of a technique used by Buder (1991b) to analyze long-term prosodic cycles in the frame of data shown in Figure 13.3. The techniques are illustrated for f_0 data but are similar in principle for intensity data (although some important distinctions will be rendered when dB data are introduced in subsequent examples). The first step is to apply appropriate transformations. For f_0, these are (a) downsampling to smooth the data from the highly microscopic domain of 30 sps to the larger viewpoint obtained with 6 sps data; (b) normalizing the data to eliminate subject differences of overall mean and variability; (c) padding of gaps in the data (using the data mean) to allow interrupted data to be submitted to a spectral analysis; and finally, (d) tapering, a procedure that smoothes off the frame onset and offset edges to reduce artifacts in spectral analysis (see Gottman, 1981, for further justification and details on this standard spectral analysis procedure). The transformed data from Figure 13.3 are displayed in the first panel of Figure 13.4.

1. Transformation of F_0

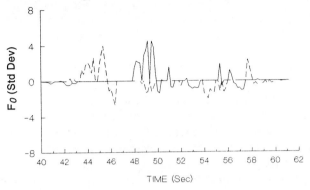

2. Cross-spectral analysis

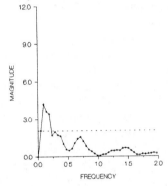

3. Individual spectral analyses

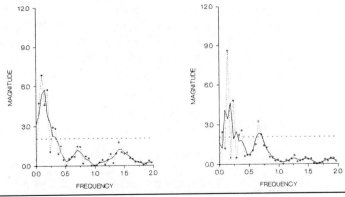

Figure 13.4. Steps used in synchrony analysis of f_0 data. See text for further explanation.

The next steps move into the frequency domain via Fourier analysis (see Bloomfield, 1976, for background and detail on Fourier-based spectral analysis; also Shumway, 1988, for assessment procedures). A spectral analysis accomplished by the Fourier transform is particularly suited for the analysis of cycles in data. The mathematical transform recasts all variation in a time series into the exact set of sinusoidal waves (with coefficients of frequency, amplitude, and phase) that would additively reconstruct the series (see VanLear & Watt, this volume). Step 2 of Figure 13.4 is a bivariate cross spectrum. This is simply the Fourier transform (with smoothing) of the covariance between two series, therefore decomposing the covariance between partners' signals into a set of frequency components. Components exceeding the noise floor beyond statistical confidence limits (the upper limit is graphed as a dashed horizontal line in the figure) can be used to guide our attention to the same frequency components in the individual partners' spectra. Step 3 displays those individual spectra. Those components identified by the cross-spectral analysis are examined for their statistical significance to find actual cycles that the partners share (see Watt, this volume, for a description of a similar procedure).

The chief periodic components of the individual data as selected by synchrony analysis can be graphed back in the time domain as sinusoidal waves. In Figure 13.5, such models are constructed using the coefficients of amplitude, frequency, and phase from the top two sinusoidal components in the synchrony analysis. The main periodic components found in these long-term data seem to correspond to the echoing of B's first sequence of utterances (Seconds 42-47) in A's next series (Seconds 48-52), although other subtleties can also be found. The shared cyclic aspect of these interactional speech data therefore seem to correspond to a rhythmic series of turn exchanges. It may have been partly the smooth coordination of such turn exchange that caused the participants to give high ratings to their interaction. The next example reveals different types of prosodic synchrony in a different temporal domain.

Comparison of Control
Conversation to Conversation
Involving a Speech Motor Disorder

To emphasize the physiological basis for speech and its relation to interaction, synchrony analysis can be applied to a conversation in

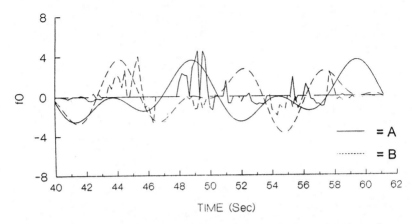

Figure 13.5. 22 seconds of *fo* data with synchrony wave models (jagged solid lines = partner A's data; smooth solid lines = partner A's model; jagged dashed lines = partner B's data; smooth dashed lines = partner B's model). See text for explanation of models.

which one participant is physiologically speech impaired. One class of diseases that impairs the body's ability to produce speech is called *dysarthria*. One type of dysarthria is due to amyotrophic lateral sclerosis (ALS), a degenerative neurological disorder sometimes called "Lou Gherig's Disease." ALS destroys both upper and lower motor neurons, resulting in muscle spasm, weakness, paralysis, and degeneration. Respiratory and speech muscles are particularly affected in many cases, causing speech that is (among other things) perceptually slow, monopitch, hypernasal, and typically marked by short phrases, inappropriate silences, and reduced intelligibility (Yorkston, Beukelman, & Bell, 1988).

In the examples below, both f_0 and dB data from a conversation between a woman (a speech clinician and professor of speech and hearing sciences) and a man of about 40 years of age with ALS are analyzed for synchrony. For comparison, conversational data obtained from the same woman and a nonimpaired man with similar characteristics (age, race, level of education) are also examined.

Control Conversation Onset

This example (see Figure 13.6) illustrates data examined in a different, smaller temporal domain than the previous example of normal

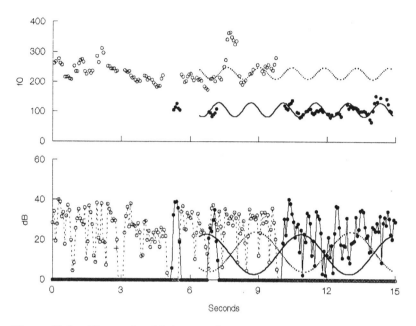

Figure 13.6. 15 seconds of f_0 (top panel) and dB (bottom panel) data from conversation between woman (hollow circles) and normal speaking male (filled circles). Dashed wave models are for woman's speech; solid wave models are for man's speech.

conversation. Here, the fine details of within-turn structure will be seen in data sampled 15 times per second and viewed through spectral windows of just over 8.5 seconds in length (contrasting with 6 sps data in 22-second windows in the previous example).

The data shown in Figure 13.6 are from the first 15 seconds of the "control" conversation. The f_0 data are displayed in the top panel and the dB data in the bottom. The woman's opening remarks (a question) are displayed as hollow circles, and the man's remarks are seen as filled circles. Three overlapping spectral frames were taken from this data, and the chief synchrony results are summarized graphically as sinusoidal models: These represent the largest periods in the individual data that also were "matched" across participants by the cross-spectral criterion outlined previously. The woman's data are modeled by the dotted sinusoids and the man's by the solid. The displayed sinusoids thus represent the chief shared periodicities in the data.

The main feature observed in this analysis is that cycles in f_0 carry across the turn juncture, as had been claimed in some of the literature reviewed above. A rhythm that is created in the woman's speech before the floor exchange is maintained by the man's speech following the exchange.

A different type of analysis is obtained in the dB data, and it should be noted that this difference is partly due to a fundamental difference in the nature of the data: Whereas f_0 data are interrupted and have no meaningful zero values (vocal folds simply do not vibrate at frequencies much lower than 80), the intensity data are continuously present, with values at or near zero being both possible and meaningful. It is therefore sensible that the main feature picked up by the dB analysis in this domain is the cyclic aspect of turn exchange itself. Although the effect is graphically more subtle due to the presence of more rapid variations, the overall intensity trends show a fundamental periodicity matched across participants. Finally, it is also of interest to note that the phase relations between participants' sinusoid models are different in the different parameters. The turn exchange cycles are 180° out of phase, whereas the shared melodic lines of the pitch models in the top panel are roughly in phase.

Disordered Conversation Onset

Figure 13.7 displays data that are formatted and analyzed identically. However, these are from the opening 15 seconds of a conversation in which the male is a speaker with fairly advanced effects of ALS. His speech is noticeably affected by the muscular difficulties he encounters, but it is still reasonably intelligible. Notice that whereas the woman still opens the conversation with a question that has a clear periodicity in the f_0, this rhythm is not echoed by her partner. (Although it appears that at the onset his speech seems to follow her sinusoid model, this pattern does not continue long enough to be picked up by the spectral analysis, and no other periodicities are dominant in his ongoing f_0 data.) In the lower panel, however, it can be seen that the disordered speaker is able to maintain some of the rhythmic aspects of turn exchange seen in the previous example.

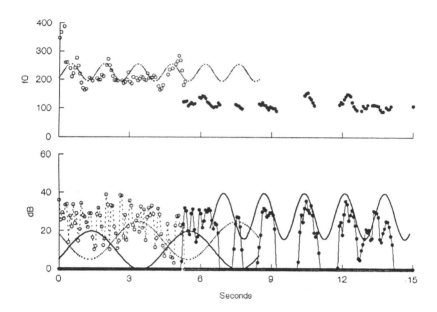

Figure 13.7.   15 seconds of f_0 (top panel) and dB (bottom panel) data from conversation between woman (hollow circles) and male with speech impairment due to ALS (filled circles). Dashed wave model is for woman's speech; solid wave models are for man's speech.

This figure includes an additional wave model to show a phenomenon that appears to be a part of the man's speech pathology. This intensity-based model, running across the latter half of the extract, captures a series of three "hyper-rhythmic" phrases (uttered between Seconds 8 and 13). This type of short phrasing is probably due to weakness in the respiratory muscles supporting speech, as if the speaker is having to constantly "catch his breath." The occurrence of this clearly cyclic pattern is of broader interest: It nicely exemplifies Chapple's (1981) idea that speakers bring physiologically based rhythmic preferences to a conversation, based in this case on a pathologic constraint that may prevent the speaker from easily entraining to other speakers' rhythms; and it clarifies that the theoretical and methodological preference for deterministic cycles advocated here need not imply that more cyclic speech is always "better." Interpersonal coordination of such cycles

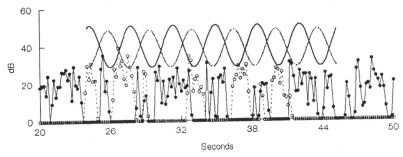

Figure 13.8. 22 seconds of dB data from conversation between woman (hollow circles) and normal speaking male (filled circles). Dashed wave models are for woman's speech; solid wave models are for man's speech.

indeed requires that speakers be able to adjust phase and periodicity to some extent.

Control Conversation Rapid Turn Exchange: 22-Second Windows

The kind of periodic turn taking that can occur in normal conversation is illustrated in Figure 13.8. This example also shows phenomena found in larger temporal domains: the data are sampled only 6 times a second (i.e., smoothed from the raw 30 sps data) and analyzed in 22-second windows. Thirty seconds of such data are shown, taken just after the sample illustrated in Figure 13.6. Here, from about Seconds 29 to 42, a "collaborative" exchange of brief remarks between the man and the woman is marked by sentence-length cycles of approximately 3 seconds in period. No such turn exchange cycling occurred in the first minute of conversation with the disordered speaker.

Synchrony Scores

The diversity of phenomena noted in the previous three subsections and figures has hopefully illustrated a key point of this chapter: that examination for cycles and dynamic patterns in speech yields quite different results depending on the parameter and temporal domain. In

TABLE 13.5   Synchrony Score Results

	Control	Disordered
25 seconds of 6 sps data		
f_0 synchrony	51	0
dB synchrony	84	116
1 minute of 15 sps data		
f_0 synchrony	16	4
dB synchrony	137	83

these examples, f_0 and dB data were analyzed in two different temporal domains. Although this brief sampling has allowed only tentative inductive interpretations, the graphic synchrony analysis technique introduced here also allows quantitative summaries. With the accumulation of enough samples, the technique can also be used in deductive research designs with testable hypotheses.

Although such a design cannot be developed here, a quantitative summary of the samples examined is still informative. Space does not permit full development of the algorithms yielding synchrony scores (see Buder, 1991b, for details), but the general idea is based on the fact that Fourier analysis decomposes data variance into additive sinusoidal components. As overviewed earlier, cross-spectral analysis allows determination of which of these components are shared between speakers. Following Warner's (1979, 1992a) rhythm index, a selection of the top five such components that significantly exceed a random noise baseline forms a "synchrony" measure. This variance can then be expressed as the proportion of total data variance to indicate the portion accounted for by shared cycles. These values are then added across analysis frames to produce a score for an extended sample. Table 13.5 presents such synchrony scores for the control-disordered conversations from which Figures 13.6 through 13.8 were drawn. Approximately 25 seconds of 15 sps data are represented as one temporal domain in the table, and a larger temporal domain is provided by examination of 1 minute of 6 sps data.

Table 13.5 shows a decrement in f_0 synchrony for the disordered subject's conversation in both temporal domains. The higher dB synchrony for the disordered subject in the 25-second sample may be a compensatory effect. The subject with ALS, lacking the muscularly more challenging ability to control f_0, can apparently still use intensity control to produce a synchronous rhythm. However, when scores from the larger temporal domain are examined, the rapid turn exchange shown in Figure 13.8 dominates, leading to a better overall synchrony score for the control conversation. Note that this is not a matter of the result stabilizing with greater sampling. The same number of frames and data points are analyzed, but different cyclic phenomena, different frequencies, are captured as a consequence of the different temporal sampling rates of the raw data.

Summary

This chapter has reviewed cycles and dynamic patterns in speech processes related to dyadic interaction. The underlying perspective developed in this review has been that speech, as a physiologically based process, is adequately modeled by deterministic cycles. The perspective was developed by a review of the cyclic units that can be found in speech, by a sampling of relevant research traditions in the literature, and by demonstrations of a technique designed to find shared cycles in speech processes. The perspective was also bolstered by inclusion of an example of conversational speech in which one participant's physiological impairment may have had an effect on the vocal interaction. The materials in this chapter will hopefully motivate further investigations into the many types of cycles and dynamic patterns that can be found in conversational speech processes.

14

Coordinated Cycles in Behavior and Physiology During Face-to-Face Social Interactions

REBECCA M. WARNER

Imagine the following situation: Two previously unacquainted college students are sitting face-to-face talking. They are participants in a study of conversation, and their instructions were to talk about anything they wish for about 40 minutes and to become acquainted. As they talk, each person's voice is picked up by a noise-canceling microphone connected to a laboratory computer. While they are talking, the computer program samples speech amplitude (loudness) four times per second and compares the speech amplitude to a preset threshold to decide whether each person is talking or silent. To see more clearly how the amount of talk varies over relatively long periods of time, the overall amount of talk is summed for each 10-second time block and converted to proportion of time spent talking. What would you expect to see when amount of talk is examined over time?

It seems likely that the decision whether or not to talk at any given moment would be influenced by many factors such as emotional or cognitive involvement in the conversation, partner behavior, momentary impulses to voice a thought that has just occurred, and so on. The fact

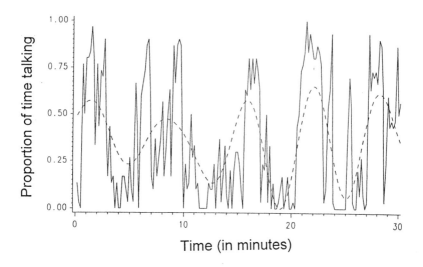

Figure 14.1. Plot of amount of talk over time for one speaker in a conversation, illustrating 6-minute cycles in amount of talk.

that so many factors could influence the decision whether or not to talk might lead us to expect amount of talk to vary in complicated and unpredictable ways over time.

In fact when the data on amount of talk from the study I have just described are plotted, strikingly clear patterns or cycles sometimes emerged. Figure 14.1 shows an example.

The jagged line shows the percentage of time this individual spent talking in each 10-second time block during 30 minutes of conversation. Superimposed on that jagged line is a smooth line representing the output from a band pass filtering procedure that highlights the cyclic tendencies in the data record.[1] The spacing between the peaks in Figure 14.1 is not perfectly regular, but it is apparent that amount of talk tends to vary rather cyclically with cycles approximately 6 minutes long. This graph illustrates the phenomenon that is the subject of this chapter: a tendency for speakers to show cyclic variations in amount of talk, with cycle lengths on the order of 3 and 6 minutes long and longer.

A second graph illustrates that such cycles can arise in physiology as well as behavior during social interaction. Each speaker's systolic blood

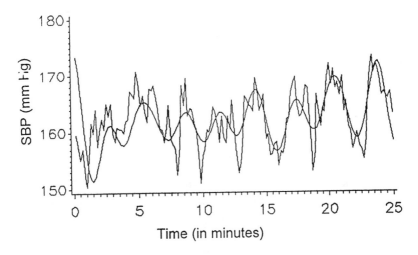

Figure 14.2. Plot of systolic blood pressure (SBP) over time for one speaker in a conversation, illustrating 3-minute cycles in blood pressure.

pressure (SBP) was monitored continuously using a Finapres noninvasive blood pressure monitor. A measurement of SBP was taken every 2 seconds, and a mean SBP was computed for each 10-second time block. Figure 14.2 shows the SBP for one male speaker during the first 23 minutes of a conversation. The jagged line shows the actual SBP measurements, and the smooth line shows the band pass filter that highlights the cyclic tendencies. In this graph, it is the relatively even spacing between the minimum blood pressures that is most striking: At minutes 8, 10, 13, 16, 19, and 22.5, there are rather sudden drops in SBP; in other words, the cycle length in this plot is about 3 minutes long.

These two examples were selected from dozens of conversations that have been recorded in ongoing research during the past few years. They are unusually clear illustrations of cycles. When analyses are done to summarize information about cycles in behavior and physiology during conversation, about half the participants in any given study have shown statistically significant cycles in behavior and physiology. For those who did not show any cyclic pattern, two different patterns emerged:

Some showed very little variability in SBP or amount of talk over time; others showed substantial variability, but the variations were random rather than cyclical. Among those who did show significant cycles in talk and SBP, only a few showed cycles as clear and consistent as those shown in Figures 14.1 and 14.2. Many subjects had wobbly or irregular cycles 3 and 6 minutes long; sometimes, longer cycles (on the order of 20 minutes or longer) also appeared.

The existence of these cycles raises many questions. Why do such cycles occur? Is the presence of cycles a mere curiosity, or are cycles important to the organization and quality of social interaction? Are a speaker's internal rhythms in SBP or other physiological variables related to that speaker's cycles in amount of talk? Are cycles in behavior and physiology coordinated between partners? Are judgments about the quality of the social interaction, the attraction between the partners, or the responsiveness of partners related to objective indexes describing how rhythmic and coordinated their behavior and physiology are during social interaction? Subsequent sections of this chapter review what is known about each of these questions. There is not as yet a substantial body of evidence to draw on, but the few existing studies suggest that these cycles do exist and are an important part of the experience of face-to-face social interaction.

Research Methods
and Data Collection

Factors That Vary in Face-to-Face
Social Interaction Research

A researcher has to make numerous design decisions that involve selection and possibly manipulation of many variables. Factors that can be varied in face-to-face social interaction research, either by selection or by manipulation, include the following:

- Composition of the dyad (e.g., parent-infant, friends, married couples, therapist and client, strangers). Most of the research reviewed in this chapter involved adult-adult stranger dyads or parent-infant dyads.

- Nature of the feelings or relationship within the dyad (e.g., distressed vs. nondistressed married couples, acquaintances who like vs. dislike each other)
- Individual characteristics of the speakers, such as gender, age, ethnicity, personality
- Nature of the social interaction task (e.g., discussion of a high-conflict issue, getting acquainted, unstructured play, etc.)
- Length of the social interaction session; the frequency of behavior sampling. These decisions will determine what range of frequencies or set of cycles can be detected in a study; the longest cycle that can be observed is equal to the length of the session, and the shortest cycle that can be detected is 2 observations long (cf. Arundale, this volume).
- Variables that are monitored (i.e., behaviors such as amount of talk, gaze, body movement; speech content or intent coded from transcripts; self-ratings or observer ratings of affect or involvement over time; physiological variables such as respiration, heart rate, blood pressure). This chapter considers on-off talk patterns; elsewhere in this volume, the focus is on different variables. For instance, variables studied may be pitch or fundamental frequency (Buder, this volume) or composite indexes of activity that combine several behaviors (Cappella, this volume).
- Setting (e.g., home vs. laboratory)

Design of Studies to Assess Cycles in Social Interaction

Early studies that looked for cycles tended to be relatively simple: The goal was simply to document the existence of cycles and other predictable activity patterns. In a typical study, a small number of dyads were asked to engage in some standard task, such as a getting-acquainted conversation (Warner, 1979). Detailed time series data are obtained for each partner, often by using automated systems to detect on-off vocal activity or to collect frequent physiological measurements. Many early studies looked at only one time series variable, such as variations in amount of talk. A spectral analysis (Bloomfield, 1976) or some related analysis such as the periodogram was done for each individual participant. Results were reported either by making general qualitative statements about the shape of spectra and locations of spectral peaks, by plotting single spectra or spectra averaged across participants, or by reporting summary statistics derived from spectral analysis such as the percentage of power contained in a particular frequency band. The goal of these early studies was mainly to document the existence of cycles in behavior and physiology during social interaction.

Current studies are typically more complex in design. Now the basic research question is how some quantitative index of cyclicity or coordination is related to external variables, either as antecedent or consequence. For instance, the percentage of power due to 10-second cycles in mother-infant interaction has been compared across groups of preterm versus full-term infants (Lester, Hoffman, & Brazelton, 1985); the behavior of preterm infants was significantly less rhythmic than that of full-term infants. Studies of adult conversations have been done to see if subsequent ratings of the interaction by participants are related to cyclicity or coordination (Warner, 1992a, 1992b). In these studies, more rhythmic conversations were evaluated more positively.

In studies such as these, larger numbers of dyads are typically run. Within each participant or within each dyad, spectral or cross-spectral analysis is performed, and for each speaker or dyad, summary indexes are extracted, such as the percentage of power contained in a certain frequency band or the coherence between partners in a certain frequency band. Other external variables are assessed (or possibly manipulated) for each person or dyad. Then, summary analyses are done to relate the index from the spectral analysis (e.g., coherence) to these external variables (e.g., preterm vs. full-term birth status). These analyses can be quite simple (e.g., correlation, t test) or more complex (e.g., multiple regression). Most of the studies have been nonexperimental and therefore do not lead to strong causal conclusions, but the studies reviewed below do show that cyclicity and coordination are systematically related to external variables such as dyad composition and evaluation of the social interaction.

The following literature review deals with these three issues:

- Early findings documenting the existence of cycles in social interaction
- Studies about synchrony and coordination
- Studies that relate cyclicity and coordination to external variables

Before reviewing the empirical literature, I first consider some theoretical speculations why cycles might arise in social interaction.

Theoretical Background: Factors That Cause or Modulate Cycles in Behavior and Physiology

Reasons Why Rhythm Might Be an Organizing Principle in Living Systems

Many theorists have speculated that the tendency to initiate and maintain social interaction is regulated in order to avoid unpleasant extremes in emotional arousal. Argyle and Dean (1965) and Patterson (1976) suggested models for the regulation of emotional arousal, which may be related to physiological arousal, in social interaction. They suggested relatively simple static equilibrium models. Essentially, these models suggest that each person has a "preferred" moderate level of arousal. When arousal becomes too high, the person engages in some form of withdrawal (less intimate topic, gaze aversion, or greater interpersonal distance) to reduce the level of arousal; when greater arousal is desired, the person will engage in some approach behavior (more intimate topic, increased gaze, closer interpersonal distance, and so on). Through these self-regulatory processes, a person could maintain a relatively constant mean level of arousal, or a static equilibrium. Such a static equilibrium model would lead us to expect somewhat cyclic patterns in approach/avoidance behaviors over time because increases in gaze that lead to increases in physiological and emotional arousal would be expected to be followed by compensatory decreases in gaze that would bring physiological and emotional arousal back to the preferred or equilibrium level.

But what if a person's "preferred" level of physiological and emotional arousal is not constant over time, but instead tends to vary depending on internal physiological states? Research on biological rhythms suggests that the equilibrium an organization is trying to maintain in most physiological processes is dynamic rather than static. For instance, human body temperature is not regulated in a way that maintains a constant 98.6° Fahrenheit at all times; instead, its equilibrium corresponds to a circadian (approximately 24-hour) cycle; the "preferred" or equilibrium body temperature is higher during the active daylight hours than at night.

Why are cycles—or dynamic equilibria—such a conspicuous feature of biological systems? Goodwin (1970) pointed out that cyclic organization provides two major advantages for organisms. First, cycles represent a form of dynamic (as opposed to static) equilibrium. Goodwin argued that dynamic equilibrium is central to the organization of physiological systems because it allows the system to adapt to a wide range of environmental conditions while retaining its essential identity and stability. Many physiological processes show cyclic or dynamic equilibrium, although the cycles are not necessarily very regular and the coordination among cycles not necessarily very close.

The existence of cycles can also facilitate coordination at two levels in physiological systems: (a) within the organism and (b) between organism and environment or between organisms. Rhythm or cycles provide timing information necessary to coordinate processes within the organism. For example, the timing of DNA replication must be coordinated with cell wall division. Cyclic organization also allows the organism to "anticipate" and adapt to a periodically varying environment such as the daily light/dark cycle and the yearly change of seasons. Also, although Goodwin did not mention this possibility, rhythm could facilitate coordination with periodic behaviors of other organisms. Goodwin's (1970) theory suggests that rhythmic organization might have evolved because it is adaptive. If rhythm confers the kinds of advantages that Goodwin suggests, then natural selection would have favored organisms that were rhythmically organized.

Other theorists have noted that rhythmic organization could have evolved independently at the social/behavioral level of organization in living systems because it provides the same advantages to social systems that it provides to biological systems (Iberall & McCulloch, 1969); or that, in fact, the rhythmically organized biological substrate could influence behaviors, such that behavioral rhythms might reflect underlying physiological rhythms (Chapple, 1970).

The most conspicuous physiological rhythms have periods on the order of 24 hours, but there are also shorter and longer cycles in physiology, with cycle lengths ranging from milliseconds to years (Iberall & McCulloch, 1969; Moore-Ede, Sulzman, & Fuller, 1985; Yates, 1972). Circadian, weekly, and monthly rhythms in physiology and mood may all have implications for social interaction patterns. The amount and positive/negative quality of social interactions may tend to vary over time. As other examples, mood and sociability and activity level differ systematically at certain times of the day (Thayer, 1989) and certain days of the week (Larsen & Kasimatis, 1990) and certain points in the menstrual cycle (Dalton, 1990). Attention and attitudes also vary cyclically, with cycles on the order of 1 minute or longer (cf. Kaplowitz & Fink, Meadowcroft, both this volume).

Chapple (1970) suggested that a person's readiness to initiate and maintain social activity varies over time as a function of the person's internal physiological states, most of which are varying cyclically. It is obvious that people's social responsiveness varies with circadian physiological rhythms: Some people are slow starters in the morning, who don't carry on much conversation until after a cup of coffee. Others fade early in the evening. However, we are interested here in more subtle ultradian (briefer than a day) cycles in physiological arousal that might influence social behavior within the course of a day or even within the duration of a conversation. Besides the well-known circadian rhythms that appear in many physiological processes, ultradian (shorter than 24-hour) cycles appear in many physiological variables when they are observed under free-running conditions.

Evidence for Ultradian Physiological Rhythms

The best known ultradian physiological rhythm is the basic rest activity cycle (BRAC), cycles about 90 to 100 minutes long that are evident in REM sleep and in adrenocortical activity and other physiological processes (Lavie, 1982). Hayes and Cobb (1979) observed that the social interactions of couples who were isolated in a lab apartment showed 90- to 100-minute cycles in amount of conversational activity, which they believe may be related to these physiological rhythms. A similar coincidence between a BRAC pattern in solitary physiological variables and in amount of social activity has been noted in dyads of rhesus monkeys (Maxim, Bowden, & Sackett, 1976).

However, there is a less well known set of physiological rhythms, with cycles on the order of 3 to 6 minutes, that have been independently reported in a number of laboratories. Human subjects show cycles of about 3 and 6 minutes in respiration at rest (Hlastala, Wranne, & Lenfant, 1973; Lenfant, 1967). Warner et al. (1983) found that these 3- to 6-minute cycles in respiration also occur during some conversations and that cycles in amount of talk may be synchronized with cycles in the speaker's respiration. Cycles of about 3 to 6 minutes long have also been recorded in human resting blood pressure (Kushner & Falkner, 1981; Warner & Stevens, 1991) and in the blood pressure of dogs

(Benton & Yates, 1990). Warner, Malloy, Schneider, Knoth, and Wilder (1987) found cycles on the order of 3 and 6 minutes long in heart rate during conversation for some speakers. Critical flicker fusion threshold, which is sometimes used clinically as an index of central nervous system arousal, also varies in cycles on the order of 3 to 6 minutes and longer (Hammond, Warner, & Fuld, 1994; Lovett-Doust & Podnieks, 1976). There are also cyclic variations in motor activity level in the human fetus and in newborns, with cycles ranging from 1 to 10 minutes long (Robertson, 1982).

The next section reviews evidence that amount of vocal activity and self-rated affect also show cycles of similar duration. This suggests the possibility of a rhythm syndrome involving 3- to 6-minute cycles in behavior, physiology, and emotion, with at least loose interconnections among all these rhythms, something like the group of loosely related physiological and behavioral rhythms that makes up the BRAC. Other chapters in this volume (cf. Kaplowitz & Fink; Meadowcroft) suggest that cycles similar in duration are manifested in attention and in attitudes.

Relationship Between Physiological and Behavioral Rhythms

Chapple's (1970) theoretical account of social interaction seemed to assume that behavioral rhythms emerge because internal physiological states, which tend to vary cyclically, influence the readiness to initiate and maintain social activity. In other words, he seems to imply that behavioral or social rhythms are caused by physiological rhythms. However, it is equally plausible that behavioral rhythms might influence physiological rhythms. Engaging in social interactions might result in mutual entrainment or coordination of physiological rhythms between partners (as in the reports of menstrual synchrony among friends, McClintock, 1971). Hofer (1984) has suggested that social relationships play an extremely important role in modulating and synchronizing physiological rhythms and in maintaining the dynamic physiological equilibrium that is essential to good physical health. McKenna, Mosko, Dungy, and McAnich (1990) have reported that sudden infant death syndrome due to respiratory failure is much less common in cultures where infants sleep with parents and attribute this to the modulation or synchronization of the infant's respiratory patterns to the adult's respiratory rhythms.

It is not clear which among these many attitudinal, attentional, be-havioral, cognitive, emotional, physiological, and social rhythms are "primary" or causal. For instance, are cyclic variations in attention or mood caused by cyclic modulations in physiology? Or are variations in physiology caused by cyclic changes in attention or mood? It is possible that all these processes can potentially influence each other and that no single process is primary in the sense of causing all the other cycles.

At this stage of research, we are merely documenting the occurrence of rhythms with a similar time course in behavior and in physiology and statistically assessing the degree of co-occurrence in these rhythms. Causal inferences would be premature. It is conceivable that physiologi-cal rhythms influence behavioral rhythms and also that behavioral rhythms could influence physiological rhythms (these two forms of influence are not mutually exclusive), or similar rhythms could arise in both behavior and physiology independently because rhythm is a "natu-ral" form of dynamic equilibrium (Goodwin, 1970), or both the behav-ioral and physiological rhythms could be "driven" by some more basic rhythm not yet identified.

Thus, it is possible that cycles in social interaction arise in part because of physiological rhythms that modulate the preferred level of arousal. However, this has not been proved. Whether this conjecture about the causes of behavioral cycles is correct or not, consistent behavioral cycles have been found; the nature of these findings is described in the next section.

Is Rhythm Always Optimal?

To suggest that a "dynamic physiological equilibrium" may be essen-tial for health does *not* mean that more cyclical or regular patterns, or more coordinated rhythms, are necessarily optimal. Some types of very regular patterning (such as Cheyne-Stokes respiration) are actually pathological; excessively tight coordination or coupling in a social system could be a sign of rigidity or pathology, as suggested by Gottman (1979b). Some degree of predictable patterning and coordination is probably necessary (although not sufficient) for a healthy system. How-ever, research to date suggests that the type of patterning and degree of coordination that are optimal for functioning depends very much on the context (e.g., the situation, the type of relationship, and the behavior under study). For instance, Cappella (this volume) reported that attrac-tion was associated with more responsiveness or co-ordination with partner behaviors in stranger dyads, whereas attraction was associated with less responsiveness or coordination in intimate dyads. Cappella suggested that the "meaning" of closely coordinated behavior and what is experienced as optimal differ in these types of dyads. For some types of dyads, a more highly structured, predictable, rhythmic, tightly coordinated pattern in behavior might be optimal; for others, a less structured or coordinated behavior pattern might be optimal. It is also conceivable that the relationship between rhythmicity and quality of the interaction is curvilinear; for instance, Warner et al. (1987) found that moderately rhythmic conversations were most positively evaluated.

Description of Cyclic Patterns
in Social Interaction

Assessing Cyclic Tendencies

Spectral analysis and related analytic techniques such as harmonic analysis provide one means of assessing the tendency for time series to contain regular cycles (Bloomfield, 1976). In some studies, the spectrum is simply visually examined, and the frequencies (or cycle lengths) that correspond to the largest peaks in the spectrum are noted. In other studies, significance tests are used to determine which peaks should be reported, or summary indexes of "rhythmicity" or "cyclicity" are calculated from the spectrum by summing the percentages of variances accounted for by particular frequency bands (cf. Wade, Ellis, & Bohrer, 1973; Warner, 1992b).

Adult-Adult Social Interaction Cycles

The one variable that has been most extensively assessed for the possible occurrence of cycles is amount of talk as it varies over the course of a conversation. These studies involve a variety of types of conversation, mostly getting-acquainted conversations between strangers. Although the cycle lengths that have been reported have varied considerably (both across studies and among the individual participants within each study), at this point the most commonly reported cycle lengths for all these variables are on the order of 2 to 3 minutes, about 6 minutes, and longer cycles ranging from 20 to 90 minutes (Warner, 1991).

These relatively long cycles (on the order of minutes) have been labeled "megaturns" (Dabbs, 1982) to distinguish them from the much briefer "turn" units reported in the landmark study by Duncan and Fiske (1977). A megaturn, or vocal activity cycle, consists of a period of about 1-2 minutes when a person is talking a lot, followed by a period of about 1-2 minutes when the person is talking relatively little; the partner's level of talk tends to be coordinated so that when A is mostly talking, B is mostly listening, and vice versa. Refer back to Figure 14.1 for an empirical example illustrating megaturns. This speaker tended to show cycles in amount of talk that were on the order of 6 minutes long. These megaturns correspond to extended periods when each speaker holds the floor, perhaps engaging in extended storytelling.

The briefest periodic rhythms or cycles that have been reported in amount of talk ranged from 32 seconds to 2 minutes (Cobb, 1973) and from 46 to 132 seconds (Dabb, 1982). Most of the studies that have looked at longer conversations have yielded cycles on the order of 2-3 minutes, 6 minutes, and longer. Several studies have yielded 3- to 6-minute cycles in initiation of social behavior or amount of talk. In the first study of this type, Kimberly (1970) reported fairly regular cycles on the order of 3 to 6 minutes long in the social behavior (attempts to initiate social interaction) of a mentally retarded woman. Spectral analysis of variations in the amount of talk during getting-acquainted conversations between pairs of college students (Warner, 1979) showed cyclic variations in amount of talk that were on the order of 3 to 6 minutes and 12 to 20 minutes.

Warner et al. (1987) also studied getting-acquainted conversations between pairs of college students and found a few major periodic components, corresponding mostly to cycles on the order of 3 and 6 minutes long. The percentage variance explained by periodic cycles in amount of talk varied considerably across individual speakers, ranging from 3.4% (not significantly above chance) to 49.4% for individual speakers. In other words, in isolated cases, these cycles in amount of talk were so regular and so large in amplitude that they explained nearly half the variance in that speaker's behavior over time.

Another variable that has also been assessed in adult-adult interaction is continuous ratings of affect. Gottman and Levenson (1985) videotaped marital interactions and then had each partner continuously rate their own affect while watching the replay of the videotape. While watching the video, each person used a dial to rate variations in affect;

positive affect was represented by turning the dial to the right, negative by turning the dial to the left.[2] Gottman and Levenson presented evidence that the couples were able to recall their affect from the interaction; the fact that their physiological arousal during the rating task tended to reproduce their physiological arousal variations during the live interaction suggested that they might be to some extent "reliving" the interaction as they did the rating task. Cycle lengths of approximately 30 to 150 seconds in the affect ratings were detected using spectral analysis. The spectral and cross-spectral analyses suggested that there may be affect cycles on the order of 1 to 2 minutes long that tend to be coordinated between spouses. It is intriguing that the cycle lengths found here are similar to those reported for cycle lengths of vocal activity, although there is not yet any direct empirical evidence that these cycles are related.

Social Interaction Cycles in Children

Similar behavioral cycles in social interaction have been found in conversations between children. Bryan (1991) examined conversations in third- and fourth-grade girls by recording amount of talk over time and then doing time domain and frequency domain analyses comparable to those in the adult-adult interaction research. She found an average cycle length of 3 minutes, with a range from 24 seconds to 8 minutes, which is quite similar to the distribution of cycle lengths reported for adult vocal activity. Field et al. (1992) did detailed analyses of conversations between previously acquainted pairs of sixth-grade children. They found cycle lengths of about 8 to 33 seconds in both on-off vocal activity patterns and global ratings of type of behavior along with cycles ranging from about 29 seconds to 6 minutes in heart rates. These two studies suggest that grade-school children may show activity cycles that are strikingly similar to those found in adult conversations.

Social Interaction Cycles in
Mother-Infant Interaction

The cycles that have been reported in mother-infant interaction (typically less than 1 minute, often on the order of 10 seconds long) have been shorter than those seen in adult interactions, but it is difficult to make comparisons between these two sets of studies because, in addition to age, there are many other differences in the design: task, setting, nature of interaction, and type of behavior that is recorded over time. In most of the mother-infant interaction studies, the variable that is studied over time is a measure of "affective involvement," such as Tronick's Monadic Phases Scale, which is coded from observable behaviors of the mother and infant. Studies of parent-infant interaction have tended to utilize much briefer observation periods (often only a few minutes long). For this reason, the cycles that can be detected are much shorter than the 3- to 6-minute cycles most often reported in adult-adult interaction. In fact, it is not clear whether the differences in the cycle lengths reported in the infant-adult and adult-adult social interaction literatures are due entirely to the differences in session length, task, and the choice of behaviors to observe or whether it reflects some real difference in the "speed" of cycling between low and high affective involvement and activity for infants versus adults. The cycle lengths (variations in affective involvement) most often reported in the infant-adult social interaction literature are on the order of 10 seconds and 1 minute long.

Mothers and infants show cyclic variations in behavior, affect, or physiology during their interactions. Early observations of this cyclicity were qualitative and did not rely on formal statistical methods to estimate cycle length or the amount of variance explained by cycles (e.g., Beebe et al., 1982; Brazelton, Koslowski, & Main, 1974; Stern; 1982). Tronick, Als, and Brazelton (1977) reported that infants tended to look away from their mothers after periods of maximum involvement, and then to look back after a rest period. Gottman (1979a) analyzed Tronick et al.'s time series data on affective involvement (which was scored using Tronick's Monadic Phases Scale), using spectral analysis to describe cyclicity. He found somewhat irregular cycles on the order of 5.55 to 7.14 seconds for the mother and 4.5 to 5 seconds for the infant in one dyad and cycles on the order of 2.27 to 2.77 seconds for the mother and 2.17 to 2.38 seconds for the infant in another. Lester et al. (1985) did a similar analysis for 3-minute long interactions involving preterm and full-term infants and found that there were cycles in the behavior of both mothers and infants, with most cycles on the order of 10 and 45 seconds. Periodicity in infant behavior was stronger at 5 months than at 3 months of age.

Cohn and Tronick (1988) reported that 5 of the 54 babies in their mother-infant interaction study had "periodic cycles" in affective involvement (with a mean period of 10 seconds). They reported other, less regular cycles for many in their sample: 18 of 54 mothers had mean cycle lengths in affective involvement ranging from 16 to 27 seconds, and 16 of 54 infants had irregular cycles, with mean cycle lengths ranging from 17 to 23 seconds. Overall, the cycle lengths reported by Cohn and Tronick (1988) seem fairly similar to those reported by Lester et al. (1985), although in their report Cohn and Tronick emphasized the irregularity of the cycles they detected.

Coordination or Synchrony of Cycles in Social Interaction

Definitions of Coordination

It is possible to define coordination in social interaction in many different ways and to use many different statistical techniques to index the strength of coordination (Warner, 1992b; also see Cappella, this volume). The type of coordination of interest in this chapter is synchronized cycles in amount of talk and other activities. Activity cycles can be in phase (if mother and infant are both showing peak levels of emotional arousal and involvement at the same moments) or in opposite phase (in talk patterns, when one person is talking, the other person is mostly silent; thus, a peak in activity for one corresponds to a low point in activity for the partner).

How can coordinated or synchronized cycles best be detected? There is no clear consensus as to the best way to assess coordination. The most obvious analytic tool to use for this is the coherence spectrum from cross-spectral analysis, which detects co-occurrence or statistical dependence between time series in the frequency domain (Porges et al., 1980). (However, in some research situations, a much simpler coordination index—a simple Pearson correlation between time series—provides equivalent information; see Warner, 1992b.) The studies reviewed below used coherence to assess coordination or synchrony between cycles.

This definition of coordination as synchronized cycles is quite different from the definition of coordination proposed by Cappella elsewhere in this volume. Cappella describes mutual influence and mutual adaptation as two distinguishable types of coordination. The data-analytic methods that are conventionally used to assess mutual adaptation involve whitening the time series data (whitening means removing trends, cycles, and any other form of serial dependence or predictable patterning) prior to assessment of statistical dependence between partners, using time series regression or related analytic methods. These data-analytic techniques tend to remove cycles, if any are present. It is important to note that the data-analytic techniques that are suitable for detection of moment-to-moment mutual adaptation (as defined by Cappella) will *not* detect shared or synchronized cycles (see Warner, 1992b, for more detailed discussion). The conventional prewhitening or preprocessing of time series data that most time series regression applications use tends to remove cycles. If coordinated cycles are the researcher's main interest, then the time series should be left intact (except for trend removal) before applying cross-spectral analysis or lagged cross-correlation analyses to detect shared cycles.

In some of the studies reviewed below, data were collected on both the behavior (amount of talk) and physiology (heart rate) of two persons in a dyadic interaction. If we measure talk and heart rate for persons A and B, we can look at the following types of coordination or synchrony:

1. How closely coordinated is person A's talk with person B's talk? This will reflect the strength of the social influence or responsiveness between them.

2. How closely coordinated is person A's talk with person A's own heart rate (and similarly, person B's talk with person B's own heart rate)? If this type of coordination is high, it could mean that talk patterns modulate heart rate or that heart rate patterns in some way modulate the likelihood of initiating or maintaining talk. Close examination of lead-lag relationships might help clarify which variable seems to be "following" the other.

3. How closely coordinated is person A's heart rate with person B's heart rate? That is, are their physiological rhythms synchronized?

In principle, it would also be possible to ask how closely coordinated person A's heart rate is to person B's talk (and person B's heart rate to person A's talk). However, none of the studies reviewed here examined that connection.

In general, the results of the few available studies consistently show that the strength of these first three types of coupling or coordination varies substantially across dyads. This suggests that the strength of coupling might possibly be useful information about differences in how well dyads "get along" or coordinate their behavior. Results so far also suggest that these first three types of coordination do vary in strength. Of the three, the coupling between the behaviors of the two persons (Item 1) is typically the strongest; the coupling between the physiology of the two persons (Item 3) is typically weakest. This is not absolutely invariant; there are individual dyads for whom the Item 2 coupling is stronger than Item 1, but usually the coupling between partner behaviors is the strongest. This suggests that, even if people's behaviors are influenced by their internal physiological states to some extent, this internal influence on behavior is generally overridden by the influence of the partner's behavior.

Synchrony/Coordination in Adult-Adult Interaction

Cross-spectral analysis can be used to assess interdependence in the frequency domain. However, as noted by Warner, Waggener, and Kronauer (1983), high coherence is a necessary but not sufficient condition in order to conclude that synchronized cycles are present. Additional information about the degree of cyclicity in each time series is essential before concluding that high coherence suggests coordinated cycles. Warner et al. (1987) used spectral and cross-spectral analysis to assess coordination of three types: between the vocal activity patterns of conversation partners; between vocal activity and the speaker's own heart rate; and between the heart rates of conversation partners. (Because only trend removal and not more drastic types of prewhitening was applied to the time series before performing cross-spectral analyses, these results are better interpreted in terms of "overall coordination" rather than as "mutual adaptation," to use Cappella's terminology.)

Weighted coherence, a summary statistic suggested by Porges et al. (1980), was used to summarize coherence across a wide band of low frequencies that explained most of the variance in each individual speaker's vocal activity. Mean weighted coherence was strongest for the coupling of vocal activity between speakers (the mean across all dyads was .595, ranging from .256 to .914 for individual dyads). This strong coupling between the talk cycles of conversation partners is not surprising because the talk-silence patterns of two partners tend to be nearly mirror image due to conversational turn taking (when A talks, B mostly listens). Mean weighted coherence was somewhat weaker for the coordination of vocal activity with the speaker's own heart rate (across dyads, the average weighted coherence across the low-frequency end of the spectrum was .444, ranging from .314 to .686 for individual dyads). This suggests that people tend to coordinate their behavioral rhythms *less* with their own internal physiological rhythms than with the behavioral rhythms of a partner, although there was some coordination within most persons between their behavioral and physiological rhythms. This finding is consistent with Field, Healy, and LeBlanc's (1989) observation that coupling between mother behavior/ infant behavior was stronger than coupling between behavior and the infant's or mother's own heart rate. These findings suggest that, although Chapple (1970) may be correct in suggesting that there is some coupling between behavioral and physiological rhythms in social interaction, the social coupling between partner behaviors tends to be stronger. The weakest coupling occurred between the heart rates of the conversation partners; in fact, there was little evidence for any direct synchrony between the physiological rhythms of the conversation partners.

A more detailed analysis of synchrony between behavioral and physiological cycles was presented by Warner et al. (1983). Band-pass filtering was used to isolate the cycles that explained the largest percent of variance in the time series data on amount of talk and respiration rate during conversation. These were plotted to assess how the cycles in one partner's vocal activity were related to cycles in the other partner's behavior within a particular frequency band. These plots made it clear that there were indeed fairly regularly recurring cycles that occurred throughout the data record and that the phase relationship between the partner's vocal activity cycles was consistent (when A was most talkative, B was least talkative; in other words, their vocal activity cycles were synchronized in opposite phase). Comparisons were also made of the cycles in ventilation rate to see whether each speaker tended to go through regular cycles of hypoventilation/hyperventilation along with cycles of more talk/less talk. Individual differences were found: Some speakers tended to show cycles in both ventilation and in talk that were closely coordinated; others showed cycles in ventilation that were essentially independent of their cycles in amount of talk; and still others showed noncyclic patterns in both speech and ventilation. It appeared that there can be close coordination between a behavioral and a physiological rhythm during social interaction; that is, a speaker's variations in ventilation rate can be very closely associated with variations in amount of talk.

However, this close coordination does not always occur, and striking instances of miscoordination were observed. One speaker actually tended to hypoventilate while talking more and hyperventilate while talking less, which is the opposite of what is generally seen in laboratory studies that assess the impact of talking tasks on ventilation rates (e.g., Bunn & Mead, 1971). According to Chapple's (1970) theory, this could be a case in which the demands of the social situation and the need to coordinate talk patterns with the partner's talk patterns may override the internal physiological rhythms that ordinarily tend to influence the amount of talk.

In summary, there is substantial evidence that adult-adult interaction partners do show behavioral cycles (variations in amount of talk) that are fairly strongly coordinated between partners. There is also some evidence that at least some individuals show some coordination between internal physiological rhythms and their behavioral rhythms, although existing studies suggest that this connection is much weaker than the coordination between partner behavior cycles. Further research is needed to assess the degree to which shared cycles are involved in the communication and sharing of affect (cf. Hatfield, Cacioppo, & Rapson, 1992).

Synchrony/Coordination
in Mother-Infant Interaction

There is some evidence that the cycles detected in mother and infant affect involvement are, in fact, coordinated between mother and infant and that observers can detect this coordination when they make global or qualitative judgments about the quality of the mother-infant interaction. Furthermore, an emerging theme in this literature is that depressed mothers may lack the ability to respond contingently and appropriately to their infant's varying level of affective involvement (cf. Field, 1985; Field et al., 1990). When the infant experiences a lack of contingency between its own behaviors and the mother's responses, this lack of contingency may contribute to the development of feelings of helplessness or even depression in the infant. Thus, when coordination of affective involvement cycles between mother and infant does not occur, this may be an indication that there is something seriously wrong that could have a negative impact on the infant's long-term emotional and social development.

Lester et al. (1985) reported coherence values in their study of variations of emotional involvement during mother-infant interaction (this study also included comparisons of interactions involving preterm and full-term infants, mentioned earlier). They reported the highest coherence values in the frequency range from .022 to .10 Hertz (corresponding to cycles ranging from 45 to 10 seconds). They also cited past research indicating that cardiorespiratory activity in infants and adults shows cycles similar in length, and they suggested that the cycles they found in mother-infant behavior may be linked to these physiological rhythms.

Field et al. (1989) examined synchrony of behavior states and heart rates in depressed versus nondepressed mother-infant dyads and found that all 16 mothers and 16 infants showed statistically significant peaks in their spectra for the behavior time series data, indicating that behavior tended to show cycles on the order of 8 to 32 seconds long. In spite of many differences in methodology, this is remarkably consistent with the cycle lengths found in the earlier mother-infant studies in other laboratories. Coherence mean estimates for mother and infant behaviors ranged from nonsignificant to .69. Phase spectrum results suggested that the mothers tended to lead the infants by less than 1 second. Mother and infant heart rate also revealed significant peaks in the spectra, corresponding to cycle lengths on the order of 2 to 9 seconds. Overall, Field et al. reported that behavioral coherence was evident for all dyads but that it was stronger for the nondepressed dyads than for the depressed dyads. The greater coherence of mother's heart rate with infant's behavior in the nondepressed dyads was tentatively interpreted as evidence of greater empathic response. Another feature of this study was comparison of the strength of coherence for different types of variables. Physiological coherence (mother's heart rate with infant's heart rate) was weaker than behavioral coherence (mother's behavior with infant's behavior).

Field et al.'s (1989) study yielded several important results. First, there were cycles in behavior and in physiology very similar in cycle length to those reported in other labs (cycles on the order of 10 seconds). Second, there was at least moderate coupling between behavioral and physiological cycles both within and between persons. Third, results confirmed earlier reports (Warner et al., 1983) that behavioral coherence or coordination is stronger than physiological coherence. This study is exemplary in the thoroughness of reporting and should serve as a model for future work along these lines.

To summarize, somewhat irregular cycles in behavior and physiology, on the order of 10 seconds long, seem to characterize brief (1- to 5-minute) mother-infant interactions. Estimates of mean cycle length have been surprisingly consistent in light of the fact that different researchers use different coding systems, settings, and dyad types. These cycles are at least moderately coupled between partners. The strength of coupling or coherence is related to individual difference variables that seem to have some relevance to interaction quality, such as preterm versus full-term birth; infant age; and maternal depression.

External Variables

Factors That Might Influence Cyclicity/Coordination

Conceivably, a great many of the factors that can be varied in social interaction research (characteristics of the members of the dyad, the nature of relationship between them, task type) could influence cyclicity, and the handful of studies that have looked at these factors have found correlations with indexes of cyclicity. However, there is no well-developed theory to make predictions. Most predictions seem to be derived from the generalized expectancy that more rhythmic functioning is adaptive and should therefore be related to positive outcomes and that coordination between partners is indicative of responsiveness or mutual involvement and should therefore also be associated with positive outcomes. This is probably an oversimplification. It is unlikely that more rhythmic/more coordinated behavior is always better, particularly in the extremes. It seems more likely that the exact type of patterning, and degree of coordination, that is optimal will vary as a function of the context (dyad type, task, behavior, etc.).

In one of the few studies that has employed any experimental interventions, Dabbs (1982) varied the type of conversation task in his study and found that there tended to be longer cycles of talk in "high cognitive load" conversations. (The high cognitive load discussion was a discussion of the fuel crisis; the low cognitive load was a getting-acquainted task.) The conversations were limited to 5 or 10 minutes in these studies, and the briefness of the conversations limited the length of the cycles that could be detected.

The question whether the nature of the relationship between partners might affect the degree of cyclicity in amount of talk was investigated in the Talmadge and Dabbs (1990) study of cycles in vocal activity in 10-minute problem discussions of 30 dating or married couples. They concluded that pairs who reported more positive affect tended to have shorter vocal activity cycles than pairs who reported more negative affect. Unfortunately, the actual cycle lengths were not documented. Another study, in which the time series variable was level of openness or self-disclosure across many conversations, found differences in the cyclic patterns of stable versus deteriorating relationships (VanLear, 1991). Stable, growing, and deteriorating relationships all showed evidence of cyclic variations in openness, but the amplitudes of the cycles in stable relationships were markedly flatter than the amplitudes of deteriorating relationships.

Group size may also affect the degree of cyclicity. Wade et al. (1973) did spectral analysis of heart rate in children engaged in free play either alone, in pairs, or in threes, and found that the tendency toward cycles about 15 to 20 minutes long in heart rate (which presumably are related to gross motor activity) was much stronger in dyads than for children playing alone or in larger groups.

The focus in mother-infant research has been mainly on coherence or coordination in relation to external variables such as infant clinical status (preterm vs. full-term) and mother clinical status (depressed vs. nondepressed). Lester et al. (1985) assessed coherence as a function of infant status (preterm vs. full-term) and infant age (3 vs. 5 months). They found that coherence tended to be higher for older infants, and it tended to be higher for full-term than for preterm infants. These results suggest that greater synchrony (as indexed by higher coherence) seemed to be related to infant health and developmental status.

Field et al. (1989) examined synchrony of behavior states and heart rates in depressed versus nondepressed mother-infant dyads. Greater coherence of both mother/ infant behavior and infant behavior/mother heart rate was found in nondepressed dyads. A similar study (Field, Healy, Goldstein, & Guthertz, 1990) involved application of spectral and cross-spectral analysis to behavior-state time series data for mother-infant interactions. This study did not find a statistically significant difference in the behavioral coherence of depressed/nondepressed dyads, although a simpler measure of co-occurrence (involving the percentage of time that mother and infant were in the same behavioral state) did differentiate depressed from nondepressed dyads.

These few initial exploratory studies suggest that the length of cycles and the coordination between partners may vary systematically as a function of several external variables including clinical status (maternal depression, infant preterm delivery), the nature of the task, and the nature of the relationship (intimate vs. nonintimate).

Possible Consequences of
Variations in Cyclicity/Coordination

A question raised earlier was whether the degree of rhythmic organization or cyclicity of behavior or physiology indicates healthy or pathological functioning of physiological and social systems. One way to assess this is to correlate ratings of the quality of social interaction with indexes that describe how cyclic or rhythmic the behaviors and physiology of partners were. Warner et al. (1987) found a curvilinear relationship between the amount of variance due to vocal activity cycles and observer ratings of participant affect. Moderately cyclic conversations were most positively evaluated. This was tentatively interpreted as evidence that there might be some "optimal" level of cyclicity. However, a later study with a larger sample correlated cyclicity with participant and observer ratings of affect and found a weak positive linear relationship (Warner, 1992b). More cyclic conversations were evaluated more favorably both by the participants and by outside observers.

Evaluations of the "quality" of mother-infant relationships may also be associated with the degree of rhythmic patterning and/or coordination. Censullo, Bowler, Lester, and Brazelton (1987) used cross-spectral analysis of Tronick's Monadic Phase Scale to assess synchrony in mother-infant dyads. They reported good agreement between global, qualitative observer judgments about the overall interaction (on such characteristics as mutual attention, positive affect, the presence of cycles of mutual turn taking, and maternal sensitive responsiveness) and the levels of coherence for the objective time series data. That is, dyads who had high coherence between their Monadic Phase Scale scores also tended to receive the most positive evaluations. This suggests that the coherence analysis taps some aspect of social interaction that observers can recognize and that influences observer judgments of the quality of the interaction. They did not report the actual coherence levels or test them for statistical significance.

Shared Physiological Rhythms
as Possible Basis for Empathy

One way that empathy can be defined is the ability to accurately recognize fluctuations in a partner's emotional state over time. It is possible that one mechanism through which people recognize or perhaps actually share their partner's emotions is through shared physiology. For instance, if both partners experience increased heart rate during the same phases of the interaction, this may reflect the fact that they are finding the same events emotionally arousing (Levenson & Ruef, 1992). Hatfield et al. (1992) used the term "emotional contagion" to refer to the sharing of emotions by interaction partners. They suggested that synchronization of physiological rhythms might be one means of facilitating such sharing of emotions. Levenson and Ruef (1992) asked couples to continuously rate the emotion of a husband or a wife in a videotaped discussion, using a dial rating device for rating affect similar to that reported in Gottman and Levenson (1985), discussed above. They found that those whose physiological changes mirrored the target person's, whose affect they were trying to rate, were significantly better at detecting negative emotions (ability to detect positive emotions was related to mean heart rate but not to the synchronization of heart rate between partners). Perhaps in future studies we can see whether it is shared cycles of affect, behavior, and physiology that mediate emotional rapport.

Conclusion

Studies conducted so far suggest that somewhat irregular cycles (in amount of talk, affect, physiology, and other variables) occur in many social interaction situations and that the occurrence of these cycles is related to evaluations of the quality of the interaction and to antecedent conditions such as the nature of the task or the dyad being studied. Analytic tools borrowed from spectral and cross-spectral analysis appear to be quite useful in describing these cyclic patterns, although more research is needed to evaluate which analytic procedures best summarize information about the cyclicity and coordination of social interaction. More than a decade ago, John Gottman (1982) called for the development of a "language of temporal form" to describe the microstructures of social interaction. The research reviewed here suggests that cycles in amount of activity and coordination of these cycles between interaction partners could be important elements of such a language of temporal form.

Notes

1. Band-pass filtering involves isolating and plotting cyclic components in a time series that fall within a specified bandwidth; unlike simpler forms of harmonic analysis described elsewhere in this volume that fit a sinusoid of constant amplitude to the entire data record, band-pass filtering captures changes in phase and amplitude that occur in the time series. A full description of the logic and procedures of band-pass filtering is beyond the scope of this chapter; further explanation, with examples, is provided in Warner, Waggener, and Kronauer (1983). Some standard spectral analysis programs such as BMDP 1T provide band-pass filtering capabilities.

2. See West and Biocca (this volume) for a discussion of the methodology of continuous response measures. See Kaplowitz and Fink (this volume) for an example of the measurement of continuous evaluations.

15

Dynamic Coordination of Vocal and Kinesic Behavior in Dyadic Interaction

Methods, Problems, and Interpersonal Outcomes

JOSEPH N. CAPPELLA

The concept of interpersonal interaction requires that the persons involved influence one another's behavior through their own behavior. This core concept is at the root of Ashby's (1963) definition of communication between systems, Hinde's (1979) definition of interpersonal relations, Davis's (1982) concept of responsiveness, and Cappella's (1987) definition of interpersonal communication.

The nomenclature used to describe the ways people affect one another's behavior in interaction has been inconsistent and confusing. Some have tried to clarify the mess (Burgoon, Dillman, & Stern, 1993). In this chapter, I draw some distinctions between *static* and *dynamic* aspects of interaction that must be kept clearly separated if research into interaction patterns is to avoid drawing inappropriate conclusions.

One pattern of interaction between partners is called *mutual influence*.[1] Mutual influence usually refers to the similarity (or reciprocity) and difference (or compensation) in *aggregate* behaviors exhibited by partners. Evidence for the presence of mutual influence is usually, but not always, static measures of sameness or difference. For example, a positive correlation in average speech rate between partners across a group of dyads would be labeled reciprocal mutual influence, even though a correlation between means does not imply that partners are affecting one another from moment to moment. They may or may not be. The data are inconclusive.

Some mutual-influence patterns do take time into account. For example, if speech rates over a lengthy interaction showed slow downward trends (due to fatigue or to partners' effects on one another), then correlations over time would be positive (reciprocal). What can one conclude from this correlation over time? Are the partners influencing one another, or are they both being influenced by a third force (fatigue)? Summaries of the research literature have not drawn fine distinctions between these two types of interactional influence.

To show that partners are influencing one another over time, another type of information is needed. The phrase *mutual adaptation* will be reserved to refer to the dynamic process by which partners respond to changes in one another's behavior during interaction. For example, if changes in one person's level of disclosure are followed by changes in the partner's levels, and vice versa, then mutual adaptation is occurring. If there is good reason to question whether partners are actually influencing one another, then it is necessary to separate mutual influence from adaptation.

Following recent work by Rosenthal (Bernieri & Rosenthal, 1991; Tickle-Degnen & Rosenthal, 1987), the term *coordination* is used to refer to general interpersonal responsiveness captured dynamically by adaptation and captured in more static form by mutual influence. Both processes can be operating within the same interaction. For example, if disclosure changes by one are being matched by the partner in direction *and* the levels of disclosure are increasing slowly over time, then both mutual adaptation (changes correlated with changes) and mutual influence (linear increase by both) are in operation.

Coordination is arguably the essential characteristic of every interpersonal interaction. The basis for this argument is fourfold.

◆ **Coordination is the defining characteristic of interpersonal communication.**

Although personal relationships have an existence apart from the interactions that mold, maintain, and destroy them, interpersonal communication is fundamentally coordination of behavior. If person A's behaviors do not affect those of B uniquely and mutually (see Cappella, 1987), then one partner cannot be said to be sensitive to alterations in the other's actions in any observable way. Without such contingent responsiveness it would be difficult to distinguish two monologists disengaged from their partners from two interactants engaged in one another's discourse.

◆ **Mutual adaptation occurs for a wide variety of interpersonal tie-signs.**

A substantial body of research indicates that social interactions among adults, children, and even infants are marked by processes of mutual influence involving automatic and deliberate behaviors (Cappella, 1981, 1991, 1994). In adult interactions, mutual adaptation has been observed among various speech behaviors including accents (Giles & Powesland, 1975), speech rate (Street, 1984; Webb, 1972), pauses (Cappella & Planalp, 1981; Feldstein & Welkowitz, 1978), latency to respond (Cappella & Planalp, 1981), vocal intensity (Natale, 1975), fundamental vocal frequency (Buder, 1991b), and turn durations (Matarazzo & Wiens, 1972). A range of kinesic behaviors exhibit adaptive patterns as well, including postural and gestural behaviors (LaFrance, 1982; Maurer & Tindall, 1983), movement synchrony (Berneri, Resnick, & Rosenthal, 1988), gaze (Klienke, Staneski, & Berger, 1975; Noller, 1984), head nods and facial affect (Hale & Burgoon, 1984), facial displays of emotion (Krause, Stemer, Sanger-Alt, & Wagner, 1989), and more generalized hostile affect (Gottman, 1979a, 1979b; Pike & Sillars, 1985).

More deliberate behaviors such as self-disclosures (Davis, 1976, 1977), excuses (McLaughlin, Cody, & Rosenstein, 1983), and stares (Greenbaum & Rosenfeld, 1978) exhibit the patterns characteristic of coordination.

◆ **Mutual adaptation operates even from the first instances of infant-mother interaction.**

Although it may not be surprising to find that children with well-developed language capacity exhibit adaptation to adult partners in noncontent speech behaviors (Street & Cappella, 1989), similar findings with the linguistically less developed are striking. Jasnow and Feldstein (1987) found matching in latency of response for mothers and their 9-month-old infants. Bernieri et al. (1988) observed greater synchrony in body movements between mothers and their 14- to 18-month-old infants than between mothers and a different infant. Adaptation of the infant to the mother has been observed even earlier with 3- and 4-month-olds by Symons and Moran (1987) and Cohn and Tronick (1987). Berghout-Austin and Peery (1983) found a statistically reliable movement synchrony between neonates 30-56 hours old and an experimenter. Movement synchrony was present in all five infants.

Together with an array of other data (Cappella, 1991; Field, 1987) the above studies suggest that adaptation occurs not only in childhood and infancy but even very early in the life of the neonate.

◆ **Mutual adaptation covaries with important relational and individual conditions.**

Positive social evaluations have been associated with certain types of coordination in interaction. Welkowitz and Kuc (1973) found that partners who were rated higher on warmth also exhibited greater similarity on speech latency. Street (1982) constructed audiotapes in which an interviewee's speech rate, latency, and duration converged, partially converged, or diverged with respect to that of an interviewer, finding that the divergent speech was evaluated more negatively.

Bernieri (1988) observed that judges' ratings of movement synchrony were positively associated with self-reports of rapport, a conclusion espoused by Tickle-Degnen and Rosenthal (1987) on the basis of their literature review. Even ratings of movement synchrony between infants and their mothers are positively associated with independent ratings of the child's positivity (Bernieri et al., 1988).

Similar patterns of covariation exist in the interactions between infants and their primary caretakers. Isabella, Belsky, and van Eye (1989) tested the coordination-attachment hypothesis. Mothers and their infants were observed interacting at 1, 3, and 9 months of age and categorized as coordinating or not. Pairs that were coordinated at ages 1 and 3 months tended to be securely attached at 1 year. Because secure attachment by the infant is central to exploration, cognitive growth, and the development of later interactional ties and is central to the functioning of all primate species (Bowlby, 1969), these data are important indications of the potential significance of adaptation to the development of the organism.

In both adult and infant-adult interactions, the results suggest the significance of coordination to relational development.

Mutual Influence Versus Adaptation

The distinction between mutual influence and adaptation is an important one, for it draws attention to the difference between aggregate similarity (or difference) and dynamic adjustment by partners to one another. The difference is profound: *Mutual influence is neither a necessary nor a sufficient condition for adaptation and vice versa.*[2] This strong statement means that the two empirical phenomena are independent of one another; therefore, explanations about empirical regularities based on one of the processes are not necessarily related to explanations about the other. Because this chapter is about the dynamics of interaction, I want to make the case that studies of the dynamics of interaction cannot be replaced by the simpler and cheaper studies of aggregate similarity and difference. The two processes are logically independent (which is not to say that they are not correlated and does not imply that both cannot be useful).

First, let me make the case for independence conceptually. The first claim to be set aside is that mutual influence is necessary and/or sufficient for adaptation. That this mutual influence is not sufficient can be seen in the following counterexample. Persons A and B each smile continuously in the first and second halves of their conversation respectively. Neither smiles during the other half. Their amount of smiling is identical (therefore they are quite similar to one another in level of smiling) but neither smiles in response to the partner and so no adaptation is present. The absence of adaptation does not imply that no mutual influence could occur as the example shows, and so mutual influence is neither necessary nor sufficient for adaptation.

Is adaptation necessary and/or sufficient for mutual influence? The absence of mutual influence does not imply the absence of adaptation. Consider a jovial Abigail interacting with a dour Benjamin. Abigail's baseline level of smiling is 60%, so that in every 30-second observational period she is smiling 18 of those seconds, whereas Benjamin's level is 20%, so that in the same period he is smiling 6 seconds of the time. They are very different in levels of smiling (3 in 5 versus 1 in 5) but this does not imply that they are not responsive to one another. For example, every time Abigail increases (or decreases) her smiling, so could Benjamin. Even though the amount might be less for Benjamin, it is the increase or decrease over baseline and the timing that determines adaptation, not the baselines themselves. Thus, adaptation is not necessary for mutual influence (i.e., similarity in the aggregate).

The same example shows that adaptation is not sufficient for mutual influence either. The example describes perfect adaptation between Abigail and Benjamin, but the overall effect of perfect correlation between their behavioral changes could be to not alter the baseline at all. If the numbers of increases and decreases in smiling are equal over and below baseline, the effect would be no change in aggregate levels of smiling even though adaptation would be perfect. Thus, adaptation is neither necessary nor sufficient for mutual influence.

I believe that the conceptual case made above is correct in general. However, the fact that adaptation and mutual influence cannot be deduced from one another does not mean that the two are always uncorrelated. It only means that having one does not guarantee the other. The burden of proving independence requires only one counterexample. If, however, baselines change over time relative to one another, then adaptation and mutual influence are related. For example, if Arnie's rate of intimate disclosures increases linearly over time and Binkie's decreases linearly over time, then, assuming they started at similar levels, they become less similar at the end of their association than at the beginning and yet both may be behaving adaptively (albeit by diverging). Similar examples can be generated by describing changes in baseline by one or both partners in response to the other partner. The conclusion is that mutual influence and adaptation can be related under conditions of temporal change in baseline.

There are two conclusions from the exercise of the previous paragraphs. The first relates to substantive claims about interaction and their explanation. Results from studies showing aggregate similarity or difference in partners' behaviors do not necessarily imply anything about the partners' dynamic responsiveness (or its lack). Such results should not be so interpreted nor explanations requiring dynamic adjustments posited. The same holds true for studies of dynamics; they do not necessarily imply anything about aggregate similarity or difference.

The second set of conclusions refers specifically to time series analyses. These techniques are sensitive to both changes in baseline and those relative to baseline. Changes in baseline are often described in terms of drifting or trending in series. These drifts and trends are usually removed statistically from the series being studied so that the dynamic relationships between series can be accurately determined apart from the drifting and trending. What should now be clear is that both components of multivariate time series are necessary for studying interpersonal interaction: the relationship between the series due to trending and drifting and the relationship between the series over and above trending and drifting. The former provides evidence about changes in baseline levels of responding and the patterns of change between partners in these baselines. The latter provides evidence of dynamic responsiveness (adaptation), but such evidence must be freed from the confounding effects of baseline trending and drifting. In short, studies of temporal coordination (that is, adaptation and mutual influence) require separate analyses of both baseline changes between series and changes relative to baseline.

Some researchers have confounded the two, arguing that changes in baseline are important and should be left in the study of relationships between series. What I have tried to show here is that, yes, changes in baseline are important, but they must be analyzed separately from changes relative to baseline.[3] How this is accomplished statistically is shown in the section on time series analysis.

Methods of Studying Coordination

Coordination, under its various pseudonyms (see Note 1), has been defined in a variety of ways. The most common approach has been to define it in terms of aggregate similarity or difference between partners in a specific behavior. Operationally, the similarity is assessed via product moment correlation between partners, across dyads (when roles are distinguishable), intraclass correlation when partners cannot be distinguished, or absolute differences. One of the problems with these measures is simply that no statistical measure of dyadic or individual coordination is possible. They are measures of similarity across groups of dyads, not within dyads. Definitions of coordination based solely on aggregate similarity bear little conceptual resemblance to the process they purport to represent.

To represent the process of coordination (i.e., adaptation), sequential behavioral data on both partners are necessary. A variety of methodologies would be consistent with such data. One common technique is experimental—employing confederates instructed to manipulate the level of an expressed behavior, increasing or decreasing it according to some design. Perhaps the best example is that of Matarazzo and Wiens (1972), who manipulated duration of response and latency to respond during specified segments of counseling and therapeutic interviews and recorded participants' responses and latencies during the ensuing period. They found, for example, that as the confederate's latencies increased so did those of the respondent and when the confederate's speed of response decreased, the respondents tended to follow, at least on average (Matarazzo & Wiens, 1967).

This methodology does capture important features of the definition of adaptation. Baseline levels of response can be taken into account either through the use of change scores or through a covariance analysis. The confederate's behavior (current and past) is being manipulated and its effect on subsequent response observed. However, certain problems with this approach remain. It is very difficult to train confederates not only in appropriate manipulation of the focal behavior but especially in the control of other behaviors that could inadvertently be the spurious cause of the partner's response. Although response to changes in the confederate's behavior is the focus of the analysis, at most one or two responses to change are observed. A lengthy sequence of confederate behavior and participant response is considered too difficult to obtain.

One alternative that yields more ethologically valid data allows relatively unconstrained interactions to be observed and assessed under various degrees of control. Typically, two or more persons interact as their actions are recorded (for later analysis) or evaluated live by coders or other instruments. The work of assessing the presence or absence of coordination is done after the fact with powerful but relatively uncommon statistical tools. Assessment procedures typically involve some form of sequential analysis using lag sequential techniques (Sackett, 1987), Markov procedures (Hewes, 1980), modified log linear modeling (Iacobucci & Wasserman, 1988), bivariate spectral analysis (Gottman, 1979b), or multivariate time series (McCleary & Hay, 1980). Which technique is most appropriate depends on the quality of the data (continuous or categorical) and the time units involved.

All the techniques can be used to assess adaptation. Each takes into account the person's own baseline effects before assessing partner effects. In the case of multivariate time series, for example, one searches for trending and drifting within the individual series along with patterns of dependence within series. Such effects are typically removed before the effects of the other person's series on the output series are ascertained. Second, each technique allows the researcher to look back at prior effects to determine how far back in time partner effects may be operating. Some of the techniques (namely, lag sequential, spectral, and time series) are especially adept at such snooping back in time. Third, each technique allows one to determine the direction and magnitude of adaptation. In the case of multivariate time series, this information is contained in the sign and magnitude of transfer function coefficients, which are analogous to regression coefficients in their interpretation.

When the data are sufficiently numerous, information on adaptation need not be aggregated across persons or dyads but can be carried out for each dyad. The advantage is that the index of adaptation itself can be evaluated for statistical reliability. The individual index can then be correlated with other measures of competence, judgment, relational well-being, and so on.

Data Requirements
for Time Series Analysis

In this chapter, multivariate time series is the focus for studying adaptation. This choice is not meant to privilege this form of sequential analysis over other types in answering questions about adaptation (see Arundale, Warner, Buder, all this volume). Rather, it simply means that we have used certain kinds of data in our research for which time series analysis (TSA) is both appropriate and powerful.

The data requirements for multivariate time series of face-to-face interaction are the following: (a) level of measurement, (b) units of time, (c) number of data points, and (d) synchrony in coding. In a nutshell, TSA applies to data that are ordered (rather than categorical), defined on fixed units of "clock" time (rather than defined by events), having cases equal to 4-5 times the longest lag studied (but probably no fewer than about 50 time points), and series that are synchronous in time.

A typical (but abbreviated) data set taken from a dyadic interaction is displayed in Table 15.1. These are the first 25 observations from an interaction between two persons who interacted for 30 minutes over topics of their own choosing. The first column is clock time in arbitrary units. The unit chosen is actually a 3-second period. The remaining six columns are three behaviors (F, G, S) for each person (A or B): Floor (speaker or listener roles), illustrative Gestures, and Smiles. The scoring is from 0 to 10 in each period—since the original time unit was 0.3 seconds—coded as 0 (off) or 1 (on) in each 0.3-second segment and then summed to yield a minimum value of 0 and a maximum of 10. The behaviors coded at each 3-second time period are relatively synchronous. To ensure this, a digital time clock was superposed on the screen during coding, and a tone (read by the computer) began the coding process.

Ordered Data

Time series analysis requires ordered rather than categorical data. Ratings, rankings, continuous judgments registered on various devices (dials, joysticks, etc.), and ratio and interval values from instruments (e.g., heart rate) when carried out at fixed intervals of time will suffice. Another alternative is frequency or percentage data like that of Table 15.1.

Time

Usually, a series of observations is obtained, each at a fixed time point determined by the clock. In Table 15.1, observations are every 0.3 seconds. One can also get observations at each event, such as a conversational turn (see Palmer, 1989).

TABLE 15.1 Multivariate Time Series Observations From a Two-Person Interaction: Frequency (or percentage if multiplied by 10) Scores for Floor, Gestures, and Smiles

Time	Person A			Person B		
	Floor	Gesture	Smile	Floor	Gesture	Smile
0.3	8	0	0	2	0	0
0.6	5	0	0	5	0	6
0.9	4	0	0	6	0	3
1.2	9	0	0	1	0	0
1.5	6	0	4	4	0	9
1.8	4	0	7	6	0	0
2.1	6	0	6	4	0	5
2.4	10	2	5	0	0	0
2.7	10	9	0	0	0	0
3.0	10	10	5	0	0	4
3.3	4	0	4	6	0	7
3.7	2	0	5	8	0	3
4.0	8	5	3	2	0	0
4.3	10	8	0	0	0	0
4.6	6	1	3	4	0	2
4.9	4	0	5	6	0	7
5.2	1	0	10	9	0	6
5.5	0	0	10	10	0	10
5.8	0	0	1	10	0	1
6.1	0	0	0	10	4	0
6.4	0	0	0	10	0	0
6.7	0	0	0	10	0	0
7.0	0	0	0	10	1	3
7.3	0	0	0	10	2	1
7.6	0	0	0	10	8	0

The frequency of sampling is a knotty theoretical problem (see Arundale, this volume) related both to problems of oversampling and to issues of seeing all the "true" changes in system state. In most of our recent work, a 3-second unit has been chosen. This unit is shorter than about 85% of the typical turn lengths in the conversations we have observed. Therefore, choosing a 3-second unit allows analyses of both within-turn and between-turn interaction. Longer time units, although potentially valuable, mask within-turn adaptation and will reduce power.

Number of Observations

Frequency of sampling is obviously related to the power of statistical tests to detect effects. There is a clear and well-known trade-off. The smaller the unit of sampling, the greater the power to detect small effects. However, in social interaction data, such as that presented here, small time units also create considerable variability. As adaptation effects are typically small, one wants many observations; however, sampling that is too fine yields high variance from the many random perturbations operating.

At a minimum, 50-70 observations or 4-5 times the length of the longest lag to be studied are needed (Hibbs, 1974). Although observations of this length are difficult to obtain, having them allows statistical evaluation of individual dyads for the presence of adaptation *at the dyad level*. If sampling is carried out at the level of the turn, a 20-minute interaction would easily yield 50-70 turns. A 10-minute interaction will produce 60 observations when sampling at 10-second intervals. Acceptable sample sizes can be generated from interactions whose lengths are common in the laboratory and the field.

When observations are too few to conduct analyses at the level of the dyad, an alternative is to pool time series and cross sections (dyads) to increase power (Kmenta, 1971; Simonton, 1977). This technique does not yield the same kind of results as individual analyses, but it is a useful compromise. The technique is not discussed further here.

Synchrony of Measures

It goes without saying that observations presumed to be at the same point in time, in fact, are. This assumption, too obvious to be made explicit with most multivariate time series data, can be a problem when one makes multiple coding passes through the same video and audio records. With frequent observations, simple mechanical failures, tape stretching, and so on can produce series that are not temporally aligned, yielding lagged effects when there should be none or no lags when there should be.[4]

From Statics to Dynamics

The dynamics of vocal and kinesic behavior have not been widely studied in adult interactions. For the most part, studies that have considered dynamics focus primarily on noncontent speech behaviors such as turn duration, latency to respond, and speech rate (Cappella & Planalp, 1981; Street, 1984; Street & Murphy, 1987), although some have used a broader range of behaviors (Street & Buller, 1987). The chief, but not always consistent, findings have been that people reciprocate latency to respond, speech rate, and interruptions but compensate in turn duration, vocalization, and illustrative gestures.

Previous studies have not always had sufficient power to allow assessment of adaptation at the level of person or dyad and so have often pooled cross sections (individuals) with time series observations. Such an approach solves power problems but does not allow the study of individual adaptation. These studies have also too often presumed that the nature of the dynamic process of adaptation is simple, involving only the immediate past behavior of the partner. Although such assumptions may ultimately prove to be sufficient, it is important for early stages of research not to foreclose options prematurely.

One important goal is to determine whether statistically reliable indices of mutual adaptation can be produced at the individual level of analysis using methods that do not prejudge the dynamic nature of the process. Studies of the dynamics of interaction with infants and mothers (Cohn & Tronick, 1988; Lester et al., 1985; Thomas & Martin, 1976) and with children (Street & Cappella, 1989) have produced results indicating that adaptation occurs over a variety of behaviors. The question remains as to whether adult patterns of interaction are as dynamically stable as those of infants and children with their partners. One question raised in our research program is whether individual dyadic interactions will yield statistically reliable dynamic models of vocal and kinesic adaptation. A subsidiary question concerns what form these models will take across dyads. We expect to find statistically reliable adaptation at the level of the individual dyad and at least rough comparability in the structure of the models representing that adaptive process.

Multivariate Time Series for
Dyadic Interaction: An Illustration

In this section, I illustrate the steps that one usually takes in conducting a TSA of multiple vocal and kinesic behaviors coded from face-to-face interaction. My purpose is to illustrate the steps with real data and present the principles behind the procedure in a conceptual way.

What Is Multivariate in
Multivariate Time Series?

Like all multivariate procedures, more than two variables are assumed to be present. With dyadic data, there are two aspects of multivariate association: between persons and within persons. Adaptation is defined between persons as the association between A's series on some behavior and B's series on some behavior. Analyses could proceed behavior by behavior, but the number of time series to be conducted, even for a few variables, would explode and become unmanageable and probably not interpretable.

An alternative to conducting a TSA for every possible pair of variables is to group behaviors *enacted by an individual* into an index, using some criterion of clustering. If groups of behaviors cluster, then one can argue that the behaviors are like parallel items on a test, measuring some latent behavioral construct (Cappella & Palmer, 1990a).

This is precisely the strategy that was pursued in Cappella, Palmer, and Donzella (1991). In this study, six behaviors were coded for each person: face-directed gaze, floor-holding (as defined by Jaffe & Feldstein, 1970), illustrative gestures, vocalization duration, adaptor gestures, and smiles. Twelve interactions of 30 minutes' duration were the database for clustering behaviors.

Table 15.2 presents the correlation matrices for the two groups of dyads, 6 low and 6 high expressive. These composites are averages of the individual correlation matrices after transformation to Fisher's z.

Visual inspection suggests that persons generate a package of behavior in holding the floor, vocalizing, gesturing through illustrators, and *averting* gaze at the same time. The average intercorrelation of these behaviors (based on the composite of the matrices in Table 15.2) is .422, which yields an effective reliability of .745 (Rosenthal, 1987, p. 10). The individual correlation matrices are similar to the composite and the typical high- and low-expressive persons do not differ from one another.[5]

Substantively, the behaviors that make up this index indicate that when people hold the floor, they tend to vocalize (rather than pause), avert gaze (rather than gaze), and gesture in support of speech (Cappella & Palmer, 1990a). The index clearly is associated with speaker and

TABLE 15.2   Average Correlations Among Behaviors Over
600 3-Second Time Units for Low- and High-
Expressive Groups

	Gaze	Smiles	Adaptors	Illustrators	Vocals	Floor
Gaze		−0.044	−0.022	−0.097	−0.321	−0.384
Smiles	0.005		0.039	−0.052	0.048	0.009
Adaptors	−0.015	0.072		−0.317	0.027	−0.005
Illustrators	−0.082	−0.051	−0.204		0.353	0.322
Vocals	−0.313	−0.004	−0.029	0.316		0.851
Floor	−0.366	−0.022	−0.030	0.312	0.849	

NOTE: *Smiles* is smiling and laughter; *Adaptors* is adaptor gestures; *Illustrators* is illustrator gestures; *Vocals* is vocalization duration; and *Floor* is duration of holding the floor. Correlations above the diagonal are for high-expressives; those below the diagonal are for low-expressives.

listener roles during the conversation, and so it is identified here as the Turn index. When it has large values, the person is most likely to be in the speaker rather than the listener role; when the values are small, the listener role is the more likely. The other behaviors (smiles and adaptors) are not discussed further in this chapter except to note that smiles and adaptor gestures do not distinguish speaker-listener roles in these data.

One solution, then, to the problem of multiple behaviors and adaptation is to search for behavioral clusters that operate together over time. The search may not always be successful, but our experience has been that longer sampling periods (0.1, 0.3, 3.0 seconds, and so on) yield larger average correlations and hence larger effective reliability. The larger the unit, though, the fewer the observations, and too few observations may miss substantively important changes in state.

Plotting Data

A useful first step in any TSA, but especially when two or more series are being studied, is visual inspection of time series plots.[6] In Figures 15.1a and 15.1b, three variables are plotted for a segment of one of the interactions: A's Turn index, B's Turn, and A's raw score on holding the floor. Two things are immediately apparent. A's and B's Turn scores are complementary (negatively correlated), so that when one is elevated the other is depressed, and vice versa. Second, A's Turn index is tracked closely by A's holding the floor.

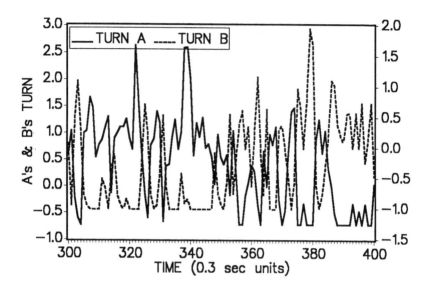

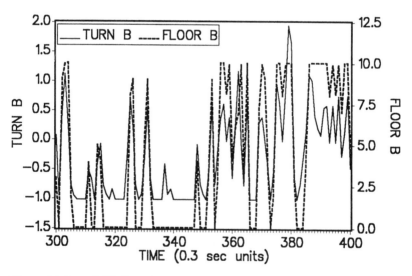

Figure 15-1a and 15-1b.   Plots of Turn indexes and floor holding for single pair of partners during 30 seconds of interaction.

Neither of these observations is surprising (and they are consistent throughout the data). The two indexes should be complementary if they are indexes of taking turns in speaking and listening. A's Turn index should be highly associated with A's holding the floor if the Turn index marks speaker role.

Not only are the results not surprising, they may also be trivial as far as adaptation is concerned. No fancy TSA is needed to demonstrate that partners alternate turns at talk. But one can still ask whether there is any form of adaptation taking place *within* the process of alternation of speaker-hearer roles.

Nonindependence Within Series

After plotting, the first analytical step in any time series modeling involves establishing the temporal structure of each input series. Time series data are usually temporally redundant (that is, each case in time is not independent of adjacent cases). The form of this redundancy within a series must be discovered (and corrected) before the relationship between series can be evaluated. Otherwise, some of the relationship between the series may be an artifact of the temporal redundancy within series (McCleary & Hay, 1980). The usual methods for assessing temporal redundancy involve generating autocorrelations and partial autocorrelations at various lags (see VanLear & Watt, this volume).

Autocorrelation and partial autocorrelation are analogous (but not numerically identical) to Pearson correlation and partial correlation. Autocorrelation (AC) is correlation between a series and itself at various lags. Partial autocorrelation (PAC) is a correlation between the series and itself at some lag but controlling for the effects of lower-level lags. The pattern of ACs and PACs indicates, sometimes clearly and sometimes not so clearly, the form of the temporal redundancy within a series. For a thorough discussion of the relationship between AC and PAC patterns and the form of redundancy, the reader is referred to McCleary and Hay (1980).

Two aspects of temporal redundancy are revealed by the AC and PAC patterns. One is the slow change in a series due to some trend (linear, curvilinear, periodic, etc.) or some slow nonregular movement, called drifting. These kinds of changes are changes in baseline behavior, which I have been calling mutual influence. The other type of temporal redundancy refers to momentary changes due to various forms of random shocks affecting the behavior while the system persists, at least in part,

TABLE 15.3   Number of Individual Series Described by Specific
Models of Temporal Redundancy: Autoregressive
(AR), Moving Average (MA), and Integrated (I)

Model Components			
Autoregressive	Integrated	Moving Average	Number
(1,	0,	0)	15
(1,	0,	1)	5
(1,	1,	1)	3
(0,	1,	2)	1
Seasonal			0

NOTE: Notation for the models is standard for ARIMA models (McCleary & Hay, 1980). For example, a (0, 1, 2) model has three components: The first is the autoregressive component of Order 0; the second is the integration component of Order 1, and the third is the moving average component of Order 2.

in its current state. These are called autoregressive and moving average processes after the form of the noise process affecting the behavior. Below, I present some of the forms of temporal redundancy that operate in the Turn index.

Because each person could be an input for the associated partner, each series was evaluated for each dyad (for a total of 24 possible series). Table 15.3 indicates the frequency of various types of temporal redundancy. Although the types of temporal redundancy could be very complex, involving distant occurrences affecting current ones and involving a mixture of types of redundancy (autoregression, moving average, and differencing), in general the form of temporal redundancy was simple.

Clearly, the first-order autoregressive model was the most common form of within-series redundancy observed. What this implies is that focusing on the behavior of the person alone (i.e., ignoring the effect of the partner), the best predictor of the current 3 seconds of behavior is the past 3 seconds of behavior. Four cases required a first difference (the "integration" component), suggesting some form of drifting within the series.

A few cases required other structures to explain the redundancy. All models satisfied the Q criterion (McCleary & Hay, 1980, p. 99) for "whiteness" with a relatively simple type of redundancy. (Roughly speaking, this criterion measures how free of temporal redundancy a series is.)

Cross Correlations

The second step in TSA uses the series from Step 1 but now transformed to remove the effect of the within-series temporal redundancy; this is called "prewhitening." For each dyad, the (pre-whitened) series for person A and person B are correlated at various lags (25 lags in the present case). The purpose of these correlations is to get some idea of the structure of the regression model predicting the A series from B's scores and vice versa. The cross correlations can also be used to determine which series is leading and which lagging the other.[7] In these data, no partner was clearly leading nor lagging the other.

The cross correlation must be generated from the differenced and whitened series; otherwise, the correlations between series will be artificially affected by the correlations within series.

Two conclusions were drawn from the patterns of cross correlation: (a) correlations at lag-0 were consistently the strongest, and (b) no significant effects beyond lag-3 were consistently observed. The results mean that no clear differences between input and output series can be made and that lags beyond lag-3 are not necessary. The most complex regression model for the effect of A's turn on B's will use only three lags back in time for a total time span of about 12 seconds (lag-0, lag-1, lag-2, and lag-3 each 3 seconds' duration).

Covariates

The plots of Figure 15.1 and the strong, negative cross correlations at lag-0 observed in all pairs of series suggest that the association between A's Turn index and B's Turn index may be nothing more than the alternation of speaker-hearer roles. When person A is holding the floor, gesturing, and looking away, the partner is listening, is not gesturing, and is likely to be looking at the partner. Because this pattern exists throughout the data, it was necessary to test the relationship between the A series and the B series after removing as much as possible the effect due to simply holding the floor.

Holding the floor was treated as a covariate in all model testing and was found to be a significant predictor in all models. Based on the cross correlations and the findings about turn taking as a covariate, the initial model identified was

$$T_a(t) = b_0 F_a(t) + b_1 F_a(t - 1) + b_2 F_a(t - 2) + b_3 F_a(t - 3)$$

$$+ d_0 T_b(t) + d_1 T_b(t - 1) + d_2 T_b(t - 2) + d_3 T_b(t - 3) + N_a(t),$$

[15-1]

where $T_a(t)$ is person A's Turn index at time t, $T_b(t)$ is person B's Turn index, $F_a(t)$ is person A's floor holding value at time t, and $N_a(t)$ is the noise (or error) component to be fit after preliminary estimates of the parameters are available.

Time Series Regressions

Equation 15-1 looks like a regression equation and behaves like a regression equation, so why isn't it handled just like a regression equation? In many ways it is. The major difference is that the form of the temporal redundancy of the input series is used to purify both the input series and the output series.[8] In effect, the redundancy is removed, allowing the number of cases in the series to be treated as if they were independent of one another. Failure to carry out this step can seriously affect significance tests, yield biased estimates of parameters (even in large samples), and confound effects due to mutual influence with those associated with adaptation. In effect, the "purification" of the series yields effects that, if they are present, are pure adaptation effects. Are the mutual influence effects lost during the purification process? More on this issue later.

How would Equation 15-1 show adaptation effects? Just as ordinary regression coefficients show relationship between variables, the d_i coefficients, when significant, show association between A's Turn and B's Turn. The sign of the coefficient indicates whether the adjustments of A to B are in the same direction (reciprocal) or in the opposite direction (compensatory). Their magnitude indicates how much of an adjustment there is. If all the d_i coefficients are nonsignificant for a particular dyad, then one concludes that the partners are not adapting to one another and that the temporal covariation between series is all due to alternation of speaker-hearer roles.

In all, 24 final time series regression models were estimated from the initial specification of Equation 15-1 according to the procedures of McCleary and Hay (1980). Space does not permit the presentation of each of the final models, but Table 15.4 gives a sense of the kind of effects obtained and their consistency across persons. In the study from which

TABLE 15.4 Average Coefficients of Adaptation, Adjusted R^2, Number of Significant Coefficients, Ranges by Group and by Lag: Turn Indexes

	Lag-0	Lag-1	Lag-2	R^2	ADAPT
LOW EXPR					
d COEFFS	−.143	.006	−.015	.783	−.298
RANGE	−.387, 0	−.058, .072	−.103, 0	.728, .849	−.795, 0
# SIGNIF*	10	3	2	12	NA
HIGH EXPR					
d COEFFS	−.092	−.007	0	.757	−.256
RANGE	−.174, 0	−.085, 0	0	.684, .845	−.575, 0
# SIGNIF*	10	1	0	12	NA

NOTE: EXPR are highs and lows in self-reported expressiveness. ADAPT are adaptation scores derived from each dyad according to procedures described in the text. The averages above are averages of coefficients that individually are each statistically significant at $p < .05$.
*Maximum number per lag that could be significant is 12.

these data are taken (Cappella, Palmer, & Donzella, 1991), one group of 6 dyads had all highly expressive partners, and the other group of 6 had low-expressive partners. The effects of the covariates are not presented in these tables, but they were substantial and consistent.

Table 15.4 presents two kinds of information: averages of those regression coefficients at lag-0, lag-1, and lag-2 that reached standard levels of significance (with nonsignificant values treated as zero) and the number of individuals having significant time series effects per group and at each lag (12 was the maximum in each case).

All lag-0 effects were negative even after controlling for holding the floor. Ten of 12 in the low-expressive group and 10 of 12 in the high-expressive group were significant. A few smaller coefficients at lag-1 and lag-2 were also significant. The negative coefficients indicate that *even after floor effects are removed* persons still compensate to their partners. A complementary or even submissive position is taken by the person as the partner exercises behaviors indicative of the speaking role. The variance explained was substantial, averaging over 75% (including covariates and noise components). The low-expressive group exhibited slightly more compensation on average than the highs, pulling back into the listening role even more strongly than the high-expressive group when the partner took responsibility for speaking. This is indicated by the slightly stronger average negative coefficient at lag-0.

Generalizing and Validating Time
Series Analysis of Interactional Data

TSA has not been applied to the study of face-to-face interaction with enough frequency as yet to have produced standards of acceptable and unacceptable results. In this section, some of the problems and concerns that are typically raised about TSA in the interactional context are raised and, where possible, resolved.

Multiple Behaviors

The basic problem is that ordinary interactions are made up of many streams of simultaneous verbal, kinesic, and vocal behavior. Exploring the associations between one stream (as a series) and another by examining one pair at a time is inefficient and ignores the possible covariation among predictor series. Indexing by clustering behaviors that occur together over time is one solution to the problem of associations between sets of behaviors. This solution may not always work, as behaviors may not cluster consistently across individuals or they simply may be independent of one another.

When predictor behaviors are mostly independent of one another, then exploration of the relation between outcome and predictor series can proceed in a bivariate way. For example, if one wanted to account for A's smiling from B's smiling, gaze, and adaptor gestures, three separate bivariate time series would be undertaken. The best predictor models in each case would be amalgamated to build the best multivariate predictive equation. At this stage, one or more predictors might drop by the wayside (McCleary & Hay, 1980). The strategy, although simple, is very tedious, especially if the goal is to develop measures of adaptation for each person in each interaction separately.

Multiple Coefficients of Adaptation

Table 15.4 shows that the final regression models describing the impact of A's Turn on B includes several coefficients of impact at various lags. When the signs of all the coefficients (that is, the d_i) are the same, then the direction of adaptation is clear. However, in some cases, the sign of the coefficients at one lag are different from the sign at other lags. How can the relative strength of the various effects be weighed to produce a single estimate of adaptation?

One solution is to use the procedure of tracing direct and indirect effects from path analysis (Kenny, 1979). The total effect of the input series on the output series depends on the number of prior lags involved, the signs and magnitudes of the direct effects, and the pattern of autocorrelation (to trace the indirect effects). The total effect is a signed value with a magnitude that indicates the overall effect of the input series on the output and that may be taken as an indicator of total adaptation. Table 15.4 lists summary values for total adaptation adjacent to those for individual effects.

This procedure has been used in two unpublished studies (Cappella & Flagg, 1992; Cappella et al., 1991) and may be carried out manually by careful application of ray-tracing procedures from path analysis. For lagged effects greater than 3 and error processes greater than lag-2, the manual procedure is cumbersome and error prone. Algebraic solutions using a simple computer program reduces the errors.

Prewhitening and Adaptation

Some researchers studying the dynamics of adaptation have argued that the accepted practice of prewhitening should be abandoned as inappropriate for work in social interaction. The argument is that if behavioral series have trends (linear, polynomial, seasonal, or whatever) and if part of the association between two series is due to these trends, then to purge the series of these trends is to remove significant and substantively interesting processes from data as if these components were irrelevant.

This is a nontrivial argument but it is misguided on both substantive and statistical grounds. The key to understanding the issue is found in the distinction between mutual influence and adaptation and the necessity of an index of overall adaptation. Prewhitening refers to removing two different types of dependency from within a series: nonstationary characteristics and temporal redundancy around a stationary series. If a series has non-stationary characteristics, such as periodic trends, linear or other trends, drifting, or systematic changes in variance, then these features need to be removed. Without removing these features, adaptation between partners, revealed by cross correlations between series, will confound mutual influence with adaptation. Both processes are of interest and both need to be studied, but by failing to rid series of nonstationarity the researcher cannot know whether significant cross correlations are indicative of one process, the other, or both.

So that information on mutual influence will not be lost, researchers should report the kind of differencing necessary to make each series stationary. Such results are potentially of substantive interest. They are not merely the dross of the interactional system.

Once series are stationary, prewhitening of the input and output series ensures that any association between the two is not confounded by association within the series themselves. Failure to prewhiten the stationary series runs the risk of producing associations between series that are inflated by the lack of independence within series. Once prewhitening of the stationary series has occurred, the use of measures of overall adaptation, as described above, reintroduces the effects of removed temporal dependencies by tracing their indirect effects from prior predictors.

Coordination is a term that should be reserved to capture both mutual influence and adaptation. Researchers should be interested in both phenomena, for they represent processes in social interaction that are potentially quite different and which potentially require very different explanations. TSA, properly done, reveals both processes providing separate, statistically reliable measures of mutual influence and adaptation. Calls to deviate from standard practice within TSA are misguided because they yield conclusions that confound the two processes and are statistically invalid.

Pooling Across Persons and Dyads

One of the purposes of this chapter has been to argue that there is a real advantage to assessing adaptation at the dyad level. One can obtain measures of coordination whose statistical reliability can be evaluated. Instead of reporting a difference score for a dyad, which may or may not be meaningful, measures of convergence or divergence, reciprocity or compensation are available along with confidence measures. Apparent patterns in a given interaction can be evaluated as real, at least in a statistical sense, and these patterns compared to interpersonal outcomes or individual differences.

At the same time, researchers are sometimes interested in variation across individual cases and not in the individual cases themselves. Two possibilities for pooling cases across time series should be considered. The first, and more complicated procedure, uses standard pooling of time series and cross-sectional (person or dyad) observations, testing a modal model of adaptation (see Kmenta, 1971). After fitting several regression-type models to individual dyads, one might be able to select a modal model to test against a complete set of time series and cross-sectional observations. The details of this procedure cannot be discussed here, but the result should be a best-fitting model for the set of dyads, with coefficients indicating the degree and type of adaptation of partners to one another. The pooled case does require that the researcher specify the structure of the modal regression model (as well as the error process) before fitting to the data set. One advantage of this pooled procedure is that interactions between coefficients of adaptation and individual or dyadic characteristics can be explored. The disadvantage is the requirement that a fixed model must be specified in advance.

A simpler alternative to pooling is meta-analysis (Hunter, Schmidt, & Jackson, 1982). Each interaction analyzed through time series can itself be treated as a study, with results in terms of coefficients of adaptation. These coefficients can be treated as input data for a meta-analysis and variation in adaptation scores related to individual or dyadic differences and outcome measures of various types.

Street and Cappella (1989) employed just such a procedure in a study of 3- to 6-year-old children. The children interacted with an adult in a play situation while their voices were being recorded. Cross correlations between the children's and the adult's speech characteristics showed that the children adapted to the adult in speech rate and in latency to respond. As a rule, both effects were reciprocal, indicating that increases followed increases, and decreases followed decreases. However, the meta-analysis also showed that there was significant variation across children in the degree of adaptation. None of the adaptation was explained by age differences, but it was explained by differences in verbal responsiveness (as measured by topical continuity) and mean length of utterance (an index of semantic and syntactic development).

This study shows both that adaptation can be evaluated at the individual level of analysis and that individual adaptation scores are related to important personal characteristics—in this case, measures of individual pragmatic and linguistic development. Pooling of dyadic differences takes the form of treating each interaction as a study, with the number of observations in each study equal to the number of time series points.

Effects at Lag-0

When there are effects between two series at lag-0, this means that, within the time period of sampling, the series are showing simultaneous effects either because there is some form of mutual causality, a spurious cause affecting both series, or the time period is insensitive to unidirectional causality because it is too gross. In the data that we have analyzed so far involving more than 100 dyads, simultaneous effects are common, even with a sampling unit as small as 3 seconds.

The presence of lag-0 effects shows up as a strong lag-0 correlation between two series. A strong lag-0 correlation does not, however, imply that person A's adaptation to B equals that of B to A. Rather, the lag-0 adaptation coefficients depend on (a) the ratio of the standard deviations of the two series and (b) the coefficients at other lags.

Substantively, lag-0 effects should not be surprising with the behaviors that we have been studying. They are relatively automatic and the absence of synchrony (which would appear statistically as effects at longer lags or no effects at all) may be experienced as a failure by the partner to be responsive.

Stability of Adaptation

Attempting to study individual dyads and categorize their interactive patterns is more likely to raise questions about just how stable these patterns are than, say, a large group of dyads being studied for characteristics of the group. If a dyad exhibits a reciprocal pattern of adaptation with a coefficient of magnitude .40 during the first third of an interaction, will that same pattern be present during other segments of the same interaction? If the index of adaptation is itself temporally unstable, then it makes little sense to categorize an interaction pattern as reciprocal or compensatory as no part of the interaction would confidently yield a conclusion about the whole.

Because the downside of every problem can also yield an upside, the presence of temporal instability may be substantively interesting, and methods of revealing such instability could be useful. A simple measure of temporal stability of adaptation coefficients divides the interaction into arbitrary segments, estimates the coefficients of the overall model within each segment, and compares the sets of coefficients using hypothesis tests in which equality of coefficients is the null. Data from Cappella et al. (1991) on smiles were tested in this way. The 30-minute interactions were divided into three 10-minute periods and adaptation coefficients for A's and B's smiling calculated for each period. The results indicate that the measures of overall adaptation are stable. All coefficients were always of the same sign (both for the total interaction and for each of the three segments). No coefficient for a 10-minute subsample deviated from the composite index of adaptation by more than 0.16, and 66 of 72 comparisons were within 0.10 of the composite. Although some differences were statistically significant, the high power of the tests would suggest that some small differences would be significant, even though inconsequential.

The substantive conclusions about the type and approximate magnitude (small, medium, large effect) of adaptation in smiles for these 12 interactions would not be affected by the segment of the interaction analyzed. Adaptation is clearly stable for this behavior and these interactions. Whether this is a general effect or not awaits further testing with a wider set of interactions and different behaviors.

A more sophisticated technique for analyzing stability in interaction patterns is illustrated in Figure 15.2. This figure plots the value of the adaptation coefficient for the effects of A's Turn index on B's at each point in the series *based on the previous data to that point.* Several features of this plot are of interest. The coefficient stabilizes at around 100 data points and changes very little thereafter (i.e., after about 4 to 5 minutes of interaction).[9] The stability of the coefficient of adaptation is visually striking after 80-100 data points. If sharp changes in the magnitude of the coefficient were visible after statistical stability had set in, then such changes might be of substantive interest and the characteristics of the interaction investigated more closely at or near the points of disjuncture.

Although one cannot have great confidence in the stability of adaptation for a broad range of behaviors or interactions, the evidence so far supports stability. Equally important, the tools for investigating the presence of stability may reveal some interesting substantive insights when interactional instability is found (see Nass & Moon, this volume, for a description of one procedure for identifying anomalous regions in a time series).

Generalizability

The data reported in an earlier section on adaptation are derived from 12 interactions. These 12 dyads had female partners only; all were

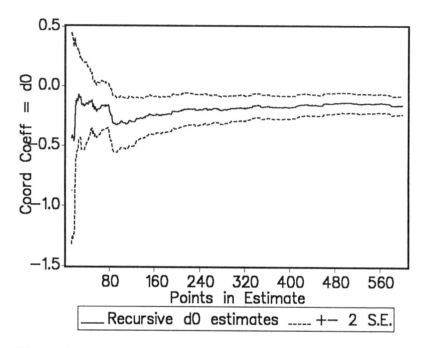

Figure 15-2. Plot of adaptation coefficient as a function of the number of time points used to estimate the coefficient.

attitudinally similar and were strangers to one another. Six of the interactions were among high-expressive partners and six among low-expressive (Cappella et al., 1991). If adaptation is as pervasive a phenomenon as I have claimed in this chapter, then it should be found in a fairly wide variety of interactional settings, although not necessarily in the same form in all contexts.

Cappella and Flagg (1992) analyzed data from 41 dyads using the same Turn index described earlier. These dyads consisted of 20 attitudinally similar pairs, 10 of whom were strangers and 10 well known to one another, and 21 attitudinally different pairs, 11 strangers and 10 well known (see Cappella & Palmer, 1990b, for details on the study's design). The partners interacted for 30 minutes; then time series regression procedures were used to analyze their behaviors for the type and quality of adaptation.

TABLE 15.5 Number of Reciprocal, Compensatory, and Null Adaptation Coefficients, Average Adaptation and R^2, by Similarity and Relational History

	Similar		Dissimilar		
Coordination	New	Old	New	Old	Total
# RECIPROCAL	1/20	1/20	0/22	2/20	4/82
# COMPENSATE	17/20	7/20	15/22	7/20	46/82
# NULL	2/20	12/20	7/22	11/20	32/82
ADAPTATION					
(SD)	−.084 (.144)	−.053 (.095)	−.139 (.168)	−.043 (.094)	−.081 (.134)
R^2 (SD)	.661 (.041)	.625 (.071)	.653 (.059)	.648 (.043)	.647 (.055)

Table 15.5 presents the results for this set of 41 dyads. Two types of information are presented: the number of persons who show statistically significant levels of adaptation (and the type) and the average magnitude of adaptation. The majority of the series showed either compensatory (46, or 56%) or null (32, or 39%) relationships, with 4 (5%) individuals exhibiting reciprocal adaptation; 32 of the persons did not adapt at all to their partners on the Turn index.

The differences among types of dyads in the type of adaptation are statistically significant with a χ^2 ($df = 6$) equal to 17.06, $p < .01$. Clearly, the new dyads showed more compensation than did the old partners who were more likely to fail to compensate or to reciprocate their partners' Turn behaviors.

The average amount of adaptation for Turn behaviors is negative, explaining about 65% of the variance. Recall that these levels of predictability are based on behavioral scores from which the roles of speaker and hearer have been removed. The variations in magnitude of adaptation across types of dyads were explored using regression analysis with orthogonal coding for the similarity and relationship conditions. The only significant difference in adaptation coefficients is for relationship length. Strangers exhibit stronger adaptation ($M = −0.111$) than do persons who know each other ($M = −0.049$), $b = 0.032$, t (80) = 2.25, $p < 0.027$. No interaction was obtained.

How do these results on adaptation compare to those presented earlier? Is there a general phenomenon of adaptation in turn behaviors over and above that due to speaker and listener roles? The results compare favorably, particularly among the partners who were strangers. If the newly acquainted pairs from the Cappella and Flagg (1992) data are compared to the group of 12 from the Cappella et al. (1991) data, 77% versus 87.5% compensated, 21% versus 12.5% showed no adaptation, and 2% versus 0% reciprocated, respectively. As noted, there are substantial differences between the new pairs and the old pairs in likelihood of adaptation, with established pairs less likely to show any adaptation in Turn behaviors (except that of ordinary speaker-hearer role differentiation).

The fact that there are no differences between attitudinally similar and different partners in adaptation suggests that initial levels of liking for the partner are not the reason for adaptation or its absence, at least in Turn behaviors. Because strangers compensate Turn behaviors even more than speaker-hearer roles would mandate, perhaps there is a kind of "hyperpoliteness" operating among newly acquainted partners, regardless of their initial liking, that manifests itself in a sharper differentiation of speaker and hearer roles than is required in general. The absence of a similar effect in established pairs (or at least a reduced form of it) may indicate that the very strong norms of speaker-listener role differentiation may take on less significance as partners' familiarity grows. Other interactional concerns may become more important than the simple differentiation of role.

Interpersonal Consequences
of Adaptation

The dynamics of interaction is interesting in its own right. How people are able to adjust to the behaviors of their partners without much awareness of what they are doing is a puzzle. Time series procedures can unravel signal from noise and detect and quantify the relationship between the partners' behaviors. Without such procedures, it would be almost impossible to know about the presence, type, and magnitude of adaptation on automatic behaviors. Although bivariate time series can reveal unanticipated patterns within interactions, thereby creating anomalies for theories of interaction to explain, one hopes that these interactional subtleties affect the more obvious consequences of relationships, such as liking and satisfaction. Are the patterns an artifact, a spurious consequence of some hidden social or psychological process,

TABLE 15.6 Correlations Between A's Adaptation Scores and
B's Liking, Satisfaction by Experimental Group:
Two Studies

	Similar		Dissimilar		
	New	Old	New	Old	Total
Study 1[a]	N = 12				
A ADAPT-B LIKE	−.430				
A ADAPT-B SATIS	−.235				
Study 2[b]	N = 20	N = 20	N = 22	N = 20	N = 82
A ADAPT-B LIKE	−.482*	.177	−.313	.156	−.103
A ADAPT-B SATIS	−.337	.145	−.155	.250	−.028

NOTE: New are stranger pairs; Old are established pairs. ADAPT refers to adaptation coefficients. *Satis* is satisfaction with the conversation.
a. Study 1 is Cappella, Palmer, and Donzella (1991).
b. Study 2 is Cappella and Flagg (1992).
* .01 < p < .05.

or are they consequential in some way to the functioning of personal relationships?

This question was asked in two different studies. The first (Cappella et al., 1991) was actually a round robin study (Kenny & LaVoie, 1984) in which each person in a group of 4 high-expressive females interacted with all possible partners. A second group of 4 low-expressives was also run. The measures of adaptation were reported earlier. Self-reports of attraction to the partner and satisfaction with the conversation were also obtained.

Using Kenny's SOREMO program, the relationship between adaptation indexes and partners' liking and satisfaction were obtained. The key association is the "relationship interpersonal" correlation. It is the adjusted correlation between person A's adaptation to person B and B's attraction to A (or B's satisfaction with the conversation). These correlations are reported in Table 15.6.

The second study (Cappella & Flagg, 1992), described previously, had 41 dyads in four conditions. Adaptation of A to B was correlated with B's attraction to A (and separately for B's satisfaction with the conversation). Both correlations indicate the degree to which one person's adjustment to the partner is linked to the partner's response. The correlations are also reported in Table 15.6.

Only 1 of the 10 correlations meets standard levels of statistical significance, the negative correlation for the similar-new dyads in the second study. Interpreting this correlation is somewhat tricky. It implies that persons who compensate more to their partners are liked more by the partners than those who compensate less. If compensation in Turn behaviors is a kind of exaggerated politeness in speaker-hearer roles, then, at least among the similar-new dyads, the more exaggerated role complementarity by one partner, the greater the attraction by the other.

The five correlations between adaptation and attraction are based on independent groups and can be treated as five separate studies in a meta-analysis (Hunter, Schmidt, & Jackson, 1982). The five groups differ at χ^2 $(df = 4) = 8.143$, $p < .08$. The variation among the five groups is due solely to the differences between the strangers and the established pairs. The three groups of unacquainted dyads are not significantly different from each other and neither are the groups of established pairs different. In short, the stronger the adaptation in turn behaviors, the more the attraction among new pairs; the opposite is more likely true among established pairs. The satisfaction outcome shows similar trends but not as distinctly.

What could account for these findings? The Turn index consists of behaviors involved in who is identified as speaker and who the hearer. After floor holding is covaried out, what is left is behaviors linked to speaker-hearer roles but, in effect, cues superfluous to the roles. Partners new to each other seem to compensate even on these superfluous behaviors in a form of exaggerated politeness, unwilling to step into each other's conversational space. The links to attraction may be the result of an implicit judgment that a strong form of interactional politeness in role complementarity is desirable or necessary and a sign of liking or respect. The fact that speaker-hearer politeness may matter more to newly established pairs in their mutual attraction than it does to established pairs may mean that exaggerated speaker-hearer separation is not consequential to a more freely flowing interaction of well-known partners. This observation is supported by the difference in correlation between adaptation and attraction for the old pairs and the fact that fewer dyads exhibit compensation among the olds.

The association between compensation and attraction found across two studies is not itself a general finding, tied as it must be to the particular behaviors and their significance to the relationship among the partners (Cappella, 1988). The finding is relevant to the general claim about coordination and rapport (Bernieri & Rosenthal, 1991) but specifically concerns adaptation on behaviors associated with speaker-hearer roles and rapport as evidenced in attraction. One should not expect all relationships nor all behaviors to exhibit the same type or magnitude of association. What has been shown is that the moment-to-moment dynamics of signaling speaker and listener roles affects partners' mutual attraction.

Conclusions

The purposes of this chapter have been to argue that certain forms of multivariate time series can reveal features of interactional structure that are otherwise hidden and to illustrate the claim in a substantive program of research. I have focused primarily on time series of individual dyads rather than groups of dyads because whether there is a pattern of dynamic adjustment is as much a question as is the question of what the pattern is related to. At least with regard to the Turn index, partners do show adaptation, and it is stable and generalizable and, for newly acquainted pairs, consequential to their attitudes toward their partners.

Notes

1. Various researchers have used different names in place of mutual influence to denote what is in essence the same process: the effect of the behavior of person A on the behavioral response by partner B over and above expectation. Jaffe and Feldstein (1970) call it congruence or sometimes interspeaker influence, Condon and Ogston (1967) call it synchrony, Chapple (1971) calls it entrainment, Giles, Mulac, Bradac, and Johnson (1987) call it convergence and divergence.

2. Some sophisticated readers might be bothered by my association of the term "mutual influence" with more static forms of interactional data. I invite them to replace mutual influence with congruence, interpersonal correspondence, or whatever terms convey more static concepts.

3. In this chapter, I focus exclusively on the dynamic aspects of interaction in the interests of providing a deeper treatment of dynamics that is less familiar to readers than is static analysis.

4. We have recently developed a time coding system that is much more precise, being accurate to about 1/30 second. This system uses time from the video frame itself as the basis for clock time. The advantage is that mechanical unreliability, tape stretching, and other sources of inaccuracy are significantly reduced.

5. Results demonstrating the similarity across groups is available from the author on request.

6. I strongly recommend using a time series program with good plotting capabilities. The emphasis should be on the ease of examining plots and not necessarily on lots of bells and whistles. I have used MicroTSP and DaDisp extensively and find their plotting features very helpful.

7. One technique for determining which is the leading and which the lagging series is called Granger causality (Granger, 1969). This procedure tests the null hypothesis that current values of a series A are *not* predicted by past A and past B values; it also tests whether B is predicted by past B and past A. Both, one, or neither of the hypotheses can be rejected or accepted. In one application with the data of Cappella and Flagg (1992), unacquainted pairs showed more unidirectional and bidirectional causality than did established pairs who showed more cases of no causality. New pairs may feel constrained to be more responsive from moment to moment than established pairs, especially with regard to the politeness of relinquishing the turn.

8. Note that prewhitening the output series in the same way as the input series does not mean that the input and output series should be differenced in the same way. Differencing to remove trends and drifting can differ for the input and output series.

9. The procedure whose output is represented in Figure 15.2 actually confounds true stability with statistical efficiency (decreased variability of an estimate as the size of the sample increases). After about 100 observations, the only way for the coefficient of adaptation to change would be through a sharp alteration in the relationship between the series. These alterations could mark for study interesting moments in the interaction.

References

Aaker, D. A., Stayman, D. M., & Hagerty, M. R. (1986). Warmth in advertising: Measurement, impact and sequence effects. *Journal of Consumer Research, 12*, 365-381.

Abbott, A. (1988). Transcending general linear reality. *Sociological Theory, 6*, 169-186.

Abell, P. (1971). *Model building in sociology*. London: Widenfeld & Nicolson.

Abelson, R. P., & Levi, A. (1985). Decision making and decision theory. In G. Lindzey & E. Aronson (Eds.), *The handbook of social psychology* (3rd ed., Vol. 1, pp. 231-309). New York: Random House.

Adam, B. (1990). *Time and social theory*. Philadelphia: Temple University Press.

Alexander, D. C. (1975, February). *Our transactional perspective; but our interactional research*. Paper presented at the annual meeting of the Western Speech Communication Association, Seattle.

Allison, P. D., & Liker, J. K. (1982). Analyzing sequential categorical data on dyadic interaction: A comment on Gottman. *Psychological Bulletin, 91*, 393-403.

Altman, I., & Rogoff, B. (1987). World views in psychology: Trait, interactional, organismic, and transactional perspectives. In D. Stokols & I. Altman (Eds.), *Handbook of environmental psychology* (Vol. 1, pp. 7-40). New York: John Wiley.

Altman, I., & Taylor, D. A. (1973). *Social penetration: The development of interpersonal relationships*. New York: Holt, Rinehart & Winston.

Altman, I., Vinsel, A., & Brown, B. (1981). Dialectic conceptions in social psychology: An application to social penetration and privacy regulation. In L. Berkowitz (Ed.), *Advances in experimental social psychology* (Vol. 14, pp. 108-160). New York: Academic Press.

Alwitt, L. F. (1985). *Monitoring the emotional flow of commercicals*. Paper presented at the midyear meeting of the Advertising Research Foundation, Chicago.

Anderson, D. R., Alwitt, L. F., Lorch, E. P., & Levin, S. R. (1979). Watching children watch television. In G. A. Hale & M. Lewis (Eds.), *Attention and cognitive development* (pp. 331-361). New York: Plenum.

Anderson, D. R., & Lorch, E. P. (1983). Looking at television: Action or reaction? In J. Bryant & D. R. Anderson (Eds.), *Children's understanding of television: Research on attention and comprehension* (pp. 1-33). New York: Academic Press.

Anderson, J. A. (1987). *Communication research: Issues and methods.* New York: McGraw-Hill.

Anderson, J. R. (1983). *The architecture of cognition.* Cambridge, MA: Harvard University Press.

Anderson, N. H. (1981). Integration theory applied to cognitive responses and attitudes. In R. E. Petty, T. M. Ostrom, & T. C. Brock (Eds.), *Cognitive responses in persuasion* (pp. 361-397). Hillsdale, NJ: Lawrence Erlbaum.

Anderson, N. H., & Hovland, C. (1957). The representation of order effects in communication research. In C. Hovland (Ed.), *The order of presentation in persuasion* (pp. 158-169). New Haven, CT: Yale University Press.

Anderson, T. W., & Goodman, L. A. (1957). Statistical inference about Markov chains. *Annals of Mathematical Statistics, 28,* 89-110.

Anselin, L. (1988). *Spatial econometrics: Methods and models.* Dordrecht: Kluwer Academic.

Aoki, M. (1987). *State space modeling of time series.* Berlin: Springer-Verlag.

Argyle, M., & Dean, J. (1965). Eye contact, distance, and affiliation. *Sociometry, 28,* 289-304.

Aronson, E., Turner, J. A., & Carlsmith, J. M. (1963). Communicator credibility and communication discrepancy as determinants of opinion change. *Journal of Abnormal and Social Psychology, 67,* 31-36.

Arundale, R. B. (1978). Sampling across time for communication research: A simulation. In P. M. Hirsch, P. V. Miller, & F. G. Kline (Eds.), *Strategies for communication research* (pp. 257-285). Beverly Hills, CA: Sage.

Arundale, R. B. (1980). Studying change over time: Criteria for sampling from continuous variables. *Communication Research, 7,* 227-263.

Ashby, R. (1963). *An introduction to cybernetics.* New York: Science Editions.

Attneave, F. (1959). *Applications of information theory to psychology.* New York: Henry Holt.

Baggaley, J. (1986a). Developing a televised health campaign: II. Skin cancer prevention. *Media in Education and Development, 19,* 173-176.

Baggaley, J. (1986b). Formative evaluation of educational television. *Canadian Journal of Educational Television, 15,* 29-43.

Baggaley, J. (1987). Continual response measurement: Design and validation. *Canadian Journal of Educational Communication, 16,* 218-238.

Baggaley, J. (1988). Perceived effectiveness of international AIDS campaigns. *Health Education Research, 3,* 7-17.

Bailey, K. D. (1990). *Social entropy theory.* Albany: State University of New York Press.

Bakeman, R., & Gottman, J.M. (1986). *Observing interaction: An introduction to sequential analysis.* Cambridge, England: Cambridge University Press.

Baker, G. L., & Gollub, J. P. (1990). *Chaotic dynamics: An introduction.* Cambridge, England: Cambridge University Press.

Bales, R. F., & Strodtbeck, F. L. (1951). Phases in group problem solving. *Journal of Abnormal and Social Psychology, 46,* 485-495.

Barnett, G. A. (1982, May). *Seasonality in television viewing: A mathematical model.* Paper presented to the annual meeting of the International Communication Association, Boston.

Barnett, G. A. (1988a). An associational model for the diffusion of complex innovations. In G. A. Barnett & J. Woelfel (Eds.), *Readings in the Galileo system: Theory, methods and applications* (pp. 55-74). Dubuque, IA: Kendall/Hunt.

Barnett, G. A. (1988b). Communication and organizational culture. In G. Goldhaber & G. Barnett (Eds.), *Handbook of organizational communication* (pp. 101-130). Norwood, NJ: Ablex.

Barnett, G. A., Chang, H. S., Fink, E. L., & Richards, W. D., Jr. (1991). Seasonality in television viewing: A mathematical model of cultural processes. *Communication Research, 18,* 755-772.

Barnett, G. A., Cho, S., & Choi, Y. (1993). Seasonality in television viewing. *Cycles, 44,* 145-149.

Barnett, G. A., & Kincaid, D. L. (1983). A mathematical theory of convergence. In W. B. Gudykunst (Ed.), *Intercultural communication theory: Current perspectives* (pp. 171-194). Beverly Hills, CA: Sage.

Baron, R. M., Amazeen, P. G., & Beer, P. J. (1994). Local and global dynamics of social relations. In R. R. Vallacher & A. Nowak (Eds.), *Dynamical systems in social psychology* (pp. 111-138). San Diego: Academic Press.

Bateson, G. (1972). *Steps to an ecology of mind.* New York: Ballantine.

Batra, N. D. (1990). *A self-renewing society: The role of television and communications technology.* Lanham, MD: University Press of America.

Bauer, C., & Fink, E. L. (1983). Fitting equations with power transformations: Examining variables with error. In R. N. Bostron (Ed.), *Communication yearbook 7* (pp. 146-199). Beverly Hills, CA: Sage.

Baxter, L. (1987). Symbols of relationship identity in relationship cultures. *Journal of Social and Personal Relationships, 4,* 261-280.

Baxter, L. (1988). A dialectical perspective on communication strategies in relationship development. In S. Duck, D. F. Hay, S. E. Hobfoll, W. Ickes, & B. Montgomery (Eds.), *Handbook of personal relationships* (pp. 257-273). London: Wiley.

Baxter, L., & Wilmot, W. (1983, February). *An investigation of openness-closedness cycling in ongoing relationship interaction.* Paper presented at the annual meeting of the Western Speech Communication Association, Albuquerque.

Beebe, B., Gerstman, L., Carson, B., Dolins, M., Zigman, A., Rosensweig, H., Faughey, H., & Korman, M. (1982). Rhythmic communication in the mother-infant dyad. In M. Davis (Ed.), *Interaction rhythms: Periodicity in communicative behavior* (pp. 79-100). New York: Human Sciences Press.

Bell, R. A., & Healey, J. G. (1992). Idiomatic communication and interpersonal solidarity in friends' relational cultures. *Human Communication Research, 18,* 307-335.

Belsley, D. A. (1991). *Conditioning diagnostics: Collinearity and weak data in regression.* New York: John Wiley.

Belsley, D. A., Kuh, E., & Welsch, R. E. (1980). *Regression diagnostics: Identifying influential data and sources of collinearity.* New York: John Wiley.

Benedetto, J. J. (1992). Irregular sampling and frames. In C. K. Chui (Ed.), *Wavelets: A tutorial in theory and applications* (pp. 445-507). San Diego: Academic Press.

Benton, L. A., & Yates, F. E. (1988). Ultradian adrenocortical and circulatory oscillations in conscious dogs. *American Journal of Physiology, 258*, R578-R590.

Berger, C. R. (1993). Goals, plans, and mutual understanding in relationships. In S. Duck (Ed.), *Individuals in relationships* (pp. 30-59). Newbury Park, CA: Sage.

Berghout-Austin, A. M., & Peery, J. C. (1983). Analysis of adult-neonate synchrony during speech and non-speech. *Perceptual and Motor Skills, 57*, 455-459.

Berlekamp, E. R., Conway, J. H., & Guy, R. K. (1982). *Winning ways for your mathematical plays.* New York: Academic Press.

Berlinksi, D. (1976). *On systems theory.* Cambridge: MIT Press.

Berlo, D. K. (1960). *The process of communication.* New York: Holt, Rinehart & Winston.

Berlo, D. K. (1977). Communication as process: Review and commentary. In B. D. Ruben (Ed.), *Communication yearbook 1* (pp. 11-27). New Brunswick, NJ: Transaction Books.

Bernieri, F. J. (1988). Coordinated movement and rapport in teacher-student interactions. *Journal of Nonverbal Behavior, 12*, 120-138.

Bernieri, F. J., Resnick, J.S., & Rosenthal, R. (1988). Synchrony, pseudosynchrony, and dissynchrony: Measuring the entrainment process in mother-infant interactions. *Journal of Personality and Social Psychology, 54*, 243-253.

Bernieri, F. J., & Rosenthal, R. (1991). Interpersonal coordination: Behavior matching and interactional synchrony. In R.S. Feldman & B. Rimé (Eds.), *Fundamentals of nonverbal behavior* (pp. 401-432). Cambridge: Cambridge University Press.

Bertalanffy, L. von. (1968). *General system theory: Foundations, development, applications.* New York: George Braziller

Beville, H. M. (1985). *Audience ratings: Radio, television, and cable.* Hillsdale, NJ: Lawrence Erlbaum.

Bhargava, S. C., Kumar, A., & Mukherjee, A. (1993). A stochastic cellular model of innovation diffusion. *Technological Forecasting and Social Change, 44*, 87-97.

Biocca, F. (1988). The breakdown of the "canonical audience." In J. Anderson (Ed.), *Communication yearbook 11* (pp. 127-132). Newbury Park, CA: Sage.

Biocca, F. (1991a). Models of a successful and unsuccessful ad: An exploratory analysis. In F. Biocca (Ed.), *Television and political advertising: Vol. 1. Psychological processes* (pp. 91-124). Hillsdale, NJ: Lawrence Erlbaum.

Biocca, F. (1991b). Viewer's mental models of political ads: Towards a theory of the semantic processing of television. In F. Biocca (Ed.), *Television and political advertising: Vol. 1. Psychological processes* (pp. 27-91). Hillsdale, NJ: Lawrence Erlbaum.

Biocca, F., & David, P. (1990, May). *Micro-shifts in audience opinions: A second-by-second analysis of the first 1988 presidential debate.* Paper presented at annual meeting of the International Communication Association, Dublin.

Biocca, F., & David, P. (1991). *How camera distance affects the perceptions of candidates during a presidential debate.* Unpublished manuscript, Center for Research in Journalism and Mass Communication, University of North Carolina at Chapel Hill.

Biocca, F., David, P., & West, M. (1990). *Micro-shifts in audience opinions: A second-by-second analysis of the Omaha vice-presidential debate.* Paper presented at annual meeting of the American Association of Public Opinion Research, Lancaster, PA.

Biocca, F., David, P., & West, M. (1994). Continuous response measurement (CRM): A computerized tool for research on the cognitive processing of communication messages. In A. Lang (Ed.), *Measuring psychological responses to media messages* (pp. 15-64). Hillsdale, NJ: Lawrence Erlbaum.

Biocca, F., Neuwirth, K., Oshagan, H., Zhongdang, P., & Richards, J. (1987, May). *Prime-and-probe methodology: An experimental technique for studying film and television.* Paper presented at the annual meeting of the International Communication Association, Montreal.

Birkenfeld, W. (1977). *Methoden zur analyse von kurzen zeitreihen* (Methods for the analysis of short time-series). Basel: Birkhauser Verlag.

Bishop, Y. M., Fienberg, S. E., & Holland, P. W. (1975). *Discrete multivariate analysis: Theory and practice.* Cambridge: MIT Press.

Bloomfield, P. (1976). *Fourier analysis of time series: An introduction.* New York: John Wiley.

Bobo, L., & Kluegel, J. R. (1991, August). *Modern American prejudice: Stereotypes, social distance, and perceptions of discrimination towards Blacks, Hispanics and Asians.* Paper presented at the annual meeting of the American Sociological Association, Cincinnati.

Borden, G. J., Harris, K. S., & Raphael, L. J. (1994). *Speech science primer: Physiology, acoustics, and perception of speech* (3rd ed.). Baltimore: Williams & Wilkins.

Bormann, E. G. (1983). Symbolic convergence: Organizational communication and culture. In L. L. Putnam & M. E. Pacanowsky (Eds.), *Communication in organizations: An interpretive perspective* (pp. 73-98). Beverly Hills, CA: Sage.

Bornstein, R. F., & Pittman, T. S. (Eds.). (1992). *Perception without awareness: Cognitive, clinical, and social perspectives.* New York: Guilford.

Bowlby, J. (1969). *Attachment and loss: Vol. 1. Attachment.* New York: Basic Books.

Box, G. E. P., & Jenkins, G. M. (1976). *Time series analysis: Forecasting and control.* San Francisco: Holden-Day.

Brazelton, T. B., Kozlowski, B., & Main, M. (1974). The origins of reciprocity: The early mother-infant interaction. In M. Lewis & L. Rosenblum (Eds.), *The effect of the infant on its caregiver* (pp. 49-76). New York: John Wiley.

Brehm, S. S., & Brehm, J. W. (1981). *Psychological reactance: A theory of freedom and control.* New York: Academic Press.

Brillinger, D. R. (1975). *Time series analysis and theory.* New York: Holt, Rinehart & Winston.

Broggi, A., d'Andrea, V., & Destri, G. (1993). Cellular automata as a computational model for low-level vision. *International Journal of Modern Physics, 4,* 5-16.

Brown, A. L., & French, L. A. (1976). Construction and regeneration of logical sequences using causing or consequences as the point of departure. *Child Development, 47,* 930-940.

Bruss, E. (1975). Beggars can't be choosers: The case of the indecisive woman. In M. Black (Ed.), *Problems of choice and decision* (pp. 550-577). Ithaca, NY: Cornell University Program on Science, Technology and Society.

Bryan, J. L. (1991). *Conversational tempo and conversation evaluation in children.* Unpublished master's thesis, University of New Hampshire, Durham.

Buchoff, R. (1990). Attention deficit disorder: Help for the classroom teacher. *Childhood Education, 67,* 86-90.

Buder, E. H. (1986). *Coherence of speech rhythms in conversations: Autocorrelation analysis of fundamental voice frequency* (Toronto Semiotic Circle Monograph No. 2). Toronto: Toronto Semiotic Circle.

Buder, E. H. (1991a). A non-linear dynamic model of social interaction. *Communication Research, 18,* 174-198.

Buder, E. H. (1991b). *Vocal synchrony in conversations: Spectral analysis of fundamental voice frequency.* Unpublished doctoral dissertation, Department of Communication Arts, University of Wisconsin, Madison.

Bunn, J. C., & Mead, J. (1971). Control of ventilation during speech. *Journal of Applied Physiology, 31*, 870-872.

Burgoon, J. K. (1978). A communication model of personal space violations: Explication and an initial test. *Human Communication Research, 4*, 129-142.

Burgoon, J. K. (1983). Nonverbal violations of expectations. In J. M. Wiemann & P. P. Harrison (Eds.), *Nonverbal interaction* (pp. 77-111). Beverly Hills, CA: Sage.

Burgoon, J. K., Dillman, L., & Stern, L. (1991, May). *Reciprocity and compensation patterns in dyadic interaction: I. Definitions, operationalizations, and statistical analysis.* Paper presented at the annual meeting of the International Communication Association, Chicago.

Burgoon, J. K., Dillman, L., & Stern, L. A. (1993). Adaptation in dyadic interaction: Defining and operationalizing patterns of reciprocity and compensation. *Communication Theory, 3*, 295-316.

Burns, J., & Anderson, D. R. (1993). Attentional inertia and recognition memory in adult television viewing. *Communication Research, 20*(6), 777-799.

Burrell, G., & Morgan, G. (1979). *Sociological paradigm and organizational analysis.* London: Heinemann.

Burridge, P. (1988), Cliff-Ord test. In S. Katz, N. L. Johnson, & C. B. Read (Eds.), *Encyclopedia of statistical sciences* (Vol. 2, pp. 119-122). New York: John Wiley.

Burt, R. S. (1982). *Toward a structural theory of action: Network models of social structure, perception, and action.* New York: Academic Press.

Burt, R. S. (1991). *STRUCTURE version 4.2* [Computer program]. New York: Center for the Social Sciences, Columbia University.

Byers, P. (1976). Biological rhythms as information channels in interpersonal behavior. In P. P. G. Bateson & P. H. Kopfler (Eds.), *Perspectives in ethology* (Vol. 2). New York: Plenum.

Calhoun, C. (1991). The problem of identity in collective action. In J. Huber (Ed.), *Macro-micro linkages in sociology* (pp. 51-75). Newbury Park, CA: Sage.

Campbell, D. T., & Stanley, J. C. (1966). *Experimental and quasi-experimental designs for research.* Chicago: Rand-McNally.

Campbell, J. (1986). *Winston Churchill's afternoon nap: A wide-awake inquiry into the human nature of time.* New York: Simon & Schuster.

Cappella, J. N. (1979). Talk-silence sequences in informal conversations I. *Human Communication Research, 6*, 3-17.

Cappella, J. N. (1980). Talk and silence sequences in informal conversations II. *Human Communication Research, 6*, 130-145.

Cappella, J. N. (1981). Mutual influence in expressive behavior: Adult-adult and infant-adult dyadic interaction. *Psychological Bulletin, 89*, 101-132.

Cappella, J. N. (1987). Interpersonal communication: Definitions and questions. In C. R. Berger & S. Chaffee (Eds.), *The handbook of communication science* (pp. 184-238). Beverly Hills, CA: Sage.

Cappella, J. N. (1988). Interaction patterns and social and personal relationships. In S. Duck (Ed.), *Handbook of social and personal relationships* (pp. 325-342). New York: John Wiley.

Cappella, J. N. (1991). The biological origins of automated patterns of human interaction. *Communication Theory, 1,* 4-35.

Cappella, J. N. (1994). The management of conversations. In M. L. Knapp & G. R. Miller (Eds.), *The handbook of interpersonal communication* (2nd ed., pp. 380-419). Thousand Oaks, CA: Sage.

Cappella, J. N., & Flagg, M. E. (1992). *Interactional adaptation, expressiveness and attraction: Kinesic and vocal responsiveness patterns in initial liking.* Paper presented at the VIth Conference of the International Society for the Study of Social and Personal Relationships, Orono, ME.

Cappella, J. N., & Green, J. O. (1982). A discrepancy-arousal explanation of mutual influence in expressive behavior for adult and infant-adult interaction. *Communication Monographs, 49,* 89-114.

Cappella, J. N., & Green, J. O. (1984). The effects of distance and individual differences in arousability on nonverbal involvement: A test of discrepancy-arousal theory. *Journal of Nonverbal Behavior, 8,* 259-286.

Cappella, J. N., & Palmer, M. T. (1990a). The structure and organization of verbal and nonverbal behavior: Data for models of production. In H. Giles & W. P. Robinson (Eds.), *Handbook of language and social psychology* (pp. 141-161). Chichester, England: Wiley.

Cappella, J. N., & Palmer, M. T. (1990b). Attitude similarity, relational history, and attraction: The mediating effects of kinesic and vocal behaviors. *Communication Monographs, 57,* 161-183.

Cappella, J. N., Palmer, M. T., & Donzella, B. (1991, May). *Individual consistency in temporal adaptations in nonverbal behavior in dyadic conversations: High and low expressive groups.* Paper presented at the annual meeting of the International Communication Association, Chicago.

Cappella, J. N., & Planalp, S. (1981). Talk and silence sequences in informal conversations III: Interspeaker influence. *Human Communication Research, 7,* 117-132.

Carley, K. M., & Prietula, M. J. (1994). Introduction: Computational organizational theory. In K. M. Carley & M. J. Prietula (Eds.), *Computational organizational theory* (pp. xi-xvii). Hillsdale, NJ: Lawrence Erlbaum.

Cartwright, D., & Harary, F. (1956). Structural balance: A generalization of Heider's theory. *Psychological Review, 63,* 277-293.

Censullo, M., Bowler, M., Lester, B., & Brazelton, T. B. (1987). An instrument for the measurement of infant-adult synchrony. *Nursing Research, 36,* 244-248.

Chaffee, S. H. (1991). *Communication concepts 1: Explication.* Newbury Park, CA: Sage.

Chaiken, S., Liberman, A., & Eagly, A. H. (1989). Heuristic and systematic information processing within and beyond the persuasion context. In J. S. Uleman & J. A. Bargh (Eds.), *Unintended thought* (pp. 212-253). New York: Guilford.

Chaiken, S., & Yates, S. (1985). Affective-cognitive consistency and thought-induced attitude polarization. *Journal of Personality and Social Psychology, 49,* 1470-1481.

Chapple, E. D. (1939). Measuring human relations: An introduction to the study of the interaction of individuals. *Genetic Psychology Monograph, 22,* 3-147.

Chapple, E. D. (1970). *Culture and biological man: Explorations in behavioral anthropology.* New York: Holt, Rinehart & Winston.

Chapple, E. D. (1971). Toward a mathematical model of interaction: Some preliminary considerations. In P. Kay (Ed.), *Explorations in mathematical anthropology* (pp. 141-178). Cambridge, MA: MIT Press.

Chapple, E. D. (1981). Movement and sound: The musical language of body rhythms in interaction. *Teachers College Record, 82*, 635-648.

Chapple, E. D., & Lui, Y. (1976). Populations of coupled nonlinear oscillators in anthropological biology systems. In *IEEE International Conference on Cybernetics and Society Proceedings* (pp. 332-335). Piscataway, NJ: IEEE Press.

Cherry, C. (1957). *On human communication.* Cambridge: MIT Press.

Chui, C. K. (1992). *An introduction to wavelets.* San Diego: Academic Press.

Clark, P. (1985). A review of the theories of time and structure for organizational sociology. In S. B. Bacharach (Ed.), *Research in the sociology of organization* (Vol. 4, pp. 35-79). Greenwich, CT: JAI.

Cliff, A. D., & Ord, J. K. (1973). *Spatial autocorrelation.* London: Pion.

Cliff, A. D., & Ord, J. K. (1980). *Spatial processes: Models, inference, and application.* London: Pion.

Cobb, L. (1973). Time series analysis of the periodicities of casual conversations (Doctoral dissertation, Cornell University). *Dissertation Abstracts International, 33*, 5105B. (University Microfilms No. 73-28, 286)

Cohen, J., & Cohen, P. (1983). *Applied multiple regression/correlation analysis for the behavioral sciences* (2nd ed.). Hillsdale, NJ: Lawrence Earlbaum.

Cohn, J. F., & Tronick, E. Z. (1987). Mother-infant face-to-face interaction: The sequence of dyadic states at 3, 6, and 9 months. *Developmental Psychology, 23*, 68-77.

Cohn, J. F., & Tronick, E. Z. (1988). Mother-infant face-to-face interaction: Influence is bidirectional and unrelated to periodic cycles in either partner's behavior. *Developmental Psychology, 24*, 386-392.

Colasanti, R. L., & Grime, J. P. (1993). Resource dynamics and vegetation processes: A deterministic model using two-dimensional cellular automata. *Functional Ecology, 7*, 169-176.

Coleman, J. S. (1968). The mathematical study of change. In M. Blalock (Ed.), *Methodology in social research* (pp. 428-478). New York: McGraw-Hill.

Collins, W. A. (1979). Children's comprehension of television content. In E. Wartella (Ed.), *Children communicating: Media and development of thought, speech, understanding* (pp. 21-52). Beverly Hills, CA: Sage.

Collins, W. A. (1983). Interpretation and inference in children's television viewing. In J. Bryant & D. R. Anderson (Eds.), *Children's understanding of television: Research on attention and comprehension* (pp. 125-150). New York: Academic Press.

Combs, A. (1993). Psychology, chaos, and the process nature of consciousness. In F. Abraham & A. Gilgen (Eds.), *Chaos theory in psychology* (pp. 129-137). Westport, CT: Greenwood.

Comstock, G. S., Chaffee, S., Katzman, N., McCombs, M., & Roberts, D. (1978). *Television and human behavior.* New York: Columbia University Press.

Condon, W. S., & Ogston, W. D. (1967). A segmentation of behavior. *Journal of Psychiatric Research, 5*, 221-235.

Condon, W. S., & Sander, L. W. (1974). Neonate movement is synchronized with adult speech: Interactional participation and language acquisition. *Science, 183*, 99-101.

Condry, J. (1989). *The psychology of television.* Hillsdale, NJ: Lawrence Erlbaum.

Conte, S. D. (1965). *Elementary numerical analysis: An algorithmic approach.* New York: McGraw-Hill.

Contractor, N. S. (1994). Self-organizing systems perspective in the study of organizational communication. In B. Kovacic (Ed.). *New approaches to organizational communication* (pp. 39-66). Albany: SUNY Press.

Contractor, N. S., & Seibold, D. R. (1993). Theoretical frameworks for the study of structuring processes in group decision support systems: Adaptive structuration theory and self-organizing systems theory. *Human Communication Research, 19,* 528-563.

Conville, R. L. (Ed.). (1994). *The use of "structure" in communication studies.* Westport, CT: Praeger.

Cook, R. D., & Weisberg, S. (1982). *Residuals and influence in regression.* London: Chapman & Hall.

Cook, T. D., & Campbell, D. T. (1979). *Quasi-experimentation: Design and analysis issues for field settings.* New York: Houghton Mifflin.

Coombs, C. H. (1964). *A theory of data.* New York: John Wiley.

Corman, S. R. (1990). A model of perceived communication in collective networks. *Human Communication Research, 16,* 582-602.

Corporation for Public Broadcasting. (1981). *A comparison of three research methodologies for pilot testing new television programs.* Washington, DC: Office of Communication Research, Corporation for Public Broadcasting.

Cortes, F. A., Przeworski, A., & Sprague, J. (1974). *Systems analysis for social scientists.* New York: John Wiley.

Crutchfield, J. P., Farmer, J. D., Packard, N. H., & Shaw, R. S. (1986). Chaos. *Scientific American, 255,* 46-57.

Cryer, J. D. (1986). *Time series analysis.* Boston: PWS-Kent.

Cushman, D. P., King, S. S., & Smith, T. (1990). The rules perspective on organizational commuication research. In G. R. Goldhaber (Ed.), *Handbook of organizational communication* (pp. 55-94). Norwood, NJ: Ablex.

Dabbs, J. M., Jr. (1982, August). *Fourier analysis and the rhythm of conversation.* Paper presented at the annual meeting of the American Psychological Association, Washington, DC. (ERIC Document Reproduction Service No. 222 959)

Dalton, K. (1990). *Once a month: The original premenstural syndrome handbook.* Claremont, CA: Hunter House.

Danes, J. E., Hunter, J. E., & Woelfel, J. (1978). Mass communication and belief change: A test of three mathematical models. *Human Communication Research, 4,* 243-252.

Davis, D. (1982). Determinants of responsiveness in dyadic interaction. In W. I. Ickes & E. S. Knowles (Eds.), *Personality, roles, and social behaviors* (pp. 85-139). New York: Springer-Verlag.

Davis, D. K., & Lee, J. W. (1980). Time series analysis models for communication research. In P. R. Monge & J. N. Capella (Eds.), *Multivariate techniques in human communication research* (pp. 429-454). New York: Academic Press.

Davis, J. D. (1976). Self-disclosure in an acquaintance exercise: Responsibility for level of intimacy. *Journal of Personality and Social Psychology, 33,* 787-792.

Davis, J. D. (1977). Effects of communication about interpersonal process on the evolution of self-disclosure in dyads. *Journal of Personality and Social Psychology, 35,* 31-37.

Davis, J. H. (1973). Group decision and social interaction: A theory of social decision schemes. *Psychological Review, 80,* 97-125.

Davis, J. H., Nagao, D. H., Spitzer, C. E., & Stasser, G. (1981). *Decisions in mock juries with multiple minorities and majorities*. Unpublished manuscript, Department of Psychology, University of Illinois at Urbana-Champaign.

Deadman, P., Brown, R. D., & Gimblett, H. R. (1993). Modelling rural residential settlement patterns with cellular automata. *Journal of Environmental Management, 37*, 147-160.

DeFleur, M. L., & Ball-Rokeach, S. (1982). *Theories of mass communication* (4th ed.). New York: Longman.

Delia, J. G. (1980). Some tentative thoughts concerning the study of interpersonal relationship and their development. *Western Journal of Speech Communication, 44*, 97-103.

Denes, P. B., & Pinson, E. N. (1993). *The speech chain: The physics and biology of spoken language*. New York: Freeman.

Dixon, W. (1990). *BMDP statistical software manual*. Berkeley: University of California Press.

Duck, S. (1993). Relationships as unfinished business: Out of the frying pan and into the 1990s. In S. Petronio, J. K. Alberts, M. L. Hecht, & J. Buley (Eds.), *Contemporary perspectives on interpersonal communication* (pp. 73-87). Madison, WI: WCB Brown & Benchmark.

Duck, S., Rutt, D. J., Hurst, M. H., & Strejc, H. (1991). Some evident truths about conversations in everyday relationships: All communications are not created equal. *Human Communication Research, 18*, 228-267.

Duncan, S., Jr., & Fiske, D. (1977). *Face-to-face social interaction: Research, methods, and theory*. Hillsdale, NJ: Lawrence Erlbaum.

Dunn, O., & Clark, V. (1990). *Applied statistics: Analysis of variance and regression* (2nd ed.). New York: John Wiley Interscience.

Eagly, A. H., & Chaiken, S. (1993). *The psychology of attitudes*. Fort Worth, TX: Harcourt Brace Jovanovich.

Ebbinghaus, H. E. (1964). *Memory: A contribution to experimental psychology*. New York: Dover.

Eckmann, J. P., & Ruelle, D. (1985). Fundamental limitations for estimating dimensions and Lyapunov exponents in dynamical systems. *Physica, 56D*, 185-187.

Einstein, A. (1961). *Relativity: The special and general theory* (R. W. Lawson, trans.). New York: Crown. (Original work published 1916)

Eisenberg, E. M. (1984). Ambiguity as strategy in organizational communication. *Communication Monographs, 51*, 227-242.

Eisenberg, E. M., & Riley, P. (1988). Organizational symbols and sense-making. In G. M. Goldhaber & G. A. Barnett (Eds.), *Handbook of organizational communication* (pp. 131-150). Norwood, NJ: Ablex.

Ellis, D. G. (1979). Relational control in two group systems. *Communication Monographs, 3*, 153-166.

Ellis, D. G., & Fisher, B. A. (1975). Phases of conflict in small group development. *Human Communication Research, 1*, 175-212.

Erickson, F., & Shultz, J. (1982). *The counselor as gatekeeper: Social interaction in interviews*. New York: Academic Press.

Fazio, R. H. (1989). On the power and functionality of attitudes: The role of accessibility. In A. R. Pratkanis, S. J. Breckler, & A. G. Greenwald (Eds.), *Attitude structure and function* (pp. 153-179). Hillsdale, NJ: Lawrence Erlbaum.

Feldstein, S., & Welkowitz, J. (1978). A chronography of conversation: In defense of an objective approach. In A. W. Siegman & S. Feldstein (Eds.), *Nonverbal behavior and communication* (pp. 329-378). Hillsdale, NJ: Lawrence Erlbaum.

Festinger, L. (1957). *A theory of cognitive dissonance.* Stanford, CA: Stanford University Press.

Feyerabend, P. K. (1963). How to be a good empiricist: A plea for tolerance in matters epistemological. In B. Baumrin (Ed.), *Philosophy of science: The Delaware seminar* (Vol. 1, pp. 3-40). New York: John Wiley.

Feyerabend, P. K. (1965). Problems of empiricism. In R. Colodny (Ed.), *Beyond the edge of certainty* (pp. 145-260). Englewood Cliffs, NJ: Prentice Hall.

Feyerabend, P. K. (1970). Consolations for the specialist. In I. Lakatos & A. Musgrave (Eds.), *Criticism and the growth of knowledge* (pp. 197-230). New York: Cambridge University Press.

Field, T. (1985). Attachment as psychobiological attunement: Being on the same wavelength. In M. Reite & T. Field (Eds.), *Psychobiology of attachment* (pp. 415-454). New York: Academic Press.

Field, T. (1987). Affective and interactive disturbances in infants. In J. D. Osofsky (Ed.), *Handbook of infant development* (2nd ed., pp. 972-1007). New York: John Wiley.

Field, T., Greenwald, P., Morrow, C., Healy, B., Foster, T., Guthertz, M., & Frost, P. (1992). Behavior state matching during interactions of preadolescent friends versus acquaintances. *Developmental Psychology, 28,* 242-250.

Field, T., Healy, B., Goldstein, S., & Guthertz, M. (1990). Behavior state matching and synchrony in mother-infant interactions of nondepressed versus depressed dyads. *Developmental Psychology, 26,* 7-14.

Field, T., Healy, B., & LeBlanc, W. (1989). Sharing and synchrony of behavior states and heart rate in nondepressed versus depressed mother-infant interactions. *Infant Behavior and Development, 12,* 357-376.

Fink, E. L., & Kaplowitz, S. A. (1993). Oscillation in beliefs and cognitive networks. In G. A. Barnett & W. Richards (Eds.), *Progress in communication sciences* (Vol. 12, pp. 247-272). Norwood, NJ: Ablex.

Fink, E. L., Kaplowitz, S. A., & Bauer, C. L. (1983). Positional discrepancy, psychological discrepancy, and attitude change: Experimental tests of some mathematical models. *Communication Monographs, 50,* 413-430.

Fink, E. L., Kaplowitz, S. A., & Wang, M.-L. (1994, August). *The cognitive effects of stereotype modification.* Paper presented at the annual meeting of the Association for Education in Journalism and Mass Communication, Atlanta.

Fink, E. L., Monahan, J. L., & Kaplowitz, S. A. (1989). A spatial model of the mere exposure effect. *Communication Research, 16,* 746-769.

Fishbein, J., & Ajzen, I. (1975). *Belief, attitude, intention, and behavior: An introduction to theory and research.* Reading, MA: Addison-Wesley.

Fisher, B. A. (1970). Decision emergence: Phases in group decision making. *Speech Monographs, 37,* 53-66.

Fisher, B. A. (1977, November). *Functions of category systems in interaction analysis.* Paper presented at the annual meeting of the Speech Communication Association, Washington, DC.

Fisher, B. A. (1978a). Information systems theory and research: An overview. In B. D. Ruben (Ed.), *Communication yearbook 2* (pp. 81-108). New Brunswick, NJ: Transaction Books.

Fisher, B. A. (1978b). *Perspectives on human communication*. New York: Macmillan.

Fisher, B. A. (1980). *Small group decision making*. New York: McGraw-Hill.

Fisher, B. A., & Drecksel, G. L. (1983). A cyclical model of developing relationships: A study of relational control interaction. *Communication Monographs, 50,* 66-78.

Fisher, B. A., & Hawes, L. C. (1971). An interact system model: Generating a grounded theory of small group decision making. *Quarterly Journal of Speech, 58,* 444-453.

Fletcher, J. E. (1985). Physiological responses to the media. In J. R. Dominick & J. E. Fletcher (Eds.), *Broadcasting research methods* (pp. 89-106). Boston: Allyn & Bacon.

Foerster, H. von. (1984). Principles of self-organization in a socio-managerial context. In H. Ulrich & G. J. B. Probst (Eds.), *Self-organization and management of social systems: Insights, promises, doubts, and questions* (pp. 2-24). Berlin: Springer-Verlag.

Ford, J. D., & Backoff, R. H. (1988). Organizational change in and out of dualities and paradox. In R. E. Quinn & K. S. Cameron (Eds.), *Paradox and transformation: Towards a theory of change in organization and management* (pp. 81-122). Cambridge, MA: Ballinger.

Freeman, H. (1965). *Discrete-time systems*. New York: John Wiley.

Freeman, L. (1979). Centrality in social networks: Conceptual clarification. *Social Networks, 1,* 215-239.

Gabor, D. (1946). Theory of communication. *Journal of the Institution of Electrical Engineers (London), 93,* Part III, 429-441.

Geary, R. C. (1954). The contiguity ratio and statistical mapping. *The Incorporated Statistician, 5,* 115-145.

Geiger, S. F., & Reeves, B. (1993). We interrupt this program . . . : Attention for television sequences. *Human Communication Research, 19,* 368-387.

Gensch, D., & Shaman, P. (1980). Models of competitive television ratings. *Journal of Marketing Research, 17,* 307-315.

Gersick, C. J. (1991). Revolutionary change theories: A multilevel exploration of the punctuated equilibrium paradigm. *Academy of Management Review, 16,* 10-36.

Gibson, J. J. (1977). The theory of affordances. In R. E. Shaw & J. Bransford (Eds.), *Perceiving, acting and knowing: Toward an ecological psychology*. Hillsdale, NJ: Lawrence Erlbaum.

Giddens, A. (1979). *Central problems in social theory: Action, structure and contradiction in social analysis*. Los Angeles: University of California Press.

Giddens, A. (1984). *The constitution of society: Outline of the theory of structuration*. Berkeley: University of California Press.

Gilbert, D. T., Krull, D. S., & Malone, P. S. (1990). Unbelieving the unbelievable: Some problems with the rejection of false information. *Journal of Personality and Social Psychology, 59,* 601-613.

Giles, H., Mulac, A., Bradac, J., & Johnson, P. (1987). Speech accommodation theory: The first decade and beyond. In M. L. McLaughlin (Ed.), *Communication yearbook 10* (pp. 13-48). Newbury Park, CA: Sage.

Giles, H., & Powesland, P. F. (1975). *Speech style and social evaluation*. London: Academic Press.

Gleick, J. (1987). *Chaos: The making of a new science*. New York: Viking.

Goffman, E. (1974). *Frame analysis: An essay on the organization of experience*. Cambridge, MA: Harvard University Press.

Goldstein, J. (1988). A far-from-equilibrium systems approach to resistance to change. *Organizational Dynamics, 17,* 16-76.

Gollwitzer P. M., Heckhausen H., & Steller, B. (1990). Deliberative and implemental mind-sets: Cognitive tuning toward congruous thoughts and information. *Journal of Personality and Social Psychology, 59,* 1119-1127.

Goode, W. J. (1960). A theory of role strain. *American Sociological Review, 25,* 483-496.

Goodhardt, G. T., Ehrenberg, A. S., & Collins, M. A. (1987). *The television audience: Patterns of viewing* (2nd ed.). London: Blackmore.

Goodwin, B. (1970). Biological stability. In C. H. Waddington (Ed.), *Toward a theoretical biology* (Vol. 3, pp. 1-17). Chicago: Aldine.

Gottman, J. M. (1979a). Detecting cyclicity in social interaction. *Psychological Bulletin, 86,* 335-348.

Gottman, J. M. (1979b). *Marital interaction: Experimental investigations.* New York: Academic Press.

Gottman, J. M. (1981). *Time-series analysis: A comprehensive introduction for social scientists.* Cambridge, England: Cambridge University Press.

Gottman, J. M. (1982). Temporal form: Toward a new language for describing relationship. *Journal of Marriage and the Family, 44,* 943-962.

Gottman, J. M., & Levenson, R. W. (1985). A valid measure for obtaining self-report of affect. *Journal of Consulting and Clinical Psychology, 53,* 151-160.

Gottman, J. M., & Ringland, J. T. (1981). The analysis of dominance and bidirectionality in social development. *Child Development, 52,* 393-412.

Gottman, J. M., & Roy, A. K. (1990). *Sequential analysis: A guide for behavioral researchers.* Cambridge, England: Cambridge University Press.

Gould, P., Johnson, J., & Chapman, G. (1984). *The structure of television.* London: Pion.

Granger, C. W. J. (1969). Investigating causal relations by econometric models and cross-spectral methods. *Econometrica, 37,* 424-438.

Granger, C. W. J. (1980). Testing for causality: A personal viewpoint. *Journal of Economics Dynamics and Control, 2,* 329-352.

Grassberger, P., & Procaccia, H. (1983). Measuring the strangeness of strange attractors. *Physica, D9,* 189-208.

Greenbaum, P., & Rosenfeld, H. M. (1978). Patterns of avoidance in response to interpersonal staring and proximity: Effects of bystanders on drivers at a traffic intersection. *Journal of Personality and Social Psychology, 36,* 575-587.

Greenhouse, S., & Geisser, S. (1959). On methods in the analysis of profile data. *Psychometrika, 24,* 95-112.

Gregory, S. W. (1990). Analysis of fundamental frequency reveals covariation in interview partners' speech. *Journal of Nonverbal Behavior, 14,* 237-251.

Gregory, S. W., Webster, S., & Huang, G. (1993). Voice pitch and amplitude convergence as a metric of quality in dyadic interviews. *Language and Communication, 13,* 195-217.

Gregson, R. A. M. (1983). *Time series in psychology.* Hillsdale, NJ: Lawrence Erlbaum.

Grings, W. W., & Dawson, M. E. (1978). *Emotions and bodily responses: A psychophysiological approach.* New York: Academic Press.

Grossberg, L., & O'Keefe, D. J. (1975). Presuppositions, conceptual foundations, and communication theory: On Hawes' approach to communication. *Quarterly Journal of Speech, 61,* 195-208.

Gutowitz, H. (1991). Introduction. In H. Gutowitz (Ed.), *Cellular automata: Theory and experiment* (pp. vii-xiv). Cambridge: MIT Press.

Hale, J. L., & Burgoon, J. K. (1984). Models of reactions to changes in nonverbal immediacy. *Journal of Nonverbal Behavior, 8*, 287-314.

Hamblin, R. L., Miller, J. L. L., & Saxton, D. E. (1979). Modeling use of diffusion. *Social Forces, 57*, 799-811.

Hammond, R., Warner, R. M., & Fuld, K. (1994). *Systolic blood pressure and flicker fusion threshold.* Manuscript in preparation.

Hanneman, R. A. (1988). *Computer-assisted theory building: Modeling dynamic social systems.* Newbury Park, CA: Sage.

Harkins, S. G., & Petty, R. E. (1987). Information utility and the multiple source effect. *Journal of Personality and Social Psychology, 52*, 260-268.

Hatch, M. J. (1987). Proximity, physical barriers, and communication in organizations. *Administrative Science Quarterly, 32*, 387-399.

Hatfield, E., Cacioppo, J. T., & Rapson, R. (1992). Primitive emotional contagion. In M. S. Clark (Ed.), *Emotion and social behavior* (Review of Personality and Social Psychology, Vol. 14, pp. 151-177). Newbury Park, CA: Sage.

Hawes, L. C. (1972a). Development and application of an interview coding system. *Central States Speech Journal, 23*, 92-99.

Hawes, L. C. (1972b). The effects of interviewer style on patterns of dyadic communication. *Speech Monographs, 39*, 209-219.

Hawes, L. C. (1973). Elements of a model for communication processes. *Quarterly Journal of Speech, 59*, 11-21.

Hawes, L. C. (1974). Social collectives as communication: Perspectives on organizational behavior. *Quarterly Journal of Speech, 60*, 497-502.

Hawes, L. C. (1975). A response to Grossberg and O'Keefe: Building a human science of communication. *Quarterly Journal of Speech, 61*, 209-219.

Hawking, S. (1988). *A brief history of time.* New York: Bantam.

Hayes, D. P., & Cobb, L. (1979). Ultradian rhythms in social interaction. In A. W. Siegman & S. Feldstein (Eds.), *Of speech and time: Temporal speech rhythms in interpersonal contexts* (pp. 57-70). Hillsdale, NJ: Lawrence Erlbaum.

Heider, F. (1958). *The psychology of interpersonal relations.* New York: John Wiley.

Heise, D. R. (1969). Separating reliability and stability in test-retest correlation. *American Sociological Review, 34*, 93-101.

Heisenberg, W. (1930). *The physical principles of the quantum theory* (C. Eckart & F. C. Hoyt, Trans.). New York: Dover.

Hess, W. (1983). *Pitch determination of speech signals: Algorithms and devices.* Berlin: Springer-Verlag.

Hewes, D. E. (1975). Finite stochastic modeling of communication processes: An introduction and some basic readings. *Human Communication Research, 1*, 271-283.

Hewes, D. E. (1979). The sequential analysis of social interaction. *Quarterly Journal of Speech, 65*, 56-73.

Hewes, D. E. (1980). Stochastic modeling of communication processes. In P. R. Monge & J. N. Cappella (Eds.), *Multivariate techniques in human communication research* (pp. 393-428). New York: Academic Press.

Hewes, D. E. (1985). A socio-egocentric model of group decision making. In R. I. Hirokawa & M. S. Poole (Eds.), *Communication and group decision making* (pp. 265-292). Beverly Hills, CA: Sage.

Hewes, D. E. (1986). A socio-egocentric model of group decision making. In R. Y. Hirokawa & M. S. Poole (Eds.), *Communication and group decision making* (pp. 265-291). Beverly Hills, CA: Sage.

Hewes, D. E., Planalp, S. K., & Streibel, M. (1980). Analyzing social interaction: Some excruciating models and exhilarating results. In D. Nimmo (Ed.), *Communication yearbook 4* (pp. 123-141). New Brunswick, NJ: Transaction Books.

Hibbs, D. A. (1974). Problems of statistical estimation and causal inference in time series regression models. In H. L. Costner (Ed.), *Sociological methodology* (pp. 252-308). San Francisco: Jossey-Bass.

Higgins, E. T. (1989). Knowledge accessibility and activation: Subjectivity and suffering from unconscious sources. In J. S. Uleman & J. A. Bargh (Eds.), *Unintended thought* (pp. 75-123). New York: Guilford.

Hinde, R. A. (1979). *Towards understanding relationships*. London: Academic Press.

Hlastala, M. P., Wranne, B., & Lenfant, C. (1973). Cyclical variations in FRC and other respiratory variables in resting man. *Journal of Applied Physiology, 34*, 670-676.

Hochberg, J. (1968). In the mind's eye. In R. N. Haber (Ed.), *Contemporary theory and research in visual perception* (pp. 309-331). New York: Holt, Rinehart & Winston.

Hochberg, J., & Brooks, V. (1978). Film cutting and visual momentum. In J. W. Senders, D. F. Fisher, & R. A. Monty (Eds.), *Eye movements and the higher psychological functions* (pp. 293-270). Hillsdale, NJ: Lawrence Erlbaum.

Hofer, M. (1984). Relationships as regulators: A psychobiological perspective on bereavement. *Psychosomatic Medicine, 46*, 183-197.

Holt, L. E. (1970). Resistance to persuasion on explicit beliefs as a function of commitment to and desirability of logically related beliefs. *Journal of Personality and Social Psychology, 16*, 583-591.

Honeycutt, J. M., Cantrill, J. G., & Greene, R. W. (1989). Memory structures for relational escalation: A cognitive test of the sequencing of relational actions and stages. *Human Communication Research, 16*, 62-90.

Hopper, R., Knapp, M. L., & Scott, L. (1981). Couples' personal idioms: Exploring intimate talk. *Journal of Communication, 31*, 23-33.

Houston, D. A., & Sherman, S. (1991). Feature matching, unique features and the dynamics of choice processes: Predecision conflict and postdecision satisfaction. *Journal of Experimental Social Psychology, 27*, 411-430.

Huckfeldt, R. R., Kohfeld, C. W., & Likens, T. W. (1982). *Dynamic modeling: An introduction*. Beverly Hills, CA: Sage.

Hunter, J. E., Schmidt, F. L., & Jackson, G. B. (1982). *Meta-analysis: Cumulating research findings across studies*. Beverly Hills, CA: Sage.

Huston, A. C., & Wright, J. C. (1983). Children's processing of television: The informative functions of formal features. In J. Bryant & D. R. Anderson (Eds.), *Children's understanding of television: Research on attention and comprehension* (pp. 35-68). New York: Academic Press.

Huston, T. L., Surra, C. A., Fitzgerald, N. A., & Cate, R. M. (1981). From courtship to marriage: Mate selection as an interpersonal process. In S. Duck & R. Gilmour (Eds), *Personal relationships 2: Developing personal relationships* (pp. 53-88). New York: Academic Press.

Iacobucci, D., & Wasserman, S. (1988). A general framework for the statistical analysis of sequential data. *Psychological Bulletin, 103*, 379-390.

Iberall, A. S., & McCulloch, W. S. (1969). The organizing principle of complex living systems. *Journal of Basic Engineering, 91*, 290-294.

Ingard, U., & Kraushaar, W. L. (1960). *Introduction to mechanics, matter, and waves.* Reading, MA: Addison-Wesley.

Isabella, R. A., Belsky, J., & van Eye, A. (1989). Origins of mother-infant attachment: An examination of interactional synchrony during the infant's first year. *Developmental Psychology, 25*, 12-21.

Iyengar, S., & Kinder, D. R. (1987). *News that matters.* Chicago: University of Chicago Press.

Jackman, M. R., & Senter, M. S. (1983). Different, therefore unequal: Beliefs about trait differences between groups of unequal status. In D. J. Treiman & R. V. Robinson (Eds.), *Research in social stratification and mobility* (Vol. 2, pp. 309-335). Greenwich, CT: JAI.

Jaffe, J., & Feldstein, S. (1970). *Rhythms of dialogue.* New York: Academic Press.

Janis, I. L., & Mann, L. (1977). *Decision making: A psychological analysis of conflict, choice, and commitment.* New York: Free Press.

Jaques, E. (1982). *The forms of time.* New York: Crane Russak.

Jasnow, M., & Feldstein, S. (1987). Adult-like temporal characteristics of mother-infant vocal interactions. *Child Development, 57*, 754-761.

Jenkins, G. M., & Watts, D. G. (1968). *Spectral analysis and its applications.* San Francisco: Holden-Day.

Johnson, B. T., & Eagly, A. H. (1990). The effects of involvement on persuasion: A meta-analysis. *Psychological Bulletin, 106*, 290-314.

Johnson, M. K., & Sherman, S. J. (1990). Constructing and reconstructing the past and the future in the present. In E. T. Higgins & R. M. Sorrentino (Eds.), *Handbook of motivation and cognition: Foundations of social behavior* (pp. 482-526). New York: Guilford.

Johnson, S. D., & Proctor, R. F., II. (1992). We cannot not process—or can we? *Spectra, 28*, 3-9.

Judd, C. M., & Krosnick, J. A. (1989). The structural bases of consistency among political attitudes: Effects of political expertise and attitude importance. In A. R. Pratkanis, S. J. Breckler, & A. G. Greenwald (Eds.), *Attitude structure and function* (pp. 99-128). Hillsdale, NJ: Lawrence Erlbaum.

Kahneman, D. (1973). *Attention and effort.* Hillsdale, NJ: Prentice Hall.

Kaplowitz, S. A., & Fink, E. L. (1982). Attitude change and attitudinal trajectories: A dynamic multidimensional theory. In M. Burgoon (Ed.), *Communication yearbook 6* (pp. 364-394). Beverly Hills, CA: Sage.

Kaplowitz, S. A., & Fink, E. L. (1988). A spatial-linkage model of cognitive dynamics. In G. A. Barnett & J. Woelfel (Eds.), *Readings in the Galileo system: Theory, methods and applications* (pp. 117-146). Dubuque, IA: Kendall/Hunt.

Kaplowitz, S. A., & Fink, E. L. (1992). Dynamics of attitude change. In R. L. Levine & H. E. Fitzgerald (Eds.), *Analysis of dynamic psychological systems: Vol. 2. Methods and applications* (pp. 341-369). New York: Plenum.

Kaplowitz, S. A., Fink, E. L., Armstrong, G. B., & Bauer, C. L. (1986). Message discrepancy and the persistence of attitude change: Implications of an information integration model. *Journal of Experimental Social Psychology, 22*, 507-530.

Kaplowitz, S. A., Fink, E. L., & Bauer, C. L. (1983). A dynamic model of the effect of discrepant information on unidimensional attitude change. *Behavioral Science, 28,* 233-250.

Kaplowitz, S. A., & Fink, E. L., with Mulcrone, J., Atkin, D., & Dabil, S. (1991). Disentangling the effects of discrepant and disconfirming information. *Social Psychology Quarterly, 54,* 191-207.

Kelly, H. H. (1955). Salience of membership and resistance to change of group-anchored attitudes. *Human Relations, 8,* 275-290.

Kelly, J. R., & McGrath, J. E. (1988). *On time and method.* Newbury Park, CA: Sage.

Kempthorne, P. J. (1989). *Identifying rank-influential groups of observations in linear regression modelling* (Sloan Working Paper No. 3018-89-MS). Cambridge: Sloan School, Massachusetts Institute of Technology.

Kenny, D. A. (1979). *Correlation and causality.* New York: John Wiley.

Kenny, D. A., & LaVoie, L. (1984). The social relations model. In L. Berkowitz (Ed.), *Advances in experimental social psychology* (Vol. 18, pp. 142-182). Orlando, FL: Academic Press.

Kent, R. D., & Read, C. (1992). *The acoustic analysis of speech.* San Diego: Singular Publishing Group.

Kerr, B. (1973). Processing demands during mental operations. *Memory and Cognition, 1,* 401-412.

Kimberly, R. P. (1970). Rhythmic patterns in human interaction. *Nature, 228,* 88-90.

Kincaid, D. L. (1987). The convergence theory of communication, self-organization and cultural evolution. In D. L. Kincaid (Ed.), *Communication theory: Eastern and Western perspectives* (pp. 209-219). San Diego: Academic Press.

Kincaid, D. L., Yum, J. O., Woelfel, J., & Barnett, G. A. (1983). The cultural convergence of Korean immigrants in Hawaii: An empirical test of a mathematical theory. *Quality and Quantity, 18,* 59-78.

Klapp, O. E. (1986). *Overload and boredom: Essays on the quality of life in the information society.* New York: Greenwood.

Kleinke, C. L., Staneski, R. A., & Berger, D. E. (1975). Evaluation of an interviewer as a function of interviewer gaze, reinforcement of subject gaze, and interviewer attractiveness. *Journal of Personality and Social Psychology, 31,* 115-122.

Kline, F. G. (1977). Time in communication research. In P. M. Hirsch, P. V. Miller, & F. G. Kline (Eds.), *Strategies for communication research* (pp. 187-204). Beverly Hills, CA: Sage.

Kloeden, P., Deakin, M. A. B., & Tirkel, A. Z. (1976). A precise definition of chaos. *Nature (London), 264,* 264-295.

Kmenta, J. (1971). *Elements of econometrics.* New York: Macmillan.

Knapp, M. L. (1978). *Social intercourse: From greeting to good-bye.* Boston: Allyn & Bacon.

Knapp, M. L., Ellis, D., & Williams, B. (1980). Perceptions of communication behavior associated with relationship terms. *Communication Monographs, 47,* 262-278.

Knoke, D., & Burt, R. S. (1983). Prominence. In R. S. Burt & M. J. Minor (Eds.), *Applied network analysis: An introduction* (pp. 195-222). Beverly Hills, CA: Sage.

Knoke, D., & Kuklinski, J. H. (1982). *Network analysis.* Beverly Hills, CA: Sage.

Kohring, G. A. (1992). The cellular automata approach to simulating fluid flows in porous media. *Physica A, 186,* 97-108.

Kolaja, J. (1969). *Social system and time and space: An introduction to the theory of recurrent behavior.* Pittsburgh, PA: Duquesne University Press.

Kratochwill, T. R. (Ed.). (1978). *Single subject research.* New York: Academic Press.

Kraus, S., & Smith, R. (1962). Issues and images. In S. Kraus (Ed.), *The great debates: Background, perspectives, and effects* (pp. 289-312). Bloomington: Indiana University Press.

Krause, R., Steimer, E., Sanger-Alt, C., & Wagner, G. (1989). Facial expression of schizophrenic patients and their interaction partners. *Psychiatry, 52,* 1-12.

Kreyszig, E. (1972). *Advanced engineering mathematics.* New York: John Wiley.

Krippendorff, K. (1970). On generating data in communication research. *Journal of Communication, 20,* 241-269.

Krippendorff, K. (1986). *Information theory: Structural models for qualitative data.* Beverly Hills, CA: Sage.

Krippendorff, K. (1987). Paradigms for communication and development with emphasis on autopoiesis. In D. L. Kincaid (Ed.), *Communication theory: Eastern and Western perspectives* (pp. 189-206). San Diego: Academic Press.

Krippendorff, K. (1993). The past of communication's hoped-for future. *Journal of Communication, 43,* 34-44.

Krueger, R. (1988). *Focus groups: A practical guide for applied research.* Newbury Park, CA: Sage.

Kuhn, T. S. (1970). *The structure of scientific revolutions* (2nd ed.). Chicago: University of Chicago Press.

Kullback, S., Kupperman, M., & Ku, H. H. (1962). Tests for contingency tables and Markov chains. *Technometrics, 4,* 573-608.

Kushner, H., & Falkner, B. (1981). A harmonic analysis of cardiac response of normotensive and hypertensive adolescents during stress. *Journal of Human Stress, 7,* 21-27.

LaFrance, M. (1982). Posture mirroring and rapport. In M. Davis (Ed.), *Interaction rhythms: Periodicity in communicative behavior* (pp. 279-298). New York: Human Sciences Press.

Landman, J. (1993). *Regret: The persistence of the possible.* New York: Oxford University Press.

Lang, A. (1990). Involuntary attention and physical arousal evoked by structural features and emotional content in TV commercials. *Communication Research, 17,* 275-299.

Lang, A. (1992). *A limited capacity approach to television viewing.* Unpublished manuscript.

Lang, K., & Lang, G. E. (1961). Ordeal by debate: Viewer reactions. *Public Opinion Quarterly, 25,* 277-288.

Lang, P. J. (1984). Cognition in emotion: Concept and action. In C. Izard, J. Kagan, & R. Zajonc (Eds.), *Emotions, cognition and behavior* (pp. 193-226). New York: Cambridge University Press.

Lang, P. J. (1985). The cognitive psychology of emotion: Fear and anxiety. In A. H. Tuma & J. Maser (Eds.), *Anxiety and the anxiety disorders.* Hillsdale, NJ: Lawrence Erlbaum.

Langer, E. J. (1978). Rethinking the role of thought in social interaction. In J. W. Harvey, W. J. Ickes, & R. F. Kidd (Eds.), *New directions in attribution research* (Vol. 2, pp. 35-58). Hillsdale, NJ: Lawrence Erlbaum.

Larsen, R., & Kasimatis, M. (1990). Individual differences in entrainment of mood to the weekly calendar. *Journal of Personality and Social Psychology, 58,* 164-171.

Latané, B. (in press). Dynamic social impact: The creation of culture by communication. *Journal of Communication.*

Latané, B., & Darley, J. M. (1970). *The unresponsive bystander: Why doesn't he help?* New York: Appleton-Century-Crofts.

Latané, B., & Nowak, A. (in press). Self-organizing systems: Necessary and sufficient conditions for the emergence of clustering and polarization. In G. Barnett & F. Boster (Eds.), *Progress in communication sciences* (Vol. 14). Norwood, NJ: Ablex.

Lavie, P. (1982). Ultradian rhythms in human sleep and wakefulness. In W. B. Webb (Ed.), *Biological rhythms, sleep and performance.* New York: John Wiley.

Lederer, W. J., & Jackson, D. D. (1968). *The mirages of marriage.* New York: Norton.

Leippe, M. R., Greenwald, A. G., & Baumgardner, M. H. (1982). Delayed persuasion as a consequence of associative interference: A context confusion effect. *Personality and Social Psychology Bulletin, 8,* 644-650.

Lenfant, C. (1967). Time dependent variations of pulmonary gas exchange in normal man at rest. *Journal of Applied Physiology, 22,* 675-684.

Lester, B. M., Hoffman, J., & Brazelton, T. B. (1985). The rhythmic structure of mother-infant interaction in term and preterm infants. *Child Development, 56,* 15-27.

Levenson, R. W., & Ruef, A. M. (1992). Empathy: A physiological substrate. *Journal of Personality and Social Psychology, 63,* 234-246.

Levy, F. (1980). The development of sustained attention (vigilance) and inhibition in children: Some normative data. *Journal of Child Psychology and Psychiatry, 21,* 77-84.

Lewin, K. (1951). *Field theory in social science.* New York: Harper & Brothers.

Lewin, R. (1992). *Complexity: Life at the edge of chaos.* New York: Macmillan.

Lewis-Beck, M. S. (1986). Interrupted times series. In W. D. Berry & M. S. Lewis-Beck (Eds.), *New tools for social scientists: Advances and applications in research methods* (pp. 209-240). Beverly Hills, CA: Sage.

Liberman, A., & Chaiken, S. (1991). Value conflict and thought-induced attitude change. *Journal of Experimental Social Psychology, 27,* 203-216.

Lieberman, P. (1967). *Intonation, perception, and language.* Cambridge: MIT Press.

Lodziak, C. (1986). *The power of television: A critical appraisal.* London: Frances Printer.

Lorenz, E. N. (1963). Deterministic non-periodic flow. *Journal of Atmospheric Science, 20,* 130-141.

Lorenz, K. (1977). *Behind the mirror.* New York: Harcourt Brace Jovanovich.

Lovett-Doust, J., & Podnieks, I. (1976). Properties of an ultradian biological clock regulating sensory perception in man: A longitudinal study. *Physiological Psychology, 4,* 523-528.

Lynn, R. (1966). *Attention, arousal and the orienting reaction.* Oxford: Pergamon.

Mabry, E. A. (1975). Exploratory analysis of a developmental model for task-oriented small groups. *Human Communication Research, 2,* 66-73.

Mackworth, N. H. (1950). Some factors affecting vigilance. *Advances in Science, 13,* 389-392.

Mair, M. W. (1978). *Steps towards principles of text regulation* (Monograph No. 2). Toronto: Toronto Semiotic Circle, Victoria College, University of Toronto.

Malik, F., & Probst, G. (1984). Evolutionary management. In H. Ulrich & G. J. B. Probst (Eds.), *Self-organization and management of social systems: Insights, promises, doubts, and questions* (pp. 105-120). Berlin: Springer-Verlag.

Mandelbrot, B. B. (1963). The variation of certain speculative prices. *Journal of Business 36*, 394-419.

Mandelbrot, B. B. (1983). *The fractal geometry of nature.* New York: Freeman.

Marple, S. L. (1987). *Digital spectral analysis with applications.* Englewood Cliffs, NJ: Prentice Hall.

Marquardt, D. W., & Acuff, S. K. (1982). Direct quadratic spectrum estimation from unequally spaced data. In O. D. Anderson & M. R. Perryman (Eds.), *Applied time series analysis* (pp. 199-227). Amsterdam: North Holland.

Matarazzo, J. D., & Wiens, A. N. (1967). Interviewer influence on durations of interviewee silence. *Journal of Experimental Research in Personality, 2,* 56-69.

Matarazzo, J. D., & Wiens, A. N. (1972). *The interview: Research on its anatomy and structure.* Chicago: Aldine.

Maurer, R. E., & Tindall, J. H. (1983). Effects of postural congruence on clients' perception of counselor empathy. *Journal of Counseling Psychology, 30,* 158-163.

Maxim, P. E., Bowden, D. M., & Sackett, G. P. (1976). Ultradian rhythms of solitary and social behavior in rhesus monkeys. *Physiology and Behavior, 17,* 337-344.

McCleary, R., & Hay, R. A. (1980). *Applied time series analysis for the social sciences.* Beverly Hills, CA: Sage.

McClintock, M. E. (1971). Menstrual synchrony and suppression. *Nature, 229,* 244-245.

McGoldrick, M., & Carter, E. A. (1980). The stages of the family life cycle. In J. M. Henslin (Ed.), *Marriage and family in a changing society* (2nd ed., pp. 43-54). New York: Free Press.

McGrath, J. E. (Ed.). (1988). *The social psychology of time: New perspectives.* Newbury Park, CA: Sage.

McGrath, J. E., & Kelly, J. R. (1986*). Time and human interaction: Toward a social psychology of time.* New York: Guilford.

McGuire, W. J. (1964). Inducing resistance to persuasion. In L. Berkowitz (Ed.), *Advances in experimental social psychology* (Vol. 1, pp. 191-229). New York: Academic Press.

McGuire, W. J. (1969). The nature of attitudes and attitude change. In G. Lindzey & E. Aronson (Eds.), *The handbook of social psychology* (2nd ed., Vol. 3, pp. 136-314). Reading, MA: Addison-Wesley.

McGuire, W. J. (1981). The probabilogical model of cognitive structure and attitude change. In R. E. Petty, T. M. Ostrom, & T. C. Brock (Eds.), *Cognitive responses in persuasion* (pp. 291-308). Hillsdale, NJ: Lawrence Erlbaum.

McGuire, W. J. (1989). Individual attitudes and attitude systems. In A. R. Pratkanis, S. J. Breckler, & A. G. Greenwald (Eds.), *Attitude structure and function* (pp. 37-69). Hillsdale, NJ: Lawrence Erlbaum.

McGuire, W. J. (1990). Dynamic operations of thought systems. *American Psychologist, 45,* 504-512.

McKenna, J. J., Mosko, S., Dungy, C., & McAnich, J. (1990). Sleep and arousal patterns of co-sleeping human mother/infant pairs: A preliminary physiological study with implications for the study of Sudden Infant Death Syndrome (SIDS). *American Journal of Physical Anthropology, 83,* 331-347.

McLaughlin, M. L., Cody, M. J., & Rosenstein, N. E. (1983). Account sequences in conversations between strangers. *Communication Monographs, 50,* 102-125.

McLeod, J., & Chaffee, S. (1976). Coorientation and interpersonal perception. *American Behavioral Scientist, 16,* 469-499.

McTaggart, J. M. E. (1927). *The nature of existence* (Vol. 2, Book 5). Cambridge, England: Cambridge University Press.

Mead, G. H. (1932). *The philosophy of the present* (A. E. Murphy, Ed.). Chicago: Open Court.

Meadowcroft, J. M., & Reeves, B. (1989). Influence of story schema development on children's attention to television. *Communication Research, 16*, 352-374.

Meadowcroft, J. M., & Watt, J. H. (1989, May). *A multi-component theory of children's attention spans*. Paper presented at the annual meeting of the International Communication Association, New Orleans.

Measuring the dimension of an attractor [Special supplement]. (1992). *The Social Dynamicist, 3*, 3-5.

Menard, S. (1991). *Longitudinal research*. Newbury Park, CA: Sage.

Menelly, N. E., Wiegel, E. K., Yan, J., & Watt, J. H. (1992, May). *The effect of instructions on attention to television*. Paper presented at the annual meeting of the International Communication Association, Miami, FL.

Merton, R. K. (1936). The unanticipated consequences of purposive social action. *American Sociological Review, 1*, 894-920.

Merton, R. K. (1963). *Social theory and social structure*. Glencoe, IL: Free Press.

Meyer, Y. (1993). *Wavelets: Algorithms and applications*. Philadelphia: Society for Industrial and Applied Mathematics.

Milenkovic, P. H. (1992). *CSpeech*, version 4.0 [Computer software]. Madison: Department of Electrical and Computer Engineering, University of Wisconsin.

Millar, M. G., & Tesser, A. (1986). Thought induced attitude change: The effects of schema structure and commitment. *Journal of Personality and Social Psychology, 51*, 259-269.

Millard, W. (1989). *Research using the Millard system ("Televac")*. Unpublished report.

Millonas, M. M. (1993). Cooperative phenomena in swarms. In N. Boccara, E. Goles, S. Martinez, & P. Picco (Eds.), *Cellular automata and cooperative systems* (pp. 507-518). London: Kluwer Academic.

Miniard, P. W., & Cohen, J. B. (1981). An examination of the Fishbein-Ajzen behavioral-intentions model's concepts and measures. *Journal of Experimental Social Psychology, 17*, 309-339.

Minus a Dukakis "home run," Bush is called winner [Editorial]. (1988, October 14). *Los Angeles Times* (National edition), pt. 1, p. 25.

Mirowski, P. (1990). From Mandelbrot to chaos in economic theory. *Southern Economic Journal, 57*, 289-307.

Monge, P. R. (1977). The systems perspective as a theoretical basis for the study of human communication. *Communication Quarterly, 25*, 19-29.

Monge, P. R. (1982). Systems theory and research in the study of organizational communication: The correspondence problem. *Human Communication Research, 8*, 245-261.

Monge, P. R. (1987). The network level of analysis. In C. R. Berger & S. H. Chaffee (Eds.), *Handbook of communication science* (pp. 239-270). Newbury Park, CA: Sage.

Monge, P. R. (1990). Theoretical and analytic issues in studying organizational processes. *Organization Science, 1*, 406-430.

Monge, P. R., & Cappella, J. N. (1980). *Multivariate techniques in human communication research*. New York: Academic Press.

Monge, P. R., & Contractor, N. S. (1988). Communication networks: Measuring techniques. In C. H. Tardy (Ed.), *A handbook for the study of human communication* (pp. 107-138). Norwood, NJ: Ablex.

Monge, P. R., Cozzens, M. D., & Contractor, N. S. (1992). Communication and motivational predictors of the dynamics of organizational communication. *Organization Science, 3*, 250-274.

Monge, P. R., & Eisenberg, E. M. (1987). Emergent communication networks. In F. Jablin, L. L. Putnam, K. H. Roberts, & L. Porter (Eds.), *Handbook of organizational communication* (pp. 304-342). Newbury Park, CA: Sage.

Monge, P. R., Farace, R. V., Eisenberg, E. M., Miller, K. I., & White, L. L. (1984). The process of studying process in organizational communication. *Journal of Communication, 34*, 22-43.

Monge, P. R., Rothman, L. W., Eisenberg, E. M., Miller, K. I., & Kirste, K. K. (1985). The dynamics of organizational proximity. *Management Science, 31*, 1129-1141.

Moon, F. C. (1987). *Chaotic vibrations: An introduction for applied scientists and engineers.* New York: John Wiley.

Moore-Ede, M. C., Sulzman, F. M., & Fuller, C. A. (1982). *The clocks that time us.* Cambridge, MA: Harvard University Press.

Morgan, D. (1988). *Focus groups as qualitative research.* Newbury Park, CA: Sage.

Morley, D. D. (1986). Revised lag sequential analysis. In M. L. McLaughlin (Ed.), *Communication yearbook 10* (pp. 172-182). Newbury Park, CA: Sage.

Mumby, D. K. (1987). The political function of narrative in organizations. *Communication Monographs, 54*, 113-127.

Mumford, L. (1934). *Technics and civilization.* London: Routledge & Kegan Paul.

Myers, R. H. (1990). *Classical and modern regression, with applications.* Boston, MA: PWS-Kent.

Natale, M. (1975). Convergence of mean vocal intensity in dyadic communication as a function of social desirability. *Journal of Personality and Social Psychology, 32*, 790-804.

National Oceanic and Atmospheric Administration (NOAA). (1991). *State, regional, and national monthly and annual precipitation.* Ashville, NC: Author.

Neisser, U. (1976). *Cognition and reality.* San Francisco: Freeman.

Nelson, C. E. (1968). Anchoring to accepted values as a technique for immunizing beliefs against persuasion. *Journal of Personality and Social Psychology, 9*, 329-334.

Nesselroade, J. R., & Baltes, P. B. (Eds.). (1979). *Longitudinal research in the study of behavior and development.* New York: Academic Press.

Neuendorf, K. A., Kaplowitz, S. A., Fink, E. L., & Armstrong, G. B. (1986). Assessment of the use of self-referent concepts for the measurement of cognition and affect. In M. McLaughlin (Ed.), *Communication yearbook 10* (pp. 183-199). Beverly Hills, CA: Sage.

Neumann, J. von. (1966). *Theory of self-reproducing automata.* Urbana: University of Illinois Press.

Newcomb, T. M. (1956). The prediction of interpersonal attraction. *American Psychologist, 11*, 575-587.

Newell, S. E., & Stutman, R. K. (1988). The social confrontation episode. *Communication Monographs, 55*, 266-285.

Newton, I. (1959). *Philosophiae naturalis principia mathematica* (Mathematical principles of natrural philosophy). Cambridge, England: Cambridge University Press. (Original work published 1687)

Nicolis, G., & Prigogine, I. (1977). *Self-organization in nonequilibrium systems: From dissipative structures through order through fluctuations.* New York: Wiley-Interscience.

Nielsen, A. C. (1991). *Report on television.* New York: Author.

Noller, P. (1984). *Nonverbal communication and marital interaction.* Oxford, England: Pergamon.

Norman, D. A., & Bobrow, D. G. (1975). On data-limited processes. *Cognitive Psychology, 7,* 44-64.

Norusis, M. J. (1993). *SPSS for Windows: Advanced statistics.* Chicago: SPSS, Inc.

Nyquist, H. (1928, April). Certain topics in telegraph transmission theory. *Transactions of the American Institute of Electrical Engineers,* pp. 617-644.

Palmer, M. T. (1989). Controlling conversations: Turns, topics, and interpersonal control. *Communication Monographs, 56,* 1-18.

Palmer, M. T., & Cunningham, R. (1987). *Computerizing the collection and coding of communication interaction data: The AIDE system.* Unpublished manuscript, Communication Arts Department, University of Wisconsin—Madison.

Patterson, M. L. (1976). An arousal model of interpersonal intimacy. *Psychological Review, 83,* 235-245.

Peters, E. E. (1991). *Chaos and order in the capital markets.* New York: Wiley-Interscience.

Petty, R. E., & Cacioppo, J. T. (1986). *Communication and persuasion: Central and peripheral routes to attitude change.* New York: Springer-Verlag.

Petty, R. E., Ostrom, T. M., & Brock, T. C. (Eds.). (1981). Cognitive responses in persuasion. Hillsdale, NJ: Lawrence Erlbaum.

Petty, R. E., Wells, G. L., & Brock, T. C. (1976). Distraction can enhance or reduce yielding to propaganda: Thought disruption vs. effort justification. *Journal of Personality and Social Psychology, 34,* 874-884.

Phillips, P. C. B., & Ouliaris, S. (1990). Asymptotic properties of residual based tests for cointegration. *Econometrica, 58,* 165-194.

Philport, J. (1980). The psychology of viewer program evaluation. In J. Anderson (Ed.), *Proceedings of the 1980 technical conference on qualitative television ratings* (pp. B1-B17). Washington, DC: Corporation for Public Broadcasting.

Piaget, J. (1926). *The language and thought of the child.* New York: Harcourt Brace.

Piaget, J. (1969). *The mechanisms of perception.* London: Routledge & Kegan Paul.

Piaget, J., & Inhelder, B. (1969). *The psychology of the child.* New York: Basic Books.

Pike, G. R., & Sillars, A. L. (1985). Reciprocity and marital communication. *Journal of Personal and Social Relationships, 2,* 303-324.

Pindyck, R. S., & Rubinfeld, D. L. (1981). *Econometric models and economic forecasts* (2nd ed). New York: McGraw-Hill.

Pittam, J. (1994). *Voice in social interaction: An interdisciplinary approach.* Thousand Oaks, CA: Sage.

Poincaré, H. (1946). *The foundation of science: Science and method* (English trans.). Lancaster, PA: Science Press. (Original work published 1913)

Pondy, L., & Mitroff, I. I. (1979). Beyond open systems models of organization. In L. L. Cummings & B. M. Staw (Eds.), *Research in organizational behavior* (Vol. 1, pp. 3-39). Greenwich, CT: JAI.

Poole, M. S. (1981). Decision development in small groups: A comparison of two models. *Communication Monographs, 48*, 1-20.

Poole, M. S. (1983a). Decision development in small groups II: A study of multiple sequences in decision making. *Communication Monographs, 50*, 206-232.

Poole, M. S. (1983b). Decision development in small groups III: A multiple sequences model of group decision development. *Communication Monographs, 50*, 321-341.

Poole, M. S. (1990, February). *A turn of the wheel: The case for a renewal of systems inquiry in organizational communication research.* Paper presented at the Arizona State University conference on "Organizational Communication: Directions for the 90s," Tempe.

Poole, M. S. (1994). Afterword. In B. Kovacic (Ed.), *New approaches to organizational communication* (pp. 271-278). Albany: State University of New York Press.

Poole, M. S., & Hunter, J. E. (1979). Change in hierarchical systems of attitudes. In D. Nimmo (Ed.), *Communication yearbook 3* (pp. 157-176). New Brunswick, NJ: Transaction Books.

Poole, M. S., & Hunter, J. E. (1980). Behavior and hierarchies of attitudes: A deterministic model. In D. P. Cushman & R. D. McPhee (Eds.), *Message-attitude-behavior relationships: Theory, methodology and application* (pp. 245-271). New York: Academic Press.

Poole, M. S., McPhee, R. D., & Seibold, D. R. (1982). A comparison of normative and interactional explanations of group decision making: Social decision schemes versus valence distributions. *Communication Monographs, 49*, 1-19.

Porges, S. W., Bohrer, R. E., Cheung, M. N., Drasgow, F., McCabe, P. E., & Keren, G. (1980). New time-series statistic for detecting rhythmic co-occurrence in the frequency domain: The weighted coherence and its applications to psychophysiological research. *Psychological Bulletin, 88*, 580-587.

Posner, M. I. (1978). *Chronometric explorations of mind.* Hillsdale, NJ: Lawrence Erlbaum.

Priestly, M. B. (1981). *Spectral analysis and time series.* London: Academic Press.

Priestly, M. B. (1988). *Non-linear and non-stationary time series analysis.* London: Academic Press.

Prigogine, I. (1980). *From being to becoming: Time and complexity in the physical sciences.* New York: Freeman.

Prigogine, I., & Stengers, I. (1984). *Order out of chaos.* New York: Bantam.

Putnam, L. L. (1983). The interpretive perspective: An alternative to functionalism. In L. L. Putnam & M. E. Pacanosky (Eds.), *Communication and organizations: An interpretive approach* (pp. 31-54). Beverly Hills, CA: Sage.

Putnam, L. L., & Pacanowsky, M. E. (Eds.). (1983). *Communication and organizations: An interpretive approach.* Beverly Hills, CA: Sage.

Ramsey, J. B., Sayers, C. L., & Rothman, P. (1988). *The statistical properties of dimension calculations using small data sets: Some economic applications.* Unpublished manuscript.

Ranson, S., Hinings, B., & Greenwood, R. (1980). The structuring of organizational structures. *Administrative Science Quarterly, 25*, 1-17.

Rapoport, A. (1968). Foreword. In W. Buckley (Ed.), *Modern systems research for the behavioral scientist* (pp. viii-xxii). Chicago: Aldine.

Rapp, P. E. (1993). Chaos in the neurosiences: Cautionary tales from the frontier. *Biologist 40*, 89-94.

Raush, H. L. (1972). Process and change: A Markov model for interaction. *Family Process, 11*, 275-298.

Read, C., Buder, E. H., & Kent, R. D. (1992). Speech analysis systems: An evaluation. *Journal of Speech and Hearing Research, 35*, 314-332.

Reardon, K. K., & Rogers, E. M. (1988). Interpersonal versus mass media communication: A false dichotomy. *Human Communication Research, 15*, 284-303.

Reeves, B., Rothschild, M., & Thorson, E. (1983). *Evaluation of the Tell-Back audience response system.* Madison: Mass Communication Research Center, University of Wisconsin.

Reeves, B., Thorson, E., Rothschild, M., McDonald, D., Hirsch, J., & Goldstein, R. (1985). Attention to television: Interstimulus effects of movement and scene changes on alpha variation over time. *International Journal of Neuroscience, 35*, 242-255.

Reeves, B., Thorson, E., & Schleuder, J. (1984). Attention to television: Psychological theories and chronometric measures. In J. Bryant & D. Zillman (Eds.), *Perspectives on media effects* (pp. 251-299). Hillsdale, NJ: Lawrence Erlbaum.

Reitman, E. (1989). *Exploring the geometry of nature: Computer modeling of chaos.* Blue Ridge Summit, PA: Windcrest Books.

Reynolds, C. W. (1987). Flocks, herds, and schools: A distributed behavioral model. *Computer Graphics, 21*, 25-34.

Rice, R. E. (1993). Using network concepts to clarify sources and mechanisms of social influence. In G. A. Barnett & W. D. Richards (Eds.), *Progress in communication science* (Vol. 12, pp. 43-62). Norwood, NJ: Ablex.

Richards, W. D. (1985). Data, models, and assumptions in network analysis. In R. D. McPhee & P. K. Tompkins (Eds.), *Organizational communication: Themes and new directions* (pp. 109-147). Beverly Hills, CA: Sage.

Robertson, S. S. (1982). Intrinsic temporal patterning in the spontaneous movement of awake neonates. *Child Development, 53*, 1016-1021.

Robinson, J. P. (1972). Television's impact on everyday life: Some cross-cultural evidence. In E. Rubinstein (Ed.), *Television and social behavior.* Washington, DC: U.S. Department of Health, Education and Welfare.

Robinson, J. P. (1981). Television and leisure time: A new scenario. *Journal of Communication, 31*, 120-130.

Robinson, M., & Sheehan, M. A. (1983). *Over the wire and on TV.* New York: Russell Sage.

Rogers, E. M., & Kincaid, L. (1981). *Communication networks: Toward a new paradigm for research.* New York: Free Press.

Rogers, L. E. (1993). The concept of social relationship from a pragmatic view. *Personal Relationship Issues, 1*, 20-21.

Rogers, L. E., & Bagarozzi, D. A. (1983). An overview of relational communication and implications for therapy. In D. A. Bagarozzi, A. P. Jurich, & R. W. Jackson (Eds.), *Marital and family therapy: New perspectives in theory, research and practice* (pp. 48-78). New York: Human Sciences Press.

Rokeach, M. (1975). Long term value change initiated by computer feedback. *Journal of Personality and Social Psychology, 32*, 467-476.

Rosenthal, R. (1987). *Judgment studies: Design, analysis and meta-analysis.* Cambridge: Cambridge University Press.

Rosser, J. B. (1991). *From catastrophe to chaos: A general theory of economic discontinuities.* Boston: Academic Press.

Rothschild, M. E., Thorson, E., Reeves, B., Hirsch, J. E., & Goldstein, R. (1986). EEG activity and the processing of television commercials. *Communication Research, 13*, 182-220.

Rovine, M., & Von Eye, A. (1991). *Applied computational statistics in longitudinal research.* Boston: Academic Press.

Rumelhart, D. E., McClelland, J. L., & PDP Research Group. (1986). *Parallel distributed processing: Explorations in the microstructure of cognition: Vol. 1. Foundations.* Cambridge: MIT Press.

Rust, L. (1985). Using test scores to guide the content analysis of TV materials. *Journal of Advertising Research, 25*, 17-23.

Sackett, G. P. (1979). The lag sequential analysis of contingency and cyclicity in behavioral interaction research. In J. Osofsky (Ed.), *Handbook of infant development.* New York: John Wiley.

Sackett, G. P. (1987). Analysis of sequential social interaction data: Some issues, recent developments, and a causal inference model. In J. Osofsky (Ed.), *Handbook of infant development* (2nd ed., pp. 878-885). New York: John Wiley.

Sahin, H., & Robinson, J. P. (1980). Beyond the realm of necessity: Television and the colonization of leisure. *Media, Culture and Society, 3*, 85-95.

Saltiel, J., & Woelfel, J. (1975). Inertia in cognitive processes: The role of accumulated information in attitude change. *Human Communication Research, 1*, 333-344.

Sandefur, J. T. (1990). *Discrete dynamical systems: Theory and applications.* New York: Oxford University Press.

Sandefur, J. T. (1993). *Discrete dynamical modeling.* New York: Oxford University Press.

Sano, M., & Sawada, Y. (1985). Measurement of the Lyapunov spectrum from chaotic time series. *Physical Review Letters, 55*, 1082.

SAS Institute. (1990). *SAS/ETS user's guide.* Cary, NC: Author.

Sayrs, L. W. (1989). *Pooled time-series analysis.* Newbury Park, CA: Sage.

Scheidel, T. M., & Crowell, L. (1964). Idea development in small group discussion groups. *Quarterly Journal of Speech, 50*, 140-145.

Schramm, W. (Ed.). (1954). *The process and effects of mass communication.* Urbana: University of Illinois Press.

Scollon, R. (1981). Rhythmic integration of ordinary talk. In D. Tannen (Ed.), *Georgetown University round table on languages and linguistics, 1981* (pp. 335-349). Washington, DC: Georgetown University Press.

Scott, W. A. (1968). Attitude measurement. In G. Lindzey & E. Aronson (Eds.), *The handbook of social psychology* (2nd ed., Vol. 2, pp. 204-273). Reading, MA: Addison-Wesley.

Shannon, C., & Weaver, W. (1949). *The mathematical theory of communication.* Urbana: University of Illinois Press.

Shumway, R. H. (1988). *Applied statistical time series analysis.* Englewood Cliffs, NJ: Prentice Hall.

Siegel, S. (1956). *Nonparametric statistics for the behavioral sciences.* New York: McGraw-Hill.

Sigman, S. J. (1991). Handling the discontinuous aspects of continuous social relationships: Toward research on the persistence of social forms. *Communication Theory, 1,* 106-127.

Simonton, D. K. (1977). Cross-sectional time-series experiments: Some suggested statistical analyses. *Psychological Bulletin, 84,* 489-502.

Singer, B., & Spilerman, S. (1974). Social mobility models for heterogeneous populations. In H. L. Costner (Ed.), *Sociological methodology: 1973-1974* (pp. 356-401). San Francisco: Jossey-Bass.

Singer, J. (1980). The power and limitations of television: a cognitive-affective analysis. In P. Tannenbaum (Ed.), *The entertainment function of television* (pp. 31-65). Hillsdale, NJ: Lawrence Erlbaum.

Smith, D. H. (1972). Communication research and the idea of process. *Speech Monographs, 39,* 174-182.

Snow, R. P. (1987). Interaction with mass media: The importance of rhythm and tempo. *Communication Quarterly, 35,* 225-237.

Sokolov, E. N. (1963). *Perception and the conditioned reflex.* New York: Pergamon.

Sorokin, P. (1957). *Social and cultural dynamics: A study of change in major systems of art, truth, ethics, law and social relationships.* Boston: Porter Sargent.

Spitzberg, B. H. (1988). Communication competence: Measures of perceived effectiveness. In C. H. Tardy (Ed.), *A handbook for the study of human communication* (pp. 67-105). Norwood, NJ: Ablex.

Sprott, J. C., & Rowlands, G. (1993). *Chaos Data Analyzer, IBM personal computer version 1.0.* New York: American Institute of Physics.

SPSS, Inc. (1993). *SPSS for Windows: Trends.* Chicago: Author.

Stern, D. (1982). Some interactive functions of rhythm changes between mother and infant. In M. Davis (Ed.), *Interaction rhythms: Periodicity in communicative behavior* (pp. 101-117). New York: Human Sciences Press.

Street, R. L. (1982). Evaluation of noncontent speech accommodation. *Language and Communication, 2,* 13-31.

Street, R. L., & Buller, D. B. (1987). Patients' characteristics affecting physician-patient nonverbal communication. *Human Communication Research, 15,* 60-90.

Street, R. L., & Cappella, J. N. (1989). Social and linguistic factors influencing adaptation in children's speech. *Journal of Psycholinguistic Research, 18,* 497-519.

Street, R. L., Jr. (1984). Speech convergence and speech evaluation in fact-finding interviews. *Human Communication Research, 11,* 139-169.

Street, R. L., Jr., & Murphy, T. (1987). Interpersonal orientation and speech behavior. *Communication Monographs, 54,* 42-62.

Suppe, F. (Ed.). (1974). *The structure of scientific theories.* Urbana: University of Illinois Press.

Symons, D. K., & Moran, G. (1987). The behavioral dynamics of mutual responsiveness in early face-to-face mother-infant interactions. *Child Development, 58,* 1488-1495.

Takens, F. (1980). On detecting strange attractors in turbulence. In D. A. Rand & L. S. Young (Eds.), *Dynamical systems and turbulence* (pp. 366-381). Berlin: Springer-Verlag.

Talmadge, L. D., & Dabbs, J. M., Jr. (1990). Intimacy, conversational patterns, and concomitant cognitive/emotional processes in couples. *Journal of Social and Clinical Psychology, 9,* 473-488.

Tannenbaum, P. H. (1967). The congruity principle revisited: Studies in the induction, reduction, and generalization of persuasion. In L. Berkowitz (Ed.), *Advances in experimental social psychology* (Vol. 3, pp. 271-320). New York: Academic Press.

Tesser, A. (1978). Self-generated attitude change. In L. Berkowitz (Ed.), *Advances in experimental social psychology* (Vol. 11, pp. 289-338). New York: Academic Press.

Tesser, A., & Shaffer, D. R. (1990). Attitudes and attitude change. In M. R. Rosenzweig & L. W. Porter (Eds.), *Annual review of psychology* (Vol. 41, pp. 479-523). Palo Alto, CA: Annual Reviews, Inc.

Tetlock, P. E. (1983a). Accountability and complexity of thought. *Journal of Personality and Social Psychology, 45,* 74-83.

Tetlock, P. E. (1983b). Cognitive style and political ideology. *Journal of Personality and Social Psychology, 45,* 118-126.

Thayer, R. E. (1989). *The biopsychology of mood and arousal.* Oxford, England: Oxford University Press.

Therrien, C. W. (1992). *Discrete random signals and statistical signal processing.* Englewood Cliffs, NJ: Prentice Hall.

Thomas, E. A. C., & Martin, J. A. (1976). An analysis of parent-infant interaction. *Psychological Review, 83,* 141-156.

Thorndyke, P. W., & Yekovich, F. R. (1979). *A critique of schemata as a theory of human story memory* (Vol. P-6307). Santa Monica, CA: RAND Corporation.

Thorson, E., & Lang, A. (1992). The effects of television videographics and lecture familiarity on adult cardiac orienting responses and memory. *Communication Research, 19,* 346-369.

Thorson, E., & Reeves, B. (1985). Effects of over-time measures of viewer liking and activity during programs and commercials on memory for commercials. In R. Lutz (Ed.), *Advances in consumer research* (pp. 549-553). New York: Association for Consumer Research.

Thorson, E., Reeves, B., Schleuder, J., Lang, A., & Rothschild, M. (1985). Effects of program context on the processing of television commercials. In *Proceedings of the American Academy of Advertising* (pp. R58-R63). Tempe: Arizona State University Press.

Thorson, E., & Zhao, X. (1988, October). *Memory for television commercials as a function of onsets and offsets in watching.* Paper presented at the annual meeting of the Association for Consumer Research, New Orleans.

Tickle-Degnen, L., & Rosenthal, R. (1987). Group rapport and nonverbal behavior. *Review of Personality and Social Psychology, 9,* 113-136.

Tourangeau, R., Rasinski, K. A., Bradbury, N., & D'Andrade, R. (1989). Carryover effects in attitude surveys. *Public Opinion Quarterly, 53,* 495-524.

Trevino, L. K., Daft, R. L., & Lengel, R. K. (1990). Understanding managers' choices: A symbolic interactionist perspective. In J. Fulk & C. W. Steinfield (Eds.), *Organizations and communication technology* (pp. 71-94). Newbury Park, CA: Sage.

Trivedi, S., & Raghavan, R. (1989). Cognitive functioning of alcoholics and its relationship with prognosis. *Drug and Alcohol Dependence, 23,* 41-44.

Tronick, E. Z., Als, H., & Brazelton, T. B. (1977). Mutuality in mother-infant interaction. *Journal of Communication, 27,* 74-79.

Tukey, J. W. (1967). An introduction to the calculation of numerical spectrum analysis. In B. Harris (Ed.), *Spectral analysis of time series* (pp. 25-46). New York: John Wiley.

Tukey, J. W. (1977). *Exploratory data analysis.* Reading, MA: Addison-Wesley.

Tuma, N. B., & Hannan, M. T. (1984). *Social dynamics: Models and methods.* Orlando: Academic Press.

Tversky, A., & Kahneman, D. (1974). Judgment under uncertainty: Heuristics and biases. *Science, 185,* 1124-1131.

Tversky, A., & Shafir, E. (1992). Choice under conflict: The dynamics of deferred decision. *Psychological Science, 3,* 358-361.

Upton, C. (1969). *Broadcast program analyzers: A century of no progress in instru- ment design.* Unpublished master's thesis, Department of Speech, University of Wisconsin—Madison.

Vallacher, R. R., Nowak, A., & Kaufman, J. (1994). Intrinsic dynamics of social judgment. *Journal of Personality and Social Psychology, 67,* 20-34.

Van Maanen, J., & Schein, E. (1979). Toward a theory of organizational socialization. In B. Staw (Ed.), *Research in organizational behavior* (Vol. 1, pp. 209-264). Greenwich, CT: JAI.

VanLear, C. A. (1983). Analysis of interaction data. In R. Bostrom (Ed.), *Communication yearbook 7* (pp. 282-303). Beverly Hills, CA: Sage.

VanLear, C. A. (1987). The formation of social relationships: A longitudinal study of social penetration. *Human Communication Research, 13,* 299-322.

VanLear, C. A. (1991). Testing a cyclical model of communicative openness in relationship development: Two longitudinal studies. *Communication Monographs, 58,* 337-361.

VanLear, C. A. (1992). Marital communication across the generations: Learning and rebellion, continuity and change. *Journal of Social and Personal Relationships, 9,* 103-124.

VanLear, C. A., & Trujillo, N. (1986). On becoming acquainted: A longitudinal study of social judgment processes. *Journal of Social and Personal Relationships, 3,* 375-392.

VanLear, C. A., & Zietlow, P. H. (1990). Toward a contingency approach to marital interaction: An empirical integration of three approaches. *Communication Monographs, 57,* 202-218.

Wade, M. G., Ellis, M. J., & Bohrer, R. E. (1973). Biorhythms in the activity of children during free play. *Journal of the Experimental Analysis of Behavior, 20,* 155-162.

Waldrop, M. M. (1992). *Complexity: The emerging science at the edge of order and chaos.* New York: Simon & Schuster.

Walster, E. (1964). The temporal sequence of post-decision processes. In L. Festinger (Ed.), *Conflict, decision, and dissonance* (pp. 112-128). Stanford, CA: Stanford University Press.

Warner, R. M. (1979). Periodic rhythms in conversational speech. *Language and Speech, 22,* 381-396.

Warner, R. M. (1988). Rhythm in social interaction. In J. E. McGrath (Ed.), *The social psychology of time: New perspectives* (pp. 63-88). Hillsdale, NJ: Lawrence Erlbaum.

Warner, R. M. (1991). Incorporating time. In B. M. Montgomery & S. Duck (Eds.), *Studying interpersonal interaction* (pp. 82-102). New York: Guilford.

Warner, R. M. (1992a). Cyclicity of vocal activity increases during conversation: Support for a nonlinear systems model of dyadic social interaction. *Behavioral Science, 37*, 128-138.

Warner, R. M. (1992b). Dimensions of social interaction tempo: A factor analytic study of time and frequency domain indexes of interaction structure. *Journal of Psycholinguistic Research, 21*, 173-191.

Warner, R. M. (1992c). Sequential analysis of social interaction: Assessing internal versus social determinants of behavior. *Journal of Personality and Social Psychology, 63*, 51-60.

Warner, R. M. (1992d). Speaker, partner, and observer evaluations of affect during social interaction as a function of interaction tempo. *Journal of Language and Social Psychology, 11*, 1-14.

Warner, R. M., Malloy, D., Schneider, K., Knoth, R., & Wilder, B. (1987). Rhythmic organization of social interaction and observer ratings of positive affect and involvement. *Journal of Nonverbal Behavior, 11*, 57-74.

Warner, R. M., & Mooney, K. (1988). Individual differences in vocal activity rhythmic: Fourier analysis of cyclicity in amount of talk. *Journal of Psycholinguistic Research, 17*, 99-111.

Warner, R. M., & Stevens, A. A. (1991, October). *Cyclic variations in blood pressure during conversation and baseline.* Paper presented at the annual meeting of the Society for Psychophysiological Research, Chicago.

Warner, R. M., Waggener, T. B., & Kronauer R. E. (1984). Synchronized cycles in ventilation and vocal activity during spontaneous conversational speech. *Journal of Applied Physiology, 54*, 1324-1334.

Watt, J. H. (1979, August). *A comparison of time and frequency domain time-series models of media coverage.* Paper presented at the annual meeting of the Association for Education in Journalism, Houston, TX.

Watt, J. H. (1988). *FATS: Fourier analysis of time series program user's guide.* Storrs, CT: Information Analysis Systems Corp.

Watt, J. H. (1994). Detection and modeling of time-sequenced processes. In A. Lang (Ed.), *Measuring psychological responses to media.* Hillsdale, NJ: Lawrence Erlbaum.

Watt, J. H., & Meadowcroft, J. M. (1990, June). *Age-related differences in children's attention span components: Harmonic models for television viewing.* Paper presented at the annual meeting of the International Communication Association, Dublin.

Watt, J. H., & van den Berg, S. (1995). *Research methods for communication science.* Boston: Allyn & Bacon.

Watts, W. A., & Holt, L. E. (1970). Logical relationships among beliefs and timing as factors in persuasion. *Journal of Personality and Social Psychology, 16*, 571-582.

Watzlawick, P., Beavin, J. H., & Jackson, D. D. (1967). *Pragmatics of human communication: A study of interaction patterns, pathologies, and paradoxes.* New York: Norton.

Webb, J. T. (1972). Interview synchrony: An investigation of two speech rate measures. In A. W. Siegman & B. Pope (Eds.), *Studies in dyadic communication* (pp. 115-133). New York: Pergamon.

Wegner, D. M. (1989). *White bears and other unwanted thoughts.* New York: Penguin.

Weick, K. (1979). *The social psychology of organizing* (2nd ed.). Reading, MA: Addison-Wesley.

Weick, K. (1983). Organizational communication: Toward a research agenda. In L. L. Putnam & M. E. Pacanosky (Eds.), *Communication and organizations: An interpretive approach* (pp. 13-30). Beverly Hills, CA: Sage.

Welkowitz, J., & Kuc, M. (1973). Interrelationships among warmth, genuineness, empathy, and temporal speech patterns in interpersonal interaction. *Journal of Consulting and Clinical Psychology, 41*, 472-473.

Werner, C. M., & Baxter, L. A. (1994). Temporal qualities of relationships: Organismic, transactional, and dialectical views. In M. L. Knapp & G. R. Miller (Eds.), *Handbook of interpersonal communication* (2nd ed., pp. 323-379). Thousand Oaks, CA: Sage.

Werner, C. M., & Haggard, L. M. (1985). Temporal qualities of interpersonal relationships. In M. Knapp & G. R. Miller (Eds.), *Handbook of interpersonal communication* (pp. 59-99). Beverly Hills, CA: Sage.

West, B. J. (1980). *An essay on the importance of being nonlinear.* Berlin: Springer-Verlag.

West, M., & Biocca, F. (1992, May). "What if your wife were murdered": Audience responses to a verbal gaffe in the 1988 Los Angeles presidential debate. Paper presented at the annual meeting of the American Association for Public Opinion Research, St. Petersburg, FL.

West, M., Biocca, F., & David, P. (1991, May). *"You're no Jack Kennedy": Audience responses to a verbal barb in the 1988 Omaha vice presidential debate.* Paper presented at the annual meeting of the American Association for Public Opinion Research, Phoenix.

White, R., & Engelen, G. (1993). Cellular automata and fractal urban form: A cellular modelling approach to the evolution of urban land-use patterns. *Environment & Planning A, 25*, 1175-1199.

Whitehead, A. N. (1929). *Process and reality.* New York: Macmillan.

Whitrow, G. J. (1972). *The nature of time.* New York: Holt, Rinehart & Winston.

Wiener, N. (1961). *Cybernetics: Or control and communication in the animal and the machine* (2nd ed.). Cambridge: MIT Press.

Wilder, D. A. (1978). Reduction of intergroup discrimination through individuation of the outgroup. *Journal of Personality and Social Psychology, 36*, 1361-1374.

Wilder, D. A. (1981). Perceiving persons as a group: Categorization and intergroup relations. In D. L. Hamilton (Ed.), *Cognitive processes in stereotyping and intergroup behavior* (pp. 213-253). Hillsdale, NJ: Lawrence Erlbaum.

Williamson, R. N., & Fitzpatrick, M. A. (1985). Two approaches to marital interaction: Relational control patterns in marital types. *Communication Monographs, 52*, 236-252.

Winer, B. J. (1971). *Statistical principles in experimental design.* New York: McGraw-Hill.

Winner, L. (1992). Silicon valley mystery house. In M. Sorkin (Ed.), *Variations on a theme park* (pp. 31-60). New York: Hill & Wang.

Woelfel, J. (1993). Cognitive processes and communication networks: A general theory. In W. D. Richards & G. A. Barnett (Eds.), *Progress in communication sciences* (Vol. 12, pp. 21-42). Norwood, NJ: Ablex.

Woelfel, J., Barnett, G. A., Pruzek, R., & Zimmelman, R. (1989). Rotation to simple processes: The effect of alternative rotation rules on observed patterns in time-ordered measurements. *Quality and Quantity, 23*, 3-20.

Woelfel, J., & Fink, E. L. (1980). *The measurement of communication processes: Galileo theory and method*. New York: Academic Press.

Wolfram, S. (1983). Statistical mechanics of cellular automata. *Review of Modern Physics, 55*, 601-644.

Wolfram, S. (1984). Cellular automata as models of complexity. *Nature, 311*, 419-424.

Wolfram, S. (1986). *Theory and applications of cellular automata*. Singapore: World Scientific Press.

Wolfram, S. (1991). *Mathematica: A system of doing mathematics by computer* [Computer program]. Champaign, IL: Wolfram Research, Inc.

Wunschel, F., III. (1982). *A predicted methodology for determining individual television program rating and share*. Unpublished master's thesis, University of Connecticut, Storrs.

Wylie, C. R. (1960). *Advanced engineering mathematics*. New York: Prentice Hall.

Yates, F. E. (1972). Modeling periodicities in reproductive, adrenocortical, and metabolic systems. In M. Ferin, F. Halberg, R. M. Richart, & R. L. Van de Wiele (Eds.), *Biorhythms and human reproduction* (pp. 133-142). New York: John Wiley.

Yorkston, K. M., Beukelman, D. R., & Bell, K. R. (1988). *Clinical management of dysarthric speakers*. Austin, TX: Pro-Ed.

Zerubavel, E. (1981). *Hidden rhythms: Schedules and calendars in social life*. Chicago: University of Chicago Press.

Zerubavel, E. (1985). *The seven day cycle: The history and meaning of the week*. New York: Free Press.

Related Readings

Altman, I. (1975). *The environment and social behavior: Privacy, personal space, territory and crowding*. Monterey, CA: Brooks/Cole.

Arundale, R. B. (1971). The concept of process in human communication research. *Dissertation Abstracts International, 32*, 1816B. (University Microfilms No. 71-23157)

Briggs, J., & Peat, F. D. (1990). *Turbulent mirror: An illustrated guide to chaos theory and the science of wholeness*. New York: Harper & Row.

Conville, R. L. (1983). Second-order development in interpersonal communication. *Human Communication Research, 9*, 195-207.

Courtright, J. A., Millar, F., & Rogers-Millar, E. (1979). Domineeringness and dominance: Replication and expansion. *Communication Monographs, 44*, 97-103.

Deetz, S. (1990, March). *Power and organizational discourse*. Paper presented at the Arizona State University conference on "Organizational Communication: Directions for the 90s," Tempe.

Dindia, K. (1982). Reciprocity of self-disclosure: A sequential analysis. In M. Burgoon (Ed.), *Communication yearbook 6* (pp. 506-528). Beverly Hills, CA: Sage.

Doggert, R. (Ed.). (1986). *Time, the greatest innovator: Timekeeping and time consciousness in early modern Europe*. Washington, DC: Folger Shakespeare Library.

Ellis, D. G., Fisher, B. A., Drecksel, G. L., Hoch, D. D., & Werbel, W. S. (1976). *RelCom: A system for analyzing relational communication*. Unpublished coding manual, Department of Communication, University of Utah.

Gottman, J., & Bakeman, R. (1979). The sequential analysis of observational data. In M. E. Lamb, S. J. Suomi, & G. R. Stephenson (Eds.), *Social interaction analysis: Methodological issues* (pp. 185-206). Madison: University of Wisconsin Press.

Grant, S. J., & Contractor, N. S. (1993, October). *Dynamic modelling of the social influence process: A networks approach.* Paper presented at the annual meeting of the Speech Communication Association, Miami, FL.

Lazarsfeld, P., & Stanton, F. (1979). *Radio research, 1942-1943.* New York: Arno.

Levy, M. (1982). The Lazarsfeld-Stanton program analyzer: An historical note. *Journal of Communication, 32,* 30-38.

Lorch, E. P., Anderson, D. R., & Levin, S. R. (1979). The relationship of visual attention to children's comprehension of television. *Child Development, 50,* 722-727.

Millard, W. (1992). A history of handsets for direct measurement of audience response. *International Journal of Public Opinion Research, 4,* 1-17.

Peterman, J. (1940). The program analyzer: A new technique in studying liked and disliked items in radio programs. *Journal of Applied Psychology, 24,* 718-741.

Rapp, P. E., Goldbert, G., & Albano, A. M. (1993). Using coarse-grained measures to characterize electromyographic signals. *International Journal of Bifurcations and Chaos In Applied Sciences and Engineering, 3,* 525-542.

Rawlins, W. K. (1983). Openness as problematic in ongoing friendships: Two conversational dilemmas. *Communication Monographs, 50,* 1-13.

Schutz, W. C. (1966). *The interpersonal underworld.* Palo Alto, CA: Science and Behavior Books.

Smith, L. A. (1988). Intrinsic limits on dimension calculations. *Physics Letters, 133A,* 283-288.

Street, R. L., Jr. (1983). Noncontent speech convergence in adult-child interactions. In R. N. Bostrom (Ed.), *Communication yearbook 7* (pp. 369-395). Beverly Hills, CA: Sage.

Taylor, D. A. (1968). Some aspects of the development of interpersonal relationships: Social penetration processes. *Journal of Social Psychology, 75,* 79-90.

Watt, J. H. (1979, May). *Periodic components in communication data: Models and hypothesis testing.* Paper presented at the annual meeting of the International Communication Association, Philadelphia.

Wilkinson, L., Hill, M. A., & Vang, E. (1992). *SYSTAT for the Macintosh, version 5.2.* Evanston, IL: SYSTAT, Inc.

Winkler, M., & Combs, A. (1993). *A chaotic systems analysis of individual differences in affect.* Paper presented at the Interamerican Congress of Psychology, Santiago, Chile.

Winkler, M., Combs, A., & Daley, C. (1992). *Further dynamical analysis of individual mood cycles.* Paper presented at the annual meeting of the Society for Chaos Theory in Psychology, Washington, DC.

Young, M., & Ziman, I. (1971). Cycles in social behavior. *Nature, 229,* 91-95.

Author Index

Subject Index

431

About the Editors

C. Arthur VanLear (PhD, University of Utah, 1985) is Associate Professor of Communication Sciences at the University of Connecticut. His interests lie in the study of interpersonal communication, and his research has focused on communication in relationship evolution and development, marital and family communication, and communication in the addiction recovery process. His primary methods of research are quantitative behavioral interaction analysis and time series analysis of longitudinal data in relationships.

James H. Watt (PhD, University of Wisconsin, 1973) is Professor of Communication Sciences at the University of Connecticut. His recent work includes articles on dynamic modeling of media use and public opinion that have appeared in *Communication Research* and *Journal of Communication.* He is coauthor of the text *Research Methods in Communication Science* and author of the computer program *FATS* (Fourier Analysis of Time Series). He is currently investigating long-term adoption and use of Internet-based computer conferencing systems.

About the Contributors

Robert B. Arundale (PhD, Michigan State University, 1971) is Associate Professor of Speech Communication at the University of Alaska, Fairbanks. His primary research interests lie in methodological problems in studying dynamic communication phenomena and in the processes of language use involved in managing social relationships in ordinary conversation.

George A. Barnett (PhD, Michigan State University, 1976) is Professor of Communication at the State University of New York at Buffalo. Currently, he is editor of *Progress in Communication Science* and *Organizational Communication: Emerging Perspectives.* His research interests deal with mathematical modeling of social and cultural processes including modeling the structure of international communication networks.

Frank A. Biocca (PhD, University of Wisconsin–Madison, 1989) is Director of the Center for Research in Journalism and Mass Communication at the University of North Carolina at Chapel Hill. His research explores how the mind absorbs and uses video and computer-based images. He has published books and a number of research articles on voter psychology and the communication aspects of virtual reality technologies and has been a consultant for ABC, NBC, *USA Today,* and other media organizations.

Eugene H. Buder is Assistant Professor of Speech Science at the University of Memphis. He received his PhD in 1991 from the University of Wisconsin—Madison's Departments of Communication Arts and Communication Disorders. He has published rticles on digital speech analysis methods, mathematical modeling of dyadic interaction, cross-linguistic studies of speech development, and the acoustic analysis of normal and disordered speech.

Joseph N. Cappella (PhD, Michigan State University, 1974) is Professor of Communication at the Annenberg School for Communication at the University of Pennsylvania. He is former editor of *Human Communication Research* and a Fellow of the International Communication Association. His research centers on social interaction, nonverbal behavior, and the effects of messages particularly in news and politics.

Sung Ho Cho (PhD, State University of New York at Buffalo, 1993) is currently employed at the Korean Broadcasting Institute in Seoul. His doctoral dissertation was entitled "Patterns of Television Viewing Behavior."

Noshir S. Contractor is Associate Professor of Communication at the University of Illinois at Urbana-Champaign where he teaches courses and doctoral seminars on organizational communication processes, communication network analysis, computer-mediated technologies, and quantitative research methods. His research interests include applications of systems theory to communication, the role of emergent communication networks in organizations, and information technologies in the workplace. His articles have appeared in *Decision Science, Organization Science, Human Communication Research,* and *Management Communication Quarterly.* He currently serves on the editorial boards of *Human Communication Research, Management Communication Quarterly,* and the *Electronic Journal of Computer-Mediated Communication.*

Steven R. Corman (PhD, University of Illinois at Urbana-Champaign, 1988) is Associate Professor of Communication and Director of the Public Communication Technology Project at Arizona State University.

His research program focuses on the relationships among communication behavior, perceived communication relationships, activity, and enactment in organizations and other social collectives. He also has interests in mathematical modeling of communication processes, communication technology, and quantitative research methods. His recent publications have appeared in *Communication Theory, Internet Research, Social Networks, Communication Monographs,* and *Communication Research.*

Edward L. Fink (PhD, University of Wisconsin–Madison, 1975) is Professor of Speech Communication, Affiliate Professor of Psychology, Affiliate Professor of Sociology, and Acting Associate Dean for Graduate Studies and Research at the University of Maryland at College Park. He is interested in the creation and testing of mathematical models of the communication process. Some of his work focuses on the cognitive processes involved in attitude change and some on the cultural and social aspects of information diffusion. He also has published work concerning the measurement and analysis problems associated with empirical research. This includes work on the theory and multidimensional scaling techniques associated with the "Galileo" system. He teaches courses in persuasion, humor, communication theory, research methods, and data analysis. In 1988, he was named a University Distinguished Scholar-Teacher.

Susan J. Grant (PhD, University of Illinois at Urbana-Champaign, 1996) is Assistant Professor in the School of Communication Studies at Kent State University. Her research interests include the development of shared meaning systems from an emergent communication network perspective, communication in occupational communities, and elaboration of systems theory in dynamic modeling.

Michael E. Kalman is a research scientist with the U.S. Navy and a doctoral candidate at the Annenberg School for Communication, University of Southern California. His background includes the identification of fleet communication requirements through dynamic analysis of advanced technologies and operations. He also has served as a liaison between federal agencies, coordinating the flow of critical information to naval scientists and engineers. He currently studies communication systems, social cooperation, and collective action in organizations.

Stan A. Kaplowitz is Professor of Sociology at Michigan State University. His research interests emphasize the measurement, structure, and dynamics of attitudes. He also studies attribution and racial attitudes and is developing research in medical social psychology.

Jeanne M. Meadowcroft is Professor in the Department of Agricultural Journalism at the University of Wisconsin—Madison. She received her PhD from the School of Journalism and Mass Communication at the University of Wisconsin—Madison and was a member of the faculty in the Department of Telecommunications at Indiana University for several years before returning to Madison. Her research addresses questions concerning how adults and children process information from the mass media.

Peter R. Monge is Professor of Communication and Co-Director of the doctoral program at the Annenberg School for Communication, University of Southern California. His research investigates communication processes in organizations, particularly communication networks and computer-based collaborative work systems. He has published articles and monographs about systems theory, communication processes, and longitudinal research methods. He is a past editor of *Communication Research* and currently president-elect of the International Communication Association.

Youngme Moon is a doctoral candidate in communication at Stanford University. She received her B.A. magna cum laude in political science from Yale University and her master's in political science from Stanford University. She has published in the *International Journal of Human-Computer Studies* and the *Proceedings of SIGCHI*. Her primary areas of interest are social responses to communication technology, personality theory, and human-computer interaction.

Clifford Nass is Associate Professor of Communication and Co-Director of the Social Responses to Communication Technology project at Stanford University. He received both his B.A. cum laude in mathematics and his doctorate in sociology from Princeton University. He has worked as a computer scientist for the IBM Research Center in Yorktown Heights and Intel Corp. He has published extensively in communication, computer science, psychology, and statistics. His primary areas of interest are social-psychological models of human-computer interaction, development of nonparametric statistics, and technology and social change.

Rebecca M. Warner (PhD, Harvard University, 1978) is Associate Professor of Psychology at the University of New Hampshire in Durham. Her research interests include development of statistical analyses tailored to research problems in social interaction, synchrony between behavioral and physiological rhythms, and expressive behavior as a basis for person perception. She is working on a book about applications of spectral analysis to social interaction data. Her articles have appeared in the *Journal of Personality and Social Psychology, Journal of Language and Social Psychology,* and *Behavioral Science.*

Mark Douglas West (PhD, University of North Carolina at Chapel Hill, 1990) is Assistant Professor of Mass Communication at the University of North Carolina at Asheville, where he teaches theory and methods courses, and is Director of the Appalachian Center for Social Research. His dissertation on time series analysis of public opinion data won awards from the International Communication Association and the Association for Education in Journalism and Mass Communication.